ROYAL HISTORICAL SOCIETY

STUDIES IN HISTORY

New Series

SCIENCE, RELIGION AND POLITICS
IN RESTORATION ENGLAND

Richard Cumberland, as bishop of Peterborough

Reproduced by kind permission of the Master and Fellows
of Magdalene College, Cambridge

SCIENCE, RELIGION AND POLITICS IN RESTORATION ENGLAND

RICHARD CUMBERLAND'S *DE LEGIBUS NATURAE*

Jon Parkin

THE ROYAL HISTORICAL SOCIETY
THE BOYDELL PRESS

First published 1999

A Royal Historical Society publication
Published by The Boydell Press
an imprint of Boydell & Brewer Ltd
PO Box 9, Woodbridge, Suffolk IP12 3DF, UK
and of Boydell & Brewer Inc.
PO Box 41026, Rochester, NY 14604–4126, USA
website: http://www.boydell.co.uk

ISBN 0 86193 241 2   1001692074

ISSN 0269–2244

A catalogue record for this book is available
from the British Library

Library of Congress Cataloging-in-Publication Data
Parkin, Jon (Jonathan Bruce), 1969–
    Science, religion, and politics in restoration England : Richard
Cumberland's De legibus naturae / Jon Parkin.
        p.   cm. – (Royal Historical Society studies in history. New
series, ISSN 0269–2244)
    Includes bibliographical references and index.
    ISBN 0–86193–241–2 (alk. paper)
    1. Cumberland, Richard, 1631–1718. De legibus naturae.
I. Title.   II. Series.
B1201.C83D424   1999
171'.2 – dc21   99–18223

This book is printed on acid-free paper

Printed in Great Britain by
St Edmundsbury Press, Bury St Edmunds, Suffolk

Contents

Publication of this volume was aided by a grant from the Scouloudi Foundation, in association with the Institute of Historical Research.

Acknowledgements

This study began life as a doctoral dissertation at the University of Cambridge. I would like to express my gratitude to the British Academy for providing the initial postgraduate funding for the project. I would also like to thank the Master and Fellows of Selwyn College, Cambridge, for electing me to the research fellowship which enabled me to complete the book. A scholar could not hope to have a more congenial atmosphere in which to live and work.

It is a great pleasure to be able to acknowledge the contribution of so many friends and colleagues. My greatest intellectual debt is to Quentin Skinner, who supervised the original doctoral project. His unflagging enthusiasm and continuing support have been an enormous encouragement. Tim Hochstrasser first suggested that I look at Cumberland, and I have been very fortunate in being able to call upon his help and advice throughout the evolution of the study. Numerous colleagues have commented upon the work at various stages in its development. Mark Goldie, Istvan Hont, John Robertson, Jonathan Scott, David Smith and Richard Tuck all found time to read and comment on various sections of the work. I have also benefited from discussion with Hans Blom, Linda Kirk, Isobel Rivers and David Stack. I hope that the finished product reflects some of the very good advice that I have received over the years. I tried out various sections of the book at seminars in Cambridge, London and Oxford, and would like to thank the participants who helped me to clarify and develop my arguments.

The work for the the book was mainly carried out in Cambridge and I am particularly grateful to the staff of the Rare Books Reading Room of the Cambridge University Library, for their helpfulness and patience. I would also like to thank the staff of Trinity College Library for allowing me to examine Cumberland's annotated copy of the *De legibus*. King's College Library not only provided me with a pleasant year's employment but also kindly allowed me access to John Maynard Keynes's rare book collection. The portrait of Richard Cumberland, as bishop of Peterborough, is reproduced by kind permission of the Master and Fellows of Magdalene College, Cambridge; the jacket illustration (plate 1) is from Jean Barbeyrac's translation of Cumberland, the *Traité philosophique des loix naturelles* (Amsterdam 1744) and is reproduced by permission of the Syndics of Cambridge University Library.

For the final shape of the text, I am particularly grateful to Sarah Meer. She read through the manuscript several times, asked awkward questions and helped make it more readable. I would also like to thank my editors at *Studies in History*, Steve Gunn and Christine Linehan, for their help and advice in preparing the book for publication. Any errors which remain are my own. Finally I would like to express my gratitude to my parents, without whose support none of this would have been possible.

Jon Parkin
August 1998

Abbreviations

CSPD	*Calendar of state papers, domestic series, of the reign of Charles II*, ed. E. Green, F. H. B. Daniell and F. Bickley, London 1860–1938
CUL	Cambridge University Library
DJBP	Hugo Grotius, *De jure belli ac pacis*, trans. F. Kelsey, Oxford 1925
DJN	Samuel Pufendorf, *De jure naturae et gentium*, ed. and trans. C. H. Oldfather and W. A. Oldfather, Oxford 1934
DLN	Richard Cumberland, *De legibus naturae disquisitio philosophia, in qua earum forma, summa capita, ordo, promulgatio & obligatio e rerum natura investigantur: quinetiam elementa philosophiae Hobbianae cum moralis tum civilis, considerantur & refutantur*, London 1672
DNB	*Dictionary of national biography*, ed. L. Stephen and S. Lee, London 1885–1900
EW	*The English works of Thomas Hobbes*, ed. W. Molesworth, London 1839–45

A Note on the Translation

Quotation of Cumberland in this work is principally based upon John Maxwell's largely accurate translation of the *De legibus naturae* (*A treatise of the laws of nature*, ed. J. Maxwell, London 1727). Maxwell attempted a word-for-word translation which usually succeeds in conveying the sense (and sometimes the confusion) of the original. In order to make the text more accessible I have used modern spelling and punctuation. I have occasionally attempted to improve the sense where Maxwell's literalism has made the translation unreadable. Where there are queries I have deferred to Cumberland's own corrected text of the first edition, held in the library of Trinity College, Cambridge. Other texts have not been modernised.

Introduction

Richard Cumberland's *De legibus naturae* is one of the most important works of ethical and political theory of the seventeenth century, but it rarely attracts much attention from historians or political theorists. When Cumberland's work is discussed, it is with reference to broader historical movements of which the *De legibus* is usually taken to be a distant, poor and sometimes rather strange relation: Cumberland has been cast as a natural lawyer, Cambridge Platonist, proto-deist, early utilitarian, premature secularist and so on. These categories, considered in isolation, fail to do justice to the range and complexity of Cumberland's work. If Cumberland is a natural lawyer, why does he spend so much of his time talking about science? If he is a secular utilitarian, why does he nevertheless invoke God as the pivot of his natural law system? If he writes against Hobbes, why does he nevertheless appear to agree with much of what Hobbes says? Cumberland and his *magnum opus* simply do not fit into the convenient boxes in which he is so often placed. The significance of the *De legibus naturae* is thus often missed. But this relative strangeness is what gives Cumberland's enigmatic work its interest. For the modern reader who comes across the text, the strange and confusing blend of ancient and modern, religious and secular, liberal and authoritarian demands explanations which no single study has managed to provide.

This book is not a biography of Cumberland. The evidence that remains of Cumberland's life and career is too sketchy to allow such an undertaking. It is, instead, the history of Cumberland's *De legibus naturae*, and the unusual ideas within it. This study asks why Cumberland used these ideas, and why the *De legibus* was written in the way that it was. It traces the political and intellectual circumstances that led to its composition, and the consequences of its publication. This process helps us to make better sense of Cumberland's own theory, which has always been interesting and intriguing in its own right. But it does more than that. By looking at seventeenth-century history through the new lens offered by a contextualisation of the *De legibus*, it becomes possible to re-examine many of the historical categories by which Cumberland's work has previously been judged. The result of this changed perspective is to alter the familiar portraits of seventeenth-century intellectual history. Some ideas and movements which have been regarded as being close together are revealed to be further apart, others, traditionally judged to be totally antipathetic, are unexpectedly discovered closer together. Understanding Cumberland's *De legibus* on its own terms thus becomes a way of examining one of the most important periods of European intellectual history.

1

The *De legibus naturae* is not an ostentatious volume.[1] The first edition of 1672 is a moderately sized quarto of 422 pages. There are no illustrations. It was printed in London for the Little Britain bookseller Nathaneal Hooke, whose stock included other Latin works, some with a scientific interest.[2] The book was advertised in the *Term catalogues* for February 1671/2 (old style) for the price of 7s.[3] This was relatively expensive. The price, and the language in which the work was written, meant that it was not designed for a popular audience, but for educated readers of Latin. Although the lists of newly published Latin texts were steadily diminishing in the second half of the seventeenth century, Latin was still the universal language of the learned treatise. Cumberland's Latin, however, was probably a challenge even to the most educated of his seventeenth-century readers, his bewildering constructions complicated by the printing errors which marred the first edition of the book.[4]

The condition of the text, coupled with its arcane Latin, did not augur well for the success of Cumberland's project. The book is difficult to read, and it is far from logically organised.[5] Cumberland's arguments ramble, wander, cross themselves. But the *De legibus* always returns to a coda-like thesis, the same central argument about the law of nature, repeated over and over again, deduced from every kind of evidence. That argument appears at first sight to be something of an oddity for the period in which it was written. The book's thesis is deceptively modern in its secular simplicity; Cumberland argues that natural law directs man to promote the good of the whole system of rational agents, in which his own good is contained as a part. In furthering the common good, man fulfils his own individual good, and the two are inseparable. This natural law is binding because there are natural rewards attached to its observation and natural punishments to its dereliction. Cumberland's theory appears to be modern because he arrives at this conclusion without referring to Scripture, and in a way that seems to generate ethical norms without the active participation of God, or a discussion of heaven and hell.[6]

---

1 Richard Cumberland, *De legibus naturae disquisitio philosophica: in qua earum forma, summa capita, ordo, promulgatio & obligatio e rerum natura investigantur: quinetiam elementa philosophiae Hobbianae cum moralis tum civilis, considerantur & refutantur*, London 1672 (hereinafter cited as *DLN*).

2 H. R. Plomer, *A dictionary of the printers and booksellers who were at work in England, Scotland and Ireland from 1668 to 1725*, Oxford 1922, 118, 160. Hooke also published Francis Glisson's *De natura substantiae energetica*, London 1672.

3 E. Arber, *The term catalogues 1668–1709*, London 1903–6, i. 98.

4 Cumberland, *DLN*, errata: this blames the textual inaccuracies upon the transcription errors of the youth who did the typesetting.

5 For comments upon Cumberland's textual inadequacies see H. Sidgwick, *Outlines of the history of ethics for English readers*, London 1886, 170; E. Albee, *A history of English utilitarianism*, London 1901, 14; F. Spaulding, *Richard Cumberland, als Begruender der Englischen Ethik*, Leipzig 1894, p. iv.

6 For Cumberland's 'modernity' see Albee, *History of English utilitarianism*, 50; this feature has also allowed his work to be used in discussion of modern ethical theory. See, for

This was not the only unusual feature of his argument. Cumberland refers to recent scientific advances to back up his ethical claims. He talks about morality in mathematical terms. But he also quotes freely from the ancients. What is one to make of this strange mixture?

Cumberland's curious 'modernity' has encouraged some historians to read Cumberland as an isolated prophet of political thought to come. For many, he was a forerunner, if not the founder, of English utilitarianism. This is an important claim, and one that has been endorsed by many of Cumberland's modern interpreters.[7] According to this analysis, Cumberland's apparently secular insistence that one should act for the happiness of the greatest number marks the genesis of an argument which would flower in the writings of Hutcheson and later utilitarians. But there are problems with this view that make it difficult to see Cumberland's theory as an isolated and premature step in a utilitarian direction. It is perhaps a source of disappointment for those seeking the origins of utilitarianism to find that Cumberland is not actually interested in elaborating a 'modern' secular theory of moral obligation based upon enlightened self-interest. In fact, his explicit purpose was to re-establish the divine obligation of natural law, to emphasise the link between God and morality.

Historians who have treated the *De legibus* as a work of natural jurisprudence have more readily appreciated the complexities of Cumberland's thesis. Richard Tuck has accurately portrayed Cumberland as a critical follower of Grotius. The *De legibus*, in this account, owed much to Grotius' *De jure belli ac pacis*, the founding text of the 'modern' theory of natural law.[8] From an eighteenth-century perspective, historians have seen Cumberland as part of a juristic tradition that transmitted natural law and state of nature doctrines to the political and economic theory of the Scottish Enlightenment.[9] Building upon these arguments, Knud Haakonssen has produced the

example, A. Carey, 'Richard Cumberland and the epistemology of ethics', unpubl. PhD diss. Washington State 1967.

7   Albee, *History of English utilitarianism*, 1–51; F. C. Sharp, 'The ethical system of Richard Cumberland and its place in the history of British ethics', *Mind* xxi (1912), 371–98; L. Kirk, *Richard Cumberland and natural law: secularisation of thought in seventeenth-century England*, Cambridge 1987 (this work is based on Kirk's London University PhD thesis 'Richard Cumberland (1632–1718) and his political theory'). Kirk describes (p. iv) Cumberland's work in summary as 'a utilitarian system of ethics based on a sensationalist psychology set in a framework of Christian belief'.

8   Richard Tuck, *Natural rights theories: their origin and development*, Cambridge 1979, 165–6, and also his 'The "modern" theory of natural law', in A. Pagden (ed.), *The languages of political theory in early-modern Europe*, Cambridge 1987, 99–122. For different interpretations of Cumberland's relationship to European natural theory see Hans-Peter Schneider, *Justitia universalis: Quellenstudien zur Geschichte des 'Christlichen Naturrechts' bei Gottfried Wilhelm Leibniz*, Frankfurt 1967, 166–75; W. Schneiders, *Naturrecht und Liebesethik: zur Geschichte der praktischen Philosophie im Hinblick auf Christian Thomasius*, Hildesheim 1971, 130–1.

9   Duncan Forbes, 'Natural law and the Scottish Enlightenment', in R. Campbell and

most effective interpretation of Cumberland's theory to date. By recovering the importance of divine obligation to the *De legibus*, Haakonssen's work has helped to correct the impression that Cumberland is a secularising utilitarian.[10] But this is still a long way from providing a fully contextualised explanation of why Cumberland should have produced the theory that he did. In particular it is more difficult to follow Haakonssen in his assertion that Cumberland's engagement with Thomas Hobbes is 'so entirely negative that it gives surprisingly little help with constructive interpretation'.[11] In fact, as I shall argue throughout this study, Hobbes and the phenomenon of 'Hobbism' are crucial to understanding Cumberland's project and its importance to seventeenth-century natural law theory. The whole point of Cumberland's attempt to unite natural law and divine obligation was to refute the challenge to that obligation posed by Hobbes.

The importance of Hobbes's work for Cumberland's thesis is often missed by those wishing to make positive claims for the arguments of the *De legibus*. Hobbes appears on almost every page, in many cases quoted directly. For many writers the running engagement with Hobbes is yet another consequence of Cumberland's disorderly method, something to be removed in order to exhume his 'real' theory.[12] But the engagement with Hobbes is the whole point of the *De legibus*; its political and ethical theory cannot be understood without it.

Cumberland was one of the most perceptive and innovative critics of Hobbes's political theory. This feature of his work has only really been noticed by historians working upon Hobbes. As the editor of the 1750 edition of Hobbes's works commented:

> Dr Cumberland's excellent Treatise *Of the Laws of Nature* was . . . written against our Author's System, and is deservedly esteemed the closest and best Book of its kind; indeed, he is the only one of all Mr Hobbes's Antagonists, that understood the Advantages the old Man had, as appears by his chusing a fresh Ground, and disputing in a way quite different from the rest.[13]

A. S. Skinner (eds), *The origin and nature of the Scottish Enlightenment*, Edinburgh 1982, 186–204. See also his *Hume's philosophical politics*, Cambridge 1975, 18–26. For other comments on Cumberland's relationship to this tradition see J. Moore and M. Silverthorne, 'Gerschom Carmichael and the natural jurisprudence tradition in eighteenth-century Scotland', in I. Hont and M. Ignatieff (eds), *Wealth and virtue: the shaping of political economy in the Scottish Enlightenment*, Cambridge 1983, 73–88; I. Hont, 'The language of natural sociability and commerce: Samuel Pufendorf and the theoretical foundation of the four-stages theory', in Pagden, *Languages of political theory*, 253–76.

[10] K. Haakonssen, 'The character and obligation of natural law according to Richard Cumberland', in M. A. Stewart (ed.), *English philosophy in the age of Locke*, Oxford forthcoming. See also his 'Moral philosophy and natural law: from the Cambridge Platonists to the Scottish Enlightenment', *Political Studies* xl (1988), 97–110, and *Natural law and moral philosophy: from Grotius to the Scottish Enlightenment*, Cambridge 1996, 50–1.

[11] Idem, 'Character and obligation of natural law', 4.

[12] Albee, *History of English utilitarianism*, 50.

[13] *The moral and political works of Thomas Hobbes*, London 1750, p. xxv, note m.

Cumberland's critique is both effective and distinctive because it seeks to refute Hobbes from his own premises. Hobbes's nineteenth-century biographer, George Croom Robertson, commented that Cumberland's effectiveness as a critic resulted from the fact that he stood 'much closer to Hobbes in method of inquiry than any other of his opponents'. John Dewey built upon this insight when he wrote that 'Cumberland, not Cudworth, was Hobbes's most intelligent opponent, and in his *De legibus naturae* we find an attempt to meet Hobbes upon his own ground.'[14] This point is of some importance when we consider the relationship between Cumberland's response to Hobbes, and his positive political theory. Cumberland's critique is not divorced from the process of construction; he seems to borrow almost as much as he criticises. Although the *De legibus* is written as a critique of Hobbes's ethical and political theory, Cumberland's work is peculiarly Hobbesian in a lot of what it has to say. Noel Malcolm has commented that 'at times the reader of Cumberland's treatise may need to remind himself that he is reading a work which was in fact intended as a refutation of Hobbes'.[15] This curious process of engagement and appropriation has never been discussed in detail before, and yet it is the key to the peculiar character of Cumberland's work.

Hobbes and Hobbism

This study of Cumberland's *De legibus* is an attempt to replace his work in its 'Hobbesian' contexts. Cumberland's book was conceived as a response to Hobbes's ideas in politics, ethics and natural philosophy. A proper examination of this context can not only explain the text's perplexing oddities, but also its relevance for Cumberland's contemporaries. To study Cumberland seriously is to study the reception of Hobbes.

Hobbes was without doubt the most notorious political philosopher in seventeenth-century England. Thomas Tenison, one of his clerical opponents, wrote in 1670 that 'there is certainly no man who hath any share of the curiosity of the present Age, or hath his conversation amongst modern books, who yet remaineth unacquainted with his name and doctrine'. Demand for Hobbesian and anti-Hobbesian works remained high throughout the Restoration period. Every year, books refuting Hobbes's central tenets, or mentioning his work, poured off the presses. John Eachard's witty attack upon Hobbes and his ideas ran into two editions in its publication year.[16] When Pepys tried to get hold of a copy of the *Leviathan* in 1668, the demand was

---

14 G. C. Robertson, *Thomas Hobbes*, London 1886, 219; J. Dewey, 'The motivation of Hobbes's political philosophy', in *Studies in the history of ideas*, i, Columbia 1918, 108
15 N. Malcolm, 'Thomas Hobbes and voluntarist theology', unpubl. PhD diss. Cambridge 1982, 254.
16 Thomas Tenison, *The creed of Mr Hobbs examined*, London 1670, 3; John Eachard, *Mr Hobbs state of nature consider'd in a dialogue between Philautus and Timothy*, London 1673.

such that he had to pay three times the original price for a second-hand copy. Even in 1680, used copies were still changing hands at more than twice the value of the first edition, even after Hobbes's own death in 1679 had encouraged the republication of many of his works.[17] This was a remarkable currency for a text that had been published in 1651.

It is reasonable to ask what factors motivated this intense interest. Explanations have traditionally focused upon the shocking aspects of Hobbes's work.[18] Even today Leviathan has the capacity to startle the reader with its striking assertion that self-interest lies at the heart of political and ethical theory. Hobbes's uncompromising materialism raised the suggestion for contemporaries that he was a dangerous and unacceptable atheist. Historians often work on the assumption that Hobbes's sheer audacity in presenting such controversial ideas was enough to attract so much critical attention from his contemporaries. This is undoubtedly true up to a point. But Hobbes was not just attacked because his work was totally alien.

Increasingly, historians have come to recognise that Hobbes's peculiar potency stemmed from a theoretical radicalism that subverted commonly accepted beliefs from within, from the inconsistency of their own terms. As a cultural critic, Hobbes had few equals. The increasingly sensitive contextual treatment now given to Hobbes reveals that many of his radical ideas were based upon premises shared with contemporaries.[19] This aspect of Hobbes's work has been explored by Noel Malcolm, who has suggested that a critical response to Hobbes could stem from an uncomfortable awareness that what Hobbes had said shockingly was not far removed from the critic's own position. Criticising Hobbes's atheism could be a means of vindicating one's own 'Hobbist' arguments from the suspicion of the heterodoxy with which Hobbes was associated. In what follows it will be argued that Cumberland's work was just such an attempt to define the relationship between Cumberland's Anglican beliefs and Hobbes's controversial ideas. Looking at Cumberland's work in this way enables us to see the De legibus as a response to specific debates from the 1660s, in which some of Cumberland's friends and

---

[17] The diary of Samuel Pepys, ed. R. C. Latham and W. Matthews, London 1970–83, ix. 298. See also E. Bysshe, Bibliotheca Bissaeana, London 1679, in which a first edition of Leviathan was sold for 18s. 6d. – the original sale price was 8s. 6d.

[18] J. Bowle, Hobbes and his critics: a study in seventeenth-century constitutionalism, London 1951; S. Mintz, The hunting of Leviathan: seventeenth-century reactions to the materialism and moral philosophy of Thomas Hobbes, Cambridge 1969.

[19] For this approach see Q. R. D. Skinner, 'Thomas Hobbes and his disciples in France and England', Comparative Studies in Society and History viii (1965–6), 153–67, and 'The context of Hobbes's theory of political obligation', in M. Cranston and R. S. Peters (eds), Hobbes and Rousseau: a collection of critical essays, New York 1972, 109–42. For more recent applications of this contextual sensitivity towards Hobbes see M. Goldie, 'The reception of Hobbes', in J. H. Burns and M. Goldie (eds), The Cambridge history of political thought 1450–1700, Cambridge 1991, 589–615; J. P. Sommerville, Thomas Hobbes: political ideas in historical context, London 1992.

colleagues were suspected by their political enemies for their use of apparently Hobbesian ideas.

Discussion of Cumberland's natural law theory often overlooks the political circumstances in which it was developed. But these circumstances are essential to understanding the purpose of Cumberland's theory. The *De legibus* was a practical response to a specific political problem. One of the primary concerns of the *Leviathan* was to endorse an erastian vision of a Church subordinated to the control of the State. This very issue lay at the heart of debates over religious toleration in the 1660s, so it is no surprise that discussion of Hobbesian ideas took on a renewed importance at this time. The *De legibus*'s engagement with Hobbes arose from the identification of Cumberland's Anglican colleagues as 'Hobbists', or followers of Hobbes. They earned this opprobrium for their insistence that the magistrate should have extensive powers to determine the form of church government. These charges grew towards the end of the 1660s, as Cumberland's colleagues adopted an increasingly authoritarian stance against those dissenting groups who were calling for liberty of conscience in matters of religion. In the powers they granted to the magistrate, the Anglicans' arguments did have much in common with the *Leviathan*. However, the basis for that power came from natural law, a position which Hobbes had infamously rejected. For this reason, Cumberland sought to demonstrate the existence of a binding natural law against Hobbes.

Natural law was one solution to the problem of religious and political conflict of the seventeenth century. As a doctrine it presupposed the existence of common norms and values which could be detected from the nature of man irrespective of his religion, culture or nationality. Hobbes embraced the language of natural law theory as the foundation for his political theory but in several key areas he deliberately subverted it. He argued that for natural laws to be binding, they had to represent the identifiable will of a superior. In the case of natural law that superior was God. This voluntarist description of natural law as the product of God's will was entirely conventional for Protestant writers. But Hobbes subverted the conventional account when he argued that man's natural reason was insufficient to identify God's will. For Hobbes, this meant that the laws of nature could not by themselves be used as the foundation of any theory of ethics or politics. In a deliberately shocking relocation of the source of moral and political authority, Hobbes argued that practical moral and political obligation could only come from the sovereign power. The implication of Hobbes's theory was that the only effective moral laws were those of the civil magistrate.

The natural law theory of Cumberland and his colleagues proceeded from the same voluntarist premises used by Hobbes. They too believed that moral obligation had to be shown to be the will of God in order to be binding. The crucial difference was that Cumberland believed that sufficient evidence of God's will could be found in nature. Cumberland's attempt to derive obligation from nature was largely shaped by ideas developed in Cambridge, where

Cumberland studied from 1649 until 1656. It is usually supposed by historians that the dominant ethical influence at Cambridge during this time was the work of the so-called Cambridge Platonists; indeed, Cumberland himself is sometimes classified as a minor figure in that school.[20] However, as this study shows, Cumberland's work, and that of his Latitudinarian colleagues, is characterised less by an affiliation to Platonism, than by what might be called Protestant Scholasticism.

The importance of Scholastic thought for Anglicanism has long been recognised in the influence of writers such as Richard Hooker, but it is often thought to have been in retreat during the second half of the seventeenth century.[21] However, the specific debts of writers like Cumberland to neo-Scholasticism, particularly the work of the Spanish natural law writers such as Suarez, have rarely been considered. By adapting the theology of these writers, Cumberland attempted to reconcile natural law doctrine with a voluntarist theology.[22]

Another powerful ingredient of this tradition which will be emphasised in this study is Cumberland's use of Stoicism. Although Cumberland's work is characterised by modern references to seventeenth-century science and mathematics, the framework of his ethical theory is classical. A great deal of Cumberland's theory is derived from Roman Stoicism, particularly from the work of Cicero. This might appear paradoxical in a work that is in many ways so 'modern', but ironically Cumberland's classical allegiances are what give his work this modern 'secular' appearance.[23] Cumberland deliberately recast his engagement with Hobbes in the mould of Cicero's debates between Stoics, who believed that nature could provide an objective morality, and Epicureans, who argued that morality was human, conventional and self-interested. This tactic allowed Cumberland to draw a distinction between the positive, constructive use of self-preservation as the basis for a system of

---

[20] J. Tulloch, *Rational theology and Christian philosophy in England in the seventeenth century*, London 1872; W. de Pauley, *The candle of the Lord*, New York 1937; G. R. Cragg, *From Puritanism to the age of reason*, London 1950; R. L. Colie, *Light and Enlightenment: a study of the Cambridge Platonists and the Dutch Arminians*, Cambridge 1957. For a corrective to these views about the nature of 'Cambridge Platonism' see C. A. Stradenbauer, 'Platonism, theosophy and immaterialism: recent views of the Cambridge Platonists', *Journal of the History of Ideas* xxxv (1974), 157–69.

[21] Of the few authors to have taken the persistence of Thomism seriously see H. R. McAdoo, *The structure of Caroline moral theology*, London 1949, and *The spirit of Anglicanism: a survey of Anglican theological method in the seventeenth century*, London 1965.

[22] The continued importance of voluntarist theology amongst Latitudinarians has only recently been addressed by John Spurr, *The Restoration Church of England 1660–1689*, New Haven 1991, esp. ch. iv, and W. M. Spellman, *The Latitudinarians and the Church of England 1660–1700*, Athens, Georgia 1993. It should be noted that this restored emphasis upon the traditional voluntarist components of Anglican thought helps to explain the tension and resonance between Hobbes and Anglicans.

[23] For Cicero's contribution to Enlightenment secularism see C. Gawlick, 'Cicero and the Enlightenment', *Studies on Voltaire in the Eighteenth Century* xxv (1963), 657–82.

universal justice, and Hobbes's 'bad' Epicurean account. Cumberland was thus able to repudiate Hobbes from the premises that they shared.

By developing his natural law theory from these sources, Cumberland was able to argue that the right of the magistrate's power was a consequence of God's will, and not simply, as Hobbes had argued, the product of human self-interest. Cumberland's theory appropriated the useful premises and lessons of the *Leviathan*, while avoiding Hobbes's controversial subversion of the natural law genre.

Although this was the primary aim of Cumberland's *De legibus*, his theory was also designed to defend another cause, similarly compromised by Hobbes: early modern science. The second half of the study deals with this debate. The *De legibus* is illustrated with a wealth of scientific examples; almost every page contains some reference to contemporary natural philosophy. This material, like Cumberland's discussion of Hobbes, has traditionally been ignored in favour of a concentration upon Cumberland's 'political' theory.[24] There are compelling reasons, however, why we should take Cumberland's scientific material more seriously. The first and most important is that the use of science was fundamental to Cumberland's novel method of discussing the law of nature. Hobbes was sceptical about the possibility of discovering evidence of God's will in nature on the grounds that such an enquiry was so uncertain as to be incapable of demonstration. In response, Cumberland argued that the application of modern scientific methodology could overcome Hobbesian doubt and provide a compelling proof of moral obligation.

The use of science to uncover moral obligation might itself be considered worthy of note, but the kind of science that Cumberland deploys in support of his moral theory is especially interesting. The argument which comes to dominate the *De legibus* is that moral relationships can be understood in the same terms as those used in mechanical physics. Cumberland argues that the laws of nature obey the same principles as the laws governing the motion of matter. The mechanical conceptions that Cumberland uses are partially borrowed from Hobbes's own work.

This form of appropriation has its roots in another controversy over Hobbism which developed in the later 1660s. Modern opinion is divided about the precise relationship between Hobbes's scientific views and his ethical and political theory, but contemporaries were confident that there was a connection between Hobbes's natural philosophy and the ethics of the *Leviathan*.[25] A reductive philosophy of matter and motion went hand-in-hand with a sceptical and atheistic moral theory. When the newly-

24 There are two notable exceptions to this: M. Forsyth, 'The place of Richard Cumberland in the history of natural law doctrine', *Journal of the History of Philosophy* xx (1982), 23–42, in which Cumberland is identified as a 'Baconian', and L. Stewart, *The rise of public science: rhetoric, technology and natural philosophy in Newtonian Britain, 1660–1750*, Cambridge 1992, 37–9.
25 For differing accounts of the relationship between Hobbes's science and his ethics see J. W. N. Watkins, *Hobbes's system of ideas*, London 1973, and T. Sorrell, *Hobbes*, London 1986.

established Royal Society began to show an interest in mechanistic theory, it attracted criticism from those concerned about the ethical implications of such interests. This criticism reached a peak in the later 1660s, when the Society came into conflict with the universities, just as Hobbes had done in the 1650s, bringing the public image, and indeed the future, of the Society and its projects into question.[26]

The scientific material in the *De legibus* is in part a defence of the Society and its mechanistic projects. Cumberland was a committed supporter of the Royal Society. He admired their projects and drew upon their *Philosophical Transactions* to illustrate his work. Although he never became a Fellow, he, like many other provincial *virtuosi*, saw the Royal Society as a flagship for the new science. For this reason, he came to the defence of the Society and mechanistic science. Cumberland's use of Hobbes was designed to show that mechanistic science did not automatically lead to Hobbesian moral theory. Indeed, Cumberland deliberately attempts to develop a closer relationship between science and ethics to show that mechanistic physics, and a philosophy of matter and motion, could be consistent with a more orthodox ethical theory. This illustrates the dilemma thrown up by Hobbes's activity as a scientist; Hobbes's unacceptable doctrines were associated with positions which he shared with many 'orthodox' scientists. As with his political ideas, Cumberland needed to refute Hobbes because his ideas were much too close for comfort.[27]

At the root of the problem was Hobbes's reaction against Aristotelian science and Scholasticism. Hobbes was determined to separate natural philosophy from discussion of theology by reducing it to a study of matter and motion. He hoped to introduce clarity and certainty to discussion of science as a way of purging the corrupted clerical influence of the Schoolmen. Hobbes's reforming scientific programme banished all discussion of incorporeal spirits, concepts of infinity and eternity, and all discussion of God from the lexicon of natural philosophy. As a result he flatly denied the possibility of using natural philosophy to discover any meaningful information about God's will.

For Cumberland and his Latitudinarian colleagues this redefinition of science was unacceptable. It was a fundamental tenet of Stoic natural law theory that an investigation of nature could yield information about ethics and politics. Where Hobbes separated science and ethics, Cumberland and his colleagues sought to bring them closer together. They attempted to do this by deploying Descartes's insight that all phenomena could potentially be

---

[26] For studies which have emphasised this period of crisis, and the role that 'Hobbism' played in bringing it about see, in particular, Michael Hunter's *Science and society in Restoration England*, Cambridge 1981, and also the articles collected in his *Establishing the new science: the experience of the early Royal Society*, Woodbridge 1989.

[27] This was a position first suggested by Noel Malcolm in 'Hobbes and the Royal Society', in G. A. J. Rogers and A. Ryan (eds), *Perspectives on Thomas Hobbes*, Oxford 1988, 43–86.

analysed by mathematics. Cumberland's critical use of Cartesianism has been noted but rarely contextualised.[28] He deliberately deployed Descartes's idea of *mathesis universalis* as a way of using mathematics to discuss the systematic basis of natural morality, and to provide an alternative to Hobbes's reductive natural philosophy. In this way, he could show that the laws of matter and motion in fact supported a more orthodox ethical theory, thereby saving mechanism and the projects of the Royal Society from the suspicion of Hobbism.

Set in these new contexts, Cumberland's work enables us to exhume the work's original purpose. This explains some its more anomalous features, and its curious 'modernity'. The *De legibus* also allows us to re-examine the relationships between Hobbes and his contemporary critics. The problem of 'Hobbism' in both its scientific and political manifestations indicates clearly that it is wrong to view Hobbes's work as being completely divorced from the common assumptions of his contemporaries. In fact, it emphasises that Hobbes's importance stemmed from his essential connection with the politics and ideas of the Restoration period. This should lead to a reconsideration of Hobbes criticism as one of the most important legacies of Hobbes's extraordinary intellectual achievement. Works like Cumberland's *De legibus*, which engaged with Hobbes on his own terms, played an essential role in preserving some of Hobbes's insights into ethics and natural philosophy. Many of Hobbes's Anglican critics, facing the dissenters' challenge to the church-state, found some of his ideas too useful to be jettisoned. Equally Hobbes's theories of matter and local motion, and his geometrical conception of what constituted true science, set an agenda that it was impossible to ignore, and important to respond to. As a result, the *Leviathan* was to be tamed and not killed.

It is often assumed that Cumberland's *De legibus* excited little positive response, but this was far from being the case. Cumberland's work, in spite of all its problems of presentation, soon gained a wide and attentive readership, precisely because it addressed so many current concerns. It would become particularly important for Protestant natural law writers who faced charges of Hobbism. As chapter 7 will show, Cumberland's work was crucial to the development of Samuel Pufendorf's theory of moral obligation. It would also come to play a role in the debate over Locke's *Essay concerning human understanding*, giving rise to James Tyrrell's English version of the *De legibus*, a work designed to defend Locke's theories from accusations of Hobbism. These examples serve to underline the central importance of Cumberland's engagement with Hobbes. In its capacity to absorb some of Hobbes's premises and conclusions, the *De legibus* helped to preserve ideas common to a natural tradition which Hobbes's apparent atheism had rendered suspect. By arguing that moral and political obligation could be discovered in nature, Cumberland replaced Hobbes's mortal God with a more sophisticated understanding

---

28 Kirk, *Cumberland*, 30.

of God's relationship with His creation. Hobbes's artificial state, and artificial science, were transformed into a product of nature. Cumberland's work effectively domesticated ideas that both he and Hobbes shared: that through a study of the natural world, individuals could come to realise that to live in accordance with nature was to live in accordance with the rules of the state.

Richard Cumberland (1632–1718)

There is remarkably little biographical material on Cumberland. The main source is the short biography written by his son-in law, prefaced to Cumberland's 1720 *Sanchoniatho's Phoenician history*.[29] The few remaining letters and records offer brief glimpses of a distinguished, if rather uneventful life. Cumberland was born in 1632, the same year as Locke, Pufendorf and Spinoza. His family was not particularly wealthy; Richard Cumberland senior had come from a farming background in Northamptonshire, but his main trade was as a tailor in London. Richard Cumberland was the youngest of two brothers and a sister.[30] He attended St Paul's School, where he became friendly with Samuel Pepys, with whom he would have intermittent contact throughout his life. In June 1649, just five months after the execution of Charles I, he entered Magdalene College, Cambridge.

Magdalene was a middle-sized college in the 1640s. It had suffered badly from the earl of Manchester's anti-Royalist purge of 1644, losing nine of its fourteen Fellows. It would also lose its Master, Edward Rainbow, when he was required to subscribe to the Engagement in 1651.[31] But for all the upheavals of the period, it was a time of relative intellectual freedom, and it was here that Cumberland developed an interest in mathematics and the new natural philosophy. He certainly became friendly with Magdalene's maverick inventor Samuel Moreland, who was a tutor at the college until 1653. Another influence may have been John Dacres, the Senior Fellow at Magdalene from 1644. Expelled in 1650 for his failure to take the Engagement, Dacres's interest in mathematics and medicine led him to become a senior physician and Gresham Professor of Geometry.[32] During Cumberland's time at Magdalene he is credited by some with the invention of the first mechanical planetary

---

[29] S. Payne, 'Brief account of the life . . . of the author', prefaced to Richard Cumberland's *Sanchoniatho's Phoenician history*, London 1720.

[30] Kirk, *Cumberland*, 12. Linda Kirk has produced the best biographical account to date in her thesis.

[31] P. Cunich, D. Hoyle, E. Duffy and R. Hyam, *A history of Magdalene College 1428–1988*, Cambridge 1994, 117, 122.

[32] Moreland is referred to as an 'honoured friend' in Cumberland's *An essay towards the recovery of Jewish measures and weights*, London 1686, 52. For Dacres see Cunich, Hoyle, Duffy and Hyam, *History of Magdalene College*, 124.

model, or orrery – an early example of his life-long interest in mechanical systems.[33]

Cumberland left Cambridge in 1656 after taking his Master's degree. He became rector of the tiny and impoverished Northamptonshire parish of Brampton Ash in 1658, a living in the gift of Sir John Norwich, baronet and a Member of the Rump Parliament. It is not known whether Cumberland, like many of his close colleagues, was secretly ordained as an Anglican. The records in Lambeth Palace indicate that he was subject to the scrutiny of three approved Presbyterian 'Triers' in order to secure the living at Brampton, but contemporary sources indicate that this was far from being a rigorous test of sectarian loyalty.[34] For a highly qualified graduate like Cumberland, the period at Brampton does not seem to have been a particularly happy one. According to Payne, he concentrated upon his studies and attempted to keep up his acquaintance with his friends in Cambridge.[35]

This rural obscurity might have signalled the end of Cumberland's significance, but in 1667 he became the client of, and possibly a domestic chaplain to Orlando Bridgeman, Lord Keeper of the Great Seal.[36] Bridgeman, Lord Chief Justice of the Common Pleas and the judge who had presided over the trials of the regicides, had been at Magdalene in the 1620s. He found work for several of Cumberland's colleagues, most notably Cumberland's particular friend, Hezekiah Burton, who would later edit the *De legibus naturae*. It was most likely on Burton's recommendation that Cumberland gained favour with the new Lord Keeper.[37]

This connection placed Cumberland and his colleagues at the centre of the religious politics of the later 1660s. During this period, Bridgeman sponsored attempts by some of Cumberland's colleagues to construct a religious compromise with Presbyterian nonconformists. Although the negotiations ultimately failed, the discussion of natural law in the debates over toleration and comprehension formed the essential background to Cumberland's own work. In 1670, at the recommendation of the Lord Keeper, the newly-married Cumberland was established in comparatively affluent livings in Stamford, which he held together with Brampton Ash by special dispensation.[38] This post, and his augmented income, gave him the opportunity to complete the

33 J. R. Millburn, 'William Stukeley and the early history of the orrery', *Annals of Science* xxxi (1974), 511–28; R. Gunther, *Early science in Cambridge*, Oxford 1937, 169.
34 Lambeth Palace, MS 999, fo. 643; CUL, MS Add. 36.
35 Payne, 'Brief account', p. vii
36 Kirk, *Cumberland*, 13.
37 For Bridgeman see Osmund Airey's article in the *DNB*.
38 Cumberland held the vicarage of All Saints and the rectory of St Peter's. In addition to this, on 22 September 1670, he married Anne Quinsey, of Aslackby, Lincolnshire, who had recently become worth some £500. All of this meant that Cumberland's financial circumstances were dramatically improved: Lambeth Palace, MS Faculty Office, fo. 11; Kirk, *Cumberland*, 13.

De legibus naturae, which was licensed in July 1671, and published in the spring of 1672, dedicated to his patron.

Soon afterwards, however, Bridgeman resigned as Lord Keeper in protest at Charles II's Declaration of Indulgence. Cumberland appears to have survived his patron's fall, and to have devoted himself to his parochial duties during the 1670s. In addition to lecturing at All Saints' in Stamford, he was elected to Convocation in 1675,[39] and in 1680 he proceeded to a doctorate. His thesis maintained (against Roman Catholics) that St Peter had no jurisdiction over the other Apostles, and (against nonconformists) that separation from the English Church was schismatic.[40]

The 1680s saw Cumberland produce two works. The first was a pamphlet dedicated to his school-friend Pepys, now President of the Royal Society, entitled *An essay towards the recovery of Jewish measures and weights* (1686). The *Essay*, originally designed as an appendix to a new edition of the Bible, attempted to translate biblical forms of mensuration into modern equivalents. Unusually, it used this information to draw political conclusions about the importance of state control of the Church, and also about the status of the Church in Hebrew society. The *Essay* became one of Cumberland's best-selling and most widely respected works.[41]

Cumberland also produced the manuscript for *Sanchoniatho's Phoenician history*. This was the first English translation of the controversial fragment of Phoenician ancient history recorded in Eusebius, together with a detailed commentary which sought to reconcile it with the Bible. The reliability of the fragment had been suspected by biblical scholars throughout the seventeenth century, but Cumberland managed to contextualise it in such a way as to make it correspond with Mosaic history.[42] As with his other works, Cumberland's scholarship was given a contemporary application. Sanchoniatho's account revealed the means by which the Phoenicians had corrupted the true sacred history to deify their own versions of biblical individuals. This corruption resulted in polytheism and idolatry, a tradition which Cumberland traced down to its most recent manifestation in the Roman Catholic Church. Cumberland argued that an understanding of the origins of idolatry, combined with the revelation that heathen accounts fundamentally agree with Scripture, 'will always tend to the establishment of men's minds in the true Religion, not only in opposition to heathenism, but also in controversy with the Romanists, who participate of the heathen corruption, both in many idolatrous practices, and in lessening the authority of the Scriptures'.[43] Although this may seem a rather indirect way of combating the Catholic

---

[39] Ibid. 14.
[40] CUL Grace Book, supplicats 1677–80.
[41] Owned by, among others, John Locke, who annotated his copy: J. Harrison and P. Laslett, *The library of John Locke*, Oxford 1965, 119.
[42] G. Parry, *The trophies of time: English antiquarians of the seventeenth century*, Oxford 1995, 328–9.
[43] Cumberland, *Sanchoniatho's Phoenician history*, 90.

threat, it is worth noting the prevalence of such scholarship and its importance to Cumberland's contemporaries. Edward Stillingfleet, Matthew Hale and even Isaac Newton devoted much time and energy to similar investigations.[44] On the eve of the Revolution of 1688, Cumberland's anti-Catholicism took on a potent significance. Indeed, Cumberland's publisher thought the work so inflammatory 'that he did not care to undertake it'. As a result *Sanchoniatho* only appeared posthumously in 1720.[45]

This seems to have been Cumberland's only contribution to the political disturbances of 1688, but in their wake he was called upon to replace the non-juring bishop of Peterborough, Thomas White. Cumberland's preferral came on the recommendation of John Tillotson, who described the author of the *De legibus* in a memo to the king as 'the most worthy and learned minister in that diocese'.[46] Cumberland was duly consecrated in July 1691, aged fifty-nine. From this time until his death, he can be occasionally glimpsed in his episcopal duties, administering his diocese diligently but with declining efficacy as old age took its toll. Cumberland regularly attended the House of Lords until 1716. Records of his activity reveal a solidly Whiggish voting profile, and conspicuous aid for Archbishop Tenison in his struggles with the lower House of Convocation.[47] Intellectually, he busied himself with studies of ancient chronology, dying 'as he had lived, without the appearance of pain or passion' on 9 October 1718.

Cumberland is often portrayed as a pedestrian academic figure far removed from the seismic upheavals of a turbulent century, and this is an impression heightened by Payne's sometimes less than flattering account of a man he had known only in aged infirmity.[48] But this is far from being the case. Placing Cumberland's *De legibus* in context reveals that it was intimately connected with the political and intellectual debates of its time; Cumberland's interests spanned questions from ethics to church politics, modern science and ancient history. His work provides a unique and wide-ranging perspective upon the connections between all of these areas. For this reason, perhaps more than any other, the *De legibus naturae* deserves to be looked at again.

---

44 For ancient chronology and its contemporary relevance see A. Grafton, *Defenders of the text: the tradition of scholarship in an age of science*, Harvard 1991, esp. pp. 20ff; F. E. Manuel, *Isaac Newton: historian*, Cambridge 1963.

45 Payne, 'Brief account', p. xxxiii. Cumberland's *Origenes gentium antiquissimae*, further essays in ancient chronology, were published in 1724.

46 Kirk, *Cumberland*, 17.

47 Ibid. 20–1.

48 Payne recorded that 'Had his life been as active, as it was innocent, he would have risen above the pitch of human Nature': 'Brief account', p. xx.

1

The Political Context

Cumberland's *De legibus naturae* combined a theory of natural law with a critique of Hobbesian ethical theory. Strikingly though, despite the *De legibus*'s explicit attack on Hobbes, Cumberland's own political theory is peculiarly Hobbesian. One of the distinctive features of the *De legibus* was its sustained defence of unlimited sovereign power, which was a doctrine commonly associated with Hobbesian absolutism. Cumberland's conception of sovereignty, far from being restricted to the civil sphere, extended 'universally to things divine and human'.[1] In other words, it dominated all sections of society. This included, crucially, the spiritual sphere, and its institutional manifestation, the Church.

Cumberland incorporated these typically Hobbesian ideas, while at the same time distancing himself from the unacceptably atheist aspects of Hobbes's methodology. This should alert us to the possibility that criticism of Hobbes was not only a negative exercise, demolishing a discredited political theory. The continuing relevance of Hobbes's work for Restoration politics meant that Hobbesian theories of sovereignty were too useful to discard, but at the same time too controversial to be passed over without comment. As a result, for writers like Cumberland, it was necessary to do battle with the *Leviathan*, both to avoid the charge of 'Hobbism' and to vindicate their own position. The *Leviathan* was thus hunted, but often with the purpose of taming rather than killing it. This was the background for Cumberland's *De legibus naturae*, and indeed, as I shall argue, much anti-Hobbesian writing of the Restoration period.

The politics of religious toleration were the driving force behind discussion of Hobbes and 'Hobbism' in the 1660s. Until recently, this political motivation for anti-Hobbesian writing has rarely been considered. Most historians have concentrated upon the uniformly hostile reactions to Hobbes's supposed atheism and materialism. These issues were, of course, enough to make Hobbes important by himself, and were important elements of the 'black legend' that grew up around the 'Monster of Malmesbury'.[2] However, an examination of Samuel Mintz's checklist of Hobbes criticism and allusion soon reveals that anti-Hobbes literature had a much more directly political focus, particularly during the later 1660s, when Cumberland was writing the

---

[1] Cumberland, *DLN* 9.7.
[2] For this particular nick-name see the anonymous *True effigies of the monster of Malmesbury: or, Thomas Hobbes in his proper colours*, London 1680.

De legibus.[3] For critics of Hobbes writing in this period, the subject that most interested them was the power of the magistrate over religion. This should not be entirely surprising, as Hobbes had gone further than any other contemporary writer in asserting that subordination of the Church to an omnicompetent State was an essential precondition for peace and stability. These ideas were now back at the top of the political agenda.

The reasons for this lay in the peculiar religious nature of the Restoration 'settlements'. The Restoration had been founded on an uneasy political alliance between moderate Presbyterians and Anglicans, an alignment which had more to do with their common antipathy to radical republican Independents than with any fundamental agreement on points of religion. Although a broad and inclusive political settlement was reached, achieving a balanced ecclesiastical agreement proved to be more difficult. Despite well-intentioned efforts to reach some kind of compromise, negotiations between representatives of the Anglican and Presbyterian parties drifted inconclusively through the later part of 1660 and into 1661. Little agreement was reached on the disputed issues of episcopal church government, the form of a revised prayer-book, and ceremonial details.[4]

Increasingly ill-tempered wrangling over scriptural interpretation led some to despair of any kind of rational settlement: 'Reason and Experience', wrote Edward Stillingfleet, 'thus give little hope of any peace if it depends on men's agreeing.'[5] Stillingfleet's scepticism, as well as his emphasis on reason and experience, were typical of younger members of the clergy who had been educated against a backdrop of sectarian enthusiasm and political unrest. Stillingfleet, born in 1635, had been fifteen when Charles I was executed; his formative years had been scarred by religious conflict. His response to this kind of conflict was to evade the intractability of scriptural dogma through an appeal to reason and prudence. This led him to eschew the contradictory and impassioned language of religious extremism, and to appeal to natural law. His *Irenicum* of 1661 was an early use of natural law theory to cut around the dogmatic claims of Anglicans and Presbyterians to be the sole professors of *iure divino* forms of church government. As both sides relied on irreconcilable readings of Scripture, Stillingfleet aimed to pitch his solution to the problem 'upon such a foundation, if possible to be found out, wherein the different parties retaining their private apprehensions, may yet be agreed to carry on the same work in common according to the peace and tranquillity of the Church of God'.

---

3 Mintz, *Hunting of Leviathan*, 157–60.
4 Narrative detail is taken from various sources: N. Sykes, *From Sheldon to Secker: aspects of English church history 1660–1768*, Cambridge 1959, ch. iii; A. H. Wood, *Church unity without uniformity*, London 1963; D. R. Lacey, *Dissent and parliamentary politics*, New Brunswick, NJ 1969; Spurr, *Restoration Church of England*.
5 E. Stillingfleet, *Irenicum: a weapon-salve for the churches wounds, or the divine right of particular forms of church government discuss'd and examin'd according to the principles of the law of nature*, London 1661, 3.

Stillingfleet began by proposing a theoretical framework for his general argument. If both sides wished to talk about church institutions by divine right, it made sense to examine exactly what this use of the term 'right' meant. If a right was something that was done with justice, then it must refer to some law which made it right. Stillingfleet maintained that rights are by their very nature dependent on laws, and that laws create two sorts of right. The first of these is a positive prescriptive right, in which the law is directive. The second type of right is a negative right, which proceeds from the silence of the law. In this instance the lack of a specific rule creates a right for the agent to do as he or she wills. To understand and clarify discussion of rights and church government, Stillingfleet thus concluded that one had to look at the relevant laws from which such rights are drawn; in this case, natural law, and the additional obligations to that law which God has imposed through Scripture.

Before he dealt with natural and positive divine laws, Stillingfleet laid down a number of hypotheses 'for our more distinct, clear and rational proceeding' in order to guide his discussion and prevent misunderstanding.[6] The first of these 'hypotheses' was that the duties of natural law were not subject to positive human law. This may seem like a rather obvious point to make, but in 1661 Stillingfleet's statement of this position revealed his awareness of its potential dangers. To use natural law theory during this period was to run the risk of association with Hobbes. The hallmark of Hobbesian natural law theory was that for the purposes of practical moral obligation, positive human laws effectively determined the obligations of natural law. Hobbes had denied that natural laws in themselves were anything other than mere theorems: products of individual reason. To make them morally obligatory, natural laws had to be authorised by the magistrate. Shockingly, Hobbes had seemed to make natural law dependent upon human law. It was this notorious inversion of the natural order which Stillingfleet sought to forestall with his prefatory hypotheses.[7]

This inoculation against Hobbism was particularly necessary for the direction of Stillingfleet's argument about rights. Having established his anti-Hobbesian credentials, Stillingfleet went on to suggest that where the law of nature is silent on an issue, *ius naturae permissivum*, or natural liberty of acting, is created. To see how this situation affected the discussion of church government, Stillingfleet proposed to examine his argument using the state of nature hypothesis. The hypothesis would allow him to discuss in isolation the duties required by natural law, a move that would allow him to detach the discussion from Scripture. The snag was that the greatest practitioner of the state of nature hypothesis, as he freely admitted in a marginal note, was Thomas Hobbes.[8]

6 Ibid. 27.
7 Ibid. 28–9.
8 Ibid. 32.

Discussion of the natural state was hardly a specifically Hobbesian inno-vation, but Hobbes's characterisation of it as warlike was a key issue for Hob-bes's critics.[9] The state of nature as a state of war may have been a hypothetical construct, but the implication that political sovereignty was constructed solely to escape such a state, negated the 'natural' institution of government. The hypothesis made it clear that political authority was made by man, and not directly ordained by God. Stillingfleet wished to use the hypothesis 'only as an imaginary state, for better understanding the nature and obligation of laws'. His refutation of Hobbes betrays the need to neutral-ise such a reading, and to reclaim natural law and the natural state from a potentially dangerous association with some of Hobbes's most notorious and atheistic theses. His marginal citation of Hobbes, from chapter 1 of the *De cive*, was cleverly designed to make the point that the state of nature had to be completely fictional, because, as Hobbes himself had stated at the end of a long annotation on the natural state, a son born to a father was automatically under some form of government.[10] Close reading of Hobbes in this instance clarified the use of supposedly Hobbesian concepts.

Stillingfleet used the hypothesis to isolate the nature of rights, like Hobbes, but with a very different kind of theory. For individuals in this natural state, outside society, whatever is not determined by positive natural law is permitted, that is, it is a right. At the same time, individuals have it within their power to restrain their own liberty in matters where they judge it necessary – they can voluntarily give up their right, if they see fit to do so. An example of this is where individuals leave their natural state and enter society, which is a positive dictate of natural law. In this instance it may not be appropriate for individuals to retain their natural rights in a social context. Public disagreement over what was previously a matter of natural liberty could conflict with the peaceful establishment of society. It is thus necessary for individuals to alienate some of their natural rights to the public authority in order to enjoy the benefits of a peaceful society. This argument was perti-nent to religion if one considered religious worship to be *ius naturae permissi-vum* in the state of nature. Although this was exercised justly by each individual in the state of nature, disagreement over religion in society could become an obstacle to peace and sociability. The implication of Stillingfleet's argument was that each side in the argument over church government should abdicate their right to decide the manner of worship to the magistrate, par-ticularly where there was no authoritative judgement of natural law or Scripture.

This discussion of the transfer of natural rights to a magisterial power might sound peculiarly Hobbesian. In Hobbes, each individual gives up his or her natural right to a sovereign power whose actions they subsequently authorise, as if they were their own. It is important to note, however, that

---

9   T. Hobbes, *Leviathan*, ed. R. Tuck, Cambridge 1991, 86–90.
10 Idem, *De cive: the English version*, ed. H. Warrender, Oxford 1983, 48.

there are crucial differences alongside the generic similarities between the arguments. For Hobbes, the state of nature is such a hostile environment that individuals are driven to seek security by a fatal necessity. This, the really distinctive feature of Hobbesian political theory, meant that individuals are forced to cede their rights to a third party. For Stillingfleet, on the other hand, individuals are not compelled to enter society so much from the fear of death, but from a natural and peaceable sociable tendency or instinct. In *Irenicum*, individuals are naturally sociable, motivated less by individual fear, than by the recognition that they have a natural obligation to the community, and the common good. Only certain potentially conflicting rights are transferred, and these voluntarily. As Stillingfleet puts it later:

> For as it is supposed that in all contracts and agreements for mutual society, men are content to part with their own liberty for the good of the whole; so likewise to part with the authority of their own judgements, and to submit to the determination of things by the rulers of the society constituted by them.[11]

The similarity between *Irenicum* and *Leviathan* lay in the necessity of giving up personal rights for a peaceful society. In this respect, both Hobbes and Stillingfleet were working with the same terms to find a solution to the problem of conflict. The crucial difference was the motivational structure in each case, and the degree of closure required. For Hobbes, creating sovereignty was an individual and negative response to the state of war – rights are alienated individually, unilaterally and necessarily, for self-preservation. Sociability was an artificial creation. For Stillingfleet, natural sociability required that individuals part with rights for the common good – alienation of right was thus for the public benefit, and not simply a calculation of self-interest. Sociability in this instance was positive, voluntary and natural.

This natural jurisprudential argument had far-reaching implications for the question of church government, implications which *Irenicum* shared with the *Leviathan*. Unless claims about the form of church government could be shown to have a basis in natural law or Scripture, then the lawful civil power had a right to constitute the Church in a form consistent with the good of society. Stillingfleet's view was that the prescription of natural law only required that there should be some form of worship. Equally, scriptural discussion was too vague to proclaim a clear divine preference. After an exhaustive search of the scriptural texts adduced to support the case on each side, Stillingfleet was forced to conclude that there was no decisive evidence that one form of government or another was divinely ordained.[12] For Stillingfleet this was proof that, for the question of church government at least, there was a *ius naturae*. In a social context, that right properly belonged to the state; neither episcopacy nor presbytery could be proved to have been divinely

---

11 Stillingfleet, *Irenicum*, 124, cf. 126.
12 Ibid. 322–3.

sanctioned. Stillingfleet concluded that it should not be the ill-grounded claims of religious zealots that should be allowed to dominate the ecclesiastical settlement. Rather it should be the prudential hand of the state, framing public worship for the common good:

> This hath been the whole Design of this Treatise, to prove that the form of Church Government is a meer matter of Prudence, regulated by the Word of God . . . that Government is best according to the principles of Christian Prudence, which comes nearest of Apostolicall practice, and lends most to the advancing the peace and unity of the Church of God.[13]

The erastian message of *Irenicum* was disturbing to those Presbyterians and Anglicans for whom the form of religious worship was defined by their understanding of Scripture. In Stillingfleet's account natural law became the basis for the state's intervention in the organisation of religion. This argument was roundly criticised for its erastianism, but also for the implication of Hobbism. In Hobbes contemporaries had a clear example of the ways in which such a position could become the basis of an arbitrary and absolute power, a power in which the obligations of natural law served merely to justify civil laws. The style and genre in which Stillingfleet had written raised the spectre of the state determining every aspect of religious life on a Hobbesian basis, defining worship, authorising Scripture and the clergy. The fine distinction between the sociable and unsociable models of natural law theory was easily overlooked by critics.

Stillingfleet felt compelled to respond to his detractors in the second edition of the *Irenicum* in 1662. This contained an appendix designed to show 'that the world may see I have not been more forward to assert the just power of the magistrate in ecclesiasticals as well as civills, than to defend the fundamental rights of the church'.[14] Stillingfleet argued that the Church was a separate, spiritual, jurisdiction, and that the right of nature did not imply that the magistrate had anything more than temporal authority. Eager to demonstrate his distance from Hobbes, Stillingfleet devoted a section to attacking the *Leviathan's* argument 'that no Precepts of the Gospel are Law, till enacted by Civil Authority'.[15] To say this, according to Stillingfleet, was to suggest that there was no higher obligation to God's own laws, which should always come, as his first hypothesis had suggested, before positive human laws.

Stillingfleet's insistence on the priority of God's laws betrayed his own unease with the boundary between temporal and divine authority. The form of church government brought out precisely this ambiguity; the Church was an institution with both spiritual and temporal identities. If civil peace was

---

[13] Ibid. 416.

[14] Idem, *A discourse concerning the power of excommunication; appendix to Irenicum*, London 1662.

[15] Ibid. 10.

the aim, it meant compromising spiritual liberty in a Hobbesian fashion; if the rights of the Church were overdependent upon problematic interpretations of God's will through Scripture, then the possibility of conflict remained. This tension fuelled Stillingfleet's defensive engagement with Hobbes; to preserve the usefulness of his natural right argument, Stillingfleet had to prove that it was not Hobbesian.[16] Hobbes may have done more than any other theorist to emphasise the utility of rights theories in resolving conflict, but he had to be discredited for those very theories to be used at all.

Stillingfleet's deployment of natural law arguments had referred primarily to the problem of deciding between *iure divino* forms of church goverment. During late 1660 and 1661, this debate was superseded by disputes at the Savoy Conference over whether the state had the right to impose forms and ceremonies which fell under the category of *adiaphora*, things indifferent. This included the wearing of surplices by ministers, the use of the sign of the cross at baptism, and the posture of kneeling to take communion. What distinguished these issues was that they were not specifically required by Scripture. As a result, they could not be said to be God's law as such, and all sides agreed on their indifferent status. The question was over who had the right to legislate on such matters; was it simply up to the individual according to his or her own conscience, or was it important for the state to regulate the public conduct of ministers and parishioners?

Again, at issue was the question of the exercise of the *ius permissivum* generated by the silence of Scripture. Inevitably the debate generated a large literature, some of which was based upon natural law. For writers like the Independent leader John Owen, and the Oxford-based don Edward Bagshaw, the absence of a positive injunction in Scripture left individuals with the right to do as they pleased in such matters. The practical consequence of this position was that as the ceremonies were in themselves indifferent and did not threaten public safety, liberty of conscience in such matters should be tolerated.[17] Any attempt to impose such things would make them necessary, and thus would violate the consciences and Christian liberty of those who did not subscribe to them.

For others, however, this championing of Christian liberty was more sinister. For the young John Locke, Bagshaw's colleague at Christ Church, it was a liberty 'for contention, censure and persecution'.[18] Locke, then in his late twenties, was a near contemporary of Stillingfleet; in his *Two tracts on govern-*

---

16 Stillingfleet was unable to escape the taint of Hobbism, particularly later in his career when he used erastian arguments against dissenters in the 1680s, for which see J. Marshall, 'The ecclesiology of the Latitude-Men', *Journal of Ecclesiastical History* xxxvi (1985), 407–27. The error still persists: Stillingfleet was identified in a recent article on seventeenth-century preachers as 'being friendly with Hobbes': S. Lehmberg, 'The writings of the English cathedral clergy 1600–1700', *Anglican Theology Review* lxxv (1993), 81.
17 J. Owen, *Two questions concerning the power of the supream magistrate about religion*, London 1659; E. Bagshaw, *The great question concerning religious worship*, London 1660.
18 J. Locke, *Two tracts on government*, ed. P. Abrams, Cambridge 1967, 120.

ment he attacked Bagshaw's defence of toleration. To understand his position in these early works it is necessary to appreciate the extent to which the religious extremism of the Interregnum had marked those who, like Stillingfleet, Locke and Cumberland, had grown up under its shadow. In this context a plea for religious liberty was indissolubly mixed with the political subversion of the 1640s and 1650s. In the *Tracts*, Locke compared the tolerationists' plea for liberty of conscience with similar demands made in the 1640s. These were, as he saw it, the 'first inlet to all those confusions and unheard of and destructive opinions'.[19]

For Locke, acts of public worship could never be as politically harmless as Owen and Bagshaw were claiming. The unbridled exercise of individual forms of devotion could only result in the destruction of the fragile peace. The only answer was to leave the determination of *adiaphora* to the civil magistrate. In arguing this, Locke had recourse to the same apparently 'Hobbesian' natural law arguments used by Stillingfleet:

> even supposing man naturally owner of an entire liberty and so much master of himself as to owe no subjection to any other but God alone, (which is the first condition we fancy him in), it is yet the unalterable condition of society and government that every particular man must undoubtedly part with his native right to his primitive liberty and entrust the magistrate with as full a power over all his actions as he himself has.[20]

As a consequence, Locke argued that 'the supreme magistrate of every nation what way soever, must necessarily have an absolute and arbitrary power over all the indifferent actions of his people'. Like Stillingfleet, Locke uses the state of nature argument to show how individuals must part with natural rights for the establishment of a government that is apparently unlimited in its jurisdiction.

The tolerationist argument against this position had been that imposition of obligation upon things indifferent violated liberty of conscience. Locke responded to this by making a Hobbesian distinction between internal and external acts. The command of the magistrate only referred to external, public acts. No command could compromise the conscience, because the conscience was beyond the reach of the public authority:

---

19 Ibid. 159.
20 Ibid. 124–5. The reference to contract theory is even more pronounced in the Latin tract, here cited in the English translation: 'But such a power can never be established unless each and every individual surrenders the whole of this natural liberty of his, however great it may be, to a legislator, granting it to him with the authority of all (by proxy, as it were), empowered by the general consent of each makes valid laws for them . . . For he concentrates in his position the authority and natural right of every individual by a general contract; and all indifferent things, sacred no less than profane, are entirely subjected to his legislative power and government': ibid. 230–1.

But the understanding and assent (whereof God hath reserved the discipline to himself, and not so much entrusted man with a liberty or pleasure to believe and reject) being not to be wrought upon by force, a magistrate would in vain assault that part of man which owes no homage to his authority.[21]

Extensive though the magistrate's powers are, he can only police external and public acts. It was physically impossible to force the conscience, and so conscience could not be violated. Stillingfleet had used the same distinction in *Irenicum* to justify the imposition of church government by the state, but this separation of public acts and private conscience was also a characteristic feature of Hobbes's argument in chapter 15 of *Leviathan*.[22]

The danger in the argument lay in the potential for hypocrisy. The way that Hobbes's scheme appeared to sanction hypocritical conformity was a staple of anti-Hobbesian works. As with the Church, the problem was to find a balance between public acts, which needed to be regulated to maintain the peace, and private conscience, which was subject to higher, divine, obligation. Hobbes's solution was a radical separation between those spheres; for writers like Owen, however, this distinction was inherently false. It created the possibility that individuals could be forced into acts which they felt might violate their own equally acceptable beliefs, with the attendant danger of incurring divine displeasure for conforming to activity which was technically scandalous.

These problems may have been part of the reason why Locke did not publish the *Tracts*. The Hobbesian tension between sovereignty and the natural law which was supposed to justify its existence, led him to explore the foundations of that natural law doctrine, and to consider Hobbes more directly. His later *Essays on the law of nature*, composed before 1664, explicitly addressed the question of what natural law was, and what it obliged individuals to do. The essays also directly attacked the means by which Hobbes had undermined the conventional account of natural jurisprudence.[23]

Both Stillingfleet and Locke thus found themselves in the position of using apparently Hobbesian arguments to justify extreme theories of sovereignty. Both felt it necessary to produce work that rebutted Hobbes's argument and clarified their own. In each case, this took the form of an examination of the true basis of natural obligation from a discussion of the law of nature. Religious conflict had required the deployment of natural law and rights theories, but that usage was dogged by the Hobbesian legacy.

In the event, the attempts to found a suitable compromise over the *adiaphora* issue were settled decisively with the advent of the 'Cavalier' Parliament. Staunchly Anglican, and determinedly reactionary, it demanded a complete restoration of the *status quo ante*. In ecclesiastical terms, this was

---

[21] Ibid. 127.

[22] Stillingfleet, *Irenicum*, 72; cf. Hobbes, *Leviathan*, 110.

[23] On the continuity between the *Tracts* and the *Essays* see von Leyden's introduction to J. Locke, *Essays on the laws of nature*, ed. W. von Leyden, Oxford 1954, 30.

embodied in the Act of Uniformity, passed on 19 May 1662. The severity of the act, which led to the deprivation of nearly a thousand non-conforming ministers in August of the same year, shocked many on all sides, not least the king, for whom a broad religious compromise had been the foundation and instrument of restoration.[24] For the moderate Presbyterians, it was a particularly bitter blow, given the close agreement which had been reached on many points of doctrine, and even over some of the ceremonies.[25] In drawing a hard and fast line between those who could and those who could not accept the Anglican 'settlement', the act effectively politicised a question which would dominate issues of Church and State until 1688.

Comprehension, toleration and Hobbism in the later 1660s[26]

Richard Cumberland's direct involvement in this debate began in the mid 1660s. It came about through his association with groups attempting to find some way of resolving the impasse over dissent. His particular acquaintances are usually known as Latitudinarians, and are commonly portrayed as a liberal, tolerant wing of the Established Church in the seventeenth century. In fact, what has become known as Latitudinarianism was far more complex, and so was the kind of politics which Richard Cumberland's De legibus naturae would ultimately come to defend.

From 1658 onwards, Cumberland had held a poor living in the tiny parish of Brampton Ash, in Northamptonshire. This was a common fate for the many clergymen unable to find substantial patronage in the seventeenth century. The rectory cannot have provided much of a challenge for Cumberland's considerable learning and experience. Payne's biography indicates that Cumberland was not idle; he busied himself with the latest books and information on scientific matters, particularly medicine. He also travelled to Cambridge frequently to keep in touch with his Magdalene friends, Burton and Hollings, a connection that would later save him from his rural exile.[27]

Cumberland's poor circumstances after the Restoration were shared by many of those educated during the Interregnum. For those who still held college fellowships, there was the immediate issue of the legality of their academic preferment under the Commonwealth and Protectorate. Many promotions had been made on the authority of Heads of Houses intruded into their

[24] For the act and Charles's attempts to ameliorate it see R. Hutton, *The Restoration: a political and religious history of England and Wales 1658–1667*, Oxford 1986, 174–6.
[25] Lacey, *Dissent and parliamentary politics*, 20–1, 269–70.
[26] For discussions of comprehension and toleration during the period see A. Thomas, 'Comprehension and toleration', in G. F. Nuttall and O. Chadwick (eds), *From uniformity to unity*, London 1962, 191–253; W. G. Simon, 'Comprehension in the age of Charles II', *Church History* xxxi (1962), 440–8; J. Spurr, 'The Church of England, comprehension and the Toleration Act of 1689', *English Historical Review* civ (1989), 927–47.
[27] Payne, 'Brief account', pp. vii–viii.

posts after the purges which accompanied the taking of the Covenant (1644) and the Engagement (1651). Anyone associated with this process found themselves objects of suspicion and distrust for their apparent complicity with the Interregnum regime. The apparent ease with which younger writers like Stillingfleet squared their allegiance to the restored regime, coupled with their espousal of a naturalistic, erastian and apparently Hobbesian ecclesiology, earned them the description of 'men of latitude'. Tarred with the stigma of Hobbism, individuals identified under this heading were popularly castigated, prompting one to write a defence of the men called abusively 'Latitudinarians'.[28]

In the years following the Restoration, these men largely left Cambridge to find employment within the legal community, as ecclesiastical positions were at that time effectively barred to them. After being ejected as the Master of Trinity College, John Wilkins's first appointment was as a preacher at Gray's Inn, which later extended residence rights to him in 1664. Stillingfleet's first patron was the barrister Sir Roger Burgoyne; he later obtained the patronage of the Master of the Rolls, Sir Harbottle Grimstone. Stillingfleet eventually became Preacher to the Rolls, and Lecturer at the Temple. John Tillotson, vindictively ejected from his fellowship at Clare College, had an unsatisfactory career as a preacher to a Puritan parish in Suffolk, before gaining a more congenial post as chaplain to Sir Edward Prideaux, Inner Temple barrister and Interregnum attorney-general. He later worked for Sir Robert Atkyns, barrister and member of parliament. Hezekiah Burton, Cumberland's friend from Magdalene, would follow in the mid 1660s by becoming chaplain to the Lord Chief Justice of the Common Pleas, Sir Orlando Bridgeman.

This distinctive pattern of migration was undoubtedly influenced by the close connections between the universities and the Inns of Court.[29] Indeed, we can see many examples of college connections providing employment; Grimstone found work for Richard Kidder, and they had both been to Emmanuel College, Cambridge. Bridgeman, an ex-Magdalene man, was patron to Burton and later Cumberland. There was also, however, a close intellectual tie between the legal community and the clergymen. Lawyers like Bridgeman and Matthew Hale had had to steer a similarly judicious course through the Interregnum to survive into the Restoration. They were all, almost to a man, friends and admirers of John Selden, who had been so influential in developing natural law ideas in England. However, the group's Seldenian connections and marked erastianism could sometimes bracket

---

28 S. P., *A brief account of the new sect of Latitude-men together with some reflections on the new philosophy*, Cambridge 1662. See also J. Glanvill, *Essays on several important subjects*, London 1676, no. 6, p. 16 (separately paginated). For a rather different account of Latitudinarianism see J. Spurr, 'Latitudinarianism and the Restoration Church', *Historical Journal* xxxi (1988), 61–82.

29 John Gascoigne, *Cambridge in the age of the Enlightenment*, Cambridge 1989, 48–9.

them with Hobbes, one of Selden's more notorious friends. It is hardly surprising to find the displaced clergymen and Seldenian legal circles finding common cause in natural law solutions to the problem of dissent. Such connections constituted the means by which such ideas could be made relevant to Restoration politics. It is also not surprising to find them suspected of Hobbism.

Cumberland's connection with these circles began in 1667, soon after Burton had been appointed as Bridgeman's chaplain. In that year, according to Payne, Cumberland was summoned to town by Bridgeman, who had been made Lord Keeper in the wake of Clarendon's fall.[30] The details and results of this meeting are not known for certain, but it is likely that Cumberland, probably on the recommendation of Burton, successfully obtained Bridgeman's patronage. Some accounts even suggest that Cumberland became a second domestic chaplain.[31]

Cumberland's involvement with Bridgeman came at a crucial time in the development of the dissent issue. Clarendon's downfall had broken the Anglican monopoly on policy-making. The new Cabal regime, although heterogeneous in many respects, was more disposed to the king's avowed aim of encouraging religious reconciliation. Dissenters looked forward to a loosening of the Clarendon Code, and greater religious freedom. A commentator from Chester reported in September 1667 that, 'the people are transported with joy upon the Lord Keeper's instalment into the ministry, and the Presbyterians big with expectations that their idol Gods, their factious ministers, should be tolerated to prate in public'.[32]

The dissenters were right to see an ally in Bridgeman, but they were wrong if they assumed, with Arlington's correspondent, that he would endorse a simple policy of toleration. Bridgeman's preferred solution, as it would be with those thinkers he patronised, would not be based upon toleration, but comprehension. These views were promoted by what Antony Wood called John Wilkins's 'Club' for comprehension and a limited indulgence.[33] Through such informal groupings, the latitude men, with the aid of their powerful legal sponsors, could attempt to influence policy. According to Wood, they met 'in the chamber of that great Trimmer and Latitudinarian, Dr Hezekiah Burton in Essex House, beyond Temple Bar, being then the

---

[30] Payne, 'Brief account', p. viii; Pepys's diary for March 1667 records what may have been the visit in question; Cumberland called on his old school friend: 'Comes my old good friend, Mr Richard Cumberland, to see me, being newly come to town, whom I have not seen in almost, if not quite, these seven years, in his plain country-parson's dress': *Diary of Samuel Pepys*, vii. 118.

[31] Kirk, *Cumberland*, 13.

[32] *Calendar of state papers, domestic series, of the reign of Charles II*, ed. E. Green, F. H. B. Daniell and F. Bickley, London 1860–1938 (hereinafter cited as *CSPD*), ccxvi. 457, 454–5.

[33] A. Wood, *Athenae Oxoniensis*, ed. P. Bliss, Oxford 1813–20, iv. 512–13. See also J. Tillotson, *The works of the Most Reverend Dr John Tillotson*, ed. R. Barker, London 1728, i, p. xii.

habitation of Sir Orlando Bridgeman'. Thomas Birch's biography of Tillotson suggests that both he and Stillingfleet were also involved, alongside Sir Matthew Hale (1609–76), the Lord Chief Baron of the Exchequer. It is tempting to imagine, and probable enough to suggest, that after his introduction into the circle of the new Lord Keeper, Cumberland was part of that group, or at least familiar with its discussions.

Toleration and comprehension are often bracketed together in discussion of the negotiations which took place in the 1660s and 1670s, but this does not reflect the very different principles which underlay tolerant and comprehensive solutions to the problem of dissent. In many ways comprehension and toleration were mutually exclusive concepts. The comprehension schemes developed by Cumberland's colleagues proceeded on exactly the same natural law premises as Stillingfleet and Locke's rejection of the principle of toleration. The natural law principle underlying comprehension was that human institutions like the Church could be constituted, as Stillingfleet put it in *Irenicum*, with regard to 'wisdom and prudence'. Stillingfleet's appeal to natural law underpinned a profoundly relativistic view of positive institutions. These, like the apostolic Church, could differ in form according to the circumstances, provided that they served the ends prescribed by the law of nature, a settled society and the orderly worship of God.[34] Accepting this approach allowed one to view institutional arrangements as being flexible, temporal expressions of a deeper continuity of purpose. This permitted room for adjustment in cases where the circumstances had changed. In the case of the dissent issue, the changing political circumstances had created a situation in which the anomaly of 'conformable' non-conforming Prebyterians like Richard Baxter could be solved. The terms of ecclesiastical settlement could be altered to allow suitable non-conformists to come within the pale of the Established Church.

This was a long way from advocacy of a principle of toleration. Toleration proceeded from the basis that the magistrate had no right to legislate upon such matters in the first place, a position upheld by John Owen and the Independents. The pro-comprehension lobby in the later 1660s were prepared to talk about the possibility of a limited toleration, but it should be stressed that this was only as a means of eventual conformity. For leading campaigners like John Wilkins, toleration was an inferior, temporary, and deliberately restrictive concession, to be completely rejected as the underlying logic of any viable settlement.[35] This was a view that was uncompromising in its requirement for religious uniformity, however that establishment was constituted or might be changed. These apparently moderate attempts at reconciliation thus concealed an extremely illiberal view of religious dissent, a fact which

---

[34] Stillingfleet, *Irenicum*, 322–3.
[35] This explains why Wilkins rejected the terms of the Declaration of Indulgence in 1672, and pursued his own unofficial comprehension schemes in his Chester diocese: B. Shapiro, *John Wilkins, 1614–1672: an intellectual biography*, Princeton 1969, 169–76, 181–4.

should be borne in mind when considering the traditionally liberal reputation of Latitudinarian churchmen.[36]

This darker side to the policy of reconciliation can be illustrated by examining the opening shot in the campaign to win the House of Commons over to the idea of comprehension. In June 1667 an anonymous pamphlet was published, entitled *A proposition for the safety and happiness of the king and kingdom*. It was designed to promote a bill drafted by Sir Robert Atkyns, one of the lawyers associated with the Cambridge divines.[37] The argument of the pamphlet was that dissenters could be dealt with by 'a conjunction with the sober part of them . . . and overcoming the rest in their weakness with forebearance, long-suffering and goodness'.[38]

The author (possibly John Humfrey, a friend of Wilkins) was not suggesting that there would be any kind of substantial intellectual compromise with dissent. Rather, he adopted the view that integrating dissenters would be the surest way to 'cure' them of their erroneous beliefs: maintaining the current separation effectively prevented dissenters from exposure to the instruction in moral duty that could be provided by the Established Church. Some of this message was clearly designed to flatter its target conformist audience, but the theme that dissent was related to moral degeneracy had deeper roots. The sentiment that dissent stemmed from an inability to perceive the natural necessity of conformity was a consistent theme of writings on the subject. Such an inability was diagnosed as a peculiar type of mental deficiency or disease and went a long way towards creating the stereotype of the religious fanatic. In a sentence which presages some of the most vitriolic attacks on nonconformists by supposedly moderate Latitudinarians, the author of the pamphlet asserts that 'a great thing that keeps these Fanaticks from the Church and the Common Prayer lies in such private odd impressions in their thicke beliefs and dark minds'.[39] Meddling with persons, he says later, only torments the body, and does nothing to heal conceptions. Thus the Act of Uniformity's attempt to politicise the pathology of fanaticism actually prevents the necessary cure, and for this reason it should be revised.

The argument behind the Atkyns Bill was not moderate in the conventional sense of the term. It suggested that the dissenter could be made to see that his or her obedience to the Established Church was necessary, whatever form it might take. In an argument designed to support comprehension, it is possible to see the authoritarian notions implicit in the assumption that the dissenter can be 'cured' of his or her erroneous conceptions. If the dissenters proved to be resilient to such cures, however, the political implications of

---

[36] For the authoritarian mood of Restoration Latitudinarianism see R. Ashcraft, 'Latitudinarianism and toleration: historical myth versus political history', in W. Kroll and R. Ashcraft (eds), *Philosophy, science and religion 1640–1700*, Cambridge 1991, 151–77.

[37] Atkyns had employed Tillotson as his chaplain: *DNB s.v.*

[38] Anon., *A proposition for the safety and happiness of the king and kingdom*, London 1667, 34.

[39] Ibid. 54.

dissent might be even more severe, as the fate of the comprehension campaign would show.

In the event, the Commons proved to be in no mood to compromise with dissent. The Presbyterian Colonel John Birch (1616–91), deputised to introduce the Atkyns Bill on 10 October, faintly attempted to raise the matter, 'but (despairing of success) sat down'.[40] Another attempt followed a few months later. Bridgeman sent Sir John Baber (1625–1704), physician to Charles II, to consult with the Presbyterian Thomas Manton (1620–77), former royal chaplain, and long-standing supporter of comprehension. Manton wrote to Baxter in January 1667/8 about the possibility of finding grounds for terms. These overtures resulted in a conference between Manton, Baxter and William Bates (1625–99), for the dissenters, with John Wilkins and Burton representing Bridgeman.[41] Agreement was reached on most of the issues discussed, but a fatal hitch emerged over the question of reordination. This raised the question of the legitimacy of an episcopal form of government – should newly conforming ministers be ordained by bishops, and if so, how should it be done? Wilkins had designed an ordination formula which had pared the ecclesiastical implications down to the bone. It was still too much for Baxter. In his autobiographical memoirs Baxter comments that 'the great stop in our treaty was about reordination, and Dr Wilkins still insisted in this, that their consciences must be accommodated who took them for no ministers who were ordained without bishop'.[42] Baxter's failure to compromise dismayed both the Anglicans and even some of his Presbyterian colleagues.[43] Worse still was the reaction of their most powerful sponsor. Bridgeman was reported to have commented in the aftermath that those 'whom I believed most ready to promote such a peaceable design will never agree in any thing; and I will have no more to do with them'.[44] Hale attempted to transform the final draft of the Bill into a more acceptably Anglican form in an attempt to salvage something, but leaked information about the discussion at the conference only succeeded in alienating the bishops, discrediting Wilkins, and generating a hostile reception for the measure in the Commons.

The session opened on 10 February with a request from the king that the House should seek to beget 'a better union and compromise in the minds of my Protestant Subjects in matters of Religion'. The Commons was entirely negative in its response. According to Thomas Barlow's account, 'the Commons that morning (before the king came to the House) upon relation of the insolent carriage and conventicles of nonconformists and sectaries in

---

40 Thomas, 'Comprehension and toleration', 198.
41 Tillotson, *Works*, i, p. xii.
42 R. Baxter, *Reliquiae Baxterianae*, London 1696, iii. 37.
43 Shapiro, *Wilkins*, 72.
44 W. Sherlock, *A vindication of the rights of ecclesiastical authority*, London 1685, 185–8. See also A. Cromartie, *Sir Matthew Hale 1609–1676: law, religion and natural philosophy*, Cambridge 1995, 186–91.

each county, voted that it should be desired (not to give indulgence but) to send out a proclamation to put the laws against non-conformity into execution'. Pepys's comment on the same day was that 'it was moved that, if any people had a mind to bring any new laws into the House about Religion, they might come, as a proposer of new laws did in Athens, with ropes about their necks'.[45] The bill was hampered and delayed, to be finally rejected on 8 April by 176 votes to 70.

The defeat of the bill, and the breakdown of the negotiations with the Presbyterians, signalled the failure of an attempt to construct a practical dialogue based around the idea of comprehension. This was particularly worrying from the Anglican side, given the fate of the limited toleration proposal which had been put before the Independents.

Wilkins's original measure had involved the imposition of financial penalties in return for indulgence. The theory was that such financial disincentives would encourage individuals back into the fold, while at the same time providing financial support for the massive project of rebuilding Anglican churches. This kind of proposal was a consistent feature of Latitudinarian discussion of toleration, designed to encourage dialogue, but also to emphasise the penal and 'second-best' quality of the dispensation. John Owen, the Independent leader, to Bridgeman's surprise, had gratefully accepted these terms. His agenda in doing so may not have been entirely innocent. Other members of the Cabal regime, particularly the duke of Buckingham, were becoming interested in the possibility of deploying royal prerogative power to authorise toleration outside the Anglican Church, without going through the Commons. Manton had detected this shift of support within the government when he wrote to Baxter in September 1668 that the 'comprehension . . . endeavoured by our friends in Court was wholly frustrated by Dr Owen's proposal of a toleration which was entertained and carried on by other persons'.[46] One of the products of the failure of the 1668 proposals was the abandonment of comprehension, and the revival of interest in a court-sponsored toleration-based solution. Toleration and liberty of conscience returned to the political agenda. As a result, so did natural law and the issue of Hobbism.

The natural language of intolerance

The rise of an assertive tolerationist lobby brought with it Anglican fears about the subversive implications of nonconformist intransigence. This new situation led writers like Stillingfleet and Tillotson, who had been in favour of the concept of comprehension and a limited toleration, to attack those for whom toleration had now become a ruling principle. Despite the usually 'liberal' reputation of divines associated with the Wilkins 'club' this was not a

---

45 *Diary of Samuel Pepys*, ix. 60.
46 P. Toon, *God's statesman: the life and work of John Owen*, Exeter 1971, 134.

paradoxical *volte-face*. In fact, there was always a latent illiberalism in their naturalistic approach to the question of Church and State, as the early works of both Locke and Stillingfleet demonstrate.[47] At the heart of their reaction was the perception that granting toleration, and thereby a controversial and potentially subversive right to worship as they pleased, fundamentally conflicted with the requirements of natural sociability. If the exercise of a right were to disturb natural sociability, and that right was *ius naturae permissivum*, then it should, by natural law, be ceded to the magistrate for the common good. This naturalistic and communitarian solution to the problem of potential religious conflict signified a return to a language of erastian authoritarianism. For many, the return to this kind of argument meant the *Leviathan* resurfacing in Anglican dress.

The changing political environment also heralded a change in the rhetoric of Anglican naturalism. A characteristic feature of dialogue with the conformable non-conformists was that discussion of comprehension was founded on an assumption of their sobriety and rationality. There was a clear sense that fundamental agreement on the importance of establishing a settlement had provided a common idiom of reasonable compromise. The breakdown of negotiation and the increasing prominence of toleration, however, drastically changed the tone and substance of the debate. Rational naturalism as a style of argument had been developed precisely to combat the conflicting claims of religious enthusiasts; it effectively got around them by finding common grounds for a discussion. Toleration implied that it was necessary to abandon any kind of common dialogue; acceptance of difference was the basis of settlement. Toleration denied that there could be a coherent natural and rational community. For those championing the cause of natural sociability and rational dialogue, this was unacceptable. To challenge the requirements of natural society and the natural community of believers could only be an unnatural conclusion resulting from a depraved process of reasoning. This kind of argument was present in the discussion over the Atkyns Bill, as we saw earlier. From 1668 it became a distinctive new method of dealing with the issue of toleration. In using it, some Anglican divines managed to turn what might have seemed to have been a benign language of natural ethics and natural community, into a pathological disorder.[48]

In analysing the cause of this 'sickness', the Anglicans made use of another topic which often appears to have a distinctively Hobbesian pedigree, the

---

[47] Both Tillotson and Stillingfleet became vocal opponents of toleration; Tillotson for his *The Protestant religion vindicated*, London 1680, and Stillingfleet for *The unreasonableness of separation*, London 1681, where he wrote that 'an Universal Toleration is that Trojan Horse, which brings in our enemies without being seen, and which after a long siege, they hope to bring in at least under the pretence of setting our gates open wide enough, to let in all our friends': Edward Stillingfleet, *Works*, London 1709–10, i. 299.

[48] For recognition of this aggressive consequence of the new Anglican moralism see P. Allison, *The rise of moralism: the proclamation of the Gospel from Hooker to Baxter*, London 1966. John Spurr follows Lecky in calling it 'religious terrorism': *Restoration Church*, 309.

abuse of language. Hobbes's entire project was based on the assumption that moral and political disorder proceeded on mistaken definition and garbled understanding of social, religious and political relationships. The purpose of his *scientia civilis* was to present these relationships definitively and demonstrably. Only by achieving that level of clarity and closure, could peace be realistically maintained. The linguistic preoccupation of Anglican naturalism was a striking feature of the work of writers such as Tillotson, Stillingfleet and Wilkins. Like Hobbes, the latitude-men identified linguistic confusion with political disorder. The crucial difference, however, was that Hobbes's rhetorical scepticism required linguistic order to be created and maintained artificially, through the creation of the state. The Latitudinarians, by contrast, retained an abiding stoic faith that plain words and clear signification represented relationships that were natural in origin. This was represented above all by John Wilkins's *Essay towards a real character and philosophical language* of 1668, written in co-operation with Tillotson. The work suggested that one could gain access to a natural and thus objective meaning which could overcome the disjuncture between rhetoric and reality. This was an overtly political statement. Wilkins suggested that by this method, the internal contradictions of irrational religious rhetoric could be exposed, clearing the way to a rational accommodation. In the dedication to the work, he spoke of his belief that his project would 'contribute much to the clearing of some of our modern differences in religion, by unmasking many wild errors, which shelter themselves under the disguise of affected phrases; which being philologically unfolded according to the genuine and natural importance of words, will appear inconsistencies and contradictions'.[49]

This linguistic turn can be seen in one of the first major works to appear in the wake of the failure of the comprehension proposals, an anonymous book entitled *A friendly debate betwixt two neighbours*. Its author was Simon Patrick (1626–1707), a preacher with an impeccably 'Latitudinarian' *curriculum vitae*. Patrick had been educated at Queens' College, Cambridge.[50] He had been forced out of his fellowship in the early 1660s, and he was most probably the author behind the initials 'S.P.' on the frontispiece of the *Brief account of the rise of the new sect of Latitude-men* – commonly held to be the definitive apologia for Anglican naturalism. Patrick was a popular preacher at St Paul's Church in Covent Garden, part of the tightly-knit network of ex-Cambridge clergymen of similar persuasions in London. Although it is difficult to say for certain whether or not Cumberland knew Patrick personally, we do know that Cumberland chose to get married at Patrick's church during the autumn of 1670.[51]

Patrick's *Friendly debate* was one of the most popular products of the anti-toleration literature of the later 1660s, being extended to a second part in

---

[49] John Wilkins, *An essay towards a real character and a philosophical language*, London 1668, 18.
[50] *DNB*.
[51] Kirk, *Cumberland*, 13, 133.

1669 and a third in 1670, not to mention numerous reprints of the original dialogue. As a debate, it was anything but friendly. The format of the work involves a rather one-sided dialogue between a conformist and his non-conforming neighbour, who is subjected to a series of arguments designed to explain the error of his ways. The intellectual link between the civil wars and dissent is constantly stressed by Patrick; he is keen to point out the continuity between the seditious confusion of the rebellion and the dangers that face the restored monarchy. The rebellion was a time when 'men ran into Excess of Riot, when there was no restraint upon them. I will not say into so much Drunkenness, but unto Whoring (I may add Atheism and Irreligion) and such-like wickednesse, which are now said to be reigning sins'.[52] That break-down had led to a breach of social discipline, reflected above all in the linguistic sphere, 'new-minted Words springing up once everything that is old is cast out'.[53] The dislocating effects of the 'new-found words, affected expressions and odd phrases' lead to the breakdown of a natural, and genuinely social, language. This anti-social tendency is represented above all by Patrick's attack on the Quakers, who had become at once the symbol and agency of the worst excesses of the Interregnum Independency. The Quakers' fanatical doctrines, on Patrick's account, lead to anti-social, and thereby unnatural behaviour. Individuals are converted from 'loving the world to hate their neighbours; from cold devotion at our churches, to a Fiery zeal against our Ministers; from undutifulnesse to Natural Parents to the Greater Contempt of Civil and Spiritual'.[54] For Patrick, the mixture of soteriological speculation, the reaching towards things outside the power of natural discourse, and the consequent misuse of metaphor and allegory, thus combine to constitute a profoundly seditious mixture.

Patrick's analysis here seems to be profoundly Hobbesian. The connection between linguistic and civil disorder, particularly that caused by the lax use of metaphor and analogy, recalls Hobbes's complaints about the abuse of language in the *Leviathan*. For Patrick, this kind of argument allows him to construct a model whereby, once the traditional bridles on licentious speech are removed, the problem posed by metaphorical language escalates until the distortion prevents effective participation in, and rejection of, natural sociability.[55] Where Patrick departs from a Hobbesian analysis is in his conviction that the teachings of Anglican ministry and the language of naturalism actually offer a route back to natural sociability. In the course of the dialogues, Patrick contrasts the rhetoric of dissent with that of Anglican naturalism. Anglican preaching avoids the obscure passages of Scripture so beloved of dissenting preachers, for the plain and predominantly social morality of the gospels. This injunction to 'live soberly, righteously and godly'

---

52 S. Patrick, *A friendly debate betwixt two neighbours*, London 1668, 153.
53 Ibid. 36–7.
54 Ibid. 56.
55 Cf. Hobbes, *Leviathan*, 33–7.

includes subordination to the lawful powers and acceptance of their dictates in matters indifferent.[56] Patrick deploys the familiar natural law argument when he says that God's laws have only given 'general rules' whereby things are to be ordered in church 'according to which our Governors are to make particular laws, and we are to obey them; or else there will be nothing else but confusion'.[57] Such external impositions do not remove Christian liberty, says Patrick, following the arguments used by Stillingfleet, because they are only intended for the civil peace, and not as an imposition on man's conscience. To those that would scruple further, he comments that there cannot be much that is godly in the disturbance of the civil peace.[58]

Patrick's argument offered a distinctive synthesis of Anglican naturalism and the new, aggressively anti-toleration position. It is indicative of this continuity that Patrick could still envisage a scenario for reconciliation with the more 'sober' part of the dissenting community, in a formula which recalled the comprehension schemes.[59] What makes his work shocking and illiberal, however, is the new strain of vitriolic attack on those, 'who, full of Folly, think they know the Mind of God more than all the Bishops and Priests in the World; and by their confidence and their bold pretence of the Spirit, would overbear all Sober Reason'.[60] The *Friendly debate* pours out page after page of dismissive invective against the irrational will-worshipping separatist, constantly attacking their 'reviling language', their 'new and monstrous expressions', connecting them directly to the kind of sedition that had caused the Civil Wars.[61] If the language of naturalism had allowed for the possibility of compromise, it could also be used to devastating effect against those for whom such a compromise was still too much. Patrick was firm in his injunction to the supporters of toleration that they should 'leave these earnest endeavours to alter the laws, and alter yourselves'.

The transition between moderation and persecution clearly made a strong impression upon the dissenters themselves, particularly among those Presbyterians who had been prepared to talk. Samuel Rolle's *A sober answer to the friendly debate*, published in June 1669, rejected Patrick's analysis of nonconformist shortcomings, and registered the change of tone: 'It almost astonisheth me', wrote Rolle, 'that a man reputed to be sober and modest as you have formerly been, should commit such outrages.'[62] Rolle identified Patrick as the standard-bearer for what he called 'the Brethren of the Rational Regiment', those 'Rational Divines' who preferred the experience of nature to the experience of faith, and who preferred Grotius to Calvin.[63] Such Lati-

---

56 Patrick, *Friendly debate*, 145, 106–7.
57 Idem, *A defence and continuation of the friendly debate*, London 1669, 421–2.
58 Idem, *Friendly debate*, 113; *Defence and continuation*, 104–7.
59 Ibid. 205.
60 Ibid. 206.
61 Ibid. 78.
62 Samuel Rolle, *A sober answer to the friendly debate*, London 1669, sig. A3r.
63 Ibid. A7r.

tudinarians, in Rolle's opinion, were in danger of a superficial understanding of faith and religion.

If Patrick's dialogues made shocking reading for dissenters, worse was to come in the shape of another 'Rational Divine', Samuel Parker, domestic chaplain to Gilbert Sheldon, archbishop of Canterbury. Parker's A *discourse of ecclesiastical politie* appeared in the autumn of 1669. Arguably the most important text to come out of the dissent-related literature in the later 1660s, it appeared to push the language of naturalism towards what many contemporaries saw as pure Hobbism.

Parker (1640–88) is not usually associated with the Cambridge divines.[64] It is probably true that the *Discourse* was written as part of an anti-toleration campaign orchestrated by Sheldon, certainly no admirer of Wilkins or his circle.[65] But although Parker was employed as the archbishop's chaplain, his immediate background had been profoundly Latitudinarian in ethos, something which might go some way towards explaining why his arguments bear a remarkable similarity to those used by Stillingfleet and Patrick.

Parker was a graduate of Wadham, where Wilkins had been Warden during the 1650s. He later repudiated his Presbyterian background to become a 'warm Anglican', under the patronage of Ralph Bathurst at Trinity. His interest in naturalism and ethics led him to produce his *Tentamina physicotheologica de Deo* of 1665, a work which repudiated Hobbesian atheism on the evidence of modern natural philosophy. This was enough to get him noticed by Sheldon, and to be made Fellow of the Royal Society, on the recommendation of Wilkins himself.[66] In his A *Free and impartial censure of the Platonick philosophy* (1666), he had attacked Platonism as a philosophical system mainly on the grounds of its linguistic extravagance. In terms that betray an affinity with Wilkins's writing on linguistic theory, and which foreshadowed his critique of dissent, Parker dismissed the Platonists' 'gaudy and extravagant phancies' on the grounds that the extensive use of allegory and metaphor led to a language unconnected with the verities of nature.[67] He quoted Stillingfleet in denying the *prisca theologia*, and he firmly rejected the use of tradition and custom rather than reason as a guide to affairs. He also attacked the Platonist doctrine of innate ideas, and embraced a solid empiricism in demanding true and exact knowledge of the 'nature of things'.[68]

---

64 Indeed, he is more usually seen as a High Church opponent. For this view see J. G. A. Pocock, 'Thomas Hobbes, atheist or enthusiast?: his place in Restoration debate', *History of Political Thought* xi (1990), 737–49. For more sympathetic treatments see R. Ashcraft, *Revolutionary politics and Locke's Two treatises of government*, Princeton 1986, 41–54; G. Schochet, 'Between Lambeth and Leviathan: Samuel Parker on the Church of England and political order', in N. Phillipson and Q. R. D. Skinner (eds), *Political discourse in early-modern Britain*, Cambridge 1993, 189–208.

65 Ashcraft, *Revolutionary politics*, 41.

66 T. Birch, *The history of the Royal Society of London*, New York 1968, ii. 90.

67 Samuel Parker, A *free and impartiall censure of the Platonick philosophy*, Oxford 1666, 76, 78–9.

68 Ibid. 91, 206, 58–9.

In the course of another work, his *The nature and extent of the divine dominion* (1666), Parker had approvingly quoted Hobbes's definition of right from the *De cive*.[69] This might raise suspicion about the origins of his later arguments. But Parker was not a simple Hobbist, as he is sometimes portrayed. It should be noted that he uses the *De cive* in the same way that Stillingfleet, and later Cumberland, would use parts of Hobbes's work to deny the larger Hobbesian project. The passage quoted a definition which suggested that right was 'that liberty which every man hath to make use of his naturall faculties according to right reason'.[70] This was not, however, a badge of Hobbesian heterodoxy. Parker immediately qualifies his usage by saying that 'Though what Exercises of Power are consistent with right Reason, and what not, I shall discourse anon.' The point is that it is a good definition. In using it, Parker concentrates on the concept of right reason, a concept which Hobbes had deliberately enervated, in order to stress, in opposition to Hobbes, that justice and injustice are intrinsically part of the divine attributes. He later attacks Hobbes, together with Calvin (a connection which would become important in his attacks upon dissenters), for upholding the suggestion that divine dominion rests upon God's power alone.[71] His point in doing so is to show that although he agrees with Hobbes and Calvin, that God's power is based upon his omnipotence, God nevertheless upholds goodness and justice voluntarily.[72] This partial agreement, but also serious disagreement, over theology, was an important part of the problematic relationship between the Latitudinarians and Hobbes, as I shall examine later.

Parker's views were developed in his *Discourse*, which was characterised by an almost hysterically abusive style. The work is peppered with long excoriating passages aimed at the 'wild and fanatic rabble', whose sects and parties 'shatter peace and common love' and who are 'utterly incapable of being either a good subject, or good neighbour'. For Parker, religious dissent was subversive of the entire fabric of Church and State.[73]

Parker's bold claim was that liberty of conscience, if allowed, would effectively undermine the social order. The argument is strikingly similar to that used by Locke in the *Two tracts*. Parker posits a direct connection between the peace of the commonwealth (which he defines as the most important end of government) and state control over public religion.[74] Uncontrolled religious expression would always be used to justify 'the most absurd excesses of the passions'.[75] Unbridled religion always meant sedition. As a consequence, it was necessary to accept the idea that 'the Supreme Government of every Commonwealth, wherever it is lodged, must of necessity be universal,

---

[69] Idem, *The nature and extent of the divine dominion*, Oxford 1666, 2.
[70] Hobbes, *De cive*, 47.
[71] Parker, *Divine dominion*, 21.
[72] Ibid. 22–3.
[73] Idem, *A discourse of ecclesiastical politie*, London 1669, pp. iv, viii, x, xxxv.
[74] Ibid. 11.
[75] Ibid. 27; cf. Locke, *Two tracts*, 160.

absolute and uncontrollable, in all affairs whatsoever, that concern the inter-ests of mankind, and the Ends of Government'.[76] Religion was to be con-trolled by the state. The argument which Parker used to justify this was the paramount importance of natural sociability as a dictate of natural law. If sociability was a necessary feature, and primary obligation, of human nature, then the state was the principal means by which natural sociability was pre-served.[77]

According to Parker, this prior obligation to society ensured that the state always retained the right to legislate on all things. It predated the idea of having a separate ecclesiastical jurisdiction. All government originated in one, temporal, patriarchal authority, where the monarchic and priestly func-tions were combined.[78] Even where religious power had been alienated, wrote Parker, citing the evidence of Old Testament monarchs, the magistrate retained overall authority. Christ never claimed temporal power, and pos-sessed no form of coercive sanction which could intrude upon the rights of the civil magistrate. On this basis, any attempts by any spiritual authority to claim some kind of temporal dominion was merely usurpation, particularly the claims of the Church of Rome. In saying this, Parker's strongly erastian position signals a powerful affinity with the Hobbesian project.

Another Hobbesian resonance lies in his discussion of language. As with Patrick, language and its abuse assumes a central position in Parker's work. The dissenters' improper claims to religious liberty are portrayed as the dis-ruptive effect of their linguistic extravagance. Parker praises the preachers of the Established Church for their deliberate use of plain and uncomplicated language. At the same time, he notes the disturbing effect of metaphor and allegory in distancing dissenters who use them from the true nature of things. Parker follows Wilkins in identifying the dangers of neologism; he remarks sarcastically that if one can devise a new language, then one can start a new religion: 'One party affect to lard their Discourses with clownish and slovenly similitudes; another delight to rail in wanton and lascivious Allegories; and a third is best pleased with odd, unusual, unintelligible, and sometimes blas-phemous expressions.' The dangers of the misuse of language prompt Parker to offer a peculiarly Hobbesian observation: he speculates frivolously that if parliament were to pass an act to prevent the use of 'fulsom and lascivious metaphors, it might perhaps be an effectual cure of our present distempers'.[79]

However Hobbesian this might seem, it should be stressed again that Parker is not a Hobbist. Parker is describing the effects of a dislocated lan-guage; his remedies are designed to defend the virtues of a plain, natural and sociable language. The assumption is that there is a stable and accessible

---

76 Parker, *Discourse*, 28; cf. Locke, *Two tracts*, 171–2.
77 Parker, *Discourse*, 28.
78 Ibid. 31.
79 Ibid. 76.

natural meaning that should be protected. Hobbes's version suggested that meanings should be determined arbitrarily. Parker, like Wilkins, Tillotson and Patrick, believed that there was a natural order which had been subverted.

The same went for Parker's erastianism. Parker's argument about the power of the state was based on an understanding of the requirements of God's immutable laws of nature. These required that man should be sociable, and that the institution of government was the best means to further this end.[80] Hobbes's account was very different; the state was constructed by individuals in order to provide a source of moral and political authority lacking in the state of nature. In Hobbes, natural law was not formally obligatory until the state had been created. Parker, by contrast, stressed that natural obligation came first. The state and its power was essentially a product of nature.

The lines were blurred, however, where the obligation to natural law and the obligation to the state overlapped. The problem with natural law was that it could only provide general rules as to practical policy. For example, the law of nature provided injunctions against the invasion of property, but how this general rule was implemented varied according to circumstances. This was also the case with public worship. Parker's argument is very close to Stilling-fleet when he suggests that examination of the law of nature necessarily reveals only very general requirements of the instituted religion. As a result Parker concludes that the lawfully constituted authority in each society can therefore adopt forms consistent with 'an honourable opinion of deity or advance of the instrument of virtue'.[81] The laws of God were to be mediated through the use of prudence, discretion, laws and prescriptions.[82] This inter-play of human and divine law at once reveals the problematic grey area at the heart of Parker's theory. How much could the laws of nature demand, when they seemed to be reduced to the justification for unlimited sovereign power? Where did the magistrate's power end? For some, this was pushing the pru-dential powers of the magistrate into a pure Hobbesian positivism.

As for the issue of liberty of conscience, Parker adhered to the position elaborated by Stillingfleet and Patrick. Individuals have liberty of conscience *de facto*. As a result, it is impossible for the civil power to legislate over the minds of men. Parker emphasises the rigid dichotomy between internal and public actions. He makes it clear that the competence of the civil power only extends to the latter: 'All Humane Authority and Jurisdictions extend no further than men's outward Actions, these are the proper object of all their Laws.'[83]

This being so, Parker extends the right of the magistrate to any public action, which must of necessity be properly ordered for the public good. In

---

80 Ibid. 78–9.
81 Ibid. 82.
82 Ibid. 194.
83 Ibid. 89.

the context of religion, this was an extreme application of the institutional scepticism which characterised the 'rational divines'; outward forms were transient superstructures of a much more important inner faith. The requirements of formal religion were tied to the changing needs of a political community, an individual's spiritual relationship with God was something different. Unfortunately for the rationalists, this was also a view shared by Hobbes in his sharp dichotomy between reason and faith. Parker suggested that outward forms were no necessary part of religion itself, and that the individual could worship as he pleased in his own soul without, as he put it, 'upsetting the Prince'. This seemed to come directly from Hobbes's suggestion that if the magistrate should demand the denial of Christ, then it was legitimate for the subject to comply while at the same time maintaining the faith in its proper sphere. Critics were quick to point out that such hypocrisy took one a long way down the road towards atheism.[84]

But for Parker, as for Hobbes, the issue at stake was the importance of preventing the dangerous, and possibly seditious, intermingling of faith and reason. The identification of religious worship as an essential part of public and political order made such a distinction necessary. To quarrel with the established religious forms 'is at once notorious schism and rebellion; for whoever openly refuses obedience plainly rebels against the Government, Rebellion being nothing else but an open denial of obedience to the civil power'.[85] Parker's conclusion was thus harsh and uncompromising:

> And for this reason, though we are not so fond as to believe the constitution of the church unalterable, yet we deem it apparently absurd to forego any of her established ceremonies out of compliance with these men's unreasonable demands: which as it would be clearly impolitick upon divers other accounts, so mainly by yielding up her Laws and by Consequence submitting her Authority to such Principles as must be Eternal and Immutable Hindrances to Peace and Settlement.[86]

To compromise with those who elevate their own irrational prejudices to principles on which society is founded is unacceptable and ultimately subversive. Not only is it subversive, but it is also extremely Hobbesian. Parker may have used some Hobbesian arguments, but he went on to devote a large amount of space in the *Discourse* to a systematic attack on Hobbes, crucially linking his arguments to the pro-toleration positions of the Independents. Parker had good reasons for doing this.

Firstly, the connection between Hobbes and the pro-toleration case was not as outlandish as it might seem. Hobbes had notoriously defended the primitive independency of the Christians in the *Leviathan*.[87] He had also cul-

---

84 Ibid. 98–9; cf. Hobbes, *Leviathan*, 343–4.
85 Parker, *Discourse*, 105.
86 Ibid. 187.

tivated links with the Independent party in Oxford in the 1650s, when Owen had been vice-chancellor.[88] In addition, the pro-toleration dissenters were increasingly publishing material appealing to the king for toleration in return for obedience. The relationship between protection and obedience was recognisably Hobbesian.[89]

Parker's second motive may have stemmed from his awareness of his own authoritarian Hobbism. The attack on Hobbes allowed him to distance his work from the *Leviathan*, at the same time giving an opportunity to emphasise the centrality of a binding natural law theory to the rational Anglican discussion of dissent. The critique was, as it would be for Cumberland, a means of developing his own natural law position.

Parker's case hinged on the understanding of what caused moral and political obligation. For Parker, political authority was the consequence of a natural tendency to sociability; government was an essential correlate of society. For Hobbes, the obligation to natural law was a product and not a cause of society or government. Society and government came about through individuals brokering their right to determine their actions in return for protection. The key point about Hobbes's theory was that because the state was founded by contracting individuals, then those individuals have the right to disobey if the state no longer protects them. Many critics had been swift to point out the implication that a Hobbesian subject was potentially subversive, primarily because Hobbes retained this natural right in a social context. Parker identified this persistence of natural liberty in a social context with the liberty of conscience which the dissenters wanted. To demand such liberties in a social context was not only inappropriate, but politically dangerous; for social involvement to be conditional upon natural liberty, whether it be to worship, or to preserve oneself, undermined the principle of natural sociability. As Locke, Stillingfleet and Parker in the *Divine dominion*, had made clear, sociability required the potential alienation of all rights for the common good. A critique of this Hobbesian point served as an attack on dissent.

Parker's argument suggested that the trouble with Hobbes's account was that he had failed to root his social contract in any kind of substantial natural law. There was no prior natural obligation which could ensure that subjects would remain loyal to the community in which they lived. Hobbes had famously argued that natural laws were merely theorems, and not sources of obligation.[90] As a consequence, according to Parker, Hobbes's covenants

[87] Hobbes, *Leviathan*, 479–80.
[88] For Hobbes's connection with the Independents at Oxford see J. R. Jacob, *Henry Stubbe, radical Protestantism and the early Enlightenment*, Cambridge 1983, 21–2.
[89] For examples of this see Charles Wolseley, *Liberty of conscience in the magistrate's interest*, London 1668, 4, 17; Anon., *A second discourse of the religion of England*, London 1668, 13.
[90] Hobbes, *Leviathan*, 111.

could not be binding. The individual remained in possession of his or her natural liberties to disturb the social order in just the way that the dissenters were doing. To suggest an account of contracts when the law of nature has no binding force, is, according to Parker, ridiculous. 'And yet', he warns darkly, 'this Hypothesis, as odd as it seems, is become the standard of our Modern Politicks.'[91]

Parker perceives that the only way to overcome this anomaly is to show that natural laws are binding. He does this by denying Hobbes's assertion that the state of nature is a lawless state of war. The state of war was the engine that drove Hobbes's self-interested men to establish a source of artificial authority. It controversially replaced the role of natural sociability in the establishment of societies. Parker, like many of Hobbes's critics, sought to combat this point with modern jurisprudential ideas about natural sociability. Men are naturally and necessarily sociable once they realise that they are not self-sufficient and cannot survive without co-operating. The extent of this interdependence is such that individuals discover a prior and natural obligation to the common good, as the only means by which their own good can be fulfilled. The law of nature thus demands that individuals should act for the common good first, and satisfy their own good in so doing. This clearly anticipates Cumberland's central argument in the *De legibus naturae*. In a passage which foreshadows Cumberland's defence of the same thesis, Parker writes:

> That as every man is obliged to act for his own Good, so also to aim for the Common Good of Mankind, because without this, the Natural Right that every man has to Happiness cannot possibly be obtain'd; so that there will plainly arise from the Constitution of Human Nature an Essential Justice, that demands every mans offices of Love and Kindness to others as well as himself; in that, without this, that Divine Providence that made it, design'd for all and every Individual of Mankind, must become utterly unattainable.[92]

To champion liberties against the common good is a necessarily self-defeating act. Parker felt that Hobbes, in founding his philosophy upon individual rights, left no bond in the state but the inevitably destructive force of misguided self-interest. If Hobbes's account were true, then man would never have left the state of war. For Parker, Hobbes's failure to come to terms with the social nature of man left him unable to construct a viable model of obligation. For the dissenters to talk about liberty of conscience had the same consequence. They had refused to understand that their first duty was to obey the laws of the society in which they lived. The lesson for the supporters of toleration was clear; the preservation of society was the most pressing duty demanded by natural law. To that end the magistrate must be obeyed, rather than risking the dangers of permitting the exercise of individual liberties in

---

91 Parker, *Discourse*, 118.
92 Ibid. 122.

matters of religion. For Parker, it was always better to err with authority, than to be right against it.[93]

In the pages of the *Discourse*, Parker had developed the Anglican natural law argument in a way which brought it much closer to Hobbes than any previous work. At the same time he had deployed criticism of Hobbes as a way of attacking dissent. Predictably, his opponents were not particularly interested in the ways in which he had refuted and gone beyond Hobbes. They chose instead to concentrate on what they felt to be the profoundly Hobbesian tenor of Parker's argument. Richard Baxter felt that Parker had 'fallen in with Mr Hobbes'. Parker was accused of having become 'a young Leviathan himself', and Andrew Marvell pronounced that his principles trod hard upon the 'territories of Malmesbury, and his arrogance surpasses by far the Leviathan'.[94] Parker's principal critic was his major target, the Independent leader John Owen, who produced his *Truth and innocence defended* (1669) in reply to the archbishop's chaplain. In that work, Owen concentrated upon what he saw as the most disturbing Hobbesian elements of Parker's position. He noted the connection between the ideas of Parker and of Patrick,[95] and the radical novelty of their style, which he noted had 'filled many people with amazement'. The idea that men could be taught to think one thing, and yet do another, Owen found indefensible. The obligation to one's conscience, he argued, could never be subordinated to requirements of the magistrate. Parker, according to Owen, had pushed the interpretative competence of the civil power over natural law too far.[96] Natural law and Scripture appeared to be subsumed beneath the all-pervasive authority of the magistrate. As for his refutation of Hobbes:

> The Hypothesis whose confutation he hath undertaken, as it is in itself false, so it is rather suited to promote what he aims at, than what he opposes. And the principles which he himself proceedeth on, do seem to border on, if not to be borrowed from his, and those which are here confuted.[97]

When Parker responded to Owen's accusations in his *Defence and continuation of the ecclesiastical politie* in 1671, he claimed that 'never did I dream that I could be accused of being so extravagant as to suggest that the law of the magistrate is the sole rule of obedience'.[98] He repeated his attack on what he saw as the Hobbesian characteristics of the dissenters' case. At the same time he

---

93 Ibid. 308.

94 Baxter, *Reliquiae*, ii. 123; J. Humfrey, *A case of conscience*, London 1669, 11, 12; Henry Stubbe, *Rosemary & Bayes*, London 1672, 18; Andrew Marvell, *The rehearsal transpros'd and the rehearsal transpros'd: the second part*, ed. D. I. B. Smith, Oxford 1971, 47. See also Robert Ferguson, *The role of reason in religion*, London 1675, 433.

95 John Owen, *Truth and innocence defended*, London 1669, 4.

96 Ibid. 68, 240.

97 Ibid. 103.

98 Samuel Parker, *A defence and continuation of the ecclesiastical politie*, London 1671, sig. A3r.

sought to distance his own theory from the allegation of Hobbism by insisting on the natural law basis of his argument:

> And therefore I never attempted (as some men have done) to devolve the entire power of judging upon the judgement of one Party; but only supposing our different Respects and Obligations to these different judgements, to propound the Safest and most moderate Principles upon which to settle and accommodate the Government of Humane Affairs, and to adjust all matters of debate between them, by such fair proposals, and upon such reasonable principles that if the parties concerned will be ingenuous to their respective capacities, will eventually secure the common peace and happiness of mankind.[99]

Parker was unrepentant about his method of championing the magistrate. In response to Owen's criticism that he was asking individuals to attend to a public conscience and not to their own, he commented that, 'this is somewhat rank Doctrine, and favours not a little of the Leviathan. But yet how can I avoid it? Are not these my own words? . . . I am content to confess that I have said something not unlike them.'[100] In admitting this much, Parker revealed the problem in applying natural law ideas to the dissent issue. Although his basic political assumptions were far from an endorsement of simple Hobbesian self-interest, his conclusions were too close to the *Leviathan* for comfort.

Distasteful though they were, Parker's arguments were not quite as isolated as all of the criticism might suggest. His use of the natural law argument, and his defence of Patrick's *Friendly debate*, earned him the support of other 'rational divines', who actively defended the *Discourse*. One example was Edward Fowler (1632–1714), whose anonymous *The principles and practices of certain moderate divines of the Church of England (greatly misunderstood)* was published in 1670. Fowler refers to the *Discourse* throughout the work, and makes it clear that Parker was seen as a Latitudinarian by Anglicans and dissenters alike.[101] Fowler aimed to defend all those whose use of the natural law argument had led their opponents to suggest that they had supported the

> embracing of any religion, and to renounce or subscribe to any doctrine, rather than incur the hazard of perfection; and that they esteem him the only heretick that refuseth to be of that religion the king or state professes . . . whos only Reason it is to temporize and transform themselves into any shape for their secular interest; and that judge no doctrine so saving, as that which obligeth to so complying and condescending a humour, as to become all things to all men, that so by any means they may gain something.[102]

---

99   Ibid. 256.
100 Ibid. 279.
101 Edward Fowler, *The principles and practices of certain moderate divines of the Church of England (greatly misunderstood) truly represented and defended*, London 1670, 247, 346.
102 Ibid. 8.

Fowler was keenly aware of the charge of Hobbism, and he sought to defend the Latitude-men by defusing it. Fowler identified the Hobbesian position as being that 'all moral righteousness is founded in the law of the Civill Magistrate, that the Scriptures are obliging only by virtue of a civill sanction: that whatsoever Magistrates command, their subjects are bound to submit to, notwithstanding Divine Moral Laws'.[103] Fowler had taken this list of Hobbesian heresies directly from the published recantation of the Cambridge 'Hobbist' Daniel Scargill, published in 1669, with whom Parker was being unflatteringly compared.[104] Fowler absolutely rejected the implication that Parker and his colleagues had been defending these ideas. These divines, he claimed,

> have proved better than anyone else that Moral Good and Evil are not onely such, because God commands the one and forbids the other; but because things are so essentially and unalterably. That there is an eternal Reason, why that which is good should be so, and required, and that which should be evil, should be so, and forbidden; which depends not so much on the divine will as the divine nature.[105]

Fowler's apologia shows the clear influence of Parker's work. It echoes the general features of the natural law language, deploying a vigorous analysis of linguistic disorder, in what seems to be a reading of Parker's *Censure*, to Platonism and Calvinism.[106] Like Parker, Fowler was prepared to claim that it was the dissenters who were the Hobbesians. He argued that they were 'not a little beholden to Mr Hobbes, as hard an opinion as they deservedly have of him'.[107]

Fowler's way of dealing with the Hobbesian charges had been to vindicate a rational, moral approach to religious questions. For other writers, an alternative strategy was to deal with Hobbes head-on. In such ways criticism of Hobbes could become a contribution to the debate over dissent. This was the approach of John Shafte, who sought to defend the Anglican natural law argument through a direct attack on Hobbes. His pamphlet, *The great law of nature*, subtitled 'self-preservation examined, asserted and vindicated from Mr Hobbes his opinions', was composed in the period 1670–1.

Shafte's tactic is to focus upon Hobbes's problematic discussion of rights. If they are pursued without reference to laws, he claimed, then there could be no foundation for obedience. As Parker had already observed, the result of this would be that individuals would constantly be in a state of war, even after a social contract, because there would be nothing to make them keep their promises. Shafte's point is that people are unlikely to act in this way; that a

---

103 Ibid. 12.
104 For Fowler's borrowing see J. Parkin, 'Hobbism in the later 1660s: Daniel Scargill and Samuel Parker', *Historical Journal* xl (1999), 85–108.
105 Ibid. 12.
106 Ibid. 110.
107 Ibid. 245.

state of war fundamentally conflicts with the idea of preserving oneself which was the supposed mainspring of Hobbes's own argument. Because individuals will naturally avoid the state of war, it could therefore be concluded that acting in a sociable manner is a practical dictate of natural law.[108] Suggesting this, and undermining the case for a state of war, allowed Shafte to show that there was no need for the creation of an artificial source of absolute moral and political authority: political society was natural, and a consequence of natural law.

Shafte claimed that he had pursued this case

> Not because it is my own opinion that there are no other grounds or foundations of good and evil, but this principle of self-preservation and equality; but to shew out of these principles granted by Mr Hobbes, that those eternal laws of Justice, Charity, Temperance, Reward, Virtue &c . . . are makers and foundations of it [natural justice], and grounded in the very nature of man, so as to oblige him to act according to them, though there were no civil magistrate in the world, or though the magistrate positively commanded the contrary.[109]

Shafte's point was that Hobbes's own principles required him to acknowledge the existence of natural law and its priority over the exercise of rights. Justice was not created with the magistrate, it operated in a peaceable state of nature as well.

This defence of natural law was the background for Shafte's Parker-like, and in some ways suspiciously Hobbesian, discussion of the rights of sovereignty. This emphasises the problem-solving role of the sovereign power. Where there are disagreements in society, argues Shafte, it is necessary to choose one or more to act as 'sole arbiter of all Causes' and, secondly, to ensure that such arbiters have sufficient rights of punishment to enforce their decisions.[110] Another condition is that the jurisdiction of such arbiters should be unlimited. By use of such arbitration, man's natural desire for individual happiness can be harmonised with the natural law requirement for sociability. Although this sounded despotic, Shafte argued that it was not. The sovereign power is guided in its decisions by the natural obligation to the common good, the good for which it was established. There are no surprises when Shafte identifies that this is the case with the English monarchy, which is far from being a Hobbesian power. 'Though there be one monarch, and the government resembling that applauded by Mr Hobbs', argued Shafte, 'yet doth he not pretend to that arbitrary and unlimited power Mr Hobbs would give his prince.'[111]

The purpose of Shafte's careful attempt to disentangle Hobbesian rights-based sovereignty from the rational divines' natural law version is revealed in

---

[108] John Shafte, *The great law of nature*, London 1673, 18.
[109] Ibid. 27.
[110] Ibid. 25–6.
[111] Ibid. 41.

the final pages. Predictably, it concerns the dissent issue. Shafte accepts that some people disagree on some of the things demanded by conscience. This notwithstanding, he suggests that the free exercise of such opinions by everyone operating at cross purposes will ultimately destroy the foundations of society. As a result, it is necessary, according to natural law, and for the common good, that the magistrate must judge 'what liberty may be or is consistent with the civil government and not every private person'.[112] As a consequence, any demand for liberty of conscience in public worship, other than what is allowed by the magistrate 'is not a thing to be desired'. Shafte argues that if toleration is introduced, 'it will certainly dissolve and bring to ruin all civil government'. The important thing to remember, according to Shafte, is that the preservation of society and the requirements of God are things that can never conflict, therefore:

> Our duty to God, and respect for the general good of mankinde, are things inseparable from our interest, there being nothing so absolutely necessary to our well-being, as to do our duty to our Creator, and to do good to our Fellow-Creatures, which is commanded by the Law of Nature, and by the example of God himself.[113]

In redefining right with reference to natural law, Shafte made duty to the common good a natural priority over individual liberty. The implication was that the preservation of society, and the common good, should come before the interests of individuals. Shafte advised those who would reject this reasoning to examine the grounds of their disobedience 'before they thrust their fingers into the fire'.

Shafte's work demonstrates the extent to which the use of a natural law argument had become inextricably linked to a discussion of Hobbism. In order to use and defend that argument effectively, it was necessary to clear it from the suspicion that it was simply the *Leviathan* in disguise. This was the reason why Richard Cumberland found it necessary to write a book in which he not only clarified the basis of the Anglican natural law argument, but also sought to demonstrate its obligatory force against Hobbes.

Cumberland, natural law and the rights of the magistrate

The most important evidence that the *De legibus naturae* was written as a part of this debate is Cumberland's master-thesis, that natural law requires that the individual acts for the common good, in which his or her own is contained as a part. This will be examined in more detail in chapter 3, but suffice it to say that this emphasis on the necessarily sociable context of natural law, and the ways in which this is developed against Hobbes, are an expansion of

---

[112] Ibid. 79.
[113] Ibid. 85.

the arguments of the *Discourse*, and the many examples of natural law usage in the debate over dissent. The *De legibus* was written to vindicate this type of argument in exactly the same way as Shafte's work linked a critique of Hobbes, and a natural law theory, with an anti-toleration theme.

Where the *De legibus* differed in its approach was in its format. The issue was clearly serious enough to warrant a magisterial vindication of the natural law argument, and this is, I would argue, what the *De legibus* was meant to be. For that reason, the complicated Latin text eschews direct reference to the religious politics of the later 1660s, just as Locke's Latinate theoretical treatments of natural law did not directly engage with the discussion of toleration which had most probably prompted their composition. In both cases, a popular debate in print had led to a reconsideration of theory. In spite of this, however, it is possible to detect evidence that Cumberland was writing with the debate over dissenters in mind. The political theory in the *De legibus naturae*, such as it is, is particularly directed to the terms of the debate over dissent during the period.

Circumstantial evidence suggests that we should read the text in this way. We know from his other writings that Cumberland was a keen opponent of toleration. His doctoral thesis of 1680 argued that separation from the English Church was schismatic. He even managed to lay out his ecclesiological preferences in his *Essay towards the recovery of Jewish measures and weights* (1686). In drawing corollaries from his careful calculations, he suggested that the

> Measure of the Tabernacle and the Temple of the Hebrews demonstrates God's early care to settle his people in the form of one entire national church . . . all differences were firmly decided within their own nation, and therein all, even Aaron, although High Priest, and elder Brother to Moses, yet was subject to Moses, who was King . . . by these means all schismatical setting of one Altar against another was prevented; National communion in solemn and decent Piety with perfect Charity was promoted.[114]

This concern for maintaining the integrity of the national Church under the authority of the secular ruler was entirely consistent with the views expressed by the Wilkins–Bridgeman circle in the later 1660s. Cumberland's dedication to his patron Bridgeman emphasises these connections. Cumberland made much of Bridgeman's connection with the Church, and particularly his financial support for the see of Chester, from 1668 occupied by Wilkins himself. Cumberland also made special mention of his desire that the book should 'prove acceptable to the Men of Letters, who rise and flourish under your Lordship's Protection'. The work was edited and prefaced by Hezekiah Burton, who saw it through the press.[115]

---

114 Cumberland, *Jewish measures and weights*, 129.
115 Idem, *DLN*, dedication, translated in *A philosophical enquiry into the laws of nature*, trans. J. Towers, Dublin 1750, appendix IV, 83–5.

The textual evidence is scattered throughout the work, but occurs particularly in chapter nine, which investigates the political corollaries of the first eight chapters. Here, Cumberland takes the criticism of Hobbes further, and spells out the implications of Cumberland's moral theory for the nature and extent of sovereign power. Examination of these arguments reveals the extent to which Cumberland was concerned to establish the validity of the authoritarian arguments used by Parker in the *Discourse*.

Cumberland begins by suggesting that concrete political lessons can be effectively drawn from his general scheme. Civil government and positive laws are both, he claims, prescribed by the law of nature, as they are necessary for the common good:

> For such societies are necessary to enforce the observance of the law of nature, to the honour of God and happiness of mankind, but especially for those who are members of such societies. And therefore, a law of nature being given which commands us to promote the end, a law is likewise given preserving the settlement and preservation of so necessary a means as society with sovereign power.[116]

The necessity of government is a fact of all human societies, from the family upwards. Cumberland views patriarchal power relationships as the natural order in his state of nature, and he does this in order to undercut the Hobbesian distinction between pre-political and political societies. Patriarchalism allows him to posit a continuity in the naturalism of political relations between the family and forms of the state, and this undercuts the idea that the state is somehow 'created' artificially by contract. In the family, the earliest and most basic form of human society, wives and children are naturally subordinate to husbands and fathers; all subsequent political societies are thus predicated upon this natural relationship: 'therefore', writes Cumberland, 'from the paternal power are we to take the copy, and deduce the origin of power both civil and ecclesiastical'. This move not only allows Cumberland to claim, like Parker, that political authority is natural, but also that it is naturally unitary. The first family is the first human society, the first civil state, and also the first human church. All of these functions are necessarily, and naturally, combined under one authority. Parker had used precisely this argument to underpin his claim that the magistrate always has an ecclesiastical jurisdiction. Cumberland appears to be following the argument of the *Discourse* when he describes how primitive political societies develop from their patriarchal origins. As their population grows, many separate societies are created, all with their own states and churches, but all nevertheless requiring due subordination of these elements as part of the law of nature's requirement for unitary sovereignty.[117]

Although Cumberland is developing an argument which stresses the

---

[116] Cumberland, *DLN* 9.5; cf. Locke, *Essays on the law of nature*, 157–9.
[117] Cumberland, *DLN* 9.6; cf. Parker, *Discourse*, 31.

power of sovereignty, he is also careful to ensure that it is distinguished from the Hobbesian stereotype by making clear its limitations. The principal limitation is, of course, that sovereign power must serve the public good for which it was created, a recurrent feature of the anti-Hobbesian arguments in Stillingfleet and Parker: 'the government, or civil power', writes Cumberland, 'is naturally and necessarily limited by the same end for which it was established. It is therefore evident, that for the honour of God, and the happiness of all nations, no government can be established that can have a right to destroy these.'[118]

The public good, however, as in Parker, proves to be a very loose bridle, and it is clear that Cumberland is more interested in magnifying sovereign power than in placing substantial conditions upon its use:

> But, since all things absolutely necessary to these ends [ie. the public good] are but few and very evident . . . the limits of the Civil Power still remain very extensive. Nothing is prohibited the supreme power but the violation of the necessary division of dominion, by which their rights are distinctly assigned to God and men.[119]

For Cumberland, then, the only limits to state power involve the violation of property rights, rights assigned by nature, and not by man, given that they are held *pro bono publico*. This still leaves an extensive sphere for government. What is more, God has appointed no power on earth that is capable of punishing the sovereign for transgressions. The implication for potential rebels is severe; any attack on a particular government is an attack on the idea of civil society itself: 'They who endeavour to subject them [sovereigns] to punishment, do, by this very action as in them lies, destroy the very nature of civil government.' This is a transgression of the law of nature. The only safeguard against tyranny that Cumberland is prepared to offer is the punishment of God – the sovereign is immune from civil law, but not from divine vengeance for illicit acts. Just as Parker had advised the oppressed to address their grievances to God, so Cumberland appealed to the same argument of passive obedience.[120]

The theme of church government is raised throughout the chapter. Cumberland makes it clear that the authority of the magistrate is not simply restricted to the secular sphere. Those things which fall within the magistrate's competence 'extend universally to things divine and human, of foreigners and fellow-subjects, of peace and war'. One consequence of this is that 'the magistrate, in order to pursue the common good, should be guardian of both tables of the decalogue'. Cumberland's sovereign not only possesses an extensive civil jurisdiction, but dominates all social actions, including those of an ecclesiastical nature. This actually goes much further than Parker,

---

118 Cumberland, *DLN* 9.7.
119 Ibid.
120 Ibid; cf. Parker, *Defence and continuation*, 258–9.

in that Parker's arguments about the limits of state power, like those of Locke, tended to focus on the idea that the sovereign had a right to legislate only in those things which affected public safety. It was the specific concern with sedition which provided the occasion to consider a more authoritarian approach to church government. For Cumberland, the discussion is not so contingent upon the idea of subversion; the magistrate's right is simply related to the common good. This creates a space for civil involvement which potentially applies to any public act of any individual, the theoretical primacy of the Hobbesian 'civil conscience' to which Owen had objected so violently.[121]

The proximity of this position to Hobbes leads Cumberland into a discussion of the way in which his methodology actually differs, and the examples that he chooses to illustrate this seem to be drawn directly from the liberty of conscience debates. Cumberland quotes chapter five of *Leviathan*, where Hobbes talks about reason. The point of the discussion in that chapter is to make it clear that what is conventionally called 'right reason' does not offer access to any kind of 'natural' truth. The consequence of this is that disagreeing individuals need to create an artificial means of arbitrating upon their dispute:

> And therefore, as when there is a controversy in an account, the parties must by their own accord, set up for right Reason, the Reason of some Arbitrator, or Judge, to whose sentence they will both stand, or their controversy must either come to blowes, or be undecided, for want of a right Reason constituted by Nature.

Cumberland challenges this sceptical position by suggesting that, in such cases, recourse can always be had to the law of nature. The criterion of the common good is always available for making an objective judgement about disputes. Although this means that Hobbes is wrong to suggest that reason cannot provide an impartial standard or rule for arbitration, in some cases, by the very logic of natural law, this will result in a decision being resolved by the civil government:

> Upon this head he is certainly so far in the right; in controversies which it is necessary to end, it makes for the common good that the contending parties willingly relinquish their decision to the reason of the commonwealth and fully aquiesce therein. And this common and right reason persuades because it is certain that this decision will either be right, or that righter cannot be had consistently with the common good.[122]

To refer controversial issues to the state is not necessarily Hobbism. Cumberland continues this theme in what could be construed as a defence against the

---

[121] Cumberland, *DLN* 9.7.
[122] Ibid. 9.9; cf. Hobbes, *Leviathan*, 32–3.

misreading of Parker as a Hobbist: 'This reasoning of Hobbes is so much the more dangerous, because it may easily lead the unwary, when they perceive the falsity of one of the premises, to suspect the useful conclusion he would infer from thence.'[123] The unwary, in this case, could plausibly be assumed to be the writers who had attacked Parker and his colleagues for their apparent Hobbism. Cumberland's objective in writing this was to clear the arbitration of the sovereign from the taint of Hobbes's *Leviathan*. The exercise of state power, far from being artificial, could, and should, be justified by natural law. As he writes, 'nothing more reproachful can be said of sovereign powers than that their laws are not dictates of right reason, but only to be taken for such, because they have now got the supreme power by their own fortune and our consent'.

Cumberland makes a similar point later in chapter nine of the *De legibus* where he discusses the proper sources of the obligation to obey the sovereign power. True obligation, he maintains, can only proceed from a rational understanding that a particular law promotes the common good. However, where the common good can be served by a variety of different means, or laws, and these Cumberland terms indifferent actions, the sovereign can legitimately choose one over another, provided the common good is served by so doing:

> Nevertheless, I own that where the same good end may be obtained by actions of a diverse kind (such actions are called indifferent) it is not to be expected that any weighty reason should be given why one indifferent action is commanded rather than another. It is sufficient that the proper end may be obtained by the method commanded. For such a command is truly rational; nor is obedience to such a command less rational, whether in affairs ecclesiastical or civil.[124]

The qualification in the last line suggests the application of the argument to the *adiaphora* issue. Indifferent actions can be determined by the sovereign power for the common good. The same issue surfaces in chapter three, and in this instance there is a clearer similarity between Cumberland's view and that of his 'rational' colleagues:

> There are many things indifferent, or concerning which human reason cannot usually pronounce, that it is necessary for the common good that the matter be transacted this way rather than that. In such cases, the different constitutions of different states take place, which although they might without a crime have been opposed before they were enacted into laws; yet once they have been established by public authority, are to be most religiously observed.[125]

In this case, the common good enables the magistrate to generate obligation in technically indifferent acts. Natural liberty is relinquished for the common

---

[123] Ibid.
[124] Ibid. 9.13.
[125] Ibid. 3.3.

good, just as Cumberland's colleagues were arguing that religious liberties should be curtailed for the same motive. The emphasis upon this creative role of the magistrate leads Cumberland into some distinctively Parker-like arguments. The primary motives for submitting to the magistrate emerge, 'both out of a conscience towards God, whose vicegerents magistrates are, and for the public happiness of subjects, which is chiefly secured by the supreme authority being preserved unviolated'. With this phrasing, the public good is tied to the existence and preservation of the sovereign power alone. Cumberland's justification for this point takes him dangerously close to Parker's supposed Hobbism:

> For it evidently conduces more to the public good, that the opinion of the magistrate should prevail in things indifferent and doubtful, and that subjects should take that for good, which seems such to the supreme power, rather than eternal broils should continue among them, whence may reasonably be expected wars and murders, which are, without all question, evil.[126]

It is hard to believe that Cumberland was writing this without the dispute over Parker's natural law theory in mind. The need for political closure at times of crisis brought them both to the point at which irreconcilable disagreement (such as that over liberty of conscience) could only be prevented from destroying the common good by accepting the arbitrary decision of the magistrate. Natural law operated not so much through the justice of the measure, but rather the justice of the means. Unfortunately for the 'rational divines', the existence of Hobbes's account meant that it was easy for critics to dismiss the notion that there was any natural justice in the means. It all looked like the Hobbesian suggestion that the civil magistrate was determining natural law. The existence of such tensions reveals exactly why it was so important to find a way of proving that the natural law obligation always existed prior to the magistrate's decision. This was ultimately the purpose of Cumberland's complicated discussion of natural law, and its simultaneous engagement with Hobbes.

Perhaps the most convincing proof of the argument that Cumberland's work was written as a response to the issues raised by the debate over the *Discourse of ecclesiastical politie*, lies in Samuel Parker's own response to the work. This will be dealt with in more detail in chapter 7, but a few observations should make the connection clear. Parker not only licensed the work, providing an enthusiastic imprimatur in July 1671, but he was so struck by it that he went so far as to produce his own popularisation of the thesis in English a few years later, the first English version of Cumberland's argument. The ease with which Cumberland's thesis sits with Parker's own contributions is a compelling demonstration of the basic congruity between their positions.

If Cumberland was going to vindicate the 'rational divines" natural law

---

126 Ibid.

language from the charge of Hobbism, he needed to prove that natural law was not simply a prudential counsel to be over-ridden when necessary. He had to demonstrate that natural law was binding, and that it did carry an inescapable obligation to the will of God. To discuss the binding power of the law of nature meant that Cumberland had to contribute to one of the central debates of ethical discussion in Protestant Europe during the seventeenth century. It is this wider intellectual context for the *De legibus naturae* that will be the subject of chapter 2.

2

The Natural Law Debate

At the beginning of *De legibus naturae*, Cumberland proclaims that his main opponents are those sceptics and Epicureans who deny the idea of a universally applicable and obligatory law of nature.[1] Cumberland's choice of enemies, and his desire to create a system of natural law relates his project to what Richard Tuck has termed the 'modern' theory of natural law, the seventeenth-century attempt to confound the implications of various forms of moral and religious scepticism.[2] According to the commentators like the natural law theorist Samuel Pufendorf, and Cumberland's eighteenth-century translator, Jean Barbeyrac, Cumberland's work contributed to this new jurisprudential tradition whose founder was Hugo Grotius. For these writers, Cumberland was one of the most important jurisprudential writers of the seventeenth century, after Grotius, and Pufendorf himself.[3]

Grotius is an important starting point for placing the *De legibus* in context. Phenomenally popular among the 'rational divines', Grotian arguments about natural law determine both the questions and the answers which Cumberland explores. But Cumberland's was not a passive and derivative adaptation. It is best seen as a response to the criticism which Grotius had attracted, particularly from his many English readers. Grotius, according to his opponents, had provided a good starting point for talking about natural law, but had remained either silent or ambiguous on the question of obligation, a question which, as the preceding chapter has shown, was central to the political use of natural law theory. It was these ambiguities that had allowed writers like Hobbes to appropriate natural law language for their own purposes. What makes Cumberland's argument distinctive is the manner in which he seeks to remedy the defects of Grotian natural law theory and render it proof against its Hobbesian mutation. By demonstrating how natural law could be compatible with a Protestant theory of moral obligation, Cumberland not only answered Hobbes, but provided a secure basis for the political use of natural law arguments. In the longer term Cumberland's reconciliation of Scholastic natural law theory and Protestant theology ensured that his work would become one of the first and most important natural law texts of the English and Scottish Enlightenments. But to understand how,

---

[1] Cumberland, *DLN* 1.1.
[2] Tuck, 'The "modern" theory of natural law', 99–122.
[3] Cumberland himself suggests that Grotius' work was the 'first of the kind': *DLN*, introduction, sect. 1. The evidence of Barbeyrac and Pufendorf is considered in Tuck, 'The "modern" theory of natural law', 107–8.

and why, Cumberland developed his theory, it is necessary to say something about Grotius and natural law.

Grotius' work dealt with the problems of religious extremism, and the political, religious and moral fragmentation that religious conflict had brought about in early seventeenth-century Europe. His goal was the restoration of religious unity, a scheme expressed in his influential *De veritate religionis christianae* (1627), and expressed through his tireless diplomatic efforts to that end in the later part of his life. His work on natural law emerged as a result of his consideration of international law, and the possibility of devising a system of justice which could operate even in the midst of conflict. This was discussed in the *De jure belli ac pacis* (1625), arguably the founding text of modern international law. On both issues, his solutions revolved around the same line of thought, that among the diversity of laws, customs and opinions, there could be some universal foundation for both law and religion on which all could agree. Montaigne and Charron had concluded that this was not an automatic possibility. For these writers, sceptical fideism and pragmatic obedience to local laws and customs had been the only conceivable response to the turmoil of the French Wars of Religion and the Dutch Revolt.

These humanist writers adopted the lexicon of classical thought to structure their intellectual response; Montaigne moving from academic scepticism to an almost Pyrrhonian doubt, Lipsius, Du Vair and Charron recognising the similarity between their own times and the darker histories of Tacitus. Grotius, too, used classical models, and when he sought to do battle with the sceptics in the *De jure belli ac pacis*, he took the field in the guise of Cicero. Cicero had not only laid out the foundations of universal justice with a theory of natural law, but he had also undertaken the task against those classical schools which had rejected such ideas, the sceptics of the New Academy and the Epicureans.

Grotius was mainly concerned to refute the moral scepticism of the New Academy. This he personified in the figure of Carneades, representative of the 'crowd' of his opponents. Carneades had drifted away from his Stoic roots to become sceptical about the possibility of there being any certainty in ethical matters beyond that provided by a concern with individual utility.[4] This was not so much an epistemological problem as one which lay in the rhetorical instability of moral language. Carneades's own notoriety lay in his ability to expose such rhetorical *lacunae* to illustrate the problems inherent in ethical discourse. The most celebrated example of this was recorded in a lost portion of Cicero's *De re publica*, reported in Lactantius, where Carneades had delivered two speeches on the subject of universal justice, one for and the other against, with equal brilliance. He had proved, by arguing *in utramque*

---

4 M. Horwitz, 'The Stoic synthesis of natural law', *Journal of the History of Ideas* xxxv (1974), 3–16.

partem, that the concept could not be discussed with any measure of certainty.[5]

If Grotius' reference to Carneades struck a chord with readers familiar with Montaigne and Charron, his response would also have been recognised by those who knew their Cicero. Building on the one premise that the sceptic would allow, Grotius asserted that the natural principle of self-preservation could become the foundation of universal laws:

> the old poets and philosophers have rightly deduced that love, whose primary force and action was directed to self-interest, is the first principle of the whole natural order. Consequently, Horace should not be censored for saying in imitation of the Academics that expediency might perhaps be called the mother of justice and equity. For all things in nature, as Cicero repeatedly insists, are tenderly regretful of self, and seek their own happiness and security. This phenomenon can be observed not only in the human race, but among the beasts also, and even in connection with inanimate objects, being a manifestation of true and inspired self-love, which is laudable in every phase of creation.[6]

Stoics, Epicureans and Peripatetics all agreed that self-preservation as a principle implied a right to defend oneself and to shun that which proves to be injurious. It also implied a right to acquire and retain those things which are useful for life.[7] A framework of rights could thus be derived from a simple observation. Although this did not go much beyond instinct, distinctive aspects of human nature meant that self-preservation did not simply stop here:

> Man is, to be sure, an animal, but an animal of a superior kind, much farther removed from all other animals than the different kinds of animals are from one another; evidence on this point may be found in the many different traits peculiar to the human species. But amongst those traits characteristic of man is an impelling desire for society, that is, for the social life – not of any and every sort, but peaceful and organized according to the measure of his intelligence, and those also of his kind; this social trend the stoics called sociableness. Stated as a universal truth, therefore, the assertion that every animal is impelled by nature to seek only its own good cannot be conceded.[8]

For Grotius, as for Cicero, the crucial difference between man and other animals is their impelling desire for sociability, or *socialitas*. The idea had roots in the Stoic concept of *oikeiosis*, by which individuals come to recognise

---

5 Cicero, *De re publica*, trans. C. W. Keyes, London 1928, III.9; Lactantius, *Divine institutes*, trans. M. F. McDonald, Washington, DC 1964, V.xiv.3–5. See also Cicero, *De finibus bonorum et malorum*, trans. H. Rackham, London 1914, III.v.8.

6 Grotius, *De iure praedae commentarius*, trans. G. L. Williams, Oxford 1950, 9; cf. Cicero, *De finibus* V.x.

7 Grotius, *De iure paedae*, 10–11; cf. Cicero, *De finibus* V.ix.24.

8 Grotius, *De jure belli ac pacis*, trans. F. Kelsey, Oxford 1925 (hereinafter cited as *DJBP*), i, proleg., sect. vi–vii.

that fellowship was a vital part of their nature as human beings. Cicero had discussed these ideas in the *De legibus* and the *De finibus* to show that individuals are fitted by nature for higher ends than self-preservation alone.[9] Man is distinguished from animals by his capacity to speak, know and act in accordance with general principles. This allows him to identify the greater good of the collectivity in addition to his own self-interest. Individuals are thus capable, on rational reflection, of identifying a higher, common, good.[10] Although self-preservation is logically prior in the order of conceptions, it necessarily leads to a sense of the common good, because it is in the common good that man's more extensive self-interest is realised.

On the basis of these premises, Grotius developed a theory of natural justice in which one necessarily has a right to life and property, and a natural obligation not to infringe the life and property of others.[11] This position suggested a natural law which was not only consistent with the observable nature of man, but which also proceeded from the main sceptical premise of self-preservation. Such a framework must represent the basis for a structure of immutable laws, laws which could carry obligatory force even if it were to be granted that God did not exist.[12]

This last statement, although recognised for the Scholastic commonplace which it had become by the time that Grotius came to write it, brought up a problem for Grotius' readers which undermined the impact of his message.[13] Grotius had suggested that the law of nature would be derived from unaided reason.[14] It was vitally important to show that the laws of nature were in fact the will of God. If they were not, this opened the question of whether they could properly be considered laws at all. How does obligation arise, if it does not come from God? How was one to tell what was obligatory according to natural law and what was not? Did such an account mean that human reason could act autonomously as a source of obligation? Grotius had not attempted at any point to elaborate on an extensive account of obligation to the laws of nature beyond their being a product of the will of God in creating the world as he had.[15] The problem with this argument was that what was being taken for the law of nature, and dictates of right reason, was subject to the vagaries of human interpretation. Grotius did attempt to demonstrate what natural law was by appealing to Cicero's suggestion that the consent of nations was a sufficient indication of it. If the same proposition was shown to be true at

---

[9] Cicero, *De finibus* II.i.1; I.ix.30; *De legibus*, trans C. W. Keyes, London 1928, I.x.29.
[10] Grotius, *DJBP* 1.2.1,2–3; cf. Cicero, *De finibus* V.ix.24.
[11] Grotius, *DJBP* 2.1.6.
[12] Ibid. proleg., sect. xi.
[13] For Scholastic use of the *etiamsi daremus* clause see Francisco Suarez, *De legibus* II.vi.14, in *Selections from three works*, trans. G. L. Williams, A. Brown and J. Waldron, Oxford 1944.
[14] Grotius, *DJBP* I.x.i.
[15] Ibid. proleg., sect. xii.

different times and different places, then that must surely demonstrate that a universal cause (i.e. God working through natural law) was in operation.[16]

Cicero's argument from consent, however, was far from offering certain proof that an obligatory law of nature existed. Adopting this position left Grotius open to the sceptical charge that it was not possible to make such judgements, given the diversity of human habits and customs. Grotius' response to this counter-argument was to suggest that one should concentrate upon examples of human behaviour taken from 'better times and better peoples' whose judgements 'are not to be slighted especially when they are in agreement with one another; for by such statements the existence of the law of nature, as we have said, is in a measure proved'.[17] This was hardly much better as an answer, and demonstration of an obligation to the law of nature remained at best an uncertain hypothesis.

Responses to Grotius: Selden and Hobbes

Many of the natural law theorists of the seventeenth century respectfully paid homage to Grotius and regularly borrowed elements of his work, but they also rejected his probabilism and criticised his failure to demonstrate moral obligation. Cumberland, so often taken to be a follower of Grotius, is no different in this respect. At the very beginning of the *De legibus naturae*, he makes a distinction between theorists who attempt to demonstrate the law of nature from effects to cause, *a posteriori*, and those who reason from causes to effects, *a priori*. Grotius is categorised among theorists who use an *a posteriori* method, in developing his proof of obligation from the evidence of human practice.[18] Although Cumberland was prepared to state that such a method was a useful way to look at natural law, he also said that the objections which had been raised were serious enough to suggest that the *a priori* method should be the more appropriate form of investigation.

Cumberland draws the reader's attention to two major objections. First, that it is impossible to derive universal tenets from the writings of a limited sample of individuals, and secondly, that any conclusions drawn lack the authority of a lawgiver and hence the obligation to give them the substantial force of law. It is true, he conceded, that normative structures may well be observable in the behaviour of various nations; some sense of religion, a basic 'humanity' prohibiting murder, theft and adultery, for example. The major problem with this kind of evidence is that it is always vulnerable to the sceptical relativist's counter-claim about how typical and 'natural' such behaviour is. At best it can only be evidence which supports rather than proves the

---

16 Cicero, *Tusculan disputations*, trans. J. E. King, London 1927, I.xiii.
17 Grotius, *DJBP*, proleg., sect. xl; 1.xii.1.
18 Cumberland, *DLN*, introduction, sect. 1.

existence of natural law. For Cumberland, the Grotian method has its place, but it was too uncertain to overcome the sceptical objection.[19]

These responses represented the reaction of Grotius' English readers to his position. They were largely sceptical about what Grotius had claimed that men could know through the exercise of their natural reason. Cumberland identifies the two objections with Thomas Hobbes and John Selden, both of whom had denied the Grotian assertion that dictates of reason in themselves could have the quality of laws. Cumberland quotes from chapter fourteen of Hobbes's *De cive* suggesting that 'the laws of nature, although they are the laid down in the writings of Philosophers, are no more, for that reason, to be looked upon as written laws, than the opinions of lawyers are laws, and that for want of a sovereign authority'.[20] Selden had argued the same point in denying that 'the conclusions of reason, considered barely in themselves, have the Authority of laws'.[21] Although these objections made the same observation about the dangers of deriving obligation from reason alone, they made it with very different ends in view, something which Cumberland was keen to stress. Hobbes had attacked the Grotian position with a view to denying that the laws of nature had any binding force above that commanded by the civil power. Selden, on the other hand, had made the objection 'upon no other account than to show the necessity of having recourse to the legislative power of God, and of proving that God has commanded our obedience to them, and, by making them known to us, has proclaim'd his laws'.[22]

This distinction was crucial to the direction which Cumberland's work would take. Hobbes and Selden had both proposed the same critique of the Grotian argument, that it was deficient as a formally defined law. Hobbes's solution to this problem had been to displace obligation to the civil power, and this answer, denying the practical reality of divine obligation, was unacceptable. Cumberland shared with Selden and Hobbes the view that Grotius had left his account of obligation underdefined, but he deliberately linked his work with Selden's more 'legitimate' account of the critique. The *De legibus naturae* can be seen as an attempt to build upon Selden's theory in a way that avoided its mutation into a Hobbesian argument.

The dangers of such a mutation were only too evident in the ambiguity of Selden's own position on the law of nature. This has been a source of confusion not only to contemporaries but also to more modern commentators, who have attempted to isolate Selden's views.[23] Selden dealt with the law of nature in a book cited by Cumberland, the *De jure naturali & gentium juxta*

---

[19] Ibid. sect. 2–3.
[20] Ibid. sect. 3; cf. Hobbes, *De cive*, 176–7.
[21] John Selden, *De jure naturali & gentium iuxta disciplinam Ebraeorum libri septem*, London 1640, bk I, ch. ix.
[22] Cumberland, *DLN*, sect. 3.
[23] See Richard Tuck, *Philosophy and government*, Cambridge 1993, 216, and Johann Sommerville, 'John Selden, the law of nature, and the origin of government', *Historical Journal* xxvii (1984), 437–47.

disciplinam Ebraeorum, published in 1640. This popular work, in spite of its apparently esoteric subject matter, influenced many English natural law writers.

The crucial passages on natural law occurred in chapters 6–9 of the first book, where Selden laid out his position on natural law and moral obligation. In chapter 6, Selden rehearsed the arguments of the Carneadean sceptic, the arguments which undermined the Ciceronian position proposed by Grotius. Selden was particularly concerned to rebut the Scholastic and Ciceronian suggestion, echoed by the Grotian definition of natural law, that the dictates of right reason could constitute an obligatory law by themselves: 'Pure, unaided reason merely persuades or demonstrates', he argued, 'it does not order nor bind anyone to their duty, unless it is accompanied by the authority of someone who is superior to the man in question.'[24] In arguing this point, Selden wanted to make a clear distinction between reason as a process by which individuals generate conclusions for themselves, and reason that carried the additional authority of a superior. Only in the latter case could there be any formal obligation, because obligation could only arise from the command of a superior. The failure to understand this distinction was, for Selden, the main problem with Scholastic and neo-Scholastic writing about natural law. Scholastic natural law writers confused the mere conclusions of reason for practical obligation because they did not recognise that obligation was a consequence of command. As he wrote in his *Table talk*: 'When the Schoolmen talke of *Recta Ratio* in morals, either they understand Reason as 'tis govern'd by a command from above, or els they say no more than a woman, when she says a thing is soe, because it is soe, that is, her reason persuades her it is soe.'[25] This confusion opened the way to the Scholastic and Grotian suggestion that there might be an autonomous natural law, the *etiamsi daremus* clause of the *De jure belli ac pacis*.

Selden made it clear that to be a law at all, natural law had to be the will and consequently the command of God, as man's superior:

> I cannot fancy to myself what the Law of Nature means, but the Law of God, how should I know I ought not to steal, I ought not to commit Adultery, unless somebody had told me, why these things are against nature? Surely 'tis because I have been told soe, 'tis not because I think I ought not to do them, nor because you think I ought not, if soe our minds might change; whence comes the restraint? From a higher power, nothing else can bind, I cannott bind myselfe (for I may untye myself againe) nor an equall cannot bind me (wee may untie one another). It must be a Superior, even God almightie. If two of us make a bargaine, why should either of us stand to it, what need you care what you say, or what need I care what I say, certainly because there is some-

---

[24] Selden, *De jure naturali*, 92–3; trans. in Tuck, *Natural rights theories*, 93–4.
[25] Idem, *Table talk*, ed. F. Pollock, London 1927, 116.

thing above me, tells me, fides est servanda, and if wee after alter our minds and make a new bargaine, there's fides servanda there too.[26]

This is what Cumberland considered to be the 'judicious hint' that Selden had given to moral philosophers 'who are wont to consider the conclusion of their own reason as Lawes, without due proof, that they have the necessary form of a law, or that they are established by God'.[27] If the conclusions of right reason were not adequate in themselves, it remained for Selden to explain how one could acquire the knowledge of God's will necessary to moral obligation. To answer this, Selden developed a controversial and distinctive solution which relied upon the suggestion that God had somehow promulgated special knowledge of his laws to Adam, and then to Noah, enjoining them to perpetual obedience. Central to this theory was the *intellectus agens*, the external intervention of the divine intellect in assisting individuals to apprehend God's will. Selden explained this unusual idea in chapter 9 of book I:

> Just as when the light is clear and shining in the appropriate direction, objects which are suitably placed are perceptible by an eye which is not diseased or badly positioned . . . so illuminated by the aid of the intellectus agens, a human mind or intellect which is not depraved and which intuits diligently is informed of these commands which are to be observed by the decree of the father of nature, and indeed, of other objects of the intellect (that is to say, of truth and falsehood as well as of good and evil).[28]

Selden identified two versions of this theory. The first, strongly Platonist version was based on a theory of emanation, that divine knowledge came from without and that God had promulgated his message directly. The second, more orthodox Thomist account suggested that the *intellectus agens* was a natural faculty of the rational soul. To endow the rational soul with such assistance, however, risked blurring the distinction between reason and command which had been Selden's critical response to the Schoolmen. Perhaps not surprisingly, the first version of the theory is the one which dominates his account of the *praeceptae noachidorum*, or those precepts by which the Jewish people were led to a special knowledge of the laws of nature. On this account, God spoke directly to Adam and Noah, and the precepts given by God were handed down in the rabbinical tradition. This choice would be particularly disappointing for writers like Cumberland, who agreed with the substance of the Seldenian critique, but for whom Selden's mystical reliance upon Hebrew tradition undermined the usefulness of his claims. In the introduction to the *De legibus* Cumberland comments on the two versions of the theory available in the *De jure naturali*, and laments that Selden

---

[26] Ibid. 69.

[27] Cumberland, *DLN*, introduction, sect. 3.

[28] Selden, *De jure naturali*, 111; translated in Somerville, 'John Selden', 440–1.

only transiently hints, in such general terms, at this latter method [the Thomist account], which however seems to me to want much explanation and proof; but he betakes himself wholly to the former, and endeavours to prove from the traditions of some Jewish Rabbins that God gave seven precepts to the sons of Noah, in the observance of which all Justice amongst Men should consist.[29]

Selden's seven principles showed, according to Cumberland, that for the Hebrew nation at least, there could be laws existing prior to the state. The problem was that Selden's solution did not answer the very objection that he himself had levelled at Grotius, namely, that such Jewish traditions were hardly representative of humanity or, indeed, widely accepted. As Cumberland put it, the seven precepts 'were not . . . manifested to all mankind; and those things which that nation [the Hebrew nation] looks upon as the greatest mysteries of religion, are by many ridiculed'.[30] For Cumberland, to place such a stress on the unwritten tradition of the learned men of one particular nation could never constitute a sufficient promulgation of the law of nature. He nevertheless hinted that some elements of Selden's second solution, the Thomist account, in which the *intellectus agens* was a faculty of the rational soul, could constitute the basis for a theory of obligation. Here again it is possible to see Cumberland attempting to rescue the substance of Selden's critical argument, and some elements of his constructive solution, while at the same time avoiding the controversial aspects of the *De jure*'s argument. This desire to supplement the hints given in the *De jure* is a striking feature of the *De legibus*, and this notion of rescuing the Seldenian heritage from heterodox interpretation was particularly important for Cumberland's cause. To understand why he should have wanted to recover an orthodox account from Selden's confusing theory, it is necessary to look at how Selden's work could be exploited for less traditional interpretations of natural law.

The most worrying aspect of Selden's approach was the way in which his sceptical analysis could undermine the connection between reason and moral obligation altogether. This was an implication discussed by many mainstream Anglican clergymen. Jeremy Taylor (1613–67) was one example of an Anglican 'Seldenian', and his 1660 work, *Ductor dubitantium*, built upon the sceptical foundation outlined in the *De jure*.

Taylor defines the law of nature as 'the Universal Law of the World, or the Law of Mankinde, concerning common necessities to which we are directed by nature, invested by consent, prompted by reason, but is to bind upon us only by the command of God'.[31] The distinction between nature's promptings and the effective sources of obligation instantly flags Selden's influence upon the work. Taylor notes that everyone agrees that there are such natural

---

[29] Cumberland, *DLN*, introduction, sect. 3.
[30] Ibid.
[31] Jeremy Taylor, *Ductor dubitantium*, London 1660, 220.

laws. However, because their content is not properly specified, natural law lacks the certainty of written law. The problem with natural law is that it is difficult to know exactly to what we are obliged.

Taylor rejects the Grotian proofs using the same arguments as Selden. He argues that the consent of nations is a good indicator to 'many degrees of probability', but the problem with this kind of evidence is that it only provides what he terms an index of the permission of nature, rather than any concrete notion of natural obligation – what one might do, and not what one must. This leads Taylor to conclude that

> the Jus Gentium, the Law of Nations, is no indication of the Laws of Nature; neither indeed is there any Jus Gentium collectively at all, but onely the distinct laws of several Nations; and therefore it is to be taken distributively; for they are united only by contract, or imitation, by fear, or neighbourhood, or necessity, or any other accident which I have mentioned.[32]

Taylor thought that Grotius' consensus argument was only probable and thus too weak to say anything about obligation. He was equally sceptical about Grotius' argument that the law of nature effectively consisted of the dictates of right reason. Taylor used Selden's distinction between reason and obligation to make the point; reason itself could only demonstrate, but it could not oblige in the formal sense required of a law. For Taylor, reason is a mere 'boxe of quicksilver', changeable, particular, and never in itself a source of obligation.[33] Like Selden, Taylor de-emphasises reason and traces obligation to the will of a superior. In the case of natural law, the lawgiver is God:

> For the Law of Nature is nothing but the Law of God given to mankinde for the conservation of his Nature and the promotion of his perfective end. A Law of which a man sees a reason and feels a necessity; *God* is the lawgiver, *Practical Reason* or *Conscience* is the *Record*, but *revelation* and expresse declaring it, was the final publication and emission of it, and until then it had not the solemnities of law, though it was pass'd in the court, and decreed and recorded.[34]

In this we can see all of the ingredients of Selden's position expressed again. Natural law does exist as a series of dictates of reason but because they lack effective promulgation by a lawgiver, they cannot properly be regarded as being laws binding upon the individual. The conclusions of reason only become obligatory when they are recognised as concrete statements of God's will. In this way, and in this way only, does science become conscience, and God 'makes that which is reasonable become law'.[35]

At this point Selden had relied upon his *intellectus agens* argument to

---

[32] Ibid. 230.
[33] Ibid. 231–2.
[34] Ibid. 233.
[35] Ibid. 235.

explain the manner in which such obligation could be discovered. For Taylor, the matter was more clear-cut. Reason might be an inadequate guide to moral obligation, but God had given man what Taylor called the 'perfect Code and Digest of Natural Law' in the words of Scripture, the Christian Law.[36] Taylor's use of revelation removed the need for a relationship between reason and God's will. Taylor claimed that this method established certainty in matters of conscience, and eased the trouble of discovering particular systems of natural law, inquiries into which had caused many disputes 'and produc'd no certainty'.

Taylor's solution was perhaps the most acceptable one to Protestant divines sceptical about the claims for reason made by Grotius. It resolved the difficulties of ascribing too close a relationship between reason and obligation, and avoided the dangerous Scholastic identification of human reason and God's will. God was satisfactorily placed as the source of moral obligation, and revelation, as the positive proclamation of his will, became the effective response to moral scepticism.

There was, however, a danger for natural law theorists in placing the burden of moral obligation upon Scripture alone. It was a danger which was fully appreciated by Selden, and probably led him to eschew this particular approach to natural law in favour of the rabbinical tradition. As Selden put it memorably in his *Table talk*, 'tho we call the scripture the word of God yet it was written by a mercenary man'.[37] The implications of this point of view are brought home when Selden challenges his interlocutor: 'You say there must bee no humane invention in the church, nothing but the pure Word. Answr: If I give any exposition but what is expressed in the Text, that is my Invencon, if you give another Exposition, yt is yor Invencon, & both are humane.'[38] For Selden, Scripture was a text with problems of authority and interpretation. It begged the question of how such a text could be used as the foundation for any kind of practical moral obligation. Selden avoided having to answer that question directly but it would become central for his friend and fellow-critic of Grotius, Thomas Hobbes.

Hobbes's connection with Selden was personal as well as intellectual. The two men became friends after Hobbes sent Selden a complimentary copy of *Leviathan* and despite the late beginning and short duration of their friendship (Selden died in 1654), they had many things in common.[39] Both were humanist scholars, committed to deploying their learning critically and sceptically against Scholastic assumptions, particularly those used politically to bolster the power of the clergy. Hobbes had sent Selden a copy of the first edition of the *De cive* in 1642, and it is not hard to detect the common

36 Ibid.
37 Selden, *Table talk*, 12.
38 Ibid. 59.
39 R. Tuck, *Hobbes*, Oxford 1989, 31–2.

themes which related it to the critique of conventional natural law theory in the *De jure*. The *De cive* registered Hobbes's distinctive impatience with the uncertainities surrounding natural law theory. As he wrote in chapter 2, 'All authors agree not concerning the definition of natural law, who notwithstanding do very often make use of this term in their writings.' He continued with a devastating attack on the inadeqacies of the *a posteriori* models of obligation proposed by Cicero and Grotius:

> One proves it hence; because it was done against the general agreement of all the most wise and learned nations: but this declares not who shall be the judge of the wisdom and learning of all nations. Another hence, that was done against the general consent of all mankind; which definition is by no means to be admitted. For then it were impossible for any but children and fools, to offend against such a law.[40]

For Hobbes, it was unreasonable that information about the laws of nature should be taken from the consent of those who more often break than observe them. Although he rejected the *a posteriori* method of deriving the content of the law of nature, Hobbes nevertheless *appeared* to endorse the Grotian and Scholastic alternative, that laws of nature could be derived from reason alone, for 'true reason is a certain law, which, since it is no less a part of human nature than any other faculty of affection of the mind, is also termed natural'.[41] This position leads Hobbes to the very Grotian conclusion that the law of nature can be defined as a 'dictate of right reason, conversant about those things which are either to be done or omitted for the constant preservation of life and members, as much as in us lies'.[42] Building upon this foundation, Hobbes generates a list of twenty such laws, premised upon self-preservation and summarised for ease of understanding by the injunction to 'do as you would be done by'.

Hobbes's laws of nature seems to create the kind of natural sociability for which Grotius had argued in the *De jure belli*, and Selden in the *De jure*. Furthermore, his argument gives the impression that it is reinforcing the conventional, Scholastic connection between reason and moral obligation. But for Hobbes the point of using this natural law language was to expose its shortcomings and redefine its terms; the orthodoxy concealed a much more critical agenda. In the *De cive*, Hobbes may have laid out his laws of nature, but he then went on to ask what would happen if the requirements of his list of laws came into conflict with the basic premise of self-preservation. In a situation where the majority of people did not obey those laws, then it would cease to be rational to observe them oneself; indeed, to do so would lead to 'a more certain, quick, destruction, and the keepers of the law would become mere prey to the breakers of it'. If it was rational to consider one's self-

---

[40] Hobbes, *De cive*, 51.
[41] Ibid. 52.
[42] Ibid.

preservation above all things, then there might be times when it might not be rational to obey what had been laid out as the laws of nature. Hobbes concluded from that that reason did not necessarily lead to a moral obligation to obey natural laws: 'It is not therefore to be imagined', he wrote, 'that by nature, that is, by reason, men are obliged to the exercise of these laws in that state of men wherein they are not practised by others.'[43]

This was an important exception. Although Hobbes conceded that reason could suggest natural laws to man, there was no sense in which individuals were obliged to obey such laws when their own self-preservation was at stake. There was not, therefore, any necessary connection between natural reason and practical obligation to conventionally sociable natural laws. As Hobbes put it: 'We must therefore conclude, that the law of nature doth always and everywhere oblige in the internal court, or that of conscience; but not always in the external court, but then only when it may be done with safety.'[44] This statement effectively redefined the obligatory nature of natural law. Rationally and internally, the products of reason still bound the individual as logical consequences of the law of self-preservation. If such actions in practice compromised self-preservation, that priority meant that those actions did not carry obligation at all. If this was true, and the laws of nature were not obligatory, were they actually laws at all? Hobbes made it clear that they were not:

> But those which we call the Laws of Nature (since they are nothing else but certain conclusions, understood by reason, of things to be done or omitted; but a law, to speak properly and accurately, is the speech of him who by right commands somewhat to others to be done or omitted) are not in propriety of speech laws, as they proceed from nature.[45]

Hobbes here has the same understanding of law as that used by Selden to undermine the easy equation between reason and obligation. Law is the command of a superior, and reason cannot issue such commands. The conclusions of reason could not, therefore, be laws by themselves. Where, then, could obligation be discovered? The traditional Protestant answer to this question, used by Taylor in 1660, was that obligation came from Scripture, as the direct command of God. In the *De cive* of 1642, Hobbes endorsed this solution in a way that qualified the radicalism of his denial of natural obligation. At the end of chapter 3, having revealed that natural laws cannot be thought of as laws, he writes that 'Yet, as they are delivered by God in holy Scriptures (as we shall see in the Chapter following), they are most properly called by the name of Laws. For the sacred Scripture is the speech of God commanding over all things by the greatest Right.'[46] Hobbes then went on in chapter 4 to demonstrate that his laws of nature could be identified through-

43 Ibid. 73; cf. *Leviathan*, 110.
44 Idem, *De cive*, 73; cf. *Leviathan*, 110.
45 Idem, *De cive*, 76.
46 Ibid.

out the Scripture. Hobbes's preparedness to take this route with the *De cive* is one reason why that work found more favour than *Leviathan* with an Anglican audience, which, like Taylor, could endorse the scriptural solution to sceptical arguments against natural law. It was not, however, his final word on the matter, and his later works made it clear that it was not his preferred solution.

When Hobbes came to write on the same topic in the *Leviathan*, his wording was almost identical, but the emphasis on Scripture had been dropped: 'But yet if we consider the same Theoremes, as delivered in the Word of God, that by right commandeth all things; then they are properly called Lawes.'[47] The elision of emphasis from Scripture to word is significant. It opened up the question of what was truly the word of God. Hobbes, like Selden, was profoundly sceptical about the kind of knowledge one could gain from Scripture. As early as the *Elements of law natural and politic* (1640) he had argued that it was far from being certain that Scripture could be said to be the word of God at all by anything other than faith.[48] These problems with the nature of Scripture led Hobbes to publish ever more sceptical accounts of the nature and coherence of scriptural texts. *Leviathan* questioned the coherence of the scriptural canon, and even questioned the authority of whole books. Hobbes's sceptical conclusion was that only the state could authorise what should be taken for Scripture, thus undermining any possibility of the text acting as an autonomous source of obligation. Although Hobbes had demonstrated that it was possible to identify his laws of nature in Scripture in the *De cive*, by 1651 he clearly felt that this was a redundant exercise – there was no equivalent chapter in the *Leviathan*.

The tension between the two accounts persisted into the 1660s. In 1658, in his critique *The catching of the Leviathan*, John Bramhall had attacked Hobbes's formulation at the end of chapter 15 of *Leviathan* for its apparent impiety. In describing the laws of nature, he argued, Hobbes 'forgetteth the God of Nature, and the main and principal laws of nature, which contain a man's duty to his God, and the principal end of his Creation'.[49] Now Hobbes rarely replied to his critics, but he did reply to this some ten years later, at that stage fearful of the consequences of leaving the direct charge of atheism unanswered. In his response to Bramhall's charge, Hobbes attempted to cover his argument by referring to the last sentences of chapter 15, where natural law was made obligatory through the word of God. He also cited chapter 4 of the *De cive*.[50] Bramhall's charge, he maintained, was therefore unjust in claiming that the *Leviathan* said nothing about divine obligation.

---

47 Idem, *Leviathan*, 111.
48 Idem, *Elements of law natural and politic*, ed. F. Tönnies, 2nd edn, intro. M. M. Goldsmith, London 1969, 1.11.8.
49 *The English works of Thomas Hobbes*, ed. W. Molesworth, London 1839–45 (hereinafter cited as *EW*), iv. 284.
50 Ibid. 284–5.

For all his protests, however, Hobbes's excuse could not disguise his progressive diminution of God's involvement in practical obligation. His response to Bramhall avoided the crucial point that the state effectively determined what constituted Scripture before its obligatory power became operational. That Hobbes was increasingly reluctant to ascribe any sort of obligation directly to God through Scripture can be seen in the Latin edition of the Leviathan, published as part of Hobbes's two-volume Opera of 1668. Hobbes had made a number of revisions to this work, and the end of chapter 15 saw yet another change to the formula. Here Hobbes drops all reference to the laws of nature being laws of God as they are in Scripture. He simply retreats to saying that natural law has to come from a lawgiver, and leaves it at that.[51] This was a typical Hobbesian move, in that the formula covered a range of constructive possibilities about who that lawgiver might be. Hobbes defused, but did not resolve, the argument by paring it down. At the same time, however, it released him from a problematic discussion of the status of Scripture, and the means by which God obliges men.

When Cumberland came to examine Hobbes's views on this issue only a few years later in the De legibus naturae, it was clear to him that Hobbes was denying the possibility that Scripture could act as an autonomous source of obligation. One of the reasons why Cumberland unusually chose to abstain from a debate with Hobbes over the sense of Scripture is because 'I cannot bring myself to believe, that he is seriously moved by its authority, as being what he looks upon to be wholly derived from the will of particular states.'[52] Cumberland focuses on the problematic passage at the end of chapter 15 as a way of pinning down his opponent and defining the nature of his task:

> [Hobbes] says indeed that, as they [natural laws] are enacted by God in scripture, then they are properly laws. But if we enquire of him whence the Holy Scripture is a law, he assumes that they to whom God has not supernaturally revealed, do not receive them, except he, who is invested with the Supreme Power in the Commonwealth; for he is the only lawgiver. Hence it follows that the law of nature, even as contained in scripture, is not properly a law except by the sanction of the state.[53]

Hobbes's insistence that it is necessary to have certain knowledge of the lawgiver leads Cumberland to conclude that 'this renders . . . what he says in the last paragraph of chapter fifteen of Leviathan wholly ineffectual'.[54]

Cumberland perceives Hobbes's wavering between Scripture and the state as an indication of basic subterfuge – an attempt to manipulate an otherwise orthodox argument in an unorthodox direction. For Cumberland, as for

---

51 Thomas Hobbes, Opera, Amsterdam 1668, ii. 79.
52 Cumberland, DLN, introduction, sect. 27.
53 Ibid. 9.13.
54 Ibid. 1.9.

many of Hobbes's critics, this was a deliberate ruse to trap the unwary reader. Cumberland proposes that Hobbes's 'real' sentiments can be discovered by looking at the way he supports or undermines the various accounts he offers. Cumberland notices that where Hobbes subscribes to the pious, orthodox, versions of his natural law theory, he crucially leaves them unsupported. This is in contrast to his impious conclusions, for which he always provides a reason.[55]

This perception of subterfuge is important for understanding why writers like Cumberland saw Hobbes's work as such a danger. Hobbes had adopted a Grotian natural law idiom, and in this he could be remarkably orthodox. He had added the reasonable scepticism about the sources of moral obligation, proposing again an acceptable solution in the use of Scripture. What he had also done, however, was to leave a question mark over the obligatory power of Scripture. This had the most dramatic consequences for his theory, because it meant that obligation needed to have some more immediate, certain and unambiguous source to be practically efficacious. Although Hobbes discussed natural law in conventional terms, his critical analysis destroyed the conventional moral relationships between those terms. Hobbes certainly did believe that God commands over all things by the greatest right, but using reason, or Scripture, to identify God's detailed commands could be potentially misleading, and dangerously uncertain. For that reason Hobbes's discussion of moral obligation always returned to the unambiguous source of authority created by men themselves, the state.

Hobbes's critical treatment of natural law theory had a number of serious implications for those who wished to use it. Hobbes eliminated the idea that natural law could bind individuals through reason, tradition or some other source. The only practical source of moral obligation rested with the state, and the civil magistrate. This necessarily subjective basis for ethics also eliminated the idea that there could be an obligatory natural morality beyond that determined by the laws of the magistrate. For Bramhall, Hobbes's vision was of an ethical world inverted, and the bishop lamented the times when 'the immutable laws of God and nature are made to depend on the mutable laws of men, just as one should go about to control the sun by the authority of the clock'.[56] These rather unpalatable consequences posed a problem for subsequent natural law theorists: Hobbes had compromised the use of natural law language as a basis for talking about moral obligation, but he had compromised it using the kind of widely accepted critique used by writers like Selden and Taylor. A number of key questions had to be answered: how could one prove that a Grotian idea of natural law could be binding through reason and nature, and yet still be the command of a superior? More particularly, could it be demonstrated against Hobbes that natural law did provide an inescapable

---

55 Ibid. 1.12.
56 *EW* iv. 372–3.

foundation for ethical theory? It was this question which would exercise Cumberland and his colleagues from Cambridge, as they attempted to find new ways to root obligation in God's natural justice.

Cambridge naturalism

Cumberland was a student at Magdalene between 1649 and 1656, at a time when England was facing the political and intellectual consequences of civil war, the execution of its anointed king, and the search for new foundations of political allegiance. In the midst of religious and political turmoil it was inevitable that political and ethical theorists would draw upon the new natural jurisprudence of Grotius, Selden and Hobbes. The publication of Hobbes's *Leviathan* in 1651, a work that both drew upon the natural law tradition, and yet at the same time fatally subverted it, was thus the occasion for much discussion, and Cambridge was at the heart of the responses to Hobbes and the new natural jurisprudential tradition.

The major innovations in British ethical thought during this period have often been ascribed to Cambridge thinkers, particularly the so-called Cambridge Platonists. However, Cumberland respectfully rejected Platonism as a response to moral scepticism, and this should make us cautious about accepting such labels uncritically. Indeed, in what follows it will be suggested that although the writers whom we know as the Cambridge Platonists did propose solutions to the problems of moral scepticism, it was their more orthodox colleagues who were to produce the distinctive fusion of Protestant theology and neo-Scholastic natural law which would characterise the work of writers like Cumberland. This tradition, which attempted to rescue the Scholastic emphasis upon reason and nature from Hobbes's critique, would be influential in shaping English ethics throughout the Restoration and into the following century. In doing battle with Hobbes, writers like Cumberland ensured that this tradition could continue to use the language of natural jurisprudence which had been compromised by the *Leviathan*. But before discussing these arguments in detail, it is necessary to examine the various Cambridge responses to the problems of ethical scepticism, and the milieu against which Cumberland developed his own ideas.

Selden had not been alone in seeing a possible response to moral scepticism in the mysteries of spiritual enlightenment. When the young Ralph Cudworth wrote to Selden praising him for his 'incomparable discourse upon the precepts of Noah', he reflected a general sympathy for Selden's approach shared amongst his Platonist colleagues.[57] Although it is problematic to identify a coherent philosophy amongst those labelled as Cambridge Platonists, the position of writers such as More, Smith and Cudworth can be

---

[57] Oxford, Bodleian Library, Selden MS supra. 109, fo. 270.

roughly sketched out along the following lines. Their response to moral scepticism took the form of an appeal to idealism, rejecting the world of sense for an attempt to recover moral and intellectual truths untainted by corporeality. True knowledge came not from the world, but from within. The resulting philosophy was an eclectic and often eccentric ethic of retreat based around spiritually enlightened reason, making possible the recovery of genuine *notitiae communes*, or innate common notions. Ethical knowledge was possible, but of a purely intellectual kind. Overcoming external scepticism about moral knowledge involved the cultivation of the inner self and the recovery of innate truths.

Henry More, of Christ's College, was perhaps the most famous representative of the neo-Platonist school. In his anti-Hobbesian *An antidote against atheism* (1653), More defined true knowledge as 'an active sagacity of the Soul, or quick recollection as it were, whereby some small business being hinted unto her, she runs out more presently into a more clear and larger conception'. Such ideas were merely activated by external stimuli, 'so that the mind of man being jogged and awakened by the impulse of outward objects is stirred up into a more full and clear conception of what was but imperfectly hinted to her from externall occasions'.[58] Rather than question the capacities of reason, as Selden and Hobbes had done, More sought to show how its operation could be purified. If true reason could be cleansed of the corruption of sense and the corporeal state, real ethical knowledge would be possible. The implication was that man could cultivate what was left of that divine common reason planted by God, while scepticism and atheism in men were consequences of corrupted reason. In *The immortality of the soul* (1659), More spoke of the brutish sensuality of men like Hobbes, who 'drown all their sober reason in the deepest Lethe of Sensuality'. In the *True way of attaining to divine knowledge*, John Smith, of Queens' College, argued the same point – any vestige of divine knowledge is utterly extinguished by the dregs of passion and sense which necessarily obscure man's fallen vision. Smith describes mankind's condition in terms of Plato's cave-dwellers, who can only hope to converse 'with sounds and shadows':

> The more deeply our Souls dive into our Bodies, the more will Reason and Sensuality run into one another, and make up a most dilute, unsavourie, and muddie kind of knowledge. We must therefore endeavour more to withdraw ourselves from bodily things to set our souls as free as may be from the miserable slavery to this base Flesh; we must shut the Eyes of Sense, and open the Brighter Eye of our Understandings.[59]

Only by doing this, argued the Platonists, could individuals free themselves

[58] Henry More, quoted in C. A. Patrides (ed.), *The Cambridge Platonists*, London 1969, 223.
[59] Ibid. 130, 139.

from their limited understandings, and attain a mystical union with God.[60] The call to open the eye of understanding to the light of God recalls the ideas used by Selden in his discussion of the *intellectus agens*, and both Smith and More used this concept to explain participation in divine knowledge.[61] In another striking parallel with Selden, More was particularly fascinated with the Hebrew cabbala; both he and Ralph Cudworth subscribed to the idea of the *prisca theologia*, whereby divinely inspired reason united elements of heathen and Mosaic beliefs in a universal intellectual tradition.

The practical consequence of this Platonic rationalism was disdain for dispute over human institutions and interpretations of Scripture. What mattered more was the enlivening and quickening spirit of God and the non-contentious essentials of holy living on which all could agree. It is striking that the Platonists were never drawn into sectarian controversy, leaving their ecclesiastical preferences deliberately ambiguous. As Ralph Cudworth put it in his celebrated sermon before the House of Commons in 1647:

> if we desire a true Reformation, as we seem to do; Let us begin here in reform-ing out hearts and lives; in keeping Christ's commandments. All outward Forms and Models of Reformation, though they never be so good in their kind; yet they are of little worth to us, without this inward Reformation of the Heart ... we must be reformed within, with a Spirit of Fire, and a Spirit of Burning, to purge us from the Drosse and Corruption of our hearts.[62]

Cudworth emphasised the inward law of the Gospel over the external requirements of particular religious positions, and declared that 'I do not urge the law written upon Tablets of stone without us but the law of Holiness written within on the Fleshy Tables of our Hearts.'

These Platonist arguments clearly ran against the grain of the voluntarist debates about the problematic status of reason, and its relationship to moral obligation. Their implication was that man's fallen rational faculty was capable of divine enlightenment, albeit of a mystical kind. This was a position diametrically opposed to the radical nominalism of writers like Hobbes, for whom the idea of spiritual illumination was a hopelessly con-fused, unhelpful and politically dangerous example of improper signification. Both More and Cudworth took up the challenge of confronting Hobbes's relativism with their own brand of moral realism; where Hobbes argued for the nominalism of matter and motion, and determinism of an inscrutable deity, they argued for the reality of spirits, human free will, and a God bound to observe an eternal and immutable morality. Although the confrontation

---

60 John Smith, *Select discourses*, ed. J. Worthington, London 1660, 377–451.

61 Patrides, *Cambridge Platonists*, 151; Henry More, *Enchiridion ethicum*, London 1668, 197, 205.

62 Ralph Cudworth, *A sermon preached ... March 31st, 1647*, Cambridge 1647, quoted in Patrides, *Cambridge Platonists*, 127.

revolved around a shared interest in natural reason and its capacities, the divergence in philosophical premises prevented a close engagement.

If the Platonism of More, Smith and Cudworth constituted one idealistic response to ethical scepticism, there were other currents of Cambridge thought which pulled in a very different direction, and which engaged much more directly with the natural jurisprudential issues raised by Grotius, Selden and Hobbes. Concentration on the Cambridge Platonists has often concealed the development of these less exotic, but arguably more influential ethical ideas in Cambridge in the 1640s and 1650s. Perhaps most important in tracing the origins of a work like the *De legibus naturae*, was the continued presence and development of Protestant Scholastic thought. It is often thought that Scholastic ideas were on the retreat throughout this period, but this is far from being the case.[63] A revival of interest in rational naturalism, against the rigours of Calvinist theology, led to a critical re-evaluation of Neo-Scholastic writings, and the creation of an enduring, if problematic, Protestant natural law tradition. This tradition, rather than the esoteric preoccupations of Cambridge Platonism, decisively shaped the political theory of Cumberland and his Latitudinarian colleagues. It also defined their ongoing conflict with Hobbes.

It may seem paradoxical to suggest that Benjamin Whichcote (1609–83) was one of the key individuals associated with the development of a Protestant Scholastic tradition. Whichcote is often portrayed as the founder of the Cambridge Platonist movement, but this view may require some reassessment.[64] Examination of Whichcote's background and extant works reveals a set of values in many ways far removed from the mysticism and eclecticism which characterised writers like More, Smith and Cudworth, although he was certainly a personal friend of the last. Indeed, far from espousing Platonism, Whichcote's work contributes to a common-sense empirical intellectual tradition which would be profoundly critical of Platonist epistemology.

The roots of Whichcote's beliefs require some examination. He had been educated at Emmanuel College, the Puritan intellectual powerhouse which would go on to provide no fewer than eleven Heads of Houses during the Interregnum.[65] The dominant influence at Emmanuel was Anthony Tuckney (1599–1670), later Regius Professor of Divinity, and an orthodox Calvinist, with whom Whichcote would later fall out over the role of reason in religion. Whichcote gained his reputation as a lecturer in Trinity Church from around 1636, where he preached ethical naturalism as an antidote to contentious

---

63 For the continued relevance of Scholastic writing to ethical thought see Spellman, *The Latitudinarians and the Church of England*, 74–7.

64 Patrides, *Cambridge Platonists*, p. xxv.

65 T. Fuller, *History of the University of Cambridge*, London 1655, 147. Emmanuel has been seen as producing the theologians of the Cambridge Platonist 'movement' in contrast to the 'natural philosophers' at Christ's: M. Nicolson, 'Christ's College and the Latitude Men', *Modern Philology* xxvii (1929–30), 35–53.

external doctrines. John Tillotson, who preached his funeral sermon in 1683 commented:

> Every Lord's Day in the Afternoon for almost twenty years together . . . he had a great number not only of the younger scholars, but of those of greater standing and best repute for learning in the university his constant and attentive auditors; and in those wild and unsettled times contributed more to the forming of the students of that university to a sober sense of religion than any man in that age.[66]

Whichcote's moderate views, and his high standing among his more orthodox colleagues, made him a natural choice as a replacement for one of the ejected Heads of Houses after Manchester's purge of 1644–5.[67] Whichcote was installed as Provost of King's in January 1645, and quickly demonstrated his commitment to reconciliation, protecting Royalist Fellows from further molestation. In an atmosphere where such sentiments were prized, Whichcote became vice-chancellor of the university in 1650, advising the Protectorate on the question of religious toleration of the Jews during the 1650s.[68] He was deprived of his office at King's at the Restoration, and retired to his rectory at Milton, just outside Cambridge. Perhaps the most compelling evidence that Whichcote was intimately linked with those dubbed 'Latitude men', or 'rational divines' was his return to prominence in the later 1660s. In 1668, through the collusion of John Wilkins and Orlando Bridgeman, Whichcote took over Wilkins's vicarage at St Lawrence Jewry in London on the latter's elevation to the see of Chester. Under Wilkins, St Lawrence Jewry had hosted guest lectures for divines such as Isaac Barrow and John Tillotson. In many ways it is possible to see Whichcote as the 'rational divines'' mentor, much more so than the more cloistered Cudworth and More (who refused church office). Whichcote's relative invisibility in such a role may be due to the fact that most of his work was only edited and published posthumously, but from the extant remains it is possible to detect a view offering a decisive contrast to classically Platonist ideas.

Whichcote's interest in ethical naturalism came as a response to religious extremism, or, in contemporary terms, 'enthusiasm'. Joseph Glanvill commented that his preaching 'contributed much to the overthrow of the Phanatical Genius of that Age',[69] and Whichcote consistently opposed uncontrolled religious passion; as he commented in one of his collected *Aphorisms*: 'Enthusiasm is the confounder, both of Reason and Religion:

---

[66] John Tillotson, *A sermon preached at the funeral of the Reverend Benjamin Whichcot . . .*, *May 24th*, London 1683. For comments on Whichcote's preaching see J. I. Cope, 'The Cupri-Cosmits: Glanvill on Latitudinarian anti-enthusiasm', *Huntington Library Quarterly* ii (1954), 269–86; Gilbert Burnet, *History of his own time*, London 1734, ii. 45, 83.

[67] J. Twigg, *The University of Cambridge and the English Revolution 1625–88*, Woodbridge 1990, 103–7.

[68] *DNB*.

[69] Cope, 'Cupri-Cosmits', 269–86.

therefore nothing is more necessary to the interests of Religion, than the prevention of enthusiasm.'[70] This attitude contrasts with some of the more permissive attitudes found amongst the Platonists where a respect for spiritual enlightenment could create sympathy for religious enthusiasm; the Magdalene College Platonist Peter Sterry defended Quakers during the 1650s, and both Cudworth and More were themselves attacked as 'enthusiasts' after the Restoration.[71] By contrast, Whichcote's position on religious toleration appears to have had more in common with his Latitudinarian friends and colleagues.[72]

For Whichcote, unwarranted confidence was the cause of irrational religious dogma. The first stage of a solution lay in scepticism about the kind of religious knowledge that men could have. The foundation of Whichcote's rationalism is sceptical, eschewing reliance upon received knowledge of any kind; as he comments in his aphorisms: 'Examine all principles of Education: for, since we are all fallible, we should suppose we may be Mistaken.' Individuals should 'keep indifferency of Judgement, till the verity of things does appear; so long as there is any uncertainty. Have no bias, but what is received from Truth'.[73]

The 'verity of the thing' is where Whichcote departed significantly from the Platonist account of moral knowledge. Throughout his work he made it clear that God had provided sufficient evidence of his law in the 'nature of things', a phrase that would be particularly important for Cumberland's *De legibus*. As his *Select notions* of 1685 made clear, man was utterly dependent upon God, not only spiritually, but through his created nature, which offered a clear guide to moral conduct. 'If we follow the dictates of nature', wrote Whichcote, 'we shall never transgress.'[74]

Although some of Whichcote's ethical naturalism came from Stoic sources, his understanding of reason combined Stoic and Scholastic, rather than a Platonist, influences. Whichcote quoted Aristotle more often than Plato.[75] In Whichcote's account, the rational faculty was created with man, but it was autonomous. This was his understanding of reason as the 'Candle of the Lord', the text from Proverbs xx.27 which became a distinctive badge

70 Benjamin Whichcote, *Moral and religious aphorisms*, ed. J. Jeffery, London 1753, no. 349.
71 *The correspondence of Anne, viscountess Conway, Henry More and their friends, 1642–1684*, ed. M. H. Nicholson, rev. edn S. Hutton, Oxford 1992, 219–21.
72 Whichcote was invited to take part in the Whitehall Conference in 1655 which discussed the possibility of readmitting the Jews to England. The guarded conservatism of the clerical participants (of whom Whichcote was an influential representative) led Cromwell to attempt to pack the conference with pro-toleration supporters like Peter Sterry: D. Katz, *Jews in the history of England*, Oxford 1994, 122–3. See also his *Philo-semitism and the readmission of the Jews to England 1603–1655*, Oxford 1982.
73 Whichcote, *Aphorisms*, no. 56, 173.
74 Idem, *Select notions*, London 1685, 127.
75 de Pauley, *Candle of the Lord*, 35–6.

of Whichcote's doctrine, subsequently to be found in the work of Nathaniel Culverwel, Simon Patrick and even John Locke.[76]

The 'Candle of the Lord' concept had two important features central to Whichcote's brand of naturalism. Firstly, it was 'lighted by God' and provided an essential means to reveal God's will, an infallible faculty for detecting true from false. The second characteristic was that it could not detect God's will on its own. Reason by itself contained no innate knowledge; Whichcote argued that 'the Understanding, as *Aristotle* well observes, is *arasa* [sic] *tabula*'.[77] Elsewhere he commented that men are born 'a sheet of white paper whereon nothing is written'.[78] The mention of Aristotle illustrates the Scholastic origins of Whichcote's views; the *tabula rasa* concept is actually a Thomist misquotation of Aristotle's comments in the *De anima*.[79] The implication of the doctrine is that knowledge must be obtained empirically, from nature illuminated by reason. Whichcote's commitment to this form of Scholastic empiricism is clear throughout his work; as he comments in the *Aphorisms*, 'None of us was born knowing or Wise: but men become Wise, by consideration, observation and experience.' Nature, created by God with this purpose in mind, provides an essential means by which the will of God is revealed, as Whichcote writes, 'Things themselves speak to us, and offer notions to our minds, and this is the voice of God.'[80]

This resolutely empirical epistemology was clearly a long way from the Platonist defence of innate ideas. The reliance upon reason and nature as a guide to God's will was also a long way from a rigorous Calvinist orthodoxy, and it was this, not Platonism, which was the cause of Whichcote's celebrated, and heated, debate with Anthony Tuckney.

The debate emerged from Whichcote's commencement sermon of 1651, in which he had delivered what Tuckney characterised as 'a large discourse of *Recta Ratio*'.[81] Tuckney objected to the implications of Whichcote's suggestions that faith could be supplemented by natural reason. His responses reassert the centrality of Scripture as the guide to God's will. It is notable that throughout the debate Platonism is only mentioned once, and by Tuckney[82] – indeed, his most frequent complaint is about Whichcote's dangerous attachment to the Schoolmen and Latinate philosophy. Tuckney argued that Whichcote should, 'affect not to speak in schoole-language; nor to runne out in schoole-notions: it is far different from the Scripture, both style and

---

[76] Whichcote, *Aphorisms*, no. 916. See also S. P., *Brief account*, 10; John Locke, *An essay concerning human understanding*, ed. P. H. Nidditch, Oxford 1975, 4.3.20.

[77] Whichcote, *Select notions*, 99.

[78] Idem, *Works*, Aberdeen 1751, 4, 215.

[79] Thomas Aquinas, *Summa theologia*, general ed. T. Gilbey, London 1964–81, *prima pars*, Q. 89, art. 1; cf. Aristotle, *De anima*, trans. R. D. Hicks, Cambridge 1907, III.iv.

[80] Whichcote, *Aphorisms*, no. 57, p. 482; cf. Cumberland, *DLN* 2.9.

[81] Whichcote, *Aphorisms*, appendix, 4.

[82] Ibid. 38.

matter: it was begot in the depth of anti-christian darkness'.[83] Tuckney suspected that Whichcote was getting his doctrine from 'Arminian' writers like Field, Jackson and Hammond, and Neo-Scholastic authorites such as Vasquez and Suarez.[84] Although Whichcote was coy about his sources, and eclectic in his method, such charges may not have been without foundation.

Whichcote's version of Scholastic rationalism preached a simple moral message. The 'Candle of the Lord' might only be a flickering and diminutive light, but from its illumination of nature, man had the opportunity to discern the path of moral virtue which God had laid down as a natural law. The process of discovery was not, however, an easy one, and in Whichcote's recognition of this it is possible to see the residual scepticism about rational knowledge which characterised Whichcote's Calvinist background. Much depended on the ability of the individual to overcome the weakness of the human condition: 'We suffer difficulty in the exercise of virtue, because our Understandings are short and fallible, our appetites diverse and contrary: but we must stay for information and control ourselves.' Reason had to be cultivated, and the passions regulated, in order to obtain true knowledge from nature.[85]

Whichcote belived that this dual process of internal reformation and empirical investigation permitted the perfection of man's nature. He wrote that 'The mind is to be informed with knowledge, and Refined by Virtue. By the several Virtues, the mind is purified and made fit to converse with God.'[86] This state of being 'fit to converse with God' constitutes a state of living in accord with man's created nature, a state in which man is made fully aware of his natural obligations to his Creator.[87] Whichcote termed this state 'Deiformity', the highest attainment of natural wisdom.[88]

Whichcote had revised a Calvinist understanding of the capacities of reason and human nature. His assertion of a natural moral order brought God's justice closer than its traditional location in the afterlife. Divine reward and punishment began on earth. Thus he wrote that:

Both Heaven and Hell have their foundation within us. Heaven lies primarily in a refined Temper; in an internal Reconciliation with the Nature of God; and to the Rule of Righteousness. The Guilt of Conscience and Emnity to Righteousness, is the inward state of Hell. The Guilt of Conscience is the fewel of Hell.[89]

---

83 Ibid. 37.
84 Ibid. 38, 80.
85 Ibid. 76.
86 Ibid. no. 229.
87 Whichcote, Select notions, 91: 'The duty of his service is the Law of his Being; hereby he holds under God, and claims of him a Man's Title to himself, is in subordination to God.'
88 Idem, Aphorisms, no. 262.
89 Ibid. no. 100, 386.

Whichcote's understanding of nature reinvested the creation with divine justice. It raised the possibility that moral laws could be read from nature by reason. Whichcote even went so far as to suggest that because of these possibilities 'we may be as certain in Morals . . . as we can be in our Mathematicks'.[90] The tantalising thought that nature, if approached in the right way, could yield this kind of certainty, would be an objective which would exercise Latitudinarian writers from Cumberland to Locke, who listed Whichcote as one his favourite preachers.[91]

It has already been observed that Whichcote did not publish anything during his lifetime, and much of what we have left is taken from his sermons and his fragmentary notes. He thus left no treatise on natural law, although nearly all his work is based around the concept. However, although Whichcote did not respond directly to the debate over natural law, one of his students did, in an important and influential work which applied Whichcote's arguments to the debate over natural law. Nathaniel Culverwell (1619–51) was also a Fellow of Emmanuel College. Although he, too, is often categorised as a Cambridge Platonist, he is much closer to the Stoic and neo-Scholastic views expressed by Whichcote. His An elegant and learned discourse of the light of nature (published in 1652 but probably delivered as sermons in 1645–6) went on to become a bestseller, with editions in 1654, 1661 and 1669. The achievement of the work was to engage the Cambridge approach with the debate over Grotian natural law theory. Culverwell develops the 'Candle of the Lord' metaphor to discuss the foundation for a truly naturalistic ethic which in many ways anticipates the work that Cumberland would do in the De legibus naturae.

Culverwell's targets in the Discourse are the religious dogmatici, the 'antinomians, seekers and seraphicks' who appear to demonstrate the 'miserable weakness of men's understanding'.[92] But the existence of religious enthusiasm is not an excuse for total scepticism. Culverwell also writes against sceptics, those 'who, by a strange kind of hypocrisy, and in an unusual way of affectation pretend to more ignorance than they have, nay, more than they are capable of'. Scepticism, for Culverwell, is not a solution, because the sceptic simply cannot live his scepticism.[93]

In investigating a suitable alternative Culverwell turns to natural law theory. The source of much of Culverwell's discussion is Suarez's Tractatus de legibus, ac deo legislatore (1612), and indeed the first half of the Discourse is virtually an English paraphrase of that work, demonstrating the manner in which Neo-Scholasticism could be referred to and used by Protestant

---

90 Whichcote, Select notions, 124–5; cf. Aphorisms, no. 298.
91 Ibid. p. xxxii.
92 Nathaniel Culverwell, An elegant and learned discourse of the light of nature, ed. R. A. Greene and H. MacCallum, Toronto 1971, 110–11.
93 Ibid. 123.

scholars.[94] But Suarez was not Culverwell's only source. He quotes Grotius' definition of natural law approvingly, translating it not only into English, but also into the natural law idiom used by Whichcote:

> The Law of Nature is a streaming of light from the Candle of the Lord, power-fully discovering such a deformity in some evil, and such a commanding beauty in some good, as that a rational being must needs be enamoured with it; and so plainly showing that God stampt and seal'd the one with his command, and branded the other with his disliking.[95]

In fact, Culverwell was broadly sympathetic to Grotius throughout the *Discourse*. Indeed, chapter 10 of the *Discourse* is devoted to a discussion of the Grotian 'proof' that natural law is indeed obligatory, but like most English responses to Grotius, Culverwell rejects the suggestion that this is the best way to discuss obligation; it is at best merely 'a secondary and additional way' in which the law of nature might be discovered.[96] Culverwell prefers to follow those whom he calls 'Criticks', by whom he means Selden in the main, who reject *a posteriori* evidence of the law of nature and who also reject the assertion that reason by itself can constitute a sufficient source of moral obligation.

At this point he directs Selden's critical humanism at those Schoolmen who would propose that the laws of nature would oblige even if God did not exist. The primary target here is Suarez, but the critique would equally apply to his follower Grotius. Natural law without a legislator, for Culverwell, as for Whichcote, was a logical absurdity. Although both writers were prepared to engage creatively with the Neo-Scholastic doctrines, their Protestant re-evaluation of nature required that the laws of nature be utterly dependent upon the will of God. For this reason, the suggestion that reason and nature alone could constitute an autonomous ethic was blasphemous. Culverwell has no problem in deploying the argument of the 'Criticks' against Scholastic right reason: 'for Reason as 'tis now does not binde in its own name'. Culverwell explains this critique in terms that were themselves reminiscent of Selden:

> For if a creature should binde itself to the observation of this Law, it must also inflict upon itself such a punishment as is answerable to the violation of it; but no such being would be willing or able to punish itself in so high a measure as such a transgression would meritoriously require; so that it must be accountable to some other legislative power, which will vindicate its own commands, and will by this means ingage a Creature to be more mindful of its own happiness, than otherwise it would be.[97]

---

94 This feature led Knud Haakonssen to call Culverwell a 'poor-man's version of Suarez's recent modification of Thomism': 'Moral philosophy and natural law', 104.
95 Culverwell, *Discourse*, 44–5.
96 Ibid. 72.
97 Ibid. 50.

If Culverwell accepted Selden's critical analysis of reason, he was not, however, prepared to adopt the solution of the *De jure*. Like Cumberland later, he rejected Selden's preoccupation with Hebrew tradition: chapter 8 of the *Discourse* ridicules the notion that the Jews have some kind of privileged status. He is prepared to admit that the Hebrews do indeed possess a greater number of revealed truths than the rest of mankind, but for all this, 'they have no greater portion of the light of nature then all men have'.[98] Culverwell rejected Selden's account of the *intellectus agens* as being both misleadingly obscure and potentially heterodox. To argue for a common intellect compromised the idea that the individual soul could go on to become immortal.[99]

Interestingly, Culverwell also points out the connections between Selden's use of the *intellectus agens* and its appeal to Platonists, who, he notes, were 'excessively enclinable to it, and were always so much conversant with spirits, which made their philosophy ever questioned for a touch of magick'.[100] This hostility to the mystical tendencies of Platonism is reinforced in chapter 11, where Culverwell, like Whichcote, clearly distances himself from the Platonist doctrine of innate ideas. To argue that moral knowledge comes from within, comments Culverwell, is like suggesting that the Candle of the Lord gives out more light than it in fact receives from the outside world. This was like Plato's mistaken belief that the eye illuminates the object. If the Platonist account suggested that intellectual light was emitted from the eye, Culverwell, like Whichcote, explicitly appealed to the Aristotelian account of sensate knowledge in proposing an empirical solution. His formulation is worth quoting in full:

> Therefore Aristotle (who did better clarifie both these kinds of vision) pluckt these motes out of the sensitive eye, and those beames out of the intellectual. He did not antedate his own knowledge, nor remember the several postures of his soul, and the famous exploits of his minde before he was born; but plainly proffest that his understanding came naked into the world.[101]

If the understanding was a blank sheet, then knowledge must come from its exposure to the external world through the senses. Culverwell developed the light metaphor further:

> Many sparks and appearences fly from the variety of objects to the understanding; the minde, that catches them all, and cherishes them, and blows them; and thus the Candle of knowledge is lighted. As he could perceive no connate colours, no pictures and portaictures in his external eye: so neither could he finde any signatures in his minde until some outward objects had made some

98 Ibid. 61–6.
99 Ibid. 70.
100 Ibid. 68.
101 Ibid. 79.

impression upon his soft and plyable understanding impartially prepared for every seal.[102]

On this model, the concept of connate notions is difficult to sustain in its Platonic form. Certainty of knowledge 'first peeps out in the sense, and shines more brightly in the understanding. The first dawnings of certainty are in the sense, the noon-day glories of it in the intellectuals.'[103] This Aristotelian formulation of empirical knowledge is Culverwell's response to the moral sceptic, and the foundation for the divine obligation to natural law. Knowledge is derived from nature, and nature is created by God. God gives man the capacity for certain knowledge of nature, which is the natural means by which man becomes aware of God's will.

This empiricism constituted the basis for Culverwell's natural law theory. The 'nature of things', as in Whichcote, provides the evidence for real ethical values: 'Nature has distinguisht good from evil, by those indelible stamps and impressions which she has graven upon both, and has set Reason as a competent judge to decide all moral controversies.' Man's rational nature allows him to apprehend such natural ethics. Whereas writers like Selden and Hobbes had required any 'law' of nature to have a legislator, clear promulgation and identifiable sanctions, Culverwell argued that his law of nature could have all of these things:

> Reason is the Pen by which Nature writes this law of her own composing; this law 'tis publisht by authority from Heaven, and Reason is the printer: This eye of the soul 'tis to spy out all dangers and all advantages, all conveniences and disconveniences in reference to such a being, and to warne the Soul in the name of its Creator, to fly from such irregularities as have an intrinsical and implacable malice in them, and are prejudicial and destructive to its nature, but to comply with, and embrace all such acts and objects as have a natural comeliness and amiableness, and are for the heightening and ennobling of its being.

Culverwell's emphasis on natural reward and punishment here echoes Whichcote's discussion of earthly judgement and the emphasis on 'deiformity'. In an equally decisive revision of ethical naturalism, Culverwell might appear to be completely abandoning his Calvinist beliefs for Scholastic heterodoxy, but Culverwell never forgets Calvinist theology. The condition of reinvesting nature with ethical significance is the total reliance of created nature upon the will of God. As a consequence, the law of nature only obliges by virtue of its status as the command of the divine legislator:

> This Law of Nature having a firme and unshaken foundation in the necessity and conveniency of its materials becomes formally valid and vigorous by the minde and command of the supreme lawgiver; so as that all the strength and

---

102 Ibid. 81.
103 Ibid. 124–5, cf. 126.

nerves, and binding virtue of this Law are rooted and fasten'd partly in the excellency and equity of the commands, but they principally depend upon the sovereignty and authority of God himself: thus contriving and commanding the welfare of his creatures, and advancing a Rational Nature to the just perfection of his being.[104]

For Culverwell, the law of nature might well be rational, but this is not the source of moral obligation, and in this he reverts to a voluntarist understanding of natural law, that its precepts only bind insofar as they are the identifiable will of God. The *Discourse* relied on the fundamental premise that the will of God could be identified through an empirical investigation of nature. This sometimes uneasy combination of voluntarism and naturalism represented an early attempt to convert what we might call Cambridge Aristotelianism or Neo-Scholasticism into a formal jurisprudential shape. The *Discourse* reveals a willingness to engage with writers such as Suarez, and also Grotius, but from the kind of critical standpoint adopted by Selden in the *De jure*, thus anticipating many features of writers like Locke and Cumberland. The *Discourse* provided an empirical riposte to those whose solutions to moral scepticism had so far relied upon innate ideas, intellectual traditions or Scripture alone.

Hobbes, of course, had proposed another solution which removed practical moral obligation from God altogether, but it should be noted that Culverwell's work was not intended as a response to Hobbes, whose work he could not have been familiar with at the time of its composition. Culverwell died before he had an opportunity to engage with Hobbes over these issues, but the argument which he supported would soon be used to neutralise Hobbes's radical redescription of natural law theory.

One writer who may have been influenced by Culverwell's formulation was John Locke. Locke had not only heard Whichcote's sermons; he listed them amongst his recommended reading. He used the 'Candle of the Lord' metaphor in book IV of his *Essay concerning human understanding*. His use of empiricism there (in work which dates back to drafts written in 1671), clearly recalls the kind of argument used by both Whichcote and Culverwell.[105] Locke also used these arguments in his writings on natural law in the early 1660s. Locke's *Essays on the law of nature* addressed the question of moral obligation in a form similar to that of the *Discourse*. To call them essays, however, is to misrepresent them, since they were written in the style of Scholastic exercises, or *quaestiones*. This, together with the fact that the essays were discovered bound into a notebook containing notes on Stoic and Ciceronian

---

104 Ibid. 65.

105 For Locke's usage of the 'Candle of the Lord' see *Essay concerning human understanding*, IV.iii.20. Locke listed Whichcote among his 'friends' to whom he gave his regards in letter to his close friend John Mapletoft in the later 1670s. For the connections between Locke and Whichcote see particularly John Marshall, *John Locke: resistance, religion and responsibility*, Cambridge 1994, 78–9, 123, 179.

references, indicates the extent to which Locke was drawing upon the same sources as Culverwell and Whichcote.[106]

The first *quaestio* asked whether there was 'a law of nature given to us?', to which Locke replied in the affirmative. The law of nature, Locke argued, is 'the decree of the divine will discernible by the light of nature and indicating what is and what is not in conformity with rational nature, and for this very reason comanding or prohibiting'. Locke's definition revealed the variety of traditions converging in his work. The basic Grotian/Ciceronian definition is recast to drop the initial emphasis upon *recta ratio*. This is replaced by the voluntarist emphasis on law as a divine decree. Locke explains this by arguing that 'reason does not so much establish and pronounce this law of nature as search for it and discover it as a law enacted by a superior power and implanted in our hearts'.[107]

The succeeding *quaestiones* examine familiar issues as Locke enquires into the origins of moral obligation. Locke rejects the consensus argument, 'for is there anything so abominable, so wicked, so contrary to all right and law, which the general consent, or rather the conspiracy, of a senseless crowd would not at some time advocate'.[108] In the second and third essays, Locke rejects the innate ideas of the Platonists, and Selden's argument that the law of nature could come from tradition. The only satisfactory method for obtaining knowledge of the laws of nature, for Locke, was sense experience.

Locke's theory demonstrated how moral obligation could be derived from empirical observation. All things must have a maker, he argued, and from this 'it is clear that men can infer from sense-experience that there exists some powerful superior who has right and authority over themselves'.[109] It is also clear, he argued, that God cannot have created the world, and man, for nothing. It is evident from nature that man is fitted for many things – discovering this purpose would thus reveal God's will, and thus natural law.[110] Locke finds that this *telos* indicates, both from man's pressing needs, and the propensities of his faculties, that man's nature above all directs him to be sociable. It is thus an obligatory law of nature that man should be sociable.

The context in which this argument had been developed, however, had been compromised by Hobbes's subversion of the genre. Hobbes had also rejected consensus, tradition and innate ideas as the basis of natural obligation. He had equally replaced it with an empirical and rational understanding of the sources of natural obligation. The problem was that Hobbes's assessment of what one could know from empirical observation was limited to those things that one could know for certain. In the case of natural law, this

---

[106] M. A. Stewart, 'Critical notice of "Questions concerning the laws of nature" ', *Locke Newsletter* xxiii (1992), 145–66.

[107] Locke, *Essays on the law of nature*, 111.

[108] Ibid. 161.

[109] Ibid. 153.

[110] Ibid. 157.

meant that the desire for self-preservation was the only inescapable right on which moral obligation could be based. Hobbes's other 'laws' of nature were not laws at all, simply prudential theorems. This meant that sociability could hardly be said to be an obligatory law of nature, as Locke wanted to suggest. Locke engaged with this directly in the sixth *quaestio*, where he comments that 'since there are some who would trace the whole value of the law of nature back to each person's self-preservation . . . it seems worth our labour to inquire what and how great is the binding force of the laws of nature'.[111] This would be the key issue, for Locke, but also for Cumberland. In order to sustain their political arguments, both needed to prove that the laws of nature were operational and obligatory, and this meant refuting Hobbes's arguments in chapter 15 of *Leviathan*. Although they shared many of Hobbes's premises in following Selden's critique of right reason, they had to find a way to distance themselves from the unpalatable implications of Hobbes's work.

Locke approached the problem with a technical definition of obligation in mind. Robert Sanderson, whom Locke was following here, had defined obligation as requiring a liability to pay a dutiful obedience to one with right and power, together with punishment 'which arises from a failure to pay dutiful obedience'.[112] Locke's answer laid stress on his identification of God as a legislator with right and power. God had created the world, and evidence of his workmanship was clearly evident; 'knowledge of God', Locke argued, 'can be concealed from no-one unless he loves blindness and darkness and casts off nature in order to avoid his duty'. The detail of natural law is promulgated with sufficient clearness in the constitution of human nature, which is perpetual and universal. This evidence, he argued, was so powerful that 'no nation or human being is so removed from humanity, so savage and beyond the law, that it is not held by the bonds of law'.[113] Locke's answer put faith in the idea that human nature could be decoded in identifiable ways. Man could be shown to be sociable, therefore this was the divine will, and thus natural law.

Locke's answer to Hobbes in the *Essays* did not go much further than this. For Locke, empirical investigation showed that there was more to moral obligation than self-interest alone. To ground natural law on such a principle could never be consistent with a truly social existence or most forms of virtue. Although this was a good and common response to Hobbes's natural law doctrine, this simple assertion of God's authorship of natural law would not be enough to save Latitude-men from association with Hobbes's ideas. The problem was one of bridging the gap between divinely ordained natural law, and the kind of Hobbesian politics required in the *adiaphora* issue. Samuel Parker's *Discourse of ecclesiastical politie* showed this only too well. Parker, too, had argued that the laws of nature required men to be sociable, but his

111 Ibid. 181.
112 Ibid. 183–5.
113 Ibid. 199.

emphasis upon political sovereignty left a serious question over the source of practical moral obligation. If natural law merely sanctioned an all-powerful magistrate, was this not simple Hobbism? To extricate this kind of natural law from association with Hobbes, several developments were necessary. Firstly, it needed to be shown in greater detail that natural law demanded sociable behaviour; secondly, and more importantly, it was necessary to demonstrate that natural law carried a divine and inescapable obligation to its precepts. This is what Richard Cumberland sought to do in *De legibus naturae*.

3

De Legibus Naturae *I*

Natural law provided attractive but problematic answers to the political and religious problems of seventeenth-century Europe. In principle, as the work of Grotius had shown, an analysis of human nature could offer the basis for some kind of discussion of rights and duties. The problem arose when one tried to establish precisely which moral actions were required by natural law, and how genuinely obligatory that behaviour was. The criticisms made by Selden and Hobbes reflected these difficulties. For both writers, the confusion over the relationship between reason and obligation required the location of a more certain source of moral authority. Selden found his authority in Hebrew tradition, but Hobbes, eschewing Scripture and tradition for a more radical naturalism, rooted moral obligation in the laws of the state.

Cumberland's *De legibus naturae* developed a new approach to moral obligation. The book attempted to show that it was possible to recover a demonstrative theory of ethics from the evidence of nature. This had been the basis of traditional Stoic and neo-Scholastic ethical theory, but in order to combat Hobbes's 'demonstration', Cumberland brought it up to date. His novel argument was that the use of modern science could allow a new and more certain way of analysing exactly what natural law did prescribe. Furthermore, Cumberland's 'scientific' method of analysing natural law could reveal that natural law was sanctioned by God as legislator. Perhaps the most far-reaching aspect of Cumberland's theory was his argument that all of this could be proved by his demonstration of the existence of natural rewards and punishments. By proving that natural law possessed both a divine legislator and sanctions attached to its observance, Cumberland refuted Hobbes and recovered natural jurisprudence for Protestant political theory.

Natural philosophy and ethical theory

The encounter between Cumberland and Hobbes turned on the question of what could be known, and known with certainty, from the evidence of nature. For both men, it was the practical constraints of nature which were the issue when it came to discussing moral obligation; only a detailed study of nature could reveal the practical extent of moral obligation. Hobbes's position made it clear that Grotius' natural law theory was too vague and uncertain to command the kind of certainty that was required to answer a moral sceptic. For Hobbes, a moral science needed to operate on principles other than an accretion of anecdotal evidence. Cumberland, on the other hand, wanted to keep faith with the Grotian and Ciceronian accounts of ethical naturalism, but he needed to show, against Hobbes, that this extensive account of natural law could be shown to be demonstrable.

Cumberland's answer to Hobbes was to argue that natural law could be known demonstrably through use of the recently developed experimental and theoretical sciences. Hobbes had claimed that his method generated *scientiae* of ethics and politics, but Cumberland sought to show that science could work for traditional understandings of natural law theory as well. Cumberland's confidence in the new natural philosophy is a defining feature of the *De legibus naturae*. It confronted Hobbes's supposedly 'scientific' defence of self-interested ethics with an equally scientific argument about man's natural sociability. This gives Cumberland's writing a peculiarly Janus-faced quality, in that he seeks to justify the natural law theory of ancient writers like Cicero, with the modern science of his contemporaries, Descartes, Huygens and Boyle. In the *De legibus*, Cartesian analytical geometry shares pages with Aristotle, Harvey is juxtaposed with Plutarch. Cumberland's work deliberately used modern science in support of ancient ethics (and at the same time ancient ethics in support of modern science). Cumberland asserted that science offered a new way to look at old problems: 'It is sufficient for us to have admonished the reader', he wrote in chapter 1, 'that the whole of moral philosophy, and of the Laws of Nature, is ultimately resolved into natural observations known by the experience of all men, *or into the conclusions of natural philosophy*' (my italics).[1] The common observations of all men, Cumberland noted, had not been enough to persuade Hobbes that natural law extended beyond self-preservation. Natural philosophy, however, for Cumberland, offered another, more precise, route to establishing moral obligation. Cumberland explains that the new science 'does not only comprehend all the appearances of natural bodies which we know from experiment, but also enquires into the nature of our souls, from observations made upon their actions, and distinguishing perfections'.[2]

Cumberland's point is that moral behaviour qualifies as a natural phenomenon which can be observed in much the same way as the behaviour of physical bodies. Just as natural philosophy deals with information about causes, effects, sum, order and duration, so these constitute the subject matter of the law of nature. This allows natural philosophy to be used in the discussion of ethics because:

Natural Philosophy does very distinctly explain what things or powers and motions of things are to others either good or evil, and how necessarily and unchangeably this is brought about. For seeing it is the only scope of this science to discover the causes of generation, duration and corruption (all which

---

[1] Cumberland, *DLN* 1.3.
[2] Ibid. 1.17.

we behold daily to happen to most bodies, but especially to men's) and to demonstrate the necessary connexion between such effects with their causes.[3]

For Cumberland, natural philosophy offered a new way of apprehending natural law, and, more importantly, a new method which was clearer, more distinct, and amenable to the kind of demonstration a writer like Hobbes had demanded. Cumberland was going to prove the verities of ancient ethics as scientifically as Hobbes, if not more so. In part, Cumberland's motive was to show that natural philosophy was not simply destructive of ethics, as its Hobbesian manifestation had suggested. But his major aim was to show that morally useful knowledge could be gained from the natural world with a reasonable level of certainty. Science, as Cumberland defined it, offered a mode of discourse which could not only overcome the moral sceptic's manipulation of rhetoric, but which could also expand the boundaries of moral knowledge beyond the narrow view of the *Leviathan*.

Cumberland's moral epistemology

Cumberland's commitment to an empirical basis for moral knowledge in many ways anticipates Locke's project in the *Essay concerning human understanding*, but it is important not to take his very suggestive arguments out of the anti-Hobbesian context of the *De legibus naturae*. The first point to make clear is that it was not Cumberland's concern to elaborate a novel epistemological theory. The arguments that he deploys are neither new, nor systematically developed with this aim in mind. Rather, Cumberland sought to re-establish an empirical theory as the basis for his defence of natural law. Cumberland's preoccupation is not with knowledge *per se*, but with moral knowledge, and it is with this objective in mind that he suggests that 'it seems necessary, especially at this time, to trace more distinctly, after what manner the power of things, as well without as within us, conspire to imprint these conclusions upon our minds, and to give a sanction to them'.[4] Cumberland's concern is to trace the mechanisms by which reason interacts with the created world through experience to generate obligatory moral propositions. 'This', he argues, 'if solidly performed, will therefore be of very great use; because thence will appear, both how our mind is, by the light of nature, let into the knowledge of the will of God . . . and what that rule is, whereby the justice and rectitude of the laws of particular states is to be measured.'[5]

Cumberland's determination to follow this empirical path leads him to reject those thinkers with whom he is so often bracketed, the Platonists. In this, as in much else, he recalls Culverwell, Locke and Parker. He argues that

---

[3] Ibid.
[4] Ibid. introduction, sect. 4.
[5] Ibid.

the Platonist solution to moral scepticism, innate ideas, is not a sufficient response to the challenge of a writer like Hobbes: 'The Platonists, indeed, clear up this difficulty [moral obligation] in an easier manner, by the supposition of innate ideas, as well of the laws of nature themselves, as of those matters about which they are conversant; but, truly, I have not been so happy as to learn the laws of nature in so short a way.'[6] Cumberland argued that it was unsafe to build moral theory on the 'hypothesis' of innate ideas, because this had been rejected 'by the generality of philosophers, as well Heathen as Christian'. Cumberland's desire to enlist the 'generality of philosophers' signals that he was not attempting to put forward a novel position in rejecting innateism; this, as we have seen, was something of a commonplace for Protestant Scholastic thinkers. What was more immediately important was that such reasoning argued past the empirical claims of writers like Hobbes, claims which Cumberland wanted to oppose on their own terms.[7]

This explains Cumberland's ambivalent attitude towards neo-Platonism. He could recognise Platonists as allies in the debate over moral scepticism, but they were allies speaking a fundamentally different language. For this reason, he resolves not to oppose Platonism 'because it is my earnest desire, that whatever looks with a friendly aspect upon piety and morality, might have its due weight'.[8] Cumberland's one concession to Platonist epistemology is to suggest, by way of consolation, that 'it is not impossible, that such ideas might be both born with us, and afterwards impress'd from without'. This last comment is often something of a disappointment for those hunting for proto-Lockean ideas in Cumberland's work, but again, it reflects a common approach to the vexed question of innateism versus empiricism. Robert Sanderson, in his De obligatione conscientiae (1660), a work which also influenced Locke, made it clear that most knowledge was acquired, but that the mind could be predisposed to assent to some kinds of proposition, such as that the whole is greater than the part.[9] Isaac Barrow, Edward Stillingfleet and many other 'Latitudinarian' writers also subscribed to this form of 'modified innateism'.[10] Cumberland was arguing something akin to this in the De legibus, but his priority here was not to discuss this question, so much as to show that the laws of nature could be demonstrated from the same empirical examination of nature recommended by Hobbes.

Hobbes's version of empiricism was uncompromisingly stark. For Hobbes, the only certain knowledge was that provided by matter and motion, perceived through the senses. The limitations of human reason meant that this

6 Ibid. sect. 5.
7 Ibid.
8 Ibid.
9 Robert Sanderson, *De obligatione conscientiae*, trans. C. Wordsworth, Lincoln 1877, 17–18.
10 Isaac Barrow, *Theological works*, ed. J. Napier, London 1858, i. 271. See also Spellman, *Latitudinarians and the Church of England*, 81–2.

sensory information could reveal little inherent ethical meaning in nature, or any kind of objective standard, norms and values. Human morality relied upon meanings generated by the interpreter, individually in the state of nature, and by the magistrate in civil society. Morality was created artificially by man. It was for this reason that self-preservation could be the only certain fulcrum on which Hobbes's laws of nature could turn, the only empirical fact of human nature which was incontrovertible. This kind of radical and sceptical nominalism was an extreme version of the Protestant critique of right reason, which both Hobbes and Cumberland shared. The Scholastic divines had suggested that man could know the mind and will of God through their common and right reason. Hobbes's devastating critique applied a nominalist razor so comprehensively, that reason and nature could not say anything certain about God's will at all.

Cumberland shared the same theological and jurisprudential roots as Hobbes, but he had to provide an alternative empirical account of morality. Such an account needed to demonstrate the possibility that some ethical knowledge could be recovered from nature. It also required some indication that the resulting ethical knowledge was genuinely the will of the divine legislator. In order to distinguish the two accounts, and to put distance between doctrines that were in many ways too closely related, Cumberland and his Latitudinarian colleagues turned to the disputes between the classical empiricists, between the Stoics and the Epicureans, as a way of negotiating a more constructive empirical theory.

The Ciceronian response to Epicurean ethics

Hobbes was identified as a neo-Epicurean almost as soon as the *Leviathan* was published, and not without reason.[11] Epicureanism had incorporated the first major attempt to develop a detailed model of empirical knowledge. Just as Hobbes had used empiricism to deflate the assumptions of the Schoolmen, so Epicurus had restricted knowledge to material, sensory information in order to release mankind from superstition.[12] If Hobbes's God was distant and unknowable, Epicurus' deities were self-contained and abstracted from the world of matter. As chapter 5 will show, Hobbes's work was closely related to Gassendi's development of neo-Epicureanism in France.

The classical response to Epicureanism, and one that shared in its empirical premises, was Stoic cognitive psychology. This relied on the argument that the natural world was the outward and meaningful manifestation of the divine *Logos*. Through experience and reflection, the Stoic sage could come

---

[11] Hobbes is identified as an Epicurean by Henry More, in his *An antidote against atheism*, London 1653, and Seth Ward in his *A philosophicall essay towards an eviction of the being and attributes of God*, Oxford 1652.
[12] See ch. 4 below.

to have an understanding of nature. Both Epicureanism and Stoicism stressed the empirical foundation of knowledge, and both acknowledged that self-preservation was the starting point for human ethics. But where the Epicurean account generated morality without the intervention of a provident God, Stoicism at least opened the possibility that divinely-inspired moral knowledge could be discovered through nature. The *locus classicus* for this debate was the work of Cicero, who provided an appropriate script for the debate between Hobbes and his Latitudinarian opponents. Much of the debate over Hobbes's work was carried out in classical guise. The *De natura deorum*, the *De finibus*, and not least the *De legibus* provided dramatised accounts of encounters between Stoics and Epicureans, and they became a characteristic motif of anti-Hobbesian works in this genre.

An early example of this, which in some ways provided the Ciceronian prototype for Cumberland's work, was Robert Sharrock's Latin work of 1660, *Ypothesis ethike: de officiis secundum naturae jus*. Sharrock (1630–84) was an Oxford friend of Boyle and editor of his works, with scientific interests of his own.[13] The *De officiis* combines the same mixture of Hobbesian critique and natural law theory that would later characterise Cumberland's work. Like Cumberland, Sharrock had accepted the thrust of the anti-Scholastic critique, and sought to give an empirical response which he needed to distinguish from Hobbes. In this work, which Cumberland mentions briefly in the introduction to the *De legibus*, Sharrock sought to transpose Hobbes into an Epicurean, and to use Cicero's dialogues against him. The aim of *De officiis* was to try and prove against Hobbes a number of hypotheses on the existence of a hierarchy of natural duties annexed to natural law. Sharrock's method followed Grotius and Cicero in amassing ancient testimony to support his arguments, and for that reason Cumberland grouped him with those writers who had adopted the *a posteriori* method of demonstrating the law of nature, from its effects, rather than its causes.[14] Although Sharrock's work met with a mixed response,[15] it led the way in applying this kind of critique systematically to Hobbes over the natural law issue.[16] Works dealing with Hobbes and the natural law issue in the succeeding decades would often adopt the Ciceronian critique and the *De legibus naturae* was no exception.

---

13 Sharrock was the author of a *History of the propagation and improvement of vegetables*, Oxford 1660. He also provided prefaces to three of Boyle's works: *Some considerations concerning the usefulness of experimental philosophy*, Oxford 1663; *New experiments physicomechanical touching the spring of the air*, London 1660; and *A defence of the doctrine concerning the spring and weight of the air*, London 1662.

14 Cumberland, *DLN*, introduction, sects 1, 24. Cumberland recommends Sharrock for his prioritising of the laws of nature, a feature of his theory which fits Cumberland's argument that there is a natural order to moral obligation.

15 Hobbes, *Moral and political works*, p. xxv.

16 Hans Blom regards Sharrock as the first of what he terms the 'Cumberlandians' in *Morality and causality: the rise of naturalism in Dutch seventeenth-century political thought*, Utrecht 1995, 131–5.

The book was written against Epicureans, and Hobbes was to be examined through a Ciceronian lens. There were many reasons for this casting; firstly, it placed clear classical water between Cumberland and Hobbes. The opposition between Cicero and the Epicureans was one which most people learned with their Latin. The distinction between the virtuous Roman Stoics, Christians in all but name, and the dissolute, impious Epicureans was a staple of pulpit oratory and moral discourse. A side-effect of this was to edge Hobbes even further away from any lingering respectability. It could be argued that much of Hobbes's peculiar potency lay in his ability to master genre and style, allowing him to subvert them from within; one can see this in his adaptaton of Grotius' natural law theory, his discussion of mathematics, and also his work as a translator of Homer, to name but a few examples.[17] This critical method could leave ambiguous signs about Hobbes's positive identity which continue to tease commentators to this day. For Hobbes's contemporaries, that ambiguity was much more dangerous, as the dispute over the Latitude-men showed only too well. Cumberland's construction of an Epicurean identity allows Hobbes to be corralled into a compromising positive position that he rarely revealed. The repeated attempts to redescribe Hobbes as an Epicurean allowed Cumberland to dismiss Hobbes's orthodox utterances as either 'confusions' or deceptions masking his true identity.[18] Hobbes was ironically displaced as the author of his work, creating an easier target and a more memorable distinction.

Another effect of the Ciceronian casting was that it allowed writers like Cumberland to engage much more closely, but at the same time, more safely, with the relevant parts of Hobbes's philosophy. Cumberland could, with much greater ease, extract those elements common to the classical positions to show that Hobbes, like the Epicureans, had got his reasoning wrong. Empiricism was one vitally contested area, natural philosophy another. It even allowed Cumberland to make the rare concession that Hobbes, in chapter 12 of *Leviathan*, was serious about the existence of God as first cause. Cumberland was pleased that 'he [Hobbes] professes to believe in the being of God, and acknowledges the force of the argument by which we discover it; for he grants that there necessarily exists one first and eternal cause of things'.[19] The Ciceronian rhetoric allowed the possibility of safe, close-quarters combat, in which Hobbes (or at least the version of Hobbes that was represented) could be seen to be beaten at his own game.

Although Cicero provided a useful theatre for the encounter between Cumberland and Hobbes, the Roman writer could not provide a compelling solution to the problem of moral obligation. This was where Cumberland's

---

[17] For Hobbes's subversion of humanistic translation see P. Davis, 'Thomas Hobbes's translation of Homer: epic and anticlericalism in late seventeenth-century England', *Seventeenth Century* xii (1997), 231–55.
[18] For example Cumberland, *DLN* 1.12.
[19] Ibid. 1.11; cf. Hobbes, *Leviathan*, 77.

contribution to the debate came in, developing the implications of Stoic epistemology for a natural law theory. In order to provide a decisive response to Hobbes's nominalism, Cumberland had to establish the method whereby God's will could be detected from the works of nature. Neither Culverwell nor Locke had managed to elaborate the means by which a more detailed understanding of moral obligation could be obtained, beyond the common experience of men. Locke had indicated his sensitivity to a possible solution by defining natural law in relation to the 'valid and fixed laws of operation' which determined the rest of creation.[20] Cumberland's contribution developed this kind of argument in suggesting that in addition to common experience, and the ordinary modes of sense experience which Hobbes had rejected, there was a new way of identifying natural law and moral obligation. By applying the detailed observational discipline of experimental natural philosophy, one could establish with a demonstrative certainty the natural necessity of the laws of nature. By adopting such a framework, one could derive propositions which would demand assent to their terms.

The essence of this solution was to reconnect God, as first cause, with nature and the capacities of human reason. If God was, as Hobbes had suggested, the author of all motion in the universe, it followed that God is author of all sense impressions received by man. As Cumberland put it,

> that a truth so evident is impressed by God as its author, is very readily shown from that natural philosophy, which shows that all impressions on our senses are made according to the natural laws of motion, and that motion was first impressed on the corporeal system by God, and is by him preserved and unchanged.[21]

It thus follows from this that if one compares conclusions or ideas derived from that sense experience, and they seem to form some kind of relationship, then that relationship is representative of a relationship which exists in the real world. This also means that it is a relationship that is willed by God. As Cumberland argues:

> God, by these motions, as by a pencil, delineates the ideas or images in our minds of all sorts of things, especially of causes and effects. And, by imprinting on us, from the same object, various notions, imperfectly representing it, he excites us to bring them together, and to compare them among themselves; and consequently determines us to form true propositions concerning things understood by us.[22]

Cumberland's argument suggested that it was possible to derive objectively 'true', and divinely ordained relationships from the confusing array of sensory information with which the individual was bombarded. As Cumberland

---

20 Locke, *Essays on the law of nature*, 109.
21 Cumberland, *DLN* 1.10.
22 Ibid. introduction, sects 8, 2.5.

argued that moral relationships can be examined in the same way as other natural, physical relationships, the implication was that divinely ordained moral knowledge could also be recovered this way. He considers the possible Hobbesian response that it would be possible to make false connections and deductions. This was an important qualification, as Hobbes's position was that all extensive theories of moral obligation were based on such misunder-standings. Cumberland proposed to overcome this kind of scepticism by applying a rigorous observational discipline to the admission of simple ideas, and here he may have been drawing upon the criteria established by Des-cartes in the third *Meditation*.[23] To gain assent, ideas needed to be clear, in that they can be observed many times; they needed to be distinct through dis-crete observation of connection concerned, and lastly they had to be ade-quate enough to be comprehended by the memory and the understanding. Care would be needed to avoid false observation, and one should be careful to consider the partial causes which could give rise to erroneous observation.[24] Cumberland was not suggesting that this was an infallible method, but that with sufficient care there was no reason why such ideas should not be regarded as being true natural relationships. This took empiricism beyond the nominal capacities suggested by Hobbes. Cumberland was arguing that if care was taken, man did have the capacity to form practical propositions which were true representations of necessary relationships in the external world as it is caused by God.

Cumberland's theory meant that every individual's reason could be tested against a common standard in the 'nature of things'. This possibility of using the nature of things as a common datum for ideas overthrew Hobbes's radical subjectivism. Cumberland thus rescued the concept of *recta ratio*, by projecting 'right' into nature. Reason, by itself, was still incapable of provid-ing information about moral obligation, and in this respect he remained faithful to Selden's critique of the Schoolmen. But by arguing that God was the author of relationships which man could perceive in nature, Cumberland made natural relationships a common standard upon which reason could operate.

The implication for moral knowledge was that a scientific analysis of human nature could offer a way of discerning divine moral obligation. Where Hobbes had used empiricism to cut back the basis of ethical theory to self-preservation, Cumberland sought to show that his method could reveal that moral obligation went much further than self-interest alone.

[23] *The philosophical writings of Descartes*, trans. J. Cottingham, R. Stoothoff and D. Murdoch, Cambridge 1985, ii. 24–36.
[24] Cumberland, *DLN* 2.9.

Beyond self-preservation

In developing a more expansive ethic, Cumberland again followed Cicero closely. Cicero's *De finibus* was a key text for the ethical question of the best goal or end to which moral philosophy should aspire. This discussion was useful for Cumberland because for the most part it revolved around the exposition of and critical response to the Epicurean assertions of Torquatus, particularly the assertion that pleasure, defined in terms of the absence of pain, is the best end.[25] This was a position which Cumberland attributed to Hobbes.[26] Cicero's distaste for this hedonistic aspect of Epicurean philosophy is a common theme throughout his work. His response was to enlist the philosophy of the Peripatetics, the Old Academy and the Stoics, to argue for the primacy of virtue and human fellowship over the pleasure and self-interest of the individual. This would also be the basis of the positive theory in the *De legibus*.

Cicero's argument, which would be taken over by Cumberland, was that Epicureanism erred in fastening on too limited criteria to provide a satisfactory account of human nature. Cicero could agree, as Cumberland could agree with Hobbes, that self-preservation and self-interest were indeed primary and natural impulses to action, as most classical philosophers had asserted.[27] However, this did not mean that the only goal of human life should be the pursuit of pleasure and the avoidance of pain. This was to do violence to the potentiality of human nature. For Cicero, as for the Stoics, man's best end lay not in his own pleasure, but in living a virtuous life in accordance with his nature.

Cumberland takes over this argument in the *De legibus*. As with the Ciceronian discussion, the starting point common both to Hobbes and Cumberland is their acknowledgement that self-interest is a fact of human nature:

> Those natural and necessary appetites, which we suppose in men, of procuring their own preservation and happiness, are confin'd within a very narrow compass, and are perfectly free from fault; as our simple sensations are free from error.[28]

This was a common feature of Latitudinarian ethics, which drew heavily upon Ciceronian sources. According to Whichcote, 'the most universal principle belonging to all kinds of things is self-preservation'.[29] John Tillotson had suggested that 'the deepest Principle that God hath implanted into our

---

[25] Cicero, *De finibus* I. ix.
[26] Cumberland, *DLN* 5.40; cf. Hobbes, *De cive*, 43 (referred to in Cumberland's annotation).
[27] Cicero, *De finibus* V.ix.24.
[28] Cumberland, *DLN* 5.40; see also 5.22, 9.2.
[29] Whichcote, *Works*, iii. 329.

Nature is the desire of our own Preservation and Happiness'.[30] John Wilkins would make the same point in the *Of the principles and duties of natural religion*, three years after the publication of the *De legibus*.[31] Although this could sometimes make the Latitudinarians sound remarkably Hobbist, they were using self-preservation in a Ciceronian sense. Self-preservation acted not so much as the basis for a hedonistic ethic, but rather as the starting point and stimulus to discover the true interest of the individual. As Thomas Traherne put it, 'It is true that self-love is dishonourable, but then it is when it endeth in oneself. . . . Had we not loved ourselves at all we could never have been obliged to love anything, so that self-love is the basis of all love.'[32] Cumberland argues that self-preservation is necessary to act as a stimulus for man to engage with nature; were it otherwise, he argues, 'there would be no hope left, either of knowing nature, or of conforming our actions to the law of nature'.[33]

Self-preservation was thus an essential part of the post-sceptical *scientia*, as Grotius had suggested, providing the essential impetus for ethical action. The ethical danger in Hobbes's usage of self-preservation was that it became both the beginning and the end of ethical action. For Hobbes (as interpreted by Cumberland), self-preservation was the first and only goal or end of human life, which should properly be oriented to avoiding pain and death.

Cumberland found this position unacceptably limiting as a description of human ethical motivation. Following Cicero's critique of Epicurean ethical stimuli in the *De finibus*, Cumberland argues that individuals are not only motivated to avoid pain alone. They are much more likely to seek to act in accordance with their nature, fulfilling their potential rather than simply avoiding inconvenience:

> no man therefore loves life, health, or such grateful motions to the nerves and spirits as we call corporeal pleasures, or desires their causes, that he may avoid death, diseases and pain; but because of their intrinsic goodness, or positive agreement (to borrow a phrase from the schools) with the nature of the body.[34]

Cumberland's point was that Hobbes and Epicurus rejected a positive theory of goods. As a consequence, Hobbes had lopped off the greater part of human ethical aspirations for goods beyond the avoidance of pain. For Cicero, and for Cumberland, this was only a partial and deeply inadequate account of human nature. The Ciceronian critique allowed Cumberland to express a purely positive theory of goods extending beyond avoidance of pain. As a

---

30 J. Tillotson, *Sermons*, ed. R. Barker, London 1704, i. 375.
31 John Wilkins, *Of the principles and duties of natural religion*, London 1675, 12.
32 Thomas Traherne, *Centuries, poems & thanksgivings*, ed. H. M. Margoliouth, Oxford 1958, i. 197.
33 Cumberland, *DLN* 5.40.
34 Ibid. introduction, sect. 14; cf. Cicero, *De finibus* II.x.32

result, self-preservation in Cumberland becomes the starting point for a per-fective theory of human nature. Drawing on Aristotle's *Politics*, he defines the good as

> that which preserves or enlarges and perfects the faculties of any one thing or several. For in these effects, is discovered that particular agreement of one thing with another, which is requisite to denominate any thing good, to the nature of the thing, rather than of others.[35]

In this way, Cumberland links the good to the preservative and perfective features of things in themselves. Good thus became an objectively 'natural' category, far from the radical subjectivism of Hobbes, for whom good meant simply what makes for the preservation of a particular individual. Good, as Cumberland insisted, was not an arbitrary and subjective category, but one determined by the nature of things:

> For the nature of good, and the efficacy of things to the preservation and per-fection of the nature of one or more persons is perfectly determined, and is estimated in the agreement of things with all the faculties of human nature, as the principle of those faculties.[36]

By arguing that human nature contained objectively perfectible faculties, Cumberland was able to suggest that good was not only natural but necessary. Good was that which operated to perfect, and evil something which detracted from human nature; as Cumberland puts it:

> It is certain that the causes generating and preserving man, for example, by efficacy of which he continues for some time and flourishes with faculties, as well of body and mind enlarged and determined in their proper function, are called good to him, but that the causes of corruption and troubles are to him naturally evil.[37]

This was a position echoed by Wilkins in his *Principles and duties*: 'Every thing is endowed with such a natural principle, whereby it is necessarily inclined to promote its own preservation and well-being . . . That which hath a fitness to promote this end is called Good. And on the contrary that which is apt to hinder it is called Evil.'[38] Cicero's understanding of self-preservation sug-gested that an objective science of natural good and evil was indeed possible.

Self-preservation had been one of the most distinctive badges of 'Hobbism', but in arguing for a positive theory of goods, Cumberland had recovered the Ciceronian meaning of the concept. He had also uncovered what he took to

---

35 Cumberland, *DLN* 3.1; cf. Aristotle, *The politics*, ed. S. Everson, Cambridge 1988, I.ii.
36 Cumberland, *DLN* 3.2.
37 Ibid.
38 Wilkins, *Principles and duties*, 12.

be its Hobbesian/Epicurean antitype. One of the central aims of the *De legibus* had been to distinguish between a 'good' Ciceronian natural law theory and Hobbes's subversion of that language. But Cumberland was not merely defending intellectual territory in the *De legibus*, or passively recycling chunks of Cicero. In response to the critical challenge issued by Hobbes, he was attempting to provide the same level of demonstrative certainty that Hobbes wished to claim for his system.

To do this, Cumberland sought to show that self-interest, even on Hobbes's terms, necessarily leads to a kind of necessary mutual benevolence. Hobbes had argued that self-interest denied the existence of natural sociability, but for Cumberland this simply was not true. True self-interest could never be genuinely anti-social, primarily because individuals are unable to maximise their happiness by themselves:

> it is well known by the experience of all men that the powers of any single person, in respect of that happiness, of which from without he is both capable and stands in need, are so small, that he wants the assistance both of many things and persons to lead his life happily. Everyone can nevertheless afford many things for the use of others, which he himself does not need at all, and which therefore can be of no use to him. But seeing we are certain, from the known limit of our powers, that we cannot compel those whose aids we want . . . to cooperate with us in the procuring of our own happiness; the only method we have left to obtain this end, is to procure their good will by making a tender to them of our service, and by a faithful performance.[39]

One can find this theme, that self-preservation necessarily leads to co-operation, throughout the book. It is very close to the enlightened self-interest model which Pufendorf had developed in his *Elementorum jurisprudentiae universalis*, published in The Hague in 1660. This work, which acknowledged a clear debt to Hobbes, argued that sociability was a product of the interplay of mutual needs, or *indigentia*. Self-interested individuals would realise that it was in their interest to co-operate peacefully.[40] This model, which seemed to base natural sociability upon the calculation of individual interest, is the basis of claims that Cumberland was developing a kind of proto-utilitarian theory.[41]

---

[39] Cumberland, *DLN* 1.21. Similar sentiments can be found scattered through the book: 'Therefore if anyone takes an exact survey of what is contained in those practical propositions, which determine every man to endeavour his own preservation, he will perceive something that dictates self-preservation to others as well as to himself, and that will hinder him from opposing any others in the same pursuit' (5.17). See also Cumberland's only surviving sermon, 'The motives to liberality considered', in *The English preacher*, London 1774, ix. 172.

[40] Samuel Pufendorf, *Elementorum jurisprudentiae universalis*, trans. W. A. Oldfather, Oxford 1931, ii, preface, p. xxx. It should be noted that there is no evidence from the text that Cumberland was familiar with Pufendorf's work.

[41] Albee, *History of English utilitarianism*, 50.

It is very easy to conclude from some of Cumberland's remarks in the *De legibus* that he is favouring this kind of utilitarian argument. This is the case in the first chapter especially, where the stress is laid upon the mechanisms by which the 'nature of things' impresses a sense of dependence upon external limits and the actions of other individuals. By focusing on the individual's perspective upon his or her natural limitations, Cumberland portrays benevolent behaviour as a function of self-interest. Cumberland makes the argument that it is profitable to make a tender of good will to others because this is the only way to obtain their services. In this instance, private utility appears to be the prior determinant of a transactionary form of moral behaviour. When Cumberland proposes that individuals can co-operate in a common end without prejudice to their own interests, his *amicitia* and consequent *socialitas* seem to bear out the suggestion that he has merely created a minimal sociability based on the individual's enlightened calculation.

Before accepting such a model, in many ways still the dominant interpretation of Cumberland's work, we should perhaps ask why Cumberland was arguing this way. Here the engagement with Hobbes is important in identifying the logic behind Cumberland's 'utilitarian' utterances. The passage quoted above was not designed to found a system on the calculation of interest alone, but to emphasise that even where Hobbes has used an acceptable premise (i.e. self-preservation), the conclusions which he draws are still not admissable. Cumberland's discussion of the necessity of co-operation runs alongside a denunciation of Hobbes's argument that the individual in a state of nature has a right to anything which they believe furthers their self-preservation.[42] Cumberland's argument is a counter to Hobbes's use of right in this instance. For Hobbes to suggest that an individual can have a theoretical right to all things ignores the natural fact that this is neither possible nor practical according to the physical limits placed upon us by the nature of our existence. Physical limits and natural laws operate to restrict the use of right. Practical reasoning, according to Cumberland, will show that it is actually in our interest only to take those things that are necessary, and to allow others to take things which are necessary to them. Only in this way can others assist us effectively:

> My readers now, I suppose, perceive the reason why I ranked that common observation, that the powers and uses of things are limited, amongst the notions chiefly necessary to the knowledge of the laws of nature: for hence both a fundamental error of Hobbes is detected, and a most useful truth is inferred, that both the uses of things and services of men, are necessarily to be divided or to be determined to one person for one time, if we design they should effect anything at all.[43]

---

[42] Cumberland, *DLN* 1.
[43] Ibid. 1.27.

Cumberland's point in all of this is to emphasise the limitations of what individuals can do under the influence of self-interest. His apparent utilitarianism is a way of responding to Hobbes. Even with the reductive emphasis on Hobbes's own suggestions as a foundation, Cumberland argues that it is impossible to live in the world without forming an idea of the necessity of co-operation, and as a result, some conception of the common good.

Human nature

The point of Cumberland's first chapter had been to demonstrate how the nature of things leads to an awareness of the limited number of 'things in our power'. The consequence of man's natural impotence is the necessity of co-operation. Cumberland's aim in chapter 2 is to look at the same issue from a more positive standpoint. As well as providing natural limitations, human nature also had positive features which had equally necessary ethical consequences. This was an important part of Cumberland's approach. The minimal sociability constructed by Grotius and taken up by Hobbes took only a few features of human nature as ethically relevant. Cumberland sought to base his ethics upon a broader range of observed characteristics. His point was to demonstrate that mankind was bound, both positively and negatively, to the demands of natural law, and not to the utility of the individual.

Cumberland first affirms that man is an animal, but one distinguished by its mind, which, *pace* Hobbes, is incorporeal. The mind is composed of the understanding and the will, understanding consisting of an ability to apprehend, compare, judge, reason and remember. The will consists in the ability to choose and refuse.[44] The mind is determined by what is put before it and what is confirmed by continued experience. Once exposed to evidence and connections apprehended from the senses, the will cannot put a stop to necessary truths. This is an important part of Cumberland's epistemological foundation, as it ensures that natural relationships can command assent by themselves. While he is loth to consider that the external world exercises its necessity upon the mind mechanically, Cumberland nevertheless concurs with Hobbes in affirming, 'that the first apprehension of things, and the desire of good and aversion from evil in general, are necessary'.[45] This agreement is an important part of Cumberland's anti-Hobbesian strategy. If the natural world necessarily and naturally imposed ideas of good and evil upon individuals, then there was little scope for Hobbes's claims that such categories were merely subjective. Cumberland therefore took Hobbes's own deterministic premises to provide the basis for his own theory. Cumberland

44 Ibid. 2.1.
45 Ibid. 2.3.

muses that, 'nor do I suppose that Hobbes, the great patron of all kinds of necessity, will contradict me here'.[46]

Cumberland shows that an examination of the powers of the mind, however, intimates that it is designed for much greater purposes than 'the preservation of the life of one inconsiderable animal'. The mind of man does more than simply gratify his immediate need for food or sustenance, 'it rather excels in those qualities which relate to the knowledge and worship of a deity, and to acts moral and civil'.[47] In other words, the more one comes to consider the nature of the human mind, the more one comes to perceive that its faculties are designed for greater things than self-preservation. This argument was something of a commonplace in Hobbes criticism, and represents the strong teleological impulse that distinguished the Latitudinarian's neo-scholasticism from Hobbes's anti-teleological nominalism. Isaac Barrow voiced a similar sentiment in his sermons:

> The frame of our nature indeed speaketh, that we are not born for ourselves; we shall find man, if we contemplate him, to be a nobler thing than to have been designed to serve himself, or to satisfy his single pleasure; his endowments are too excellent, his capacities too large for so mean and narrow a purpose.[48]

Cumberland illustrates this point by examining the powers of reason which mankind has been given, abilities which allow individuals to apprehend ideas and goals above mere self-preservation. These include the power to form universal ideas about the world and the power to use speech to represent and communicate these ideas. The knowledge of number, weight and measure allow men to compare and contrast relative good. By these means, men not only have the ability to observe order, but also to create it.[49]

Cumberland, following his Roman Stoic mentors, also stresses the power of restraint that man has. Far from being dominated by the passions, man can raise, stop and moderate them. Reason can exert sufficient control to allow a man to direct his bodily force to desire greater goods than animals that are devoid of reason, and ruled by the passions, could comprehend. To live in accordance with man's true nature is thus to exercise these faculties, and to desire those goods which are suggested by nature.[50]

The most important natural goods, for Cumberland, are those to do with living in society. The discussion in the first chapter had shown the necessary interdependence of individuals from the point of view of need or want. The

---

[46] Ibid.
[47] Ibid. 2.4.
[48] Barrow, *Theological works*, iii. 400; cf. Whichcote, *Works*, iv. 212; Richard Burthogge, *Divine goodness explicated and asserted*, London 1671, 115; Locke, *Essays on the law of nature*, 157.
[49] Cumberland, *DLN* 2.4.
[50] Ibid.

second chapter now reinforces this by arguing that human rational capacities are designed to be used in a sociable context. Through an examination of nature, individuals can perceive that they are bound, both by their limitations and their potentiality, to a common social good. The logical consequence of this is that right reasoning about human nature will propose a natural good that is a higher fulfilment of human nature than mere self-preservation alone. Because the common good is thus a greater realisation of human nature than self-preservation by itself, the individual should, rationally, place this before his or her own self-interest. The common good thus becomes prior in the order of goods sought by the individual (since his or her own good is necessarily contained therein). This, according to Cumberland, should always be the primary rule of action.

There was nothing particularly revolutionary in this. That the common good should take priority over individual needs was a commonplace of Aristotle, Aquinas, and any number of neo-Scholastic philosophers. What makes Cumberland interesting in his use of this argument is his emphasis on the interdependence of the common and the private good which always coincide. The common good remains a priority not only because it fulfils the potential of mankind, but also because it is the most effective way of promoting one's own good.

But Cumberland's conception of the common good does not stop at temporal forms of *socialitas*. At this point in his argument, Cumberland seeks to universalise his *socialitas*, to form a general and universal proposition which applies to all rational agents, including God. As Cumberland puts it, 'there is naturally in men so large and noble a faculty, which can comprehend and pursue that vast good, the greatest united happiness of all rational agents'.[51] This is possibly the most crucial theoretical concept in the *De legibus*, because it re-establishes the suggestion that God and man participate in the same rational nature; participation which makes them members of a common rational society or system: 'The mind of man is naturally fitted to become a member of the greatest society (consisting of all [rational] beings with God at their head) and that it neglects its principle use and loses the best fruits of its natural dispositions if it do not enter therein.'[52] God, for Cumberland, constitutes reason in perfection, and this allows him to consider God to be part of a common rational society. His source in this instance is Cicero, for whom this common rational society of gods and men was the very foundation of natural law:

therefore, since there is nothing better than reason, and since it exists both in man and in God, the first common possession of man and God is reason. But those who have reason in common must also have right reason in common. And since right reason is law, we must believe that men have law in common

51 Ibid. 2.3.
52 Ibid. 2.4.

with the gods. Further, since those who share law must also share justice; and also those who share these are to be regarded as members of the same commonwealth. . . . Hence we must now conceive of this whole universe, as one commonwealth of which both gods and men are members.[53]

Cumberland's use of Cicero jars with his Protestant theology. If the law of the greatest society were reason, then there was the danger of making right reason superior to God's will, the very problem that English writers had deplored in Grotius and the Scholastics. One can detect this tension when Cumberland feels constrained to apologise for this juxtaposition of God and men within the same rational society.[54] Nevertheless, Cumberland is prepared to use this approach and argument in order to universalise his proposition. His purpose is to demonstrate the possibility of, if not at this point the practical obligation to, universal justice and the law of nature. God's participation was the effective guarantee of its objectivity. This represented the most complete inversion of Hobbes's reductive nominalism, and a means by which human nature could be 'read' for the purposes of natural law. It allowed Cumberland to formulate his 'practical proposition' which emerged from a proper consideration of man and nature, that man's proper action should be 'an endeavour, according to our ability, to promote the common good of the whole system of rationals. This includes our love of God, and of all mankind, who are part of this system. God, indeed, is the principal part. Man, the subordinate part'.[55]

This was Cumberland's antidote to Hobbes's 'laws' of nature built on self-preservation alone. The main problem with this however, was that Cumberland's practical proposition was still just that, a hypothesis derived from the observation of human nature, with the same non-obligatory status as Hobbes's theorems. If Cumberland wanted to argue that his proposition was properly a natural law, he would have to prove that it could meet those criteria by which Hobbes and Selden had rejected Grotius and the Scholastics. Cumberland's proposition had to be shown to be the will of God as legislator, published with sufficient clearness, with sanctions annexed. Cumberland's solution to this problem would be his main contribution to the natural law debate.

Rewards and punishments

Cumberland's 'practical proposition' could be said to be natural law in the sense that it was a product of man's reflection on God's creation of the world. God's will was manifested through the motion that the senses perceived,

---

53 Cicero, *De legibus* I.vii.22.
54 Cumberland, *DLN*, introduction, sect. 10.
55 Ibid. sect. 15.

therefore the rational conclusions drawn from such sensory evidence indicated natural law. This empirical argument had constituted the defence of natural law theory in the work of Culverwell and Locke. However, it was vulnerable to the Hobbesian critique. Although it was possible to ascribe the products of sense data to the will of God, there was the problem of interpretation. Did specific rational conclusions necessarily have anything to do with the will of God? Hobbes's point was not that such conclusions were irrational, or incorrect, but that there was no certain proof that such conclusions, beyond self-preservation, were obligatory. Natural law, as a consequence, boiled back down to self-preservation, and self-obligation.

Cumberland's answer to this problem would be his major contribution to the development of the obligation question. His solution depended upon identifying God's sanctions in nature, and in revealing the structure of natural justice. It would not be a complete and demonstrative answer to Hobbes, but it sought to show that, from the evidence of nature, it was possible to detect the workings of divine justice with sufficient probability to cast doubt on Hobbes's reductive model of ethical naturalism, and to provide evidence that his 'practical proposition' was in fact natural law.

This was an unusual way of solving the problem of moral obligation, and one which emerged from Cumberland's desire to refute Hobbes from his own premises. Culverwell and Locke had both argued that knowledge of moral obligation had to come from an *a priori* understanding of what God intended. If God was just and rational, then it followed that God should will just and rational conclusions, such as those of natural law. Cumberland, too, discussed this method of coming to the knowledge of God's will. The method assumed that God was endowed with reason, wisdom, prudence and constancy; perfections which man can observe in himself, but which must be perfected in his maker. On this basis, right reasoning must agree with the will of God over both ends and means; if a person rightly judges that the common good is better than one individual's interest, then God must think the same. The conclusion is that God should therefore will that particular end.[56] Another argument, along the same lines, present in Locke and Pufendorf (its probable source), was that the power that gives rise to man should wish for his preservation and perfection. God's will to create, as maker, gives the will that man should be preserved, and thus the obligation to that will.[57]

Cumberland considers this approach, but rejects it as an answer to Hobbes. His reason for this was that 'our adversaries will hardly grant anything relating thereunto, and all the attributes of God are to be deduced by us in the analytical method (*a posteriori*), from his effects'.[58] Hobbes had famously rejected this kind of argument as being anthropomorphic, and therefore unsound. He had argued that it was impossible to know anything

---

[56] Ibid. 5.19.
[57] Locke, *Essays on the law of nature*, 153.
[58] Cumberland, *DLN*, 5.19.

meaningful about God's attributes aside from negatives and superlatives. Human assumptions and characteristics were not, therefore, much of a guide to the divine will.[59] Cumberland was determined to answer Hobbes on his own terms, and for this reason he sought knowledge of the details of God's will in the same sensory information that Hobbes would allow. In doing this, Cumberland was pushing his moral epistemology into areas where previous writers in the genre had been reluctant to go. Cumberland argued that from a knowledge of God's effects, one could apprehend rewards and punishments for acts subject to natural law. As he puts it, 'God, in his ordinary government of the world, has so ordered and adjusted the powers of all things, that such actions [in accordance with the law of nature] should be rewarded, and the contrary punished.'[60] Cumberland's discussion of rewards and punishments suggested that the natural world contained explicit and divinely sanctioned ethical meaning.

Before Cumberland's work, rewards and punishments had played a rather different role in the discussion of God's justice. Although one could argue that God was essentially just, this interpretation seemed to be rather at odds with a world in which, more often than not, the virtuous were afflicted and the vicious appeared to flourish. One was, of necessity, forced to posit the rewards and punishments of the afterlife as the probable divine sanction attached to natural law. This offered the believer a version of Pascal's Wager; John Tillotson's sermon of 1664, *The wisdom of being religious*, appealed to enlightened self-interest when he suggested that sin simply was not worth the risk of eternal damnation.[61] At best, one could feel the pangs and guilt of conscience as an anticipation of future judgement, something that Whichcote had used to argue for the temporal origins of heaven and hell.

It should be stressed that Cumberland did not wish to overthrow this framework of punishment and reward in the afterlife. Indeed, the whole point of his theory was to underpin it more thoroughly. Cumberland argued that if one carefully analysed the causal relationship between moral acts and their consequences, one could perceive a natural, necessary and thus divinely willed, connection between such acts and natural rewards and punishments, according to the law of nature. This, understood clearly from sense-data, would provide a more effective communication of the obligatory force of God's laws. It would also encourage the rational expectation in less clear examples that punishment and reward would occur at some later time. As Cumberland puts it, 'if anything necessary to this end be wanting in this life, it will be supplied by God in a life to come'.[62] Cumberland's point was not to prove that all moral acts have earthly rewards and punishments, as a deistic reading of his work might suggest. Rather he argued that there was a natural

---

59 Hobbes, *De cive*, 190–2.
60 Cumberland, *DLN*.
61 Tillotson, *Works*, i. 1–27, esp. pp. 24–7.
62 Cumberland, *DLN* 5.26.

principle of justice which did operate, and which should form the basis for moral acts. Cumberland refers to this idea from the first chapter of the *De legibus*:

> The laws of nature have an intrinsic and essential proof of their obligation, taken from the rewards, or increase of happiness, which attends the benevolent person from the natural efficacy of his actions, and follows the man who studiously observes those laws, and from the punishments or degrees of misery which, whether they will or no, they bring upon themselves, who either do not obey, or do oppose the conclusions of right reason.[63]

By arguing that the law of nature carries rewards for observance and punishments for dereliction, it has been suggested that Cumberland was embracing a form of ethical hedonism, in which the need for God as legislator almost entirely disappears. The fact that nature provides sanctions suggests that obligation might not arise from God at all, but rather from the natural principles with which men were endowed, of seeking natural good, and shunning evil.[64] There is no doubt that Cumberland, in taking this line, was in danger of submerging his account of obligation into a discussion of nature alone, removing the necessity for God as legislator. But this was certainly not his intention. Indeed, the whole point of the *De legibus naturae* was to prove that an account of ethical naturalism could be compatible with the voluntarist account of natural law. Obligation could only arise from the will of God, and nothing else; as Cumberland made clear in chapter 5:

---

[63] Ibid. 1.12.

[64] Linda Kirk perceived two accounts of natural law in the *De legibus naturae*, a 'conventional' voluntarist account, and a 'utilitarian' formulation by which obligation simply arises from the good consequences of rational actions. She ingeniously bases her assertion around the two different versions of the definition of the law of nature which were printed in the first edition of the *De legibus*. The first reads: 'Lex Naturae est propositio natura rerum ex voluntate primae causae menti satis aperte oblata vel impressa, quae actionem agentis rationalis possibilem communi bono maxime deservientem indicat, & integram singulorum foelicitatem exinde solum obtineri posse.' The 'corrected' version reads after 'impressa': 'actionem indicans Bono Rationalium communi observientem, quam si praestetur praemia, sin negligatur poenae sufficientes ex Natura Rationalium sequuntur' (*DLN* 5.1). The continuation of the second version introduces the voluntarist emphasis upon lawgiver, precept and sanction, for which the first version has no equivalent: Kirk, *Cumberland*, 31. Knud Haakonssen has suggested that a conflict between the accounts is inadmissible on the basis of Cumberland's own assertions, especially in 5.3 where Cumberland argues that although the initial definition seems to omit the concepts of commanding, forbidding, punishing and rewarding, 'nevertheless I acknowledge that [the law of nature] to have all those powers': Haakonssen, 'Character and obligation of natural law'. I hope that my placing of Cumberland in context has shown that firstly there was, as Kirk perceived, a tension between the naturalist and voluntarist accounts, as the debate over Grotius had suggested, but that the whole point of the *De legibus* was to reassert the connection between voluntarism and naturalism, to demonstrate that natural law could carry all of the formal qualities of natural law which Hobbes had denied.

Men's love of their own happiness, which causes them to consider and be moved by rewards and punishments, is no cause of obligation; that proceeds wholly from the law and the lawgiver. It is only a necessary disposition in the subject, without which the laws and penalties of the law would be of no force to induce men to the performance of their duty.[65]

If individuals were merely motivated by rewards and punishments immediately administered, then there would be no opportunity for them to exercise their moral responsibility. Cumberland wished to use earthly rewards and punishments as evidence of the general application of his practical proposition. For this reason, such evidence could not be certain, but it could act as a demonstration that Hobbes was wrong in his extreme reduction of ethics to self-interest.

Cumberland's use of rewards and punishments developed his assumption that God's will, and his justice, were both essential to, and inherent in, nature itself. Essentially, he was building upon the distinctive providentialism latent in a natural theology which sought to detect in nature signs of God's providential government.[66] In its simplest form, this was the kind of almost superstitious response which characteristically emerged in response to catastrophes like the 1665 plague and the Fire of London. The supposedly rationalist divines were immediately ready to posit direct connections between national disasters and national apostasy.[67] In Cumberland, this providentialism, transformed through the plenistic system-based physics of the new mechanics, isolated ways in which natural mechanisms of cause and effect could generate natural rewards and punishments. These could then act as the final proof of moral obligation to Cumberland's 'practical proposition', and a rather neat refutation of Hobbes's neo-Epicurean position.[68]

Cumberland's rewards and punishments take various forms, ranging from the sanctions of conscience, as they had been discussed by preachers like Whichcote, through to more complex forms of natural sanctions. On the former, he takes a conventional approach which stresses the apprehension of divine and human retribution for immoral acts:

> For it is impossible to separate from the crime all degrees of anxiety of mind, arising from the struggle between the sounder dictates of right reason, which

---

65 Cumberland, *DLN* 5.22.
66 Richard Burthogge pursued a similar argument in his *Divine goodness*. He stressed that God's laws were binding from the evidence of rewards and punishments, amongst which were wars and social disharmony. To answer sceptics like Hobbes, he argued that the chains of providence required more investigation. He also discussed the ways in which one could perceive God's operation in the world as a theory of 'signatures, impressions or sacred characters': *Divine goodness*, 32.
67 John Spurr, ' "Virtue, religion and government": the Anglican uses of providence', in *The politics of religion in Restoration England*, ed. T. Harris, P. Seaward and M. Goldie, Cambridge 1990, 29–48; Spellman, *Latitudinarians and the Church of England*, 110.
68 Cumberland, *DLN* 5.41.

enforce our duty, and those rash follies which hurry men on to wickedness. These, likewise, ensure fears (which cause present grief) of vengeance, both divine and human, and an inclination to the same crimes, or even worse; which, because it hurts the faculties of mind, seems to me that it ought also to be reckoned among punishments. Even the very malice and envy, which are essential to every invasion of another's right, do necessarily and naturally torture every malevolent mind; and so the wicked man drinks deep of the poisoned draught of his own mixture.[69]

In addition to this, however, Cumberland takes a more interesting and innovative approach to the demonstration of moral obligation. What marks out his approach here is his understanding of the relationship between rational agents. Cumberland, deploying his scientific approach to ethics, sees the system of rational agents like a closed and tightly inter-related physical system. Any action contrary to the determination of the system as a whole will damage that actor through the harm caused to the common good. This is one form of sanction, but not the only one to emerge from this model. Cumberland argues that in addition to damaging the common good, any attempt to subvert that good will of necessity incline other rational agents to punish the wrong-doer. The reason for this public-spiritedness is that each individual will be looking to preserve the public good, in which their own is contained as a part. Just as every individual is obliged to seek their own self-preservation and perfection, so each individual necessarily has a right to punish those who thwart the common good on which their own is dependent. It is thus in everyone's individual interest to preserve the system against those who attempt to undermine it.[70]

Cumberland uses this theory as a way of refuting Hobbes's discussion of the state of nature. In Hobbes's account, men in the state of nature can justly do whatever they please to secure their own preservation. Because there is no over-arching social obligation, the state of nature thus becomes a state of war. In response Cumberland argues that Hobbes is misreading the relationship between self-interest and the resulting violence. The war and destruction of the Hobbesian state of nature are in fact natural punishments for breaking the law of nature.[71] Selfish behaviour undermines the common good and encourages non-cooperative and violent responses. In this situation, self-preservation then dictates violent actions against those who endanger life and well-being. Because such actions are prompted by right reason, argues Cumberland, then they are properly punishments, 'and this marks that practical propositions are properly laws'.[72]

Ironically, it is because men are rational beings that their reaction to subversion of the common good is so severe. The more rational the individual,

69 Ibid. 5.36.
70 Ibid. 1.26.
71 Ibid. 5.24.
72 Ibid. 5.35.

the more attuned that individual will be to the common good, and the more he or she will react to behaviour which undermines that good. As Cumberland puts it, 'If someone is so unnatural as to commit a villainy, he cannot be secure because men whose interest it is that a most extensive benevolence and justice should take place universally are almost certain to discover and punish the most secret crimes.'[73] Cumberland's system is designed to react to any breach of its integrity, like feedback in physical and biological systems, in this case structured to punish the malefactor. The committing of acts against the natural law gives an incitement to others to punish, and thus, 'by injuries we give being at least to one, and that the first, cause of our destruction'. There is always a reasonable expectation 'that others will concur to restrain or destroy such by condign punishment'.[74]

The severity envisaged by Cumberland is so great that the attempt of a housebreaker to violate the property rights of his victim gives the latter a legitimate right of war against the former. Reason dictates extreme measures as a means of demonstrating the force of the obligation to natural law. This logic accounts for why such 'horrible revenges' are sometimes necessary in wartime.[75] Here men's reversion to savagery is itself a natural punishment for failure to observe the law of nature. In arguing this, Cumberland had managed to invert Hobbes's use of the state of war. For Hobbes, conflict was a natural feature of relations between men in the state of nature.[76] For Cumberland, that same conflict was the awful punishment for unnatural, selfish and malevolent behaviour. Hobbes had been right to see a connection between self-interest and conflict, but wrong to diagnose it as the natural state of man. Subversion of the common good placed one outside the normal bonds of benevolent behaviour; Cumberland remarks upon the 'unreasonableness of expecting that men should willingly labour to make those happy whom they know to be in themselves malevolent, ungrateful, inhuman'.[77]

Even if the culprit appears to get away with a crime, there is still no respite from natural justice, since his destruction of the common good has effectively destroyed his or her own happiness: 'every action proceeding from a malevolence towards others, has a natural endless tendency to produce other malevolent actions of the like kind, thwarting the common happiness and consequently diminishing that of the malevolent person himself'.[78]

Cumberland's sanctions do not just include punishments, although these provide the must effective response to Hobbes. Actions in accord with the common good, which Cumberland identifies with the traditional virtues, are

---

73 Ibid. 1.26.
74 Ibid. 5.29.
75 Ibid. 5.25.
76 Hobbes, *Leviathan*, 88.
77 Cumberland, *DLN* 5.29.
78 Ibid. 5.37; cf. Cicero, *On duties*, ed. M. T. Griffin and E. M. Atkins, Cambridge 1991, V.22.

rewarded with happiness. In arguing this, Cumberland reconciles his account to the Stoic belief that virtue is its own reward:

> Much has been advanced by philosophers, especially the stoics and academics, which with strength and perspicuity demonstrates that the virtues necessarily bring happiness along with them, as essentially connected therewith . . . it is sufficient that I readily acknowledge them to be the principal parts of human happiness, so that no man can ever be happy without them.[79]

Virtue is thus the best means of promoting the law of nature, and a means which is rewarded by happiness. As Cumberland puts it, 'it adds vast weight to arguments drawn from the pleasures consequent upon virtuous action if they be consider'd as rewards annexed to virtue by the will of the first cause'.[80] Such rewards not only include the 'tranquility and joy' of conscience, but also the concrete benefits of peace, prosperity and security.

As with the discussion of punishments, Cumberland is keen to make it clear that it is not the pleasure in itself which is the cause of obligation. Pleasure acts as a stimulus to the individual to recognise his or her proper end, and to develop a more accurate conception of the law of nature.

This discussion of rewards and punishments was Cumberland's most significant contribution to the debate over natural law. By arguing that moral acts did have identifiable consequences, which could be seen as rewards and punishments, Cumberland was able to claim that natural justice could be seen to be operating in the world. What was more, he was able to argue that his practical proposition was not simply a rational theorem, as Hobbes had suggested, but was in fact a law according to the criteria that Hobbes himself had used. Natural law was declared through nature, and made accessible to man through the use of his reason. Cumberland's scientific methodology, revealing natural rewards and punishments, provided evidence that the natural law of sociability was in fact a law of God, a general principle which applied to all rational agents. The greatest society of rational agents, rather than the individual, was man's most important, and ultimately natural, end.

For those writers struggling to accommodate ethical naturalism and a voluntarist theology, Cumberland's solution soon became an attractive addition to their armoury. Cumberland offered a way of combining the two approaches, while at the same time explicitly dealing with the problematic relationship to Hobbes. Through the process of criticism and construction in the *De legibus*, Cumberland cleansed the language of natural jurisprudence of its heterodox associations, and established what was, and what was not valid in Hobbes's work. This meant that Hobbes's political insights could now be used safely, as Cumberland explains after he has demonstrated the natural obligation to the laws of nature:

---

[79] Cumberland, *DLN* 5.43.
[80] Ibid.

And now, when I treat of obligation, which is the proper effect of laws, and becomes known to our senses by the rewards and punishments consequent upon observation and violation of those laws, and is therefore a proper evidence that they are laws; I may assume what Hobbes has with reason granted, provided I take care to avoid the many errors he has intermixed therewith.[81]

The *Leviathan* had been tamed.

---

[81] Ibid. 5.37.

4

The Royal Society and Hobbism

The *De legibus naturae* is a book dominated by the science of its time. Almost every page contains some reference to contemporary natural philosophy in fields as diverse as mathematics, physics, biology and anatomy. Despite the prevalence of this material it has rarely, if ever, been discussed.[1] The main cause of this neglect has been the preoccupation with teasing out the political implications of Cumberland's natural law theory. From this point of view, the scientific material is problematic, appearing as digression, or even self-indulgent irrelevance. Cumberland emerges from this kind of analysis as an over-enthusiastic amateur *virtuoso* in an age when such allusion might be considered to be merely fashionable.[2]

But there are reasons why we should take Cumberland's use of science seriously. The first is that it was fundamental to his novel method of 'demonstrating' the law of nature. Cumberland's thesis rested on the idea that natural philosophy could be used to found a system of ethics. This in itself might be considered worthy of note, but what makes it even more interesting is the kind of natural philosophy which Cumberland deploys in support of his *scientia moralis*. The key conception that dominates the argument of the book is that moral relations between men, and between men and God, can be understood in the same terms as were used in contemporary discussions about mechanical physics. Ethical relations, according to Cumberland, could be understood in the same terms as physical systems, obeying the same kind of laws as those governing the motion of matter. The only other writer to have put forward a theory in which natural philosophy was so closely related to ethics was Hobbes.

Hobbes's claim to have founded a demonstrative science of human behaviour overshadowed early modern natural philosophy. His contemporaries were confident in their assertion of an inescapable connection between Hobbes's science and his ethics. A reductive and materialistic philosophy of matter and motion went hand in hand with a sceptical moral theory; political, moral and scientific theory were embedded in the same primarily theological matrix. The problem for the scientific community was that Hobbes's

---

[1] One exception is Murray Forsyth, who suggests that Cumberland should be considered first and foremost as an empirical 'Baconian'. Although Forsyth is right to draw attention to the science in the *De legibus naturae*, the influence of science on his natural law theory extends far beyond a simple 'Baconianism', which is in itself a problematic concept: Forsyth, 'The place of Richard Cumberland', 23–42.

[2] Kirk, *Cumberland*, 6.

heterodoxy, like his natural law theory, arose from a theological position which many 'orthodox' scientists shared. As with his political ideas Hobbes proved to be objectionable because his controversial ideas were too close for comfort.[3] This fatal association with Hobbes and atheism haunted the discussion of mechanism in the later 1660s. For this reason, Cumberland set out to reclaim mechanism for a more conventional ethics. The *De legibus naturae* sought to demonstrate that natural philosophy in general, and the mechanical hypothesis in particular, could both support orthodox ideas about morality, and at the same time demolish Hobbes's own usage of such evidence. As with Hobbes's natural law theory, Cumberland sought to reclaim natural philosophy from the imputation of Hobbism and atheism.

Cumberland was no mere dilettante when it came to natural philosophy. He was, it is true, first and foremost a clergyman, with a deep commitment to his calling. But he was also an accomplished scholar in many branches of learning. Payne noted that he was 'thoroughly acquainted with all the Branches of Philosophy; he had good judgement in Physick, knew everything that was curious in Anatomy'. Above all, his greatest interest was 'Mathematicks in all its parts'.[4] The roots of this interest lay in Cumberland's education at Cambridge, at a time when there was an unprecedented expansion and acceleration of interest in natural philosophy in all of its forms.

Cambridge was still a stronghold of traditional Scholastic learning when Cumberland arrived there in 1649. However, interest in the new learning, and Cartesianism in particular, was developing during these years through the agency of tutors like Henry More, and more publicly through John Smith's lectures on geometry, which began in 1648. For some, the new mathematics offered the key to unlocking the secrets of nature. As John Hall wrote in 1649 mathematics could become 'nimble and apt to find the fountain-head of every Theoreme, and by degrees, as we may hope, inable us to the solution of any Probleme without any more assistance than pen and inke'.[5] This confidence in the possibilities of what Descartes had called *mathesis universalis*, a universal mathematical science, would be crucial to Cumberland's mathematical understanding of *scientia moralis*.

Cumberland's concern to apply mathematics to the physical world manifested itself in his love of mechanics. This interest was probably fostered by Samuel Moreland, a maverick inventor, Fellow of Magdalene in the early 1650s and Cumberland's 'Honoured Friend'.[6] During his time at Magdalene Cumberland may have invented the first orrery or planetary model. His interest in mechanics also led to a life-long interest in clockwork, and he is credited with the application of an adjustable pendulum to clocks, and also with

3   Malcolm, 'Hobbes and the Royal Society', 43–86.
4   Payne, 'Brief account', p. xxi.
5   John Hall, *The advancement of learning*, ed. A. K. Crosten, Liverpool 1953, 39–40.
6   Cumberland, *Jewish measures and weights*, 52.

devising an astronomical clock with a three-wheel action.[7] Cumberland was clearly fascinated with mechanical order, and the inter-relationship of mechanical systems from terrestrial timepieces to the systematic movements of the heavens, all of them linked by the natural laws of mathematics. These preoccupations were central to his method in the De legibus naturae, which sought to represent moral relations between individuals as a kind of mechanical system.

Cumberland was fortunate in having many friends at Magdalene who were also interested in the new natural philosophy. He was part of a circle of ex-St Paul's students including Samuel Pepys, an old school friend and later President of the Royal Society; John Hollings, a doctor of medicine, who provided some of the medical references for the De legibus naturae; Hezekiah Burton, later chaplain to Orlando Bridgeman and editor of De legibus; and Joseph Hill, who, as a 'universal scholar', was to be involved in the abortive plan for a new university at Durham in the later 1650s.[8]

As the 1650s wore on, and the fate of both the universities and the Church began to come into doubt, it is possible that Cumberland may have undertaken some medical training with a view to an alternative career. This was not uncommon at the time. As Walter Charleton wrote in 1654: 'Our late warres and Schisms, having almost wholly discouraged men from the study of theologie and brought the civil law into contempt; the major part of young scholars in our universities addict themselves to Physic.'[9] For Samuel Rolle, the motive was the threat to the universities, 'the Great Suspition which [he] had of the Approaching ruine of Schollars', which affected both enrolment and choice of study.[10] The result was that many students, including Cumberland's near-contemporaries, Thomas Tenison and Isaac Barrow, became familiar with medical science.[11] Nature and natural philosophy became a refuge from political strife and theological controversy. The striking recurrence of organic and medical metaphors in the work of Cumberland, and indeed all of the 'rational divines', undoubtedly owes much to these experiences.

Cumberland's departure from Magdalene to the rural obscurity of Northamptonshire and the parish of Brampton Ash in 1657 might ordinarily have marked the end of a productive scientific career, but Cumberland appears to have kept himself busy, and in touch with his Cambridge friends. Payne records that 'in this rural retirement he minded little else than the Duties of his Function and his Studies. His Relaxation from these were very few besides

---

[7] Millburn, 'William Stukeley and the early history of the orrery', 511–28; Gunther, Early science in Cambridge, 169.
[8] DNB, s.v.
[9] Walter Charleton, The darkness of atheism dispelled by the light of nature, London 1654, 40.
[10] E. Calamy, Calamy revis'd: being a revision of Edmund Calamy's account of the ministers and others ejected and silenced, 1660–2, ed. A. G. Matthews, Oxford 1934, 416.
[11] E. Carpenter, Thomas Tenison, archbishop of Canterbury: his life and times, London 1948, 7; Barrow, Theological works, i, p. xii.

his journies to Cambridge which he made to preserve a correspondence with his learned Acquaintances in that Place.'[12] Maintaining these connections paid dividends when he gained the support of Bridgeman, through his old friend Burton, in 1667. This patronage yielded the living in Stamford, and the resources to put together the materials for *De legibus naturae*.

It was during this period that Cumberland appears to have become very interested in the scientific work of the Royal Society. Cumberland never became a Fellow of the Society, but this was not uncommon for *virtuosi* who were not resident in London, particularly after the Society began to limit its expansion from the mid 1660s. In spite of this, the *De legibus naturae* is full of references to the activities of the Royal Society between 1667 and 1669, mostly drawn from the *Philosophical Transactions*. The earliest refer to Robert Hooke's work on respiration in 1667, and the latest to July 1669.[13] This could give us a rough date for the composition of the work in the period 1669–70. The presence of some material of this kind might not be considered unusual in a Latitudinarian divine from the period concerned, but Cumberland's obsessive concern to incorporate so much of the science of the Royal Society into an anti-Hobbesian ethical theory has deeper roots in a more specific debate.

During the 1660s, the Royal Society became the focus for increasing concerns about the potentially atheistic implications of the new natural philosophy. The anomalous position of the Society outside the traditional university structure allowed its detractors to draw attention to its subversive implications for both Church and State. These charges centred around allegations that the Society was propagating ideas that were excessively materialistic, and by implication irreligious and immoral. The Royal Society could even be perceived as being Hobbesian in its disregard for orthodox moral ideas. The extensive use of natural philosophy in Cumberland's *De legibus* was in part a response to this kind of criticism. By using the Royal Society's scientific material, Cumberland sought to vindicate the Society, and some of its projects, from the suspicion of Hobbism and atheism.

---

12 Payne, 'Brief account', p. vii.

13 Cumberland, *DLN* 5.24, 2.18; Hooke's work was published in the *Philosophical Transactions* on 21 Oct. 1667; the latest mention of the Royal Society is a reference to hydrophobia reported to the Royal Society on 8 July 1669. The most readily datable references refer to, among other things, reproductive anatomy (discussed at the Royal Society in 1668), Wren and Huygen's work on the laws of motion (1668), Wren's engine for making lenses (1669), Holder's *Elements of speech* (1669) and Lower's *Tractatus de corde* (presented in 1669). For more details of the use of this work see ch. 6.

The Royal Society in the 1660s

If Richard Cumberland was convinced of the importance of natural philosophy in forming the foundation for *scientia moralis*, he was also convinced that the Royal Society had a vital role to play in that undertaking:

> To resolve the visible world into its most simple principles, matter, variously figured, and motion, differently compounded, and after geometrical investigation of the property of figures, and of compounded motions, from phaenomenon faithfully observed, to show the history of the whole corporeal system exactly conspiring with the laws of matter and motion; but that is an undertaking not only unequal to the abilities of any one man, but of an age. It is, nevertheless worthy of the united endeavours, and unwearied industry of those great geniuses of which the Royal Society is composed: Worthy of his most excellent majesty, King Charles, its founder, patron and example. We may safely commit so important and difficult an affair to so faithful and skillful hands.[14]

This passage is interesting for several reasons. Not only does it indicate Cumberland's attachment to the Royal Society, but it also makes several important assumptions about the nature of the work which the Society was undertaking. To suggest that the Society should aim to resolve the universe into the mathematical principles of matter and motion was a controversial statement of the Society's methods and objectives. It was a contentious agenda which many contemporaries felt uncomfortable about. It was also a type of natural philosophy that came to the fore in the Society's work during the period 1668–9, when an experimental programme was inaugurated which aimed to do exactly what Cumberland was outlining in the passage above. To understand the background to this controversial agenda, it is necessary to examine the early history of the Royal Society, and its relationship to Hobbes and Hobbism.

The Royal Society occupied an anomalous position in the first decade of the Restoration. Although Charles II was its patron, it relied on private subscription, and was in character and outlook more akin to a gentleman's club than an official organ of state enthusiasm for natural philosophy.[15] The Society's membership remains notoriously difficult to classify. Attempts to identify a common political outlook among the Fellowship have been less than successful, and the leading historian of the Society has quite properly warned against over-simplistic generalisations, or assertions of a common programme or policy.[16] The Fellows ranged across the political and religious

---

14 Cumberland, *DLN*, introduction, sect. 3.
15 Q. R. D. Skinner, 'Thomas Hobbes and the nature of the early Royal Society', *Historical Journal* xii (1969), 217–39; M. Hunter, *Science and society in Restoration England*, Cambridge 1981, 44.
16 For this view see the many works of Michael Hunter: *Science and society: the Royal Society and its Fellows*, Chalfont 1982; *Establishing the new science: the experience of the early*

spectrum, incorporating Catholics, Anglicans and Presbyterians. Intellectu-ally, the breadth of opinion ranged from the neo-Aristotelian Sir Kenelm Digby, to the exotic combination of Cartesianism and Platonism espoused by Henry More. The one feature that could be said to unite the Society's hetero-geneous membership was an attachment to a loosely defined Baconian utili-tarianism.[17] This is not to suggest that 'Baconianism' could pretend to any substantial intellectual coherence; Bacon was a broad symbol for the 'Grand Design of Improving Natural Knowledge for the glory of God, the Honour and Advantage of the Kingdom and the Universal Good of mankind'.[18] Although this could be, and has been, interpreted as a sign of intellectual naivety on the part of the Society's founders, it is as well to remember that the Baconian banner did much to provide a broad spectrum of support in the Society's early years. Cumberland himself felt the need to locate his scientific enquiry into natural law within a wider Baconian project, when he argued that, 'our countryman, Lord Verulam, has reckoned such an enquiry among the things that are found wanting'.[19] Bacon's authority was taken very seri-ously by writers like Cumberland, who were enabled to envisage the work of the Society as a crucial focus for a wider, inclusive, philosophical community, a community in which intellectual dissent could be subsumed beneath a common mantle. Bacon became an icon for much-needed social and political unity.

This adaptation of Bacon as the patron saint of the advancement of learn-ing was perhaps too successful. It was successful in that it responded to a political need to provide legitimacy for a new institution through the use of a universally respected pre-civil war figure. But it was too successful in the way that this ambiguous public image concealed a range of mutually contradictory and controversial intellectual positions. This may have been appropriate in the wake of the Restoration, which witnessed concerted efforts to bring about a political and religious compromise over the shape of the Restoration polity. Within a very short time, however, the collapse of eirenic aspirations in the face of a conservative reaction left the Royal Society, with its conspicuous lack of an institutional identity, as an object of suspicion and distrust. In a politically divisive context, the meagre intellectual resources of Baconianism could do little to prevent the Society from association with every variety of

---

Royal Society, Woodbridge 1989. For attempts to categorise the Fellowship upon ideological grounds see L. Mulligan, 'Civil war politics, religion and the Royal Society', *Past and Present* lix (1973), 92–116, and 'Anglicanism, Latitudinarianism and science in seventeenth-century England', *Annals of Science* iii (1973), 213–19.

[17] P. Rattansi, 'The social interpretation of science', in P. Mathias (ed.), *Science and society 1600–1900*, Cambridge 1972, 28–32.

[18] *Philosophical Transactions* 1 (1665), preface. For similar Baconian statements see Francis Bacon, *Works*, ed. J. Spedding, R. C. Ellis and D. Heath, London 1858–74, i. 47–8, 79.

[19] Cumberland, *DLN*, introduction, sect. 4. For this purpose behind 'Baconianism' see M. B. Hall, *Promoting experimental learning: experiment and the Royal Society 1660–1723*, Cam-bridge 1991, 9–23.

Restoration anxiety, from conventicle to crypto-Catholicism. Far from meeting with little resistance in its first decade, the Royal Society was placed in a necessarily defensive posture. It needed to redefine itself and its projects.

This problem of identity emerged as the Society's stated aims to further practical knowledge were seen to be at odds with the diverse and often esoteric work produced by its Fellows.[20] The *ad hoc* experimental programme was characterised by a lack of intellectual definition. Even more perilous was the Society's failure, or inability, to commit itself to a well-defined public statement of purpose. This created an opportunity for individuals to interpret or represent the Society's position in ways which were only partially representative of its heterogenous composition. This left the Society exposed to the excesses of even its own apologists.

This can be seen most clearly in the case of Joseph Glanvill and, to a lesser extent, Samuel Parker. Their representations of the Royal Society were instrumental in mobilising nervous hostility against it. Glanvill's writings have often been taken to be the official propaganda of the Society and its projects, but we should be cautious before accepting this uncritically.[21] Glanvill's overstated agenda alienated key portions of the Society's natural constituency, and could even be said to have helped create the debate which was to put the Society at risk in the later 1660s. Glanvill's iconoclastic deployment of sceptical and anti-Scholastic rhetoric was far from being shared by the majority of the Society's active membership. Some writers voiced fears that such arguments might fatally compromise the political position of the experimental science, not least because Glanvill's scepticism and materialism seemed to have much in common with Hobbes.

Sceptical young men: the danger of Hobbism

Glanvill was in some ways an unlikely defender of the Royal Society. He was surprisingly remote from the main body of the Fellowship, spending much of the 1660s, for example, in the West Country, on the provincial, corresponding fringe of the Society's activities.[22] The point applies intellectually as well as geographically; although Glanvill was at Oxford during the 1650s at a time when some of the founding members of the Royal Society were carrying out crucial experimental work, he seems not to have cared much for experimental science. Indeed, he even said that he wished he had been sent to

---

[20] Hunter, *Science and society in Restoration England*, 90, 105–6; R. H. Syfret, 'Some early critics of the Royal Society', *Notes and Records of the Royal Society* viii (1950), 20–64; Charles Webster, 'Henry More and Descartes: some new sources', *British Journal for the History of Science* iv (1969), 370.

[21] For this view see J. Cope, *Joseph Glanvill: Anglican apologist*, St Louis 1956.

[22] Glanvill was rector of Frome Selwood from 1662, rector of Bath in 1666, and rector of Streat and Walton in 1672: *DNB, s.v.*

Cambridge instead, such was his enthusiasm for Cartesianism and the Platonism of Henry More.[23] This attachment to neo-Platonist humanism characterised his early works, some of which sought to defend Origenic ideas about the pre-existence of the soul.[24] Glanvill's Platonist enthusiasm fused with a sceptical approach to natural philosophy, and his first work on this topic deployed the humanist's sceptical tools in a critique of Scholastic learning.

The *Vanity of dogmatizing*, published in 1661, argued firmly against 'confidence in uncertainties' as the greatest enemy to true certainty. Glanvill made it clear that he was not endorsing Pyrhonnism *per se*, but rather using scepticism to undermine false pretence to philosophical authority. His aim was to clear the way for a new science.[25] His target was Scholasticism, the 'notional way' of philosophy, a tradition which had corrupted the ideas of Aristotle to such an extent that they had reduced philosophical discourse to litigious nonsense:

> The Volumes of the Schoolmen, are deplorable evidence of Peripatetick depravations . . . there, the most obvious verity is subtiliz'd into niceties, and spun out into a thread indiscernable by common Optickes, but through the eyes of the adored Heathen. This hath robb'd the Christian world of its unity and peace; and made the church the stage of everlasting contentions; and while Aristotle is made the Centre of Truth and Unity, what hope of reconciling?[26]

For Glanvill, Scholastic dogmatising was the cause of political dysfunction, and for this reason it needed to be replaced with the more sceptical analysis of writers like Descartes, whose mechanistic science replaced dogma with more open-ended hypotheses based upon sounder principles.[27] For some of his readers, Glanvill's polarisation of Scholasticism and modern philosophy was forgivable juvenile excess,[28] but for others his scepticism had darker implications. Thomas White, then developing a neo-Aristotelian version of the new science,[29] attacked the *Vanity* in 1663 for resurrecting ancient scepti-

---

23 Wood, *Athenae*, iii. 1244; Glanvill matriculated into Exeter College in 1652, graduated BA in 1655, transferring to Lincoln College in 1656. He proceeded MA in 1659: *DNB*.
24 Cope, *Glanvill*, 127–43.
25 Joseph Glanvill, *The vanity of dogmatizing*, London 1661, epistle dedicatory, sig. A3r.
26 Ibid. 166–7.
27 Ibid. 250.
28 J. Worthington, *Diary and correspondence*, ed. J. Crossley and R. C. Christie, Manchester 1847, i. 299–301.
29 White replied to Glanvill in *Sciri, sive scepti et scepticorum a iure disputationis exclusio*, London 1663. This was translated in 1665 as *An exclusion of sceptics from all title to dispute* after Glanvill had republished his views in the *Scepsis scientifica*, London 1665. For White's neo-Aristotelian science see John Henry, 'Atomism and eschatology: Catholicism and natural philosophy in the Interregnum', *British Journal for the History of Science* li (1982), 211–40. For White's arguments against Glanvill see B. C. Southgate, 'Cauterising the tumour of Pyrhonnism: Blackloism vs skepticism', *Journal of the History of Ideas* liii (1992), 631–45.

cism, which, he suggested, ought to be returned to its rightful place in the grave. He also ominously identified Glanvill's approach with the teachings of Pierre Gassendi, whose Neo-Epicureanism challenged Scholastic natural philosophy with a science of matter and motion.

Glanvill linked his controversial work with the name of the Royal Society in 1664, when he became a Fellow and also republished his views in the *Scepsis scientifica*.[30] The *Scepsis* followed the same line of argument as the *Vanity*, with a more austere prose style, mentions of the Royal Society's work, and a toning down of the praise for Descartes. The emphasis upon the importance of scepticism and the disparagement of the Schools nevertheless remained. Glanvill was to a certain extent justified in associating the Society with his sceptical project. The critical use of sceptical ideas was common among some of the more famous society members; Robert Boyle adopted Carneades as his *alter ego* in the *Sceptical chymist* of 1661; John Hoskins had written to John Aubrey in the same year describing the Fellowship as 'our philosophical scepticks'.[31] Glanvill took advantage of this outlook to draw the Society into his rhetorical opposition between dogmatic 'ancients' and sceptical 'moderns', inserting a prefatory address to 'the most learned and ingenious Society in Europe'.[32]

Although this presented a positive image of the Society, some feared that Glanvill might be claiming too much. Henry Oldenburg, the Society's secretary, became worried that Glanvill was generating higher expectations than the Society's limited resources could justify.[33] Perhaps more worrying was the persistent identification of the sceptical novelty attached to the Society's programme, an identification which would soon be reinforced by Samuel Parker's *Free and impartiall censure of the Platonick philosophy* (1666).

Ironically Parker's book had been promoted by the virtuoso John Beale as a counterweight to Glanvill's exoticism.[34] The book combined advocacy of the Royal Society with a condemnation of Platonism. However unorthodox Platonist thinking might sometimes be, it was nevertheless a respected tradition widely held to be reconcilable with Christianity, and in attacking it, Parker was venturing into dangerous territory. In a work that was already complicated by apparently favourable references to Hobbes, Parker's discussion sounded alarmingly iconoclastic. He wrote at one point that he had 'lately grown such a despairing Sceptick in all Physiologicall Theories, that I cannot concern myself in the Truth or Falsehood of any one Hypothesis'. He added that he preferred the mechanical and experimental hypothesis not on any

---

30 T. Birch, *A history of the Royal Society of London*, New York 1968, i. 500–1. Glanvill's membership was proposed by Lord Brereton.
31 Cope, *Glanvill*, 121.
32 Glanvill, *Scepsis scientifica*, preface.
33 Hunter, *Science and society in Restoration England*, 13.
34 *The correspondence of Henry Oldenburg*, ed. A. Rupert Hall and M. B. Hall, Madison 1965–75, iii. 155.

ideological grounds, but rather because it offered the best method by which to obtain some certainty in the knowledge of nature.[35] It was on these sceptical grounds that he advocated the Royal Society:

> And therefore we may expect a greater improvement of Natural Philosophie from the Royal Societie (if they pursue their design) then it has had in all former ages; for they having discarded all particular hypotheses and wholly addicted themselves to exact Experiments and Observations, they may not only furnish the World with a compleat History of Nature . . . but also lay firm and solid foundations to erect Hypotheses upon.[36]

Although these statements were consistent with a basic 'Baconian' empiricism, Parker's emphasis upon scepticism, his disrespect for ancient learning and his taste for mechanism combined to create alarm among some of his readers. Richard Baxter, the Presbyterian leader, attacked Parker explicitly in the appendix to *The reasons of the Christian religion* (1667). Baxter was concerned to defend the immortality of the soul against what he saw as the rampant materialism of the age. In particular he focused upon the brash confidence of young writers 'who have received prejudice against the Peripateticks, the Platonists and the Stoicks, before they ever did thoroughly study them'. These were men whose sceptical outlook and headlong desire for novelty had driven them to endorsement of what he saw as the interchangeable and equally pernicious doctrines of neo-Epicureanism or Cartesianism. The sceptical young men cited specifically were Joseph Glanvill and Samuel Parker, both Fellows of the Royal Society.[37]

Baxter had been acquainted with Glanvill, and Glanvill had even sent him a copy of the *Vanity of dogmatizing* in 1661.[38] Five years later, however, with the added evidence of Parker's *Censure*, Baxter was increasingly troubled at the dangerous implications of their arguments. In the *Reasons*, he argued that excessive scepticism of the kind demonstrated by Glanvill and Parker led to an over-concentration upon matter and motion alone, the philistine rejection of ancient learning, and ultimately the casting aside of the first, divine, cause. Baxter saw this as Epicureanism by the back-door. Gassendi, Descartes and Hobbes had turned the heads of gullible and easily-influenced young philosophers. Immersion in matter led men to look too closely at the organ and, as a consequence, overlook the agency of God. This kind of materialist scepticism also concealed an unacceptable moral agenda:

> With Nature, you deny the Being of Morality. For if there be no difference of Beings, but in quantity, figure, motion and size; and all motion is Locomotion, which moveth by natural necessitating, than as a man moveth as a stone,

---

[35] Parker, *Censure*, 46.

[36] Ibid. 47–8.

[37] Richard Baxter, *The reasons of the Christian religion*, London 1667, 497–8.

[38] Cope, *Glanvill*, 6–7.

because it is irresistably moved, and hath no power to forbear any act which it performeth, or to do otherwise than it doth. For if there be no power, habit or disposition antecedent to the motion, there is one and the same account to be given of all actions good and bad . . . then there is no virtue or vice, no place for Laws and moral government.[39]

This argument against sceptical scientists would have had an unavoidable resonance for any informed contemporary; it was precisely that used by John Bramhall in his famous confrontation with Hobbes over the issue of free will. Hobbes was perhaps the most notable proponent of natural necessity, and the role of local motion in analysing natural phenomena. Bramhall argued that such necessitarian doctrines removed liberty and, as a consequence, responsibility from moral actions.[40] For Baxter, the scepticism of Parker and Glanvill, taken to be representative of the Royal Society, led to Epicurean materialism, and a Hobbesian disregard for conventional morality.

Baxter was not the only writer concerned about the excesses of the sceptical young men. Henry More sensed the recrudescence of the materialist atheism he had fought against in the 1650s. His *Divine dialogues*, published in 1668, satirised the 'young, witty and well-moralised materialist' in the character of Hylobares.[41] More, like Baxter, sensed the impious implications of mechanism:

> For I have very much wondered at the devotedness of some men's spirits to the pretense of pure mechanism in solving the phenomena of the universe, who yet otherwise have not been of less pretension to Piety and Virtue. Of which mechanic pronity, I do not see any good tendency at all. For it looks more like an itch of magnifying their own, or other men's Wit, then any desire of glorying God, in his wise and benign contrivances in the work of nature; and cuts off the most powerful and popular argument for the existence of a Deity, if the rude career of agitated matter would at last necessarily fall into such a structure of things. Indeed, if such a Mechanical Necessity in the nature of Matter were really discoverable, there were no help for it: And the almighty seeks no honor from a man's lye.[42]

This kind of charge worried senior members of the Royal Society. Oldenburg wrote to Robert Boyle in December 1667 that

> Dr Baxter inveighes in his Book written to assert ye Reasons of ye Christian Religion, against ye Corpuscularianism (called by him, ye somatical) Philosophy, and traduces it as if it supplanted our future Estate. This our good friend,

---

[39] Baxter, *Reasons*, 520.
[40] Hobbes, *EW* v.
[41] Although Hylobares sounds very like Parker, in fact he represents one of More's Cambridge students, Thomas Baines. The book nevertheless ran into trouble with Parker for its Platonism; as licenser, Parker delayed the publication of the book for a year: *Conway correspondence*, 255, 294.
[42] Henry More, *Divine dialogues*, London 1668, i. 44–6.

would fain have rightly stated, to prevent ill-effects, like to follow ye popular discoursing of a popular man.[43]

The 'ill-effects' of the Society's controversial reputation were soon in evidence. When, in 1667, Robert South preached against atheism in Westminster Abbey, he characterised his targets as being of 'such a peculiar stamp of Impiety, that they seem to be a set of fellows got together, and formed into a kind of Diabolicall Society, for the finding out new experiments in Vice'.[44] The desire to have the Society's position 'rightly stated' against burgeoning criticism led to the completion of the most famous, if also one of the most misunderstood, works in defence of the new learning, Thomas Sprat's *History of the Royal Society* (1667). Sprat's work is often considered to be an 'official' statement of the Society's positive programme, but historians of the Society are increasingly coming to realise that Sprat's project was far more defensive in tone and content.[45] The *History* illustrates the essentially defensive posture which the Society found itself in towards the end of the 1660s. What is more, it demonstrates the growing anxiety about the potential link with apparently Hobbesian forms of natural philosophy.

The *History of the Royal Society*

As the concern of Petty, Evelyn and Oldenburg had shown, the Fellowship was aware from an early stage of the problem of institutional definition. As early as May 1663 Robert Moray informed Christopher Huygens that there were plans afoot to produce a small apologetic work.[46] In April of that year Thomas Sprat, a young graduate of Wadham and protégé of John Wilkins, had been elected Fellow. Sprat was no great scientist, but he was a talented writer, and the express purpose of his election seems to have been the production of the work.[47] Initial hopes that the work would be finished by 1664 were disappointed, although in 1665 Sprat did fulfil part of his defensive function by providing an indignant response to Samuel Sorbière's *Relation d'un voyage en Angleterre* (1663), a work which forms an interesting prelude to the *History*. Sorbière, friend of Gassendi and regular correspondent with Hobbes,

---

[43] *Correspondence of Henry Oldenburg*, vi. 80.

[44] Robert South, *Sermons preached upon several occasions*, Oxford 1823, ii. 373–5. For South's complex attitude towards the new science see G. Reedy, *Robert South 1634–1716: an introduction to his life and sermons*, Cambridge 1992, 4.

[45] M. Purver, *The Royal Society: concept and creation*, London 1967, 9. For the revised view see Michael Hunter's fine essay, 'Latitudinarianism and the "ideology" of the Royal Society: Thomas Sprat's History of the Royal Society reconsidered', in his *Establishing the new science*, 45–72.

[46] C. Huygens, *Oeuvres*, La Haye 1889, iv. 343.

[47] P. B. Wood, 'Methodology and apologetics: Thomas Sprat's History of the Royal Society', *British Journal for the History of Science* xliii (1980), 1–26.

had been elected an honorary Fellow of the Society in 1663 during his visit. In his subsequent published account, he described the Royal Society as being composed of two main groups, the *literati*, inspired by a Gassendist view of natural philosophy, and the mathematicians, largely influenced by Descartes. Although, for reasons that will be discussed later, this might have been a rather canny assessment of the most important factions in the early history of the Society, it was the very last thing many of the Fellows wanted to hear in public. Both institutional autonomy and philosophical orthodoxy were compromised by the suggestion that the Society was factionalised around dubious and imported philosophical movements. Sprat sought to put the record straight; he wrote that 'neither of these two men [Gassendi or Descartes] bear any sway amongst them: they are never named there as Dictators over men's Reasons; nor is there any extraordinary reference to their judgements'.[48] Sprat was even more defensive when Sorbière had the temerity to suggest a stylistic affinity between the Society's patron-saint Bacon, and his one-time amanuensis Thomas Hobbes. Sprat assures his English audience that there is in fact 'no more likeness, than there was between *St George* and the *Waggoner*. . . . I scarce know two men in the world, that have more different colors of speech'.[49] Sprat's message was clear enough; the Royal Society's pedigree was native, English and Baconian, nothing to do with foreign traditions and their English offshoots like Hobbes. This emphasis would carry through to his writing in the *History*.

Sprat's tardiness with the *History* caused considerable concern among interested Fellows as criticism of the Society grew.[50] John Beale was so worried that, in addition to sponsoring Samuel Parker's *Censure*, he began to write his own apologetic work. The growing hostility in 1666–7 caused Wilkins, Sprat's main supervisor, to hurry the work along, adding a third part in 1667 which sought to quell the kind of criticism being levelled by Baxter. The resulting work is not a Latitudinarian manifesto, but rather, as Michael Hunter has suggested, a register of the criticism faced by the Royal Society, and Sprat's attempts to deal with it.[51] Sprat felt compelled to apologise for the 'larger and more contentious' style than one might expect to find in a normal history, but he put blame squarely upon the Society's critics.[52]

For all Sprat's panegyric enthusiasm, he was soon defending the Society against the 'very hard usage' of those who gave the Fellows of the Royal Society 'scornful titles of Philosophers, Schollars or Virtuosi'. Sprat listed the Society's assailants by character: those individuals who thought of them as hopelessly divorced from the real world, or, at the other extreme made them

---

48 T. Sprat, *Observations on monsieur de Sorbière's voyage into England*, London 1665, 241.
49 Ibid. 332–3.
50 For John Wallis's concern see *Correspondence of Henry Oldenburg*, iii. 49.
51 Hunter, 'Latitudinarianism and the "ideology" of the Royal Society', 45–72.
52 T. Sprat, *The history of the Royal Society of London for the improving of natural knowledge*, ed. J. I. Cope and H. W. Jones, St Louis 1958, preface.

out to be mere drudges. 'Over-zealous divines' like Baxter attacked natural philosophy as 'a carnal knowledge, and a too much minding worldly things'; 'men of the world', or of business said that the Society's activities were only an 'idle matter of fancy', preventing more useful activity.[53]

Against this hail of criticism, Sprat sought to make a distinction between 'good' forms of natural philosophy, carried out by the Royal Society, and the kind of 'bad' science with which the Society might be erroneously associated. Topping the list of forms of 'bad' science, which the Royal Society did not represent, was that which went too far in rejecting the ancients, creating new theories as tyrannical as the old.[54] Sprat's charge seems to aim at several of what he calls the 'modern dogmatists', but Descartes, Gassendi and, of course, Hobbes were all likely candidates. Sprat attacks what he sees as the limited ambition of much of the new science. What use would it be, he argues, if such philosophers did find the true principles of natural philosophy, if all they did was limited to 'the solving of appearances'. This was possibly an attack on the nominalism of Gassendi in particular, but also on Hobbes and Descartes, for their reduced aspiration to provide hypothetical explanations for physical events, rather than attempting to analyse the nature of things. Just as the Society did not limit its enquiries to the study of appearances, so it also rejected other reductive and dogmatic methods of analysing natural phenomena. Sprat uses the example of the man 'who discovered that all things were ordered by Nature in Motion', and who refused to proceed beyond this. Sprat, as the pious virtuoso, ostentatiously refrains from naming names, but the reference to Hobbes is unmistakable, and recurs in Sprat's characterisation of the modern dogmatist's frame of mind:

> This is a Temper of Mind, of all others the most pernicious; to which I chiefly attribute the slowness of the increase of knowledge amongst men. For what greate things can be expected, if men's understandings shall be (as it were) always in a Warlike State of Nature, one against the other?[55]

The rhetorical flourish plays upon the most distinctive feature of Hobbes's natural law theory. Hobbes the dogmatist behaves as his unacceptable political theory dictates.

Sprat is equally crushing in denouncing those who simply reject the Schoolmen for another patron such as Epicurus, Democritus or Philolaus, thus establishing a new tyranny of ancient thought. Sprat's target here is Gassendi, who is attacked alongside those 'Chymists' whose interest in occult phenomena obstructs the pursuit of true natural philosophy. In doing this, Sprat aimed to define what the Royal Society was not: not Gassendist, not Cartesian and certainly not Hobbesian.

Sprat also attempted to counter the charge that the Society was out to

[53] Ibid. 26–7.
[54] Ibid. 28–30.
[55] Ibid. 33.

undermine ancient philosophy.[56] Far from denouncing ancient learning, he was careful to explain that the Society's intention was only to free natural philosophy from an absolute servitude to ancient texts. Sprat consistently stresses a reconciliatory collaboration between ancient and modern. The *History* suggests that the new learning continues in the spirit of the old in a way that blind imitation cannot.[57] This can best be seen as an attempt to counter the sort of criticism which had emerged from the attacks launched by Glanvill and Parker upon the Schoolmen and the Platonists. It betrayed the need to patch up relations with the more traditional natural philosophers, and also with the universities, who, by the late 1660s, would come to see the Society's iconoclastic image as a threat.

These tensions recur in part III of the work, probably written in 1667 explicitly to deal with the problems which had emerged by that date. Sprat went further in denouncing those who had gone too far in rejecting the authority of the ancients, and desperately attempted to defuse the antagonism between 'old' and 'new' learning, a position familar from the writings of Hobbes and Descartes, but one newly restored to prominence by the writings of Parker and Glanvill:

> I confess that there have not been wanting some forward *Assertors* of *the new philosophy*, who have not us'd any kind of *Moderation* towards them [the ancients]: but have presently concluded, that nothing can be well-done in *New Discoveries*, unless all the Ancient Arts be first rejected, and their Nurseries abolish'd. But the rashness of these men's proceedings, has rather prejudic'd, than advanc'd, what they make show to promote. They have come as furiously to the purging of *philosophy* as our *Modern Zealots* did to the *Reformation of Religion*.[58]

Sprat's strategy was to draw a distinction between the Society's prudent reform and the kind of radical reform which had been proposed during the Interregnum by writers like Hobbes. Hobbes referred on many occasions to the universities as nurseries of Scholastic absurdity, and frequently recommended their reform as an essential means of checking the malign influence of bad philosophy.[59] It is the spectre of Hobbes and the 1650s that lurks behind Sprat's anodyne assurances that the Society's natural philosophy does no harm to Church and State. Sprat's philosophical polity is less a positive political image than a defensive anti-Hobbesian statement.

In spite of this, the points of contact still remained. Sprat gloried in the achievements of the Royal Society in the study of matter and motion, and cited work which had Epicurean origins. He argued that although the Society and some of his modern dogmatists had some things in common, this did not

56 Ibid. 46.
57 Ibid. 51, 54.
58 Ibid. 328.
59 Hobbes, *Leviathan*, 14, 19, 462, 491.

mean that the methods of philosophy themselves were entirely to blame. Some writers, it was true, 'by their carelessness of a Future Estate, have brought a discredit on *knowledge* itself'. But this raised the question whether or not this was necessarily to do with their science? 'Must we', Sprat asks, 'strait believe that their Impiety proceeds from their philosophy?' Sprat argued that it was possible to look at such individual philosophers and mistake the causes of their heterodoxy. Where vice was mixed with good philosophy, people were often 'apt to imagine the bad to arise from the good, and so condemn both together; whereas perhaps it sprung from some hidden cause of which they took no notice'.[60] The science itself was not to blame; the impiety of writers like Hobbes who used it stemmed not from the intrinsic nature of the natural philosophy itself, but rather from the peculiarities of the individual practitioner. The Royal Society may well have had methodological characteristics in common with Gassendi and Hobbes, but this did not mean that it necessarily subscribed to their questionable conclusions. In arguing this point, Sprat sought to cleanse natural philosophy of its heterodox associations, and distance the Society's position from that of Hobbes.

However subtle these distinctions may have been, Sprat was treading a dangerous path in confronting this overlap between a godly and an atheistic science. Sprat himself, as a result of the book, was regarded with some suspicion. For John Worthington, corresponding with Henry More in February 1668, Sprat was a 'perfect Hylobares', one of those devoted to 'nothing but what gratifies external sense, or what sense doth reach'.[61] The characterisation of Sprat himself as a sceptical materialist was an ominous sign, and in the tense political atmosphere of the later 1660s, with its increasing sensitivity to Hobbism in all of its forms, Sprat's assurances were an ambiguous protection against such charges. This would be a danger which would re-emerge after the publication of another controversial work by Glanvill.

The early response to the *History*, from the Fellowship at least, was quite positive. Beale felt that 'it will prove an Invincible Light to all the World, & for all ages'. Nathaniel Fairfax felt that it had captured the 'life and soul' of the Society.[62] Oldenburg's review in the *Philosophical Transactions* was enthusiastic, but the secretary felt the need to supplement Sprat's account with some practical information about the contributions which the Society had made, in response to the accusation that their achievement had been minimal.[63] The feeling that Sprat had not adequately answered this point led Oldenburg to seek a means of publicising the Society's contribution, and just such an opportunity emerged in the shape of a new project by Glanvill. Glanvill had been considering another apologetic work before the publication of

---

60 Sprat, *History*, 375.
61 Worthington, *Correspondence*, ii. 265.
62 Hunter, 'Latitudinarianism and the "ideology" of the Royal Society', 61; *Correspondence of Henry Oldenburg*, iii. 491–2.
63 *Philosophical Transactions* ii (1667), 505.

Sprat's *History*, but John Beale, Glanvill's near neighbour, had reservations about the kind of contribution that Glanvill would make. He wrote to Boyle that it would be necessary to 'ballast him from Origenian Platonism and extravagant adventures', but feared that 'his genius is apt for sublime adventures'.[64] Oldenburg, however, was willing to use Glanvill's work as a publicity vehicle to remedy the deficiencies of Sprat.[65] He went to the trouble of providing Glanvill with unpublished information relating to Boyle's experimental work, and other details of the Society's activities. There is little indication in Oldenburg's comments that he suspected that any problem might emerge over his semi-official endorsement of what would become Glanvill's *Plus ultra*, possibly the most controversial piece of work to emerge from the debate over the Society.[66]

The problem with *Plus ultra* was not the information about the Society *per se*. This, as Oldenburg hoped, extended the discussion in Sprat's *History*, and provided an answer to the carping about the Society's achievements.[67] Controversy over *Plus ultra* developed instead from the local political context in which Glanvill had developed the work. The polemical tone of the work took its keynote from Glanvill's encounter, in 1667, with the Aristotelian divine and ex-Presbyterian Robert Crosse, vicar of Chew Magna, a living that Crosse had taken in preference to the Regius Chair of Divinity at Oxford. A showcase debate was arranged between Glanvill and Crosse, which ended with Crosse accusing Glanvill and the Royal Society of 'downright atheism'. For Glanvill, in physical danger from dissenter agitation in his own parish, the Scholastic ex-Presbyterian's defence of ancient learning was too much. *Plus ultra* was never simply going to be an appendix to Sprat. There was the greatest urgency in aggressively promoting the new science as an antidote to the politically dangerous Scholastic dogma peddled by dissenting sympathisers.[68]

For this reason, *Plus ultra* combines apologetics for the Royal Society with a sustained attack on Scholasticism. It represented the achievements of the Society in a manner which many found objectionable. Glanvill specifically juxtaposed modern advances in natural philosophy with unfavourable references to ancient work. He also aligned Society mathematicians such as John Wallis and Seth Ward with Cartesian advances in analytical geometry.[69] He appeared to claim that the Society had been instrumental in the develop-

---

[64] *The works of the Honourable Robert Boyle*, ed. T. Birch, London 1772, vi. 418.
[65] Birch, *History*, ii. 197n.
[66] Joseph Glanvill, *Plus ultra, or the progress and advancement of knowledge since the days of Aristotle in an account of some of the most remarkable later improvements of practical useful learning*, London 1668. The work was presented to the Society by Oldenburg on 18 June 1668.
[67] Ibid. 83–4, 90.
[68] N. H. Steneck, 'The "Ballad of Robert Crosse and Joseph Glanvill", and the background to *Plus ultra*', *British Journal for the History of Science* xlvi (1981), 59–74.
[69] Glanvill, *Plus ultra*, 46.

ment of modern scientific equipment, and singled out five examples, the telescope, microscope, thermometer, barometer, and Robert Boyle's celebrated air-pump.[70] The extent to which Glanvill could claim these advances for the Royal Society was, to say the least, questionable, given the complex interplay of personnel and ideas between the universities and the Society. More objectionable was the continued emphasis on the Society's removal of the 'rubbish' of former times, rubbish that for Glanvill meant Scholasticism in all of its forms. The harsh treatment of the Schoolmen, familiar from the *Vanity* and the *Scepsis*, was liberally reapplied.[71]

The experimental philosophy of the Royal Society emerged as the antidote to a disease that was more than philosophical. Scholasticism for Glanvill was intimately related to political and religious divisions because it fundamentally distorted all forms of human knowledge. Sceptical, experimental learning, by contrast, 'rectifies the *grand abuse* which the *Notional* knowledge hath so long foster'd and promoted the *hindrance* of Science, the *disturbance* of the World, and the prejudice of the *Christian faith'*.[72] This true philosophy is thus a 'specific against Dispute and Division', a sceptical solution to political problems placed squarely at the door of Scholastic modes of thought.

Glanvill's renewed attack on Scholasticism and his exaggerated account of the Royal Society's contribution, although born of the need to answer the Society's critics, generated an inevitably hostile reaction from the universities. Glanvill had trodden on a nerve which had its roots in university anxieties over threats to abolish the ancient seats of learning in the 1650s. After the Restoration, many in Oxford and Cambridge were deeply suspicious of new, and particularly new royal, institutions trespassing upon their ancient prerogatives.[73] Equally there was much concern about the dangers of divorcing the study of the liberal arts from the new philosophy, much of which had been developed in the two universities. Glanvill's work reopened old wounds and attracted a critical response, particularly from those university dons who were themselves involved in the new science; individuals, ironically, who in other circumstances might be considered the Society's natural constituents.[74]

Glanvill's philistinism soon came under attack from the well-respected classical scholar Meric Casaubon.[75] Casaubon was concerned about the

---

70 Ibid. 53.

71 Ibid. 124.

72 Ibid. 148.

73 For concerns about royal treatment of the universities see J. Axtell, 'The mechanics of opposition: Restoration Cambridge v. Daniel Scargill', *Bulletin of the Institute of Historical Research* xxxviii (1965), 102–11.

74 Hunter, *Science and society in Restoration England*, 145.

75 Casaubon, son of the famous Isaac, had served as one of Laud's chaplains. He was most noted for his work as an editor and a translator of Marcus Aurelius. He also wrote A *treatise concerning enthusiasm*, London 1655, which looked at enthusiasm as a psychological condition, and contributed to the 'rule of faith' controversy in 1665, replying to John Sergeant's

dangers presented by Hobbesian and Epicurean forms of natural philosophy, and as a result he was already engaged in an attempt to promote a 'middle way' between scepticism and dogmatism, which he published in 1670 under the title *Of credulity and incredulity*. After finishing the first part of that work, Casaubon had spent some time in Cambridge, where his friend Peter du Moulin, an enthusiastic supporter of the new science, showed him a copy of Glanvill's new work. Glanvill's devotion to Descartes, mirrored by enthusiasm among Cambridge undergraduates, led Casaubon to compose a short tract *On learning* in July 1668, in which he lamented that the addiction to Descartes 'makes solid learning and reading go out of fashion', This was to be followed by the publication of a subsequent letter to du Moulin, *Concerning experimental natural philosophie* (1669).[76]

As with other university critics, Casaubon was far from being hostile to the new science. He was more concerned with the context in which it was being pursued. Casaubon was careful to make clear that it was not the limited claims of cautious writers like Boyle that aroused his ire, but rather the unrestrained experimental enthusiasm of those like Glanvill. In his response to Glanvill, he argued that experimental philosophy on its own is:

> very apt to be abused and to degenerate into atheism. Men that are much fix'd upon matter and secondary causes and sensual objects, if great care be not taken, may in time (there be many examples) and by degrees forget that there are such things as Spirits, substances really existing and of great power, though not visible, or palpable by their Nature; forget, I say, and consequently discredit supernatural operations: and at last that there is a God, and that their soul is immortal. This is a great precipice; and the contempt of all learning an ill-presage.[77]

It was with good reason that a concerned Beale wrote to Evelyn of the 'huge clatter' that would come from remarks made by 'so great a Name amongst the Critics and Antiquaries'.[78] John Wallis, the Oxford mathematician, wrote to Oldenburg in April 1669 urging him to restate the Society's position *vis à vis* the universities.[79] It seemed that a backlash against the Society was inevitable.

The worst fears of the *virtuosi* were realised over the following months. In Cambridge, Peter Gunning, Regius Professor of Divinity and Master of St John's College, refused to license a poem by Du Moulin in praise of the Society.[80] In November 1668 Edmund Boldero, vice-chancellor of the uni-

---

Sure footing in Christianity, or rational discourses on the rule of faith, London 1665. For Casaubon and the debate over science see M. R. G. Spiller, *Concerning natural experimental philosophie: Meric Casaubon and the Royal Society*, The Hague 1980.

76 Reproduced ibid.

77 Meric Casaubon, *Concerning experimental natural philosophie*, London 1669, 30.

78 Hunter, *Science and society in Restoration England*, 139.

79 *Correspondence of Henry Oldenburg*, v. 500.

80 Gascoigne, *Cambridge*, 54–6.

versity, forbade the use of Cartesian ideas in disputations. This may have been a response to the activities of Daniel Scargill, a junior Fellow of Corpus Christi College who defended controversial Cartesian and Epicurean theses in the Schools. Scargill, clearly a supporter of the new science, was forced to recant as a Hobbist in July 1669.[81] When Cosimo Medici visited the university in the same year, the Copernican hypothesis was publicly opposed in a showcase disputation. At Oxford, influential figures such as John Fell, Dean of Christ Church, Obadiah Walker, Master of University College, Thomas Pierce, Master of Magdalen and Thomas Barlow, Bodley's Librarian and later bishop of Lincoln, joined the chorus of disapproval.[82] The antagonism was such that in July Robert South could deliver a crushing sermon at the opening of the Sheldonian Theatre, which had the *virtuosi* present (including, ironically enough, the architect) squirming in their seats. As Wallis reported to Boyle:

> Dr South, the University orator made a long oration. The first part of which consisted of satyrical invectives against Cromwell, fanaticks, the Royal Society, and new philosophy; the next of encomiasticke, in praise of the archbishop, the theatre, the vice-chancellor, the architect and the painter; the last of execrations against fanaticks, comprehension and the new philosophy; damning them *ad infernos, ad gehennam*.[83]

South's choice of targets juxtaposed the new philosophy with Cromwell and religious extremism; in this rhetoric, the Royal Society was linked with the excesses of the Interregnum. The inclusion of comprehension in South's execrations demonstrates how Latitudinarian religious aspirations were attacked in the same way as their scientific activities. The 'rational divines" efforts in favour of comprehension and the Royal Society had attempted to create an inclusive unity from the disorder of conflict. Now both projects were simultaneously compromised by polarising politics.

The criticism continued into 1670, when the Society was assaulted by its most celebrated and inveterate opponent, Henry Stubbe. Like most of the Society's critics, Stubbe, a physician, was a keen follower of the new science. He had even contributed a history of chocolate (*The Indian nectar, or a discourse concerning chocolata*) to the Royal Society in 1662.[84] This had been dedicated to Boyle, with whom he maintained a correspondence throughout the 1660s.[85] Extracts from Stubbe's account of a voyage to Jamaica were read to the Society as late as May 1668.[86] However, upon his acquaintance with

---

[81] Axtell, 'The mechanics of opposition'; Parkin, 'Hobbism in the later 1660s', 85–108.
[82] Gascoigne, *Cambridge*, 54–6.
[83] Boyle, *Works*, vi. 459.
[84] Henry Stubbe, *The Indian nectar, or a discourse concerning chocolata*, London 1662.
[85] Boyle, *Works*, i, pp. lxxxxix–xcvi.
[86] Birch, *History*, ii. 292.

Crosse in 1669, Stubbe took up the argument against Glanvill, producing *Plus ultra reduced to a non-plus* in 1670.[87]

Stubbe sought to systematically demolish Glanvill's claims for the Society. The instruments which Glanvill had claimed for the Society were invented by others; even Boyle's Air-Pump was invented by Guericke.[88] So-called 'modern' advances were traced back to Aristotelian origins; Stubbe argued that even Harvey's work was a synthesis of the Peripatetic anatomy of Caesalpinus.[89] Even where advances had been made, the Royal Society could not claim credit; Thomas Willis, Stubbe revealed, had written his *De fermentione* before he even became a Fellow of the Royal Society. Stubbe was quite prepared to acknowledge the shortcomings of Scholastic interpretations of Aristotle, but he argued in response that critics should 'blame the abuse, and not the philosophy'.[90] In any case, he argued, 'Are not the Principles of Descartes, and the figur'd Atoms of Gassendus as precarious as those of Aristotle, and less subjected to sense[?]'.[91]

After his initial assault upon Glanvill, Stubbe's attacks played upon the instability of the Society's identity, and some of the ambiguous utterances of the apologetic works. Sprat's *History* was accused of promoting a crypto-Catholic plot.[92] Stubbe's ingenious use of just about every form of Restoration anxiety reflected the Society's vulnerability as political identities became increasingly important.

Particularly damaging was Stubbe's exploitation of the Society's internal incoherence over its policy towards mechanical explanation of natural phenomena. He sought to use Henry More's disillusionment with Descartes, and his burgeoning hostility to mechanical science in the *Divine dialogues*, against the Society. In *A letter to Dr Henry More*, Stubbe charged the Society with promoting an exclusively mechanical natural philosophy. He argued that

> as for all the philosophy of the universe, they make it all out to be matter in motion. . . . Out of which it is manifest, that they suppose not onely that the material part of every thing in the Corporeal Universe is Body or Corpuscular-

---

87 Stubbe later fell out with Crosse, but the latter's dispute with Glanvill seems to have been the occasion for Stubbe's involvement. There is also an unsubstantiated story that Stubbe was put up to the job by the President of the Royal College of Physicians, Benjamin Hamey, who saw the Society as attempting to usurp the position of the college in medical research: H. Brown, *Scientific organisations in seventeenth-century France*, Baltimore 1934, 255; Hunter, *Science and society*, 138; Spiller, *Meric Casaubon*, 29.

88 Henry Stubbe, *Plus ultra reduced to a non-plus*, London 1670, 9.

89 Ibid. 113.

90 Ibid. 12.

91 Ibid. 13.

92 Idem, *A censure upon certaine passages contained in the History of the Royal Society, as being destructive to the established religion and Church of England*, Oxford 1670, and *Campanella revived: or an enquiry into the history of the Royal Society, whether the virtuosi there do not pursue the projects of Campanella for the reducing of England unto popery*, Oxford 1670.

ian, but that the Vicissitudes and Phaenomena occurring therein, even in the generation of man, are the result of Corpuscles moving mechanically.

Stubbe plays with a pseudo-Hobbesian description of the Society's mechanical endeavours, and enlists More's testimony that 'this mechanical philosophy doth lead to Atheism'.[93] The pamphlet also cited passages from the *Divine dialogues* in which Hylobares was attacked for his Hobbesian attachment to mechanism. By enlisting More's work, Stubbe turned the Society's internal wrangling against itself.

Stubbe's targeting of mechanism was certainly astute, and identified a crucial weakness in the armoury of the Society's defenders. Both Sprat and Glanvill had promoted the mechanical hypothesis, but in terms which pushed it towards the boundaries of orthodoxy. Sprat, for example, had claimed much for the developing experimental programme of Christopher Wren. Wren had worked on an experimental project to discover more about the behaviour of bodies in impact, using pendula and other apparatus. According to Sprat, Wren's work with the Royal Society could lay claim to have devised

> The Doctrine of Motion, which is the most considerable of all others, for establishing the first Principles of Philosophy, by Geometrical Demonstrations. This Des Cartes had before begun. . . . But some of his conclusions seeming very questionable. . . . Dr Wren produced before the Society, an instrument to represent all sorts of impulses, made between two hard globous Bodies, either of equal, or of different bigness or swiftness, following or meeting each other, or the one moving, or the other at rest. From these varieties arose many unexpected effects; all of which he demonstrated the true Theories, after they had been confirmed by many hundreds of Experiments in that Instrument. These he proposed as the Principles of all Demonstrations in Natural Philosophy: Nor can it seem strange, that those Elements should be of such universal Use; if one considers that Generation, Corruption, Alteration and all the vicissitudes of Nature, are nothing else but the effects arising from the meeting of little Bodies, or of differing Figures, Magnitudes and Velocities.[94]

Sprat was correct in his detailing of Wren's project, but he had perhaps unwisely embroidered the philosophical implications of Wren's work. The final sentences of the paragraph were paraphrased from Walter Charleton's explicitly neo-Epicurean and pro-Hobbesian *Physiologia-Epicuro-Gassendo-Charletonia* of 1654.[95] Perhaps not surprisingly, Stubbe would cite this passage in his *Letter* to More as an indication of the Society's unhealthy interest in mechanism.

93 Idem, *A letter to Dr Henry More*, London 1671, 16.
94 Sprat, *History*, 311–12.
95 Walter Charleton, *Physiologia-Epicuro-Gassendo-Charletonia: or a fabrick of science natural, upon the hypothesis of atoms*, London 1654, 435.

But it was not only at the polemical level that the Society was putting out confusing signals about the nature of its projects. Renewed interest in mechanical theories of motion emerged in the autumn of 1668, when Robert Hooke proposed that 'experiments of motion . . . be prosecuted, thereby to state at last the nature and laws of motion'.[96] Oldenburg was instructed to contact both Wren and Huygens to collect their theoretical and experimental ideas. He did so in terms which seemed to indicate a thoroughly mechanistic agenda. Oldenburg's letter to Wren announced that the intention was to 'study ye nature & laws of motion, as ye foundation for all Philosophie and Philosophical Discourse'.[97] The project involved the commissioning of research into extant ideas, as well as the mobilisation of Society members including the Oxford mathematician John Wallis. But as with other Society projects, the philosophical premises underlying the study soon came into question. Simple assumptions about the use of experiment became complicated as theoretical and mathematical ideas came to dominate discussion of the topic. Oldenburg, for one, was worried about the abstract mathematical nature of Wallis's contribution, which appeared to supersede the Society's trademark experimentalism altogether. Wallis replied that nature could be analysed in this way:

> Ye Hypothesis I sent is indeed of ye Physical Laws of Motion but mathematically demonstrated. For I do not take ye Physical and Mathematical Hypotheses to contradict one another at all. But what is physically performed, is Mathematically measured. And there is no other way to determine ye Physical Causes of Motion exactly, but by applying ye Mathematicall measures and properties to them.[98]

Wallis's statement may seem obvious today, but his mathematical investigation into motion moved a long way from a simple faith in collecting facts from experiments.

Worse was to come. The most significant achievement of the project came in December 1668. Wren presented the findings of his experimental work to the Society in the form of a law.[99] These were published in the *Philosophical Transactions* of January 1668/9 as 'The law of nature in the collision of Bodies'. Here, the Royal Society had claimed to have discovered a law of nature through the use of its experimental programme. The use of the term 'laws of nature' however was provocative, and immediately raised philosophical objections. Another Fellow, the mathematician William Neile, immediately objected that Wren's experiments were not a sufficient basis on which to discuss the laws of nature, primarily because they revealed nothing about the causes of the phenomena concerned. Wren needed to state the theory

---

[96] Birch, *History*, ii. 315.
[97] *Correspondence of Henry Oldenburg*, v. 117–18.
[98] Ibid. 220–1.
[99] Birch, *History*, ii. 335.

which lay behind his experiments. As Neile put it, Wren was against 'finding a reason for the experiments of motion (for aught I see) and says that the appearances cause reason enough in themselves as being the law of nature. I think it is the law of nature that they should appear, but not without some causes.'[100] Although experiment constituted a common activity of the Fellowship, it was clear that they had very different ideas about what it could prove and how it should be used. Instead of analysing the effects of nature, argued Neile, science should investigate its causes. He also challenged theoretical assumptions which underlay the empirical work of Hooke and Wallis, who had both assumed that qualities like momentum were simply transferred from body to body. In fact he argued that one needed to look at what momentum might be, and how it might be caused mechanically. Neile proposed that a materialist theory of collision be adopted instead.[101]

As the experiments on motion went on into the new year, Neile was asked to prepare a more detailed version of his theory to answer Wallis and Wren. When his theory was presented in April 1669, just at the time that criticism of the Society was growing, Neile again produced a theory of motion. This included ideas which, he wrote, 'I gladly acknowledge taking from the books of Mr Hobbes.' Neile had drawn much of his theory from Hobbes's *De corpore*. The attempts to discover the laws of nature scientifically had led back to Hobbes, and the debates surrounding knowledge of their causes.[102]

The laws of motion project had raised many questions about the nature of the Royal Society's work. Neile had denied that 'laws of nature' could be gleaned from the Society's experimentalism alone. His alternative was a Hobbesian account of mechanical physics. But did this kind of mechanical theory necessarily lead to atheism, as the writing of Baxter, More, Casaubon and Stubbe seemed to indicate? The Society's image, and its programme into discovering the laws of nature, had been compromised by the disparate nature of its fellowship, the incoherence of its projects, and the failings of its apologists. For those, like Cumberland, who had faith in the possibility of using natural philosophy, and particularly mechanistic forms of natural philosophy, to discover the laws of nature, whether moral or physical, the challenge would be to try and show that mechanical natural philosophy did not automatically lead to atheism.

Several writers took up this challenge, including the indefatigable Glanvill who published *Philosophia pia* in 1671. This work explicitly responded to the criticisms made by Baxter, and attempted to clear the Royal Society of the charge of atheism. Glanvill argued that it was the

perverse Opinion of hasty, inconsiderate Men, that the study of Nature is prejudicial to the Interests of Religion; and some who are more zealous than

---

[100] *Correspondence of Henry Oldenburg*, v. 263–5.
[101] Ibid. 519–28.
[102] Ibid. 542.

they are wise endeavour to render the Naturalist suspected of holding secret Correspondence with the Atheist.[103]

Glanvill defended the Royal Society and mechanistic philosophy by arguing that atheists who used mechanism to analyse matter and motion alone were bad scientists. The proper study of mechanism led the true natural philosopher back to a better understanding of God: 'The shallow naturalists rest in nature. But the true Philosopher shows the vanity and unreasonableness of taking up so short; and discovers infinite Wisedom at the end of the Chain of Causes.' Glanvill defended the investigation into matter and motion because 'the more we understand the Laws of Matter and Motion, the more we shall observe the necessity of a wise mind to order the blind and insensible Matter, and to direct the original motions'.[104] Mechanistic philosophy, far from being a vehicle for atheism, was, according to Glanvill, an essential part of the armoury of the modern churchman against the atheist. Never was there a greater need, he argued, for priests to be philosophers. Called upon to defend religion and ethics against the atheist, the saducee and the epicure, ''tis the knowledge of God in his Works that must furnish us with some of the most proper Weapons of Defence'. The atheist must be 'met by a Reason instructed in the knowledge of Things, and fought in their own Quarters, and their Arms must be turned upon themselves'.[105]

Cumberland's De legibus naturae, published in 1672, did precisely this. Cumberland's explicit objective, in developing his scientific approach to the laws of nature, was to show that the 'mechanical' philosophy and the laws of matter and motion did not automatically lead to atheism of a Hobbesian variety. His central concern, expressed in the same language as Glanvill's rallying cry, was to show that

the foundations of piety and moral philosophy were not shaken (as some would insinuate) but strengthened by mathematics and natural philosophy that depends thereon; and that therefore those natural philosophers, who endeavour to overturn the precepts of morality, by weapons drawn from matter and motion, may, by their own weapons, be both opposed and confuted.[106]

Just as he had sought to show that the use of ethical naturalism did not lead automatically to Hobbism, so Cumberland attempted to vindicate natural philosophy from the same charge. Science did not just undermine conventional ethics, as the work of Hobbes had suggested; it could also strengthen it.

For this reason, the De legibus naturae should also be seen as a kind of apologetic work for the Royal Society at a difficult moment in its history,

---

[103] J. Glanvill, Philosophia pia, or, a discourse of the religious temper and tendencies of the experimental philosophy which is profest by the Royal Society, London 1671, 1–2.
[104] Ibid. 24.
[105] Ibid. 139.
[106] Cumberland, DLN, introduction, sect. 29.

similar in many respects to Glanvill's contemporaneous *Philosophia pia*. Cumberland's use of Royal Society science in searching out natural law was carefully attuned to the controversial agendas of the later 1660s and the laws of motion project in particular. Cumberland identified the Royal Society as a body which was capable of showing 'the history of the whole corporeal system exactly conspiring with the laws of matter and motion', using mathematics and geometry as a pattern.[107] Cumberland wanted to place his work within the same project. The *De legibus* explicitly referred to the work of Wren and Huygens on the physical laws of nature.[108] Cumberland sought to reconcile the use of empirical experiment with the deductive use of mathematics. But *De legibus* primarily sought to deal with the question of the causes of the laws of nature, the issue which Neile had raised in 1669, and to which he had supplied a Hobbesian answer.

Cumberland's task would be a difficult balancing act. The mechanical science endorsed by both Hobbes and Cumberland shared the same sceptical, nominalist emphasis upon matter and motion, and, as the reaction of More, Baxter and Casaubon had suggested, many felt that this kind of enquiry led in only one direction. Discrediting Hobbes as a scientist would be one important tactic. But it had to be shown how mechanism and natural philosophy in general could link up with orthodox morality and religion. In doing this Cumberland drew upon a tradition of science very much at odds with Hobbes's nominalist account. These opposed traditions will be discussed in chapter 5.

[107] Ibid. introduction, sect. 3.
[108] Ibid. 2.14.

5

Voluntarism and Natural Philosophy

Thomas Hobbes's use of science attached the stigma of atheism to any project involving the study of matter and motion. However innocuous the Royal Society might claim to be, the theological dangers of a materialist approach to nature generated criticism and hostility. The Society's apologists had to show that Royal Society science, and its mechanistic projects in particular, led in more orthodox ethical directions.

For the supporters of the Society's work, though, there was a serious problem. Hobbes might have been tainted with atheism, but in many ways his science had been logically, if ruthlessly, consistent. He had systematically addressed the question of what a nominalist science of matter and motion could be like. Writers such as Boyle, Locke and even Cumberland shared Hobbes's sense that God was distant and in many ways unknowable. This shared nominalism meant that Hobbes's reductive, causal emphasis on matter and motion made a great deal of sense. The problem was that Hobbes's position had placed extreme boundary conditions upon the ethical and theological relevance of any natural information gleaned this way. Far from using science as a way of expanding man's access to God's truths, Hobbes's natural philosophy had become the means by which that access was systematically contracted, to the point at which it was doubtful that man could have any natural knowledge of God at all. The only certain knowledge of which man was capable was knowledge of matter and motion. The logical consequence of Hobbes's materialism was the systematic exclusion of everything else from ethical discourse, most controversially, spirit, and the nature and attributes of God. For those writers, like Cumberland, who in part shared Hobbes's deeply nominalist theology, the crucial issue was whether matter and motion, mechanism and geometry, could be won back to support an orthodox ethics, and a deeper knowledge of God's will.[1]

This was where Cumberland's *De legibus naturae* was designed to play a part. One of the distinguishing features of the work is its use of Hobbesian science. Although Cumberland draws a great deal of his scientific inspiration from Descartes, in many cases he takes his examples, particularly mechanics,

---

[1] For discussion of this common theological tradition see E. Klaaren, *The religious origins of modern science: belief in creation in seventeenth-century thought*, Grand Rapids 1977; R. Hookyaas, *Religion and the rise of modern science*, Edinburgh 1972; F. Oakley, *Omnipotence, covenant and order: an excursion into the history of ideas from Abelard to Leibniz*, Ithaca 1984; F. Oakley and E. W. Urdang, 'Locke, natural law and God', *Natural Law Forum* xi (1966), 92–109.

directly from Hobbes's own writings, most notably from the *De corpore*. This was intended to demonstrate that Hobbes had used the right theory for the wrong purpose. There was more to this, however, than the simple assertion that Hobbes had got his science 'wrong', although this was, and still is in many cases, a popular and persistent interpretation of Hobbes's natural philosophy. Cumberland was suggesting that the science which Hobbes had used could be consistent with a more orthodox ethical end. His work is thus a reminder that we should not neglect the ethical and theological dimensions of scientific methodology, and that it is as well to remember that these 'non-scientific' factors were crucial to the development of such methodologies and indeed the shape of modern experimental science.

The *De legibus naturae* is a book about how individuals can discover the precepts of natural law and the divine obligation which lies behind it. By using science as a new way of discovering natural law and its obligatory character, Cumberland showed that the new science was consistent with an acceptable ethical framework. By arguing this, Cumberland was contributing to a debate which emerged from the development of natural philosophy during the seventeenth century. This addressed the crucial question of whether natural philosophy was capable of revealing any information about God's will. Could, or should, natural philosophy claim to be able to reveal substantial information about the nature of God's will, and also divine obligation? For writers who accepted a voluntarist and nominalist understanding of the relationship between God and man (both Cumberland and Hobbes), this was not an easy question to answer. The voluntarist distinction between God and the creation posited by this tradition meant that statements about the nature and purposes of God were extremely problematic. But although Cumberland and Hobbes shared aspects of a theology and natural philosophy, the ethical implications which they drew from them were very different. Both men produced a voluntarist science of morality, but while Hobbes sought a radical redefinition of the relationship between science and ethics which put the former in danger of association with atheism, Cumberland attempted to rescue science, and a science of morality, from those implications.

Matter, motion and morality

When Cumberland set out to demonstrate the inadequacies of Hobbes's science, he did so by identifying the source of Hobbes's error in his Epicureanism. Throughout the *De legibus* Hobbes is presented as an Epicurean. Hobbes's master is Epicurus, his opinions are akin to Epicurus, and both acknowledge principles in common. Hobbes is, by turns, Velleius of Cicero's *De natura deorum*, and Torquatus in the *De finibus*.[2] We have already dis-

---

2 Cumberland, *DLN* 1.1; 5.40–1; 5.18; 5.20

cussed Cumberland's use of the debates from Cicero's philosophical works to restructure Hobbes's philosophical identity, but when discussing the use of science in the *De legibus*, the accusation of Epicureanism takes on a still more potent and contemporary significance.

In chapter 5, Cumberland focuses upon the inadequacies of Epicurean natural philosophy, which must be 'resolved into certain principles, which assume many suppositions not to be granted'. Among the 'suppositions' to which Cumberland takes exception is the idea that all things are 'composed of atoms moving through the void with a double natural motion, one perpendicular, the other inclining, and that they are by these motions given an innate gravity'. This atomic hypothesis, which operated without the guiding hand of God, showed that Epicurus 'was a perfect stranger to the laws of motion, nor did he sufficiently consider that remarkable order, connection and dependence, which is conspicuous in those innumerable complicated motions'. The natural order of the universe, rather than Epicurean chaos, should be what natural philosophers studied, particularly through the use of mathematics, the ultimate science of order. But Epicurus' incapacities in this respect led to his poor science. Cumberland could only lament that 'Epicurus was so utter a stranger to mathematics, that he was not sensible of the spherical figure of the earth, contending that it was a plane, which is easily refutable from the first elements of geometry.'[3]

Epicurus' natural philosophy was thus characterised as 'flat-earth' nonsense. It is worth noting, however, that Cumberland's denunciation of Epicurus and his natural philosophy was more than an idle exercise in classical allusion. Although Cumberland may have assured his readers that the bare recital of Epicurus' opinions 'in an age of such great discoveries, is a sufficient confutation', his concentrated efforts to subvert Epicurean science masked a contemporary concern about the popular vogue enjoyed by Neo-Epicurean forms of natural philosophy. Cumberland himself acknowledged that Epicurus' 'herd' was 'lately increased'. Meric Casaubon pointed out in 1670 that Epicurus had shed his traditional odium, and had become a saint to many.[4] Neo-Epicureanism was in fact a credible and influential force in Restoration natural philosophy. It drew some of its strongest English support from Fellows of the Royal Society. This was primarily because Epicureanism, revived and baptised, as it were, appeared to be an attractive natural philosophy to accompany the voluntarist theology which many of the English scientific community, including Hobbes, shared.[5] Cumberland's juxtaposition of Hobbes and Epicurus was significant because it associated Hobbes with Neo-

---

[3] Ibid. 5.41.

[4] Ibid; M. Casaubon, *Of credulity and incredulity in things divine & spiritual*, London 1670, 200.

[5] For the relationship between Epicureanism and voluntarism see M. J. Osler, *The divine will and the mechanical philosophy: Gassendi and Descartes on contingency and necessity in the created world*, Cambridge 1994.

Epicureanism in all of its forms. Hobbes was not alone in his use of a new science to propose a new relationship between science and ethics. Cumberland was not simply combating Hobbes, he was confronting an influential alternative view of science. To understand these relationships, it is necessary to explore the common roots of the association between Epicureanism, theological voluntarism and Hobbism.

Seventeenth-century Neo-Epicureanism, as Cumberland recognised, owed much to the work of Pierre Gassendi (1592–1655).[6] Gassendi began his career as a rising star of the same Scholastic establishment that he would later seek to replace. His latent dissatisfaction with the style of Scholastic scholarship blossomed into open hostility with the first of a projected seven-book series of *Exercitationes paradoxicae adversus Aristoteleos* (1624). Gassendi appealed to sceptical arguments in combating problematic Scholastic doctrine, but, possibly under the influence of Marin Mersenne, this developed into an interest in establishing new, post-sceptical forms of knowledge. This project settled around the possibility of reviving ancient Epicurean doctrines.

To revive Epicurus was a controversial move. The 'Philosopher of the Garden' was without doubt one of the chief villains of Greek philosophy for the Stoically-inclined Christian tradition. The main objectionable features of Epicureanism were its hedonism and its denial of an actively providential deity. The former manifested itself in a philosophy which regarded pleasure, defined as the absence of pain, as the *summum bonum*. Although Epicurus' apologists were keen to emphasis that true pleasure actually derived from the exercise of the traditional virtues, this did not prevent Epicureanism from being associated with the cultivation of more worldly lusts. Epicurus' Garden was popularly portrayed as *hortus deliciarum*, with Epicurus as *patron voluptatis*.

If Epicurean psychology jarred with a Christian emphasis upon moral virtue, Epicurean comments upon the nature of the gods had even less to satisfy a Christian audience. Epicurus did allow that men had some proleptic knowledge of the gods' existence as perfected beings. Unfortunately, this perfection required that Epicurean deities should be removed from the cares and vicissitudes of the physical universe. Epicurean gods were happy, immortal and free from the problems of physical existence, inhabiting the interstices of the universe but fundamentally unconcerned with it.[7] As a result, the universe did not operate according to active divine providence, but according to chance. Epicurus adopted the atomism of Democritus and Leucippus to explain how this occurred. Discrete atomic particles proceeding downwards

---

6   Cumberland, *DLN* 5.41. In discussing Gassendi I have drawn upon the following studies: L. S. Joy, *Gassendi the atomist: advocate of history in an age of science*, Cambridge 1987; B. Brundell, *Pierre Gassendi: from Aristotelianism to a new natural philosophy*, Dordrecht 1987; H. Jones, *Pierre Gassendi 1592–1655: an intellectual biography*, Nieuwkoop 1981; O. Bloch, *La philosophie de Gassendi, nominalisme, materialisme et metaphysique*, The Hague 1971.

7   Lucretius, *De rerum natura*, ed. and trans. C. Bailey, Oxford 1947, I.44–9; II.646–51; VI.146–55; Cicero, *De natura deorum*, trans. H. Rackham, London 1933, I.49–53.

in the universal void were somehow endowed with a swerve, or *clinamen*. This created the conditions for random collision resulting in the formation of larger bodies.[8] The apparently uncaused swerve, and the attribution of the formation of the world to random processes was particularly hard for writers like Cicero to swallow. Epicurus, as Cicero, and later Cumberland, would argue, was a pseudo-philosopher whose natural philosophy was at best the product of ignorance, and at worst of deliberate malice.[9]

As a result, Epicureanism became a throw-away tag for hedonistic, impious excess. But there was at the same time a certain amount of ambiguity associated with Epicurean doctrine. Although Epicurean hedonism could be seen to encourage indulgence in sensual pleasure, it was also defended as justifying the pleasure to be derived from the exercise of virtue.[10] This latent ambiguity lent itself to the textual enthusiasms of early Italian humanists, who used these ideas to suggest that there might be more to the Christian tradition than austere Stoic virtue and the suppression of sensuality. Epicureanism thus became a critical tool for appraising the disparate philosophical ingredients of medieval Christianity.[11] This encouraged some critical effort to elicit the truth about Epicurus, and this kind of interest stimulated Gassendi to look at Epicureanism afresh.

Gassendi sought to exhume the historical Epicurus from the mass of contradictory opinions about the man and his creed. This began with an examination of the Epicurean remains reproduced in book X of Diogenes Laertius' *Lives of the ancient philosophers*, but it soon developed to become a project with more far-reaching aspirations. Recognising the potential of ancient atomism, Gassendi discovered in Epicureanism an alternative to Scholastic physics and metaphysics which would be compatible with the sceptical objections he had raised in his earlier work.

What made Epicureanism peculiarly attractive to Gassendi was the moral agenda which lay behind its use of natural philosophy. Epicurus made no secret of the fact that he regarded natural philosophy as being merely instrumental to his ethical ends. If the *summum bonum* of Epicurean philosophy was a tranquillity characterised by freedom from pain and disturbance, natural philosophy was an essential tool for carrying this out. This ethical objective shaped the character and priorities of Epicurean natural science. The main purpose of natural investigation was to undermine false belief and superstition.[12] An understanding of the proper efficient causes in nature was a vital tool in banishing faulty reasoning and misunderstandings about physical

---

8 Diogenes, *De clarorum philosophorum vitis*, trans R. D. Hicks, London 1925 (hereinafter cited as *Lives*), X.40–2; Lucretius, *De rerum natura* II.216.
9 Cicero, *De finibus* I.iv.17–21.
10 Diogenes, *Lives* X.131–2.
11 L. S. Joy, 'Epicureanism in renaissance moral and natural philosophy', *Journal of the History of Ideas* liii (1993), 573–83.
12 Cicero, *De finibus* I.xix.63.

and metaphysical phenomena. Natural philosophy was tailored to the capabilities and limitations of men rather than reaching beyond human experience or reason.

It was for this reason that Epicurus denied God's activity in the maintenance of the universe. The impossibility of reasoning in anything but abstract terms about the nature of the gods meant that they could be relegated to the interstices of the universe, where they could no longer present any cause of anxiety to mortals. Equally, the Epicurean doctrine that the soul was mortal, and that it would inevitably dissolve after death, quietened men's fear of death and possible judgement in the afterlife.[13] This pragmatic aspect carried through to all aspects of Epicurean natural philosophy; it sought to give rationalised materialistic hypotheses for physical phenomena, but in such a way that it could prevent the harmful assertion of dogmatic opinion.

It is easy to see why this should have appealed to Gassendi given his dissatisfaction with Scholasticism. Scholastic Aristotelianism was the chief purveyor of the kind of discussion which an Epicurean science would banish. Scholastic knowledge created disturbance, confused disputation and empty syllogism, a science which was, in Gassendi's terms, *obscura* or *occulta*. This would be contrasted with an Epicurean science which would be *perspicua*, if a little less ambitious. The Epicurean account of natural philosophy offered the possibility of a reconstruction of knowledge which could prevent superstition, and also cleanse Christianity of its unstable Scholastic baggage. The revival of Epicureanism was thus not simply an exercise in reconstructing a dead philosophy, but an essential task in defence of the true faith.

This view of Gassendi's motivation helps to explain why he undertook what might seem in hindsight to have been a rather difficult and controversial task. The congruence of the moral agenda underlying the Gassendian and Epicurean projects could not disguise the difficulty of importing many ideas which could at times be painfully at odds with Christianity. Nevertheless, Gassendi laboured to achieve a synthesis which could effectively baptise the key elements, offering an antidote to obscurity, dogma and superstition.[14]

An important starting point lay in the reconciliation of God's providential activity with the atomism of Epicurus. Atoms no longer required the uncaused *clinamen* as a starting point for randomly generated natural phenomena because, Gassendi maintained, God had infused motion to particles.[15] Gassendi's voluntarism was the key to preserving the Epicurean idea of a distant and remote deity. Gassendi maintained that God was beyond human understanding, unrestricted by all anthropomorphic considerations of rationality, barring non-contradiction. God could even dispense with

---

13 Lucretius, *De rerum natura* I.311.
14 M. J. Osler, 'Baptising Epicurean atomism: Pierre Gassendi on the immortality of the soul', in M. J. Osler and P. Farber (eds), *Religion, science and world-view: essays in honour of R. S. Westfall*, Cambridge 1985, 163–84.
15 Pierre Gassendi, *Opera omnia*, Lyons 1658, i. 280b.

secondary causes altogether should He will it.[16] This put natural knowledge of God's will beyond man's capabilities. The impossibility of human knowledge of God's will through nature thus gelled with Epicurus' assumption of a remote deity. Natural philosophy could thus only be defined with reference to the subjective sense-based perspective of a man-centred universe. As a result, faith in Christianity could coexist with a sceptical science custommade to reform religious belief.

Epicurus and the English

Through his 'baptism' of Epicureanism, Gassendi had provided the basis for a post-sceptical *scientia* based on a voluntarist theology. This formulation became attractive to English philosophers who shared the same voluntarist theology.[17] Not the least of these was Hobbes, whose acquaintance with Gassendi began during his exile in Paris in the 1640s.[18] Upon reading a manuscript of Gassendi's *Animadversions*, he pronounced the work to be 'as big as Aristotle's philosophy, but much truer and excellent Latin'. It is not hard to see why Hobbes should have been so taken with Gassendi's work; Hobbes and Gassendi shared the same critical humanist enterprise, combining a strongly voluntarist theology with a willingness to deploy the same sceptical tools against the Schoolmen. It is likely that Hobbes had developed his own solipsistic materialism before his exposure to the French philosopher, but Hobbes's scientific elaboration of these ideas owed a great deal to Gassendi's formulation.[19] It should be stressed that Hobbes was not a pure Epicurean, or even a follower of Gassendi, but the ethical and scientific framework which Gassendi had teased out of the Epicurean corpus was something which he shared in part. This connection explains the pointed recurrence of the anti-Epicurean motif in Cumberland.

The common thread linking the two writers was a sceptical voluntarism which rested on the radical distinction between God and the creation. Both Hobbes and Gassendi were concerned to clarify what one could and could not say about the relationship between the two. Hobbes was uncompromising in his assertion of the primacy of God's will in determining the world, but this

[16] Ibid. 309.

[17] For studies of Epicureanism in England see T. F. Mayo, *Epicurus in England 1650–1725*, Dallas 1934; R. F. Kroll, *The material word: literate culture in the Restoration and early eighteenth century*, Baltimore 1991.

[18] For evidence of Hobbes's relationship with Gassendi see L. Sarasohn, 'Motion and morality: Pierre Gassendi, Thomas Hobbes and the mechanical world-view', *Journal of the History of Ideas* xlvi (1985), 363–80; T. Sorrell, 'Seventeenth-century materialism: Gassendi and Hobbes', in G. H. R. Parkinson (ed.), *The renaissance of seventeenth-century rationalism*, London 1993, 235–72.

[19] Although this was not a debt that Hobbes would choose to acknowledge: EW vii. 340–1.

determinism was balanced by the fact that God's will was inscrutable and beyond the analysis of mortal powers of reasoning. As he made clear in his examination of Thomas White's *De mundo* (1643), human reasoning could say little that was relevant to the being of God, as God was not to be defined by the limited understandings of his creatures. God was fundamentally incomprehensible to the finite and inferior understanding of men. Any attempt to incorporate discussion of the nature of God into philosophical discourse would inevitably lead to logical absurdity. Scholastic writers presumed to dispute upon the nature of God and God's will, and this, in Hobbes's view, was not only fruitless but dangerously misleading. The pretension to knowledge of God's will, for Hobbes, was the foundation of priestcraft, and the temporal political authority wielded by clerics.[20]

Hobbes's answer to this problem was a post-sceptical *scientia*. This deployed a nominalist natural philosophy as an antidote to the political, religious and ethical dangers of philosophical obscurity. Natural knowledge would be defined according to the known capacities of man. This meant a reductive emphasis upon the basic building blocks of perception, the apprehension of matter and motion. The subject of philosophy was thus every kind of body that individuals could conceive materially. This rigorously excluded theology, discussion of angels, God or his attributes.[21] Both Hobbes and Gassendi thus subscribed to a view which placed knowledge of God's will beyond the reach of human understanding. A materialist natural philosophy was an essential tool in clarifying the epistemological limits of philosophical discourse.

These common interests came together in their juxtaposed objections to Descartes's *Meditations*, published in 1641. Descartes had argued that knowledge of God's existence and non-deceiving nature offered an escape route from hyperbolic doubt. Hobbes was unhappy with what he saw as Descartes's ungrounded assumptions about the nature of God. It was impossible, he maintained, to talk about the nature and attributes of God in a meaningful way.[22] Descartes, according to Hobbes, could have 'no idea which we can say is the idea of that eternal Being'. Gassendi agreed that the nature and purposes of God's will were beyond the reach of human understanding: 'God is infinitely beyond anything we can grasp, and when our mind addresses itself to contemplate him, it is not only in darkness, but is reduced to nothing. Hence we have no basis for claiming that we have any authentic idea which represents God.'[23]

---

[20] This was a long-running theme that unites all of Hobbes's writing, but these nominalist points are explored in detail in his *Thomas White's De mundo examined*, trans. H. W. Jones, Bradford 1976, chs xxx–xxxviii, pp. 361–480.

[21] Hobbes, *EW* i. 10–11.

[22] Idem, in *Philosophical writings of Descartes*, ii. 171, 180.

[23] Ibid. ii. 287, 305–6.

Both Gassendi and Hobbes found that Descartes's discussion of the *cogito* presented similar problems of tautological obscurity. For Hobbes, the perception that one is thinking can lead only to the acknowledgement of a material existence.[24] In a common association of reductive monism, both writers attacked the Cartesian dichotomy of mind and body on the grounds that the notion of thought acting reflexively harked back to Scholastic tautology. Ideas and thoughts must surely signify a physical relationship with the material world. For Hobbes, thoughts proceeded from the apprehension of motion; for Gassendi, they arose from the senses.[25] For both writers, the discussion of thought abstracted from a material reality was the worst kind of Scholastic absurdity.

Hobbes and Gassendi may have agreed over this nominalist critique of Descartes, but they were to differ irreconcilably over the issue of fatalism. Although both could agree that man was liberated from any kind of rational connection or direct knowledge of God, thereby enjoying a kind of intellectual liberty, Hobbes argued that all physical motion in the universe was fatally determined by the first cause, or God.[26] Controversially, Hobbes had extended this to human actions, traditionally thought to be the province of human free will. Hobbes argued that although an individual might think he or she was free, in fact this was an illusion stemming from an inability to perceive the means by which he or she was determined.[27] Gassendi, who believed in the freedom of the will, could not accept Hobbes's rigorously materialist position. Thus while the two men could agree upon a voluntarist critique of both Scholasticism and Cartesianism, their agreement over the philosophical constitution of 'nature' could conceal substantial differences between their theological beliefs.

It was the similarities between the ideas of Hobbes and Gassendi which would prove to have the greatest significance for Hobbes's critical reception. But Hobbes was not the only English philosopher to be struck by the potential of Epicureanism for the reform of natural philosophy. Leading members of the Royal Society were attracted by Gassendi's formulation, and would develop work similar in many respects to Hobbes's own. In such instances, Epicurean natural philosophy was understood to be an acceptable philosophical expression of a rigorous voluntarist theology, rather than simple atheism. This was one of the principal reasons why Hobbes was not categorised as an atheist by those who were involved in constructing such nominalist forms of natural philosophy. To such writers Hobbes's position was comprehensible in terms of their shared theological foundation.

---

[24] Ibid. ii. 173.
[25] Ibid. ii. 280–2, 286.
[26] For Hobbes's fatalism see L. Damrosch, 'Hobbes as a reformation theologian', *Journal of the History of Ideas* xl (1979), 339–52. Hobbes explicitly associated himself with reformed theologians such as Luther, Melanchthon and Calvin: *EW* v. 64.
[27] Ibid. 55.

Perhaps the most important example of this attitude towards Epicurean-ism and Hobbes is Walter Charleton (1619–1707).[28] In the early 1650s Charleton became the main conduit for the transmission of Epicurean ideas to England with the publication of *The darkness of atheism dispelled by the light of nature* (1654). In that work, Charleton explicitly associated himself with the anti-Scholastic critique offered by Gassendi and Hobbes.[29] He followed this up with his major work, the *Physiologia Epicuro-Gassendo-Charletonia* of 1654, which attempted to market Epicureanism as an effective antidote to superstition and misguided belief. Charleton argued that, with a few correctives, 'the poisonous part of Epicurus's opinion may be converted into one of the most potent Antidotes against our Ignorants: The Quantity of Atoms sufficing to the Motivation of all Concretions and their various Figures and Motions to the Originations of their Qualities and Affections'.[30]

Following Gassendi, Charleton tempered the Epicurean denial of God's providential government by self-consciously adopting the Ciceronian critique.[31] The endorsement of the design argument, however, ran alongside scepticism about how much man could know of God's purposes in creating the world as he had. His approach coincided with Hobbes when he argued that although providence did operate, man was fundamentally ill-equipped to perceive it. As he put it in the *Darkness of atheism*: 'The wayes of God in the World are past finding out . . . there is a Sanctum Sanctorum in the Ark of Providence, into which blind mortality cannot look.'[32] Nature, for Charleton, was 'an immense ocean, wherein are no shadows, but all Depths – men fancy themselves to be Eagles, but are grovelling moles'.[33] The implication of this sceptical assessment of human capacities was that science should focus on what human knowledge could reasonably aspire to know. In a combination of the physics of Gassendi and Hobbes, Charleton suggested that the solution might lie in the sensory investigation of motion.[34]

Charleton held Hobbes in high esteem. In 1650, he referred to Hobbes as that 'Noble Enquirer into Truth', who had published that 'inestimable manual of humane nature' in the same year. This was an opinion that Charleton kept into the Restoration, when, as a Fellow of the Royal Society, he could refer to 'our Incomparable Mr Hobs' in his *Concerning the different wits of men* (1669).[35] He continued to borrow extensively from the full range of

---

28 For Charleton see N. R. Gelbart, 'The intellectual development of Walter Charleton', *Ambix* ix (1971), 149–78; L. Sharp, 'Walter Charleton's early life 1620–59, and his relation to natural philosophy in mid seventeenth-century England', *Annals of Science* xxx (1973), 311–40.
29 Charleton, *Darkness of atheism*, sig. B3r, 10–12.
30 Idem, *Physiologia*, London 1654.
31 Idem, *Darkness of atheism*, 63–78.
32 Ibid. 125.
33 Idem, *Physiologia*, 5.
34 Ibid. 435.
35 Idem, *Deliramenta catarrhi*, London 1650, sig. A1v. For Charleton's many subsequent

the Hobbesian corpus, reproducing Hobbes's natural law theory from the *De cive* in his anonymous production of 1682, *The harmony of natural and positive divine laws*.[36] Charleton's voluntarist framework and Epicurean sympathies meant that he could appreciate Hobbes's ethical theories without recoiling from their supposedly atheistic implications.

Gassendi's approach also impressed other English natural philosophers, particularly Robert Boyle, who wrote to Samuel Hartlib in 1647 that 'Gassendes is a great favourite of mine.'[37] Boyle's approach to natural philosophy was conditioned by his intense theological voluntarism. It is perhaps no surprise, therefore, to find that he should refer favourably to Gassendi's 1649 *Syntagma* in his unpublished papers 'Of ye Atomicall Philosophy', or that Hartlib should pass some of Boyle's early work to an interested Hobbes.[38] Boyle would also be heavily influenced by Charleton's formulation of Gassendi's ideas.[39] Although Boyle was to become one of Hobbes's bitterest opponents after the Restoration, it is worth noting the considerable similarities in their attitudes towards the new natural philosophy, informed, as they were, by a shared theology and critical purpose. Boyle made it clear on many occasions that the radical distinction between God and man made it difficult to obtain information about the nature and intentions of the deity from a knowledge of nature. Such things were properly the province of Scripture.[40] Boyle's fideist, and sceptical, approach to natural philosophy in many ways placed him closer to writers like Charleton and Hobbes than it did to Latitudinarians like Wallis and Wilkins.

Another notable Fellow of the early Royal Society to become involved in the Epicurean revival was John Evelyn. Evelyn translated a portion of Lucretius' *De rerum natura* with the aim of bringing knowledge of Epicureanism into the English language.[41] In exposing the original source of much modern Epicureanism to light, Evelyn had been aware of the dangers of presenting Lucretius 'naked' and sought counsel from his friend Jeremy Taylor. It is clear from Taylor's correpondence with Evelyn that Taylor did not regard Epicure-

---

references to Hobbes see C. D. Thorpe, *The aesthetic theory of Thomas Hobbes*, Michigan 1940, 176–88.

[36] Walter Charleton, *The harmony of natural and positive divine laws*, London 1682, 8–10; Charleton cites ch. iv of the *De cive*, where Hobbes confirmed that the laws of nature were contained in Scripture. This emphasis was dropped in *Leviathan*.

[37] Boyle, *Works*, vi. 77.

[38] R. Westfall, 'On ye atomicall philosophy: unpublished papers of Robert Boyle', *Annals of Science* xii (1956), 111. For Hobbes's involvement see Boyle, *Works*, v. 257; M. Boas, *Robert Boyle*, Cambridge 1958, 17–18.

[39] R. Kargon, 'Robert Boyle and the acceptance of Epicurean atomism in England', *Isis* xlv (1964), 184–92.

[40] Boyle, *Works*, iii. 515. See also J. E. McGuire, 'Boyle's conception of nature', *Journal of the History of Ideas* xxxiii (1972), 523–42.

[41] John Evelyn, *An essay on the first book of T. Lucretius Carus De rerum natura interpreted and made English by John Evelyn*, London 1656.

anism as being necessarily harmful to Christianity.[42] Taylor's sceptically voluntarist outlook and sometimes rather Hobbesian positions have been referred to elsewhere, but the essential point was that an Epicurean *deus absconditus* and a radically nominalist view of the role of natural philosophy were not automatically viewed as atheistic aberrations. Indeed, the process of redefining natural philosophy along Epicurean lines could be taken as essential in purging philosophy of the unwarranted assumptions of the Schoolmen, and in establishing more godly forms of science.

Hobbes was not unique in proposing a nominalist science of matter and motion; many committed Protestant writers, who shared the same theological and ethical objectives could find such a project congenial to their aims. It is noteworthy that during the hard years of the Restoration, when he faced year after year of relentless assault upon his theories, Hobbes would find friends and allies amongst those sympathetic to Epicureanism. Even amongst his enemies, the potency of his arguments about the relationship between science and religion would have an enduring legacy.

English Cartesianism

The other major, and in many ways opposed, continental tradition shaping English natural philosophy was the philosophy of Descartes.[43] Descartes was the dominant influence behind Cumberland's own natural philosophy. There are more references to Descartes in *De legibus naturae* than to any other single philosopher apart from Hobbes. Cumberland's enthusiasm for a mathematised universal science, of ethics as well as physics, had a distinctively Cartesian pedigree. Cumberland refers to the Cartesian notion of *mathesis universalis*, uses Cartesian physical theories and deploys Cartesian analytical geometry to a moral as well as a scientific end.

There is much evidence to suggest that Descartes's work was well-known in Cambridge by the time that Cumberland arrived at Magdalene in 1649.[44] Henry More, at Christ's College, had become fascinated with Cartesianism in the mid 1640s, and, through the mediation of Samuel Hartlib, had begun corresponding with Descartes from 1648. More had expressed almost embar-

---

42 *Diary and correspondence of John Evelyn*, ed. W. Bray, London 1908, iii. 218.

43 On the reception of Descartes see S. P. Lamprecht, 'The role of Descartes in seventeenth-century England', *Studies in the History of Ideas* iii (1935); M. Nicolson, 'The early stages of Cartesianism in England', *Studies in Philology* xxvi (1929), 356–74; J. E. Saveson, 'Descarte's influence on John Smith, Cambridge Platonist', *Journal of the History of Ideas* xx (1959), 255–63; A. Armitage, 'René Descartes (1596–1650) and the early Royal Society', *Notes and Records of the Royal Society* viii (1950), 1–19; A. Gabbey, 'Philosophia Cartesiana triumphata: Henry More 1646–71', in T. M. Lennon (ed.), *Problems of Cartesianism*, Montreal 1982, 171–250.

44 J. B. Mullinger, *The University of Cambridge from the election to the chancellorship in 1626 to the decline of the Platonist movement*, Cambridge 1911.

rassing praise for the French philosopher, when he wrote that 'all the masters of the secrets of Nature, who have ever existed, or who now exist seem, in comparison with you, mere dwarfs and pygmies'. What attracted More was the high degree of systematic coherence of Cartesian science. Descartes's ideas were, he observed, 'so co-ordinated and so consistent with each other and with nature, that the human mind and reason could hardly hope for a more agreeable and joyful sight'.[45]

This consistency fitted well with More's syncretic Platonist project to establish a universal synthesis of knowledge. Descartes's concern to demonstrate the existence of God, and the distinction between spirit and matter, within the context of a new form of universal natural philosophy, formed a useful adjunct to More's scheme. This initial enthusiasm would wane as More became increasingly aware of the drawbacks of Cartesian metaphysics; Descartes's rigid distinction between *res cogitans* and *res extensa* had the effect of separating the realms of spirit and matter which More sought so assiduously to bring together. By the time he came to write the *Divine dialogues* in the 1660s, More saw Cartesian mechanism as another route to the dangerously reductive emphasis upon matter and motion which he had sought to combat in Hobbes.[46]

Although More's response to, and disillusion with, Descartes is the best documented in an English context, it should be noted that his often idiosyncratic views were not shared by all his Cambridge contemporaries. It was suggested in chapter 2 that some of the novel adaptations of naturalism in Cambridge during the 1640s and 1650s proceeded from Protestant Scholastic ideas. For those sympathetic to this approach, the work of Descartes was assimilated in other ways. The young Isaac Barrow, for example, a near contemporary of Cumberland, was also impressed with Cartesianism's distinctive rigour. In his Master of Arts oration of 1652, he stated that Descartes had given the best philosophical account to date by virtue of his 'extraordinary skill as a mathematician, his unwearied thought concerning the nature and use of meditation, his judgement stripped of all prejudice and disengaged from the snares of popular error'. Barrow also commended Descartes's empirical work and the clarity of his presentation which allowed him 'not only to think clearly and simply, but also to explain his own mind fully and lucidly in the fewest possible words'. Such praise, however, was mitigated by Barrow's critique of the French philosopher's *a priori* procedure:

> it seemed good to him, not to learn from things, but to impose his own laws on things . . . first, he collected and set up metaphysical truths which he considered suitable to his theory from notions implanted in his own mind . . . next, from these, he descended to general principles of nature, and then generally

45 Henry More, *Collection of several philosophical writings*, London 1662, 61.
46 Idem, *Divine dialogues*, preface.

advanced to particulars which, forsooth, he had framed without consulting Nature.[47]

Barrow's theological voluntarism made him as wary of Cartesian intellectualism as both Hobbes and Gassendi had been. The essential difference, however, was that Barrow's empiricism remained wedded to the Scholastic idea that one could and should obtain knowledge from the 'nature of things' before anything else. In this respect Barrow was close to the language of Scholastic naturalism which was present in the sermons of Benjamin Whichcote. Like Whichcote, and Culverwell, Barrow was influenced by Neo-Scholastic learning, and writers like Suarez.[48] Culverwell had similar grounds for being critical of Descartes. His *Discourse*, published one year before Barrow's oration, contained one of the earliest English critiques of Descartes along the same lines. Culverwell argued that 'if Des-Cartes, the French Philosopher resolves all his assurances into thinking what he thinks, why not into thinking what he sees?'[49]

Although there was a reluctance to endorse the detail of Cartesian metaphysics, it was possible to accept much of Descartes's mechanical theory on the grounds that it was presented as hypothesis only. This was crucial to the endorsement and use of Cartesianism by English natural philosophers. Such hypotheses allowed explanatory and causal models to be devised without suggesting that the model proposed was a definitive representation of the natural world. The empiricism required by a nominalist theology could thus be rendered compatible with *a priori* theory, provided that such theory was only accepted as probable and hypothetical. As a result, Cartesian suggestions about the nature of matter and the operation of vortices could be accepted provisionally, but could be replaced and updated as more empirical information improved the knowledge available. This provides an important qualification to labelling Cumberland as a Cartesian. Cumberland, like Glanvill and Parker, consistently qualifies his Cartesian borrowings on this basis. 'Other hypotheses', Cumberland noted in the *De legibus*, 'according to the laws of matter and motion, nevertheless may and ought to be invented, if the appearance of things so require.'[50]

More important than the detail of Descartes's theory, however, was the methodological impact of his suggestions for a universal and exact science of proportions based upon geometry, *mathesis universalis*. Descartes had remarked in the *Regulae* of 1628 that mathematics offered a framework for analysing any kind of order or measure. This made him realise that 'there must be a general science which explains all the points that can be raised

---

[47] Barrow, *Works*, ix. 79–104.

[48] As Abraham Hill recorded in his *Life* of Barrow, preceding the 1687 editions of his works: Isaac Barrow, *Works*, ed. J. Tillotson, London 1686–7, i, pp. xxxvii–liv.

[49] Culverwell, *Discourse*, 126.

[50] Cumberland, *DLN*, introduction, sect. 29.

concerning order and measure irrespective of the subject matter'.[51] The guiding mathematical influence behind *scientia moralis* in *De legibus naturae* is this notion of *mathesis universalis*. Cumberland wrote that 'The science of morality and politics both can and ought to imitate the analytic art (in which I comprehend not only the extraction of roots, but also the whole doctrine of specious arithmetic or algebra) as the noblest pattern of science.'[52]

Cumberland's elaboration of *scientia moralis* will be dealt with in greater detail in chapter 6, but it should be noted that Descartes's new mathematics and its potential application to natural philosophy opened the possibility of extending the conclusions of science beyond the limits of a simple nominalism. Mathematics, combined with experimental knowledge, could become a new key to deciphering nature, and a new way of apprehending God's will. It is striking that the first English writers to explore this constructive potential of Cartesian geometry were scholars, like Cumberland, associated with the new Cambridge naturalism. John Wallis (1616-1703), the premier English exponent of analytical geometry, had been taught by Whichcote at Emmanuel. Wallis had defended Aristotelian empiricism against the Platonists Peter Sterry and Lord Brooke in his 1643 work *Truth tried*.[53] As Savilian Professor of Geometry from 1649, Wallis would take a leading role in developing the new mathematical sciences. His colleague, Seth Ward (1617–89), of Sidney Sussex College, would apply geometrical principles to planetary movement;[54] he would also go on to write one of the most famous defences of the use of philosophy in religion, the *Philosophicall essay towards an eviction of the being and attributes of God* (1652). With so much enthusiasm for the possibilities of mathematical science, it is easy to see why Hobbes's claim to have arrived at a demonstrative, and mathematical science of politics and ethics should have found such a ready audience amongst the scientific community.

Behemoth against Leviathan[55]

Hobbes's work appeared at first to promise much for English natural philosophy. Before 1651 Hobbes had deployed his nominalism to make useful points about political sovereignty, hinting at the development of a fully-formed

---

51 *Philosophical writings of Descartes*, i. 19.
52 Cumberland, *DLN* 4.4.
53 John Wallis, *Truth tried*, Cambridge 1643, 49.
54 Seth Ward, *Astronomiae geometricaes*, Oxford 1656; Cumberland refers to this work in the *De legibus naturae*: *DLN* 4.4.
55 This was Hobbes's own suggestion for the title of an anti-Hobbesian work. Both creatures came from Hobbes's favourite Book of Job, which summed up a great deal of his thinking on the subject of God and his relationship to natural justice (or the lack of it): *EW* v. 27; P. Springborg, 'Hobbes's biblical beasts: Leviathan and Behemoth', *Political Theory* xxiii (1995), 353–75.

post-Scholastic science founded on mathematically demonstrated principles. His considerable reputation, however, was based upon promise rather than achievement, so that it was far from certain what Hobbes's scientific approach would look like. Early responses suggest that Hobbes was viewed with excitement as an English version of Descartes and Gassendi rolled into one. In the preface to the 1650 edition of the first half of the *Elements of law*, published under the title *Humane nature*, the writer (who was probably Seth Ward), commended Hobbes's philosophy as being constructed 'upon such principles and in such order as are used by men conversant in demonstration'.[56] Ralph Bathurst, President of Trinity College and a friend of Ward and John Wilkins, contributed a poem comparing Hobbes to Archimedes. In an enthusiastic letter to Hobbes he wrote that

> I hope your learned booke of Optickes, and that other de Corpore, if it be now yet finished, may no longer lie concealed: especially since now the best wits, as well here as in other countries, are so greedy to listen after works of that nature, and to vindicate themselves from the superficiall doctrines of the schools.[57]

This kind of endorsement soon rebounded severely upon the English natural philosophers and their ambition to promote the new science. The publication of *Leviathan* irreversibly changed the public image of Hobbes and his new methods. Hobbes's philosophical nominalism, previously accepted by many, was now presented shorn of the intellectual safeguards which had shielded work like the *De cive* from accusations of atheism. Scriptural and clerical authority was systematically undermined, obligation to the laws of nature enervated, and all placed within the matrix of an uncompromising materialism. Philosophy should deal only in propositions composed of definitions which could be perfectly understood by those using them. To meet that requirement, such definitions had to be based ultimately upon the reductive experience of matter in motion.

This ruthless closure of philosophical discourse was a response to the linguistic confusion which Hobbes felt had bred conflict and civil war. Loose speculation and inexact definition had led to 'wandering amongst innumerable uncertainties; and their end, contention, and sedition and contempt'.[58] Of particular concern to Hobbes was the manner in which religious language had become infected with such errors of signification. Clergymen could talk of incorporeal substance (for Hobbes, a contradiction in terms),[59] and confidently assert their knowledge of the attributes and the will of God. In these ways, clerics had fortified their privileged status as interpreters of God's will, and with it their political power. Hobbes's philosophy was designed to be the

---

56 Hobbes, *EW* iv, 'To the Reader'.
57 *Correspondence of Thomas Hobbes*, i. 180–1.
58 Hobbes, *Leviathan*, 36.
59 Ibid. 30.

antidote to this clerical perversion of natural knowledge, particularly of the knowledge that men could claim to have of God. A proper understanding of God could only yield an acknowledgement of his incomprehensible nature. Any other kind of discussion was positively blasphemous:

> disputing of Gods nature is contrary to his Honour: For it is supposed, that in this naturall Kingdome of God, there is no other way to anything, but by natural Reason; that is, from the Principles of naturall Science; which are so farre from teaching us any thing of Gods nature, as they cannot teach us our own nature, nor the nature of the smallest creature living. And therefore, when men out of Principles of natural Reason, dispute of the Attributes of God, they but dishonour him: For in the attributes which we give to God, we are not to consider the signification of Philosophicall Truth; but the signification of Pious Intention, to do him the greatest Honour we are able.[60]

Hobbes's use of reason and demonstration effectively closed down extensive theological speculation. Clerical members of the scientific community were understandably concerned that such a position compromised the position of natural philosophy. Although Hobbes's theological position had much in common with the nominalist tenor of contemporary natural philosophy, the *Leviathan* went too far, and brought natural philosophy itself into disrepute. In one of the earliest responses to Hobbes, in his *Philosophicall essay* of 1652, Seth Ward quickly retracted his apparent endorsement of Hobbes's project. He carefully explained that he had 'a very great respect and a very high esteem' for Hobbes, but

> he must ingenuously acknowledge that a great proportion of it is founded on a belief & expectation concerning him, and an expectation of those Philosophicall and Mathematicall works, which he hath undertaken; and not so much what he has published to the world, and that he does not see reason from thence to recede from anything upon his Authority, although he shall avouch his Discourse to proceed Mathematically. That he is sure he hath much injured the Mathematicks, and the very name of Demonstration, by bestowing it upon some of his discourses, which are exceedingly short of the evidence and truth which is required to make a discourse able to bear that reputation.[61]

Hobbes had gone further than anyone had expected, and had pushed his nominalism to extremes. Ward could agree with Hobbes that discussion of God and his attributes was difficult. Hobbes could argue that he himself did not have knowledge of God. But to elevate that position to the status of a science was not acceptable:

> to imagine that no man hath an apprehension of the god-head, because he may not perhaps think of him so much as to tear a strip off the corporeal

---

[60] Ibid. 252.
[61] Ibid. sig A3r.

circumstances wherewith he doth use to fancy him; or to conclude every man under the sentence of being non-sensicall, whosoever have spoken or written of incorporeal circumstances, he doth conceive of things not to be made good by the authority of Mr Hobs.[62]

Ward spelled out the difference with a revealing simile in which he likened their common endeavours to those of astronomers looking at Jupiter; Hobbes with his naked eyes, Ward using the telescope of his reason to overcome the limitations of his natural condition in order to make out the features of the planet: 'The reason why M. H[obbes] denies those beings whilest other men apprehend them, is that he looks at them with his Fancy, they with their minde.'[63] Hobbes may have proceeded from similar premises to Ward about the importance of empirical investigation, but Hobbes's absolutist conclusions, which denied scope for any meaningful discussion about God and his nature, were beyond the pale.

Ward's own account of what science could do was outlined in the rest of the *Essay*. Against atheists, epicures and sceptics, Ward urged the use of empiricism that was Aristotelian in inspiration and which was designed to prove that spirits and attributes of God 'are from the Creation of the World clearly seen'.[64] Ward suggested that, through an empirical examination of nature, the understanding 'climbs up by degrees, and through the continued chain of causes till it come to that link which is fastened to the chair of God'. In following such lines of enquiry, man 'attains to a kinde of mastery over the works of Nature . . . and so imitates God and nature in great and marvellous conclusions'. This 'imitation' of God recalls Whichcote's idea of 'deiformity'. Through an exploration of nature, individuals could acquire knowledge of God and his attributes, precisely the kind of knowledge that Hobbes had denied was possible.[65]

Ward's *Essay* became a bestseller, running to five editions by 1677. It was widely quoted both against Hobbes, and in support of the new science. Joseph Glanvill saw it as the original anti-Hobbesian apologetic for natural philosophy, and he dedicated his *Philosophia pia* (1671) to Ward for that reason. Cumberland, too, referred to Ward's work in defence of the idea of incorporeality of the mind.[66]

By 1652, however, it was clear that in spite of Ward's protests, Hobbes's extreme nominalism had compromised the moral status of the new sciences. This made it imperative that his influence be neutralised. Ward, together with John Wilkins, renewed the assault in 1654 in the *Vindiciae academiarum*. The work was a response to the critique of university learning in John Webster's *Academiarum examen*. Webster's book had questioned the utility of

---

62 Ibid. A3v.
63 Ibid. A4r.
64 Ibid. 13.
65 Ibid. 65.
66 Glanvill, *Philosophia pia*, dedication; Cumberland, *DLN* 2.1.

university learning, a position which he to some extent shared with Hobbes, who had decried the universities as the breeding grounds of Scholasticism and clerical conspiracy.[67] Ward and Wilkins took the opportunity offered to attack *Leviathan* as well as Webster.

The attack was designed to vindicate and distinguish university natural philosophy from Hobbes's project, which was portrayed as eccentric, ill-informed and out of date. Wilkins was still prepared to concede that Hobbes was a man of 'good ability and solid parts', but otherwise he was 'highly magisterial, and one that will be very angry with all that do not presently submit to his dictates, and for advancing of his own skill, cares not what unworthy reflexions he casts upon others'.[68] These unworthy reflexions included his assaults upon the universities, which were, according to Ward and Wilkins, simply inaccurate. Modern natural philosophy was alive and well, they argued; furthermore, Hobbes's own ideas lagged way behind in terms of novelty and importance. Ward and Wilkins systematically undermined Hobbes's claims to innovation and influence by portraying him as a plagiarist and a fraud. His novel doctrine of motion was, they argued, a corrupted amalgam of the work of Gassendi, Descartes and Kenelm Digby. Ward and Wilkins claimed that his optical theories were stolen from Walter Warner.[69]

Aside from any dubious truth any such accusations might contain, charging Hobbes with plagiarism was a useful tactic; it allowed Ward and Wilkins to acknowledge the worth in Hobbes's scientific writings but removed his authority from it. This process of prising Hobbes's name away from his methods and arguments would become an important part in cleansing natural philosophy of his influence.

Hobbes's nominalist natural philosophy was published as the *De corpore* in 1655. It declared that the subject of philosophy was properly every body of which man could conceive. Discussion of God or his attributes was rigorously excluded. Hobbes argued that it was impossible to subject God to rational analysis because he was eternal and ungenerable, with no components to divide or compound. Where there were no bodies, he argued, there could be no ratiocination, and thus discussion of God was not a subject for philosophers, but only for theologians and the words of Scripture.

The study of matter and, more importantly, matter in motion was presented as the definitive means of analysing all phenomena.[70] For Hobbes, the only true sciences were those capable of definitional certainty. Geometry was the prime example of such a science, because it could be known from its causes (διοτι) which were precise definitions. This was contrasted with natural knowledge drawn from physical effects (οτι), which could only be

---

67 Hobbes, *Leviathan*, 236–7.
68 Seth Ward and John Wilkins, *Vindiciae academiarum*, Oxford 1654, 6–7.
69 Ibid. 53.
70 Hobbes, *EW* i. 70.

hypothetical and probabilistic assumptions.[71] Hobbes argued that the task of the natural philosopher was to establish analysis of natural phenomena upon true first principles, which enabled knowledge of causal mechanisms. These true first principles proceeded from the observation of matter in motion. Natural investigation was thus limited to explanations or hypotheses based upon the first principles of matter in motion. In so doing, Hobbes attempted to provide a certain causal understanding of natural phenomena. Rational explanations could be created for a consistently materialist account of the physical world. These would banish the obscurity and inconsistencies of Scholastic accounts.

Hobbes took the opportunity to attack Ward for what he portrayed as Scholastic loyalties. Ward had discussed the mathematical concepts of infinity and eternity in his *Essay*. His purpose there was to prove, mathematically, that the world could not be eternal. Such words were, for Hobbes, classic examples of Scholastic absurdity because they were literally meaningless. Hobbes wrote that 'as soon as they are entangled in the words infinite and eternal, of which we have in our mind no idea, but that of our own insufficiency to comprehend them, they are forced either to speak something absurd, or, which they love, to hold their peace'. Hobbes warned Ward and his colleagues to stick to Scripture, while he discoursed about true natural philosophy.[72]

The *De corpore* confirmed the dangers of the *Leviathan*. Writers like Ward and Wilkins had hoped that science might offer new possibilities for extending and confirming the conclusions of conventional ethics and theology. Hobbes's natural philosophy seemed to have been turned into an instrument with the express design of reconstituting the basis of the relationship between science and religion. The university scientists needed to show that Hobbes's natural philosophy was either erroneous, or misused, in order to prove that their own work was not a threat to religion.

Hobbes's opponents were not slow to take up the challenge. John Wallis, Savilian Professor of Geometry, and a friend and colleague of Ward, immediately attacked the mathematical foundations of the *De corpore* in his *Elenchus geometriae Hobbianae* (1655). In his dedicatory epistle to John Owen, then vice-chancellor of Oxford, Wallis argued that Hobbes needed to be opposed for three reasons. The first was that Hobbes's mathematical conceit should be deflated. Hobbes, Wallis made it clear, was not to be regarded as a mathematician of any stature at all. The second and related point was that in doing this 'others less skilled in geometry, may know that there is no more to be feared from this Leviathan upon this account, since its armour . . . is easily pierced'. Mathematics would be decoupled from the ethical implications of *Leviathan*. Wallis also wished to attack Hobbes 'so that outsiders (if they saw

---

[71] Ibid. i. 66–7.
[72] *De corpore* XXVI. i.

him maintain such things unchecked) might not think all men who practise Geometry here are like him'.[73]

Wallis's attack was designed to systematically undermine Hobbes's claims to scientific eminence, but also to clear those sciences from their association with him. The *Elenchus* would be the opening salvo in a recurrent conflict between the two men lasting until Hobbes's death in 1679. The peculiar bitterness of the dispute has often left historians puzzling over why both men should have persisted for so long when, with hindsight, it is possible to see that Hobbes was mistaken in much of his mathematics, and Wallis clearly had the better of the technical disputes. There was more at stake, however, than the abusive wrangling of two inveterately stubborn individuals, and hindsight, in this instance, can be misleading.

For Hobbes, his new form of geometrical demonstration was the finest example of what a nominalist science could achieve. It offered demonstrably certain knowledge. The creation and interaction of lines could be clearly conceived as a product of matter in motion, whose properties could be demonstrated with the highest level of certainty. The complicated diagrams of complex geometrical constructions which adorned the pages of the *De corpore* were demonstrations that Hobbes felt carried an inescapably compelling proof.

Wallis, by contrast, was the foremost English exponent of Cartesian analytical geometry. He had gone further than any of his contemporaries in applying the new methodology which was based upon the Cartesian insight that geometrical relationships could be expressed through arithmetical and algebraic analysis. This had resulted in his work upon conic sections, *De sectionibus conicis* (1655), and also his pioneering work on the integration of infinite quantities into arithmetical operations, the *Arithmetica infinitorum* (1655). It is emblematic of the philosophical distance between Wallis and Hobbes that the former could incorporate symbolic representation of infinity, decimal fractions and irrational numbers into arithmetical operations. Such a level of abstraction was anathema to Hobbes for whom the whole basis of Cartesian analysis was flawed by its reliance upon symbols and algebraic representations of geometrical constructions. Such things could only be used as mathematical shorthand: 'Though it be very easy to discourse by symbols of very remote propositions; yet whether such discourse deserves to be thought very profitable, when made without any idea of the things themselves, I know not.'[74] Hobbes's typically renaissance view of mathematics required that his demonstrations should be represented by line and point, rather than esoteric and obscure symbols, part of his nominalist campaign to reform natural philosophy.[75]

---

[73] John Wallis, *Elenchus geometriae Hobbianae*, London 1655, epistle dedicatory.
[74] Hobbes, *EW* i. 315–16.
[75] For Hobbes's mathematics see H. Grant, 'Hobbes and mathematics', in T. Sorrell (ed.), *The Cambridge companion to Hobbes*, Cambridge 1996, 108–28.

In the *Elenchus*, Wallis focused his attack upon Hobbes's claim that he had squared the circle using the methods he had described in the *De corpore*. Wallis ridiculed Hobbes's efforts, picking up on the fact that Hobbes had produced not one, but three, attempts at solving the problem by his new method with varying degrees of failure. Some of Wallis's palpable hits forced Hobbes to tidy his treatment of the problem in the English *De corpore* of 1656, but Hobbes inevitably detected a more sinister agenda behind both the attack, and the style of mathematics that Wallis was using.

In his *Six lessons to the professors of mathematics* (1656), an attack on both Ward and Wallis, Hobbes identified the Oxford mathematician's crusade against him as the latest recrudescence of Scholasticism. Hobbes had already written to Sorbière in 1655 that his controversy was not merely scientific, but ideological. His dispute was 'with all the Ecclesiastics of England at once, on whose behalf Wallis wrote against me'.[76] For Hobbes the mathematical assault was a priestly attempt to win back science for Scholastic obscurity and irrational dogma. In particular Hobbes identified the introduction of the concept of infinity by the Presbyterian Wallis as a tell-tale marker of a new Scholasticism. Infinite quantities were fundamentally inconceivable, and thus could have no place in the one demonstrably certain science.[77] If they were to be allowed, they would become tools enabling the Schoolmen to perpetuate confusion and their own false authority in mathematics and all forms of science. Hobbes regarded the *Arithmetica infinitorum* as 'that scurvy book', which, like Wallis's work on conic sections, was covered with the 'scab of symbols', poisoning the study of geometry and reducing it to yet another arcanum of Scholasticism.[78] Hobbes was not slow to identify what he saw as a priestly conspiracy on the part of the new Schoolmen to pervert the development of natural philosophy for their own ends. He connected their science to their new forms of rational religion:

> your arguing from natural reason the incomprehensible mysteries of religion, and your malicious writing, are very shrewed signs that you are none of those which you say do freely philosophize; but that your philosophy and your language are under the servitude, not of the Roman religion, but of the ambition of some other doctors, that seek, as the Roman clergy did, to draw all human learning to the upholding of their power ecclesiastical.[79]

Although Hobbes's anticlerical paranoia does much to dramatise his accounts of his opponents, neither Wallis or Ward were averse to being labelled as

---

[76] *Correspondence of Thomas Hobbes*, i. 429.

[77] For Hobbes's discussion of infinite quantities and their problematic status see P. Moncosu and E. Vailati, 'Torricelli's infinitely long solid and its philosophical reception in the seventeenth century', *Isis* lxxxii (1991), 50–70.

[78] Hobbes, *EW* vii. 238, 329. For Hobbes's many comments on the dangers of symbols see ibid. 242, 245, 247, 261.

[79] Ibid. 348.

School-divines as well as natural philosophers. In 1656 Ward, who had already signalled the compatibility of the old and new philosophies in the *Essay* and the *Vindiciae*, produced a section-by-section rebuttal of the Hobbesian corpus in his *In Thomae Hobbii philosophiam exercitatio epistolica*, dedicated to John Wilkins. Ward reaffirmed his belief in the incorporeality of the mind and soul, and the possibility of establishing the nature and attributes of God.[80] In response to Hobbes's charge that he was 'carrying double', a mutually exclusive mixture of theology and natural philosophy, Wallis responded by arguing that Hobbes's alternative was completely unacceptable. By collapsing theology into a nominalist natural philosophy, one could only be left with two equally unpalatable consequences; either God did not exist, or if he did, then he had a material nature. One could, suggested Wallis, be both a mathematician and a School-divine, provided that one was careful to observe the proper relationship between the two spheres.[81]

The dispute between Hobbes and his Oxford antagonists thus turned upon their contrasting views of the proper function of a nominalist natural philosophy. Hobbes's science was predicated upon the need to generate the kind of closure which could prevent the priestly manipulation of obscure knowledge. For his clerical opponents, by contrast, the possibilities of new sciences offered a more expansive and open-ended form of natural philosophy. Cartesian analysis allowed mathematics to be used as a way of investigating all kinds of natural relationships from geometrical problems to the movements of heavenly bodies. For Isaac Barrow, mathematics allowed man to comprehend 'the huge Fabrick of the Universe, admire and contemplate the wonderful Beauty of the Divine Workmanship'.[82] As Cumberland would later hope to prove, the new mathematised sciences could offer a new way to perceive the operation of God in the world, and to demonstrate the existence of his natural laws. Both approaches had the study of matter and motion in common, but Hobbes's extreme nominalism required his exposure as an atheist.

It is important to remember, however, that given the political and theological context to this debate, the clerics were far from being conventional in this view, and that Hobbes was far from being completely unacceptable in opposing it. This becomes clearer if one considers the shaky political credentials of Hobbes's major opponents. These reveal them not to be the comfortable establishment figures that their writings might suggest. Ward and Wallis were both Cambridge men who had been intruded into their Chairs after the ejection of Royalist scholars John Greaves and Peter Turner.[83] Wallis had

---

[80] Seth Ward, *In Thomae Hobbii philosophiam exercitatio epistolica*, Oxford 1656, cited in Cumberland, *DLN* 2.1.
[81] John Wallis, *Due correction for Mr Hobbes*, Oxford 1656, 31–3.
[82] Isaac Barrow, *The usefulnesse of mathematical learning*, trans. J. Kirkby, London 1684, p. xxx. See also M. Feingold, 'Isaac Barrow; divine, scholar and mathematician', in M. Feingold (ed.), *Before Newton*, Cambridge 1991, 54.
[83] *DNB*.

gained notoriety for his services to the Assembly of Divines, and also for the use he had made of his expertise in cryptography.[84] Equally, Wilkins trod a narrow path, alienating Royalists for his personal connections with the Cromwell family, and gaining the odium of republicans for sheltering Royalists at Wadham.[85] To orthodox Schoolmen like Alexander Rosse, men like Wilkins were promoting novel doctrine at least as dangerous as Hobbes's own.[86] To more radical Protestant dons, the new emphasis upon the capabilities of man's reason and the stress upon natural morality could be more suspicious than the radical nominalism of a writer like Hobbes. Just as Whichcote had come under fire from Anthony Tuckney for his attachment to Scholastic moralism, so Ward and his colleagues in Oxford, according to his biographer, were subject to criticism from 'peevish people' to whom they were 'mere moral men'.[87] The rational divines were an embattled minority, suspicious to both Independents and Royalists alike, whose view of Hobbes was far from being universally accepted.

This can be seen in the critical appreciation that Hobbes's own work gained in some quarters during the 1650s. Hobbes himself had noted in the *Six lessons* that his doctrine was generally well received and his opponents were in a minority.[88] Athough Hobbes was not inclined to be modest when it came to his own popularity, the evidence does suggest that he was finding an approving audience. The level of concerned response to the *Leviathan* betrayed this anxiety. Alexander Rosse feared that he might be attacked himself for opposing such a fashionable work.[89] William Lucy in 1656 noted 'this book [*Leviathan*] I find admir'd by many Gentlemen'.[90] In 1657 George Lawson commented that he had undertaken the refutation of Hobbes because 'many gentlemen and young students in the Universities were revealing a distressing tendency to take the Leviathan as a rational piece'.[91]

---

84 Wallis was rumoured to have used his skills to decipher Royalist correspondence after the Battle of Naseby, a charge capitalised upon by Henry Stubbe in his *A severe equiry into the late oneirocritica*, London 1657. A further cause of distress to Royalists was Wallis's acquisition of the post of *custos archivorum* over the Royalist candidate Richard Zouch, again challenged by Stubbe in *The Savilian Professor's case stated*, London 1658.
85 Wilkins had replaced the ejected John Pitt at Wadham in 1648. He married Cromwell's sister in 1656: *DNB, s.v.*
86 Rosse responded to Wilkins's popularisations of Galilean thought, *A discourse concerning a new planet*, Oxford 1640, with *The new planet no planet, or, the earth no wandring star, except in the wandring heads of Galileans*, London 1646. Although Rosse's position might seem ridiculous, Wilkins's interests were nevertheless exotic for a churchman.
87 Walter Pope, *Life of the Right Reverend Father in God, Seth, lord bishop of Salisbury*, London 1697, 43.
88 Hobbes, *EW* vii. 333.
89 Alexander Rosse, *Leviathan drawn out with a hook*, London 1653, preface
90 William Lucy, *Observations, censures and confutations of divers errors in the first two chapters of Mr Hobbes his Leviathan*, London 1656, sig. A3r.
91 George Lawson, *An examination of the political part of Mr Hobbs his Leviathan*, London 1657, sig A2r.

It was not only the students of the universities who were finding much to admire in Hobbes. His dispute with the Presbyterian Wallis attracted allies amongst the ascendant Independent faction at Oxford. In 1656 Hobbes began a correspondence with Henry Stubbe, the future critic of the Royal Society, then under-librarian at the Bodleian Library and client of John Owen, the Independent vice-chancellor. Stubbe assisted Hobbes in his attacks on Wallis and even began a Latin translation of the Leviathan.[92] To Stubbe and his Independent colleagues, Hobbes's anticlericalism could be used to combat Presbyterianism within the university.[93] This was not the first, or indeed the last time, that Hobbes's ideas would be endorsed by Independent writers, capitalising upon Hobbes's anticlericalism and his loathing for Presbyterians like Wallis.

It was also far from clear that Hobbes's fellow natural philosophers and mathematicians recoiled from the implications of Hobbesian science in the way that Ward, Wilkins and Wallis had done. Alternative neo-Epicurean philosophies showed a similar distrust of Cartesian approaches. Wallis's application of algebraic and arithmetical ideas was not universally accepted, even by more generally sympathetic writers such as Robert Boyle. Like Hobbes, Boyle was consistently sceptical about the esoteric use of mathematical symbols. Such practices reduced the possible membership of the scientific community to mathematical experts and generated unnecessary obscurity.[94] This is a point of some interest when modern opinion has been so ready to condemn Hobbes's natural philosophy upon the basis of his mathematical ineptitude. Hobbes maintained connections with Sir Charles Scarborough's circle of mathematicians into the late 1650s,[95] so that it is certainly not the case that his conflict with the notoriously difficult Wallis automatically excluded him from serious discussion. Hobbes also retained the friendship of individuals such as William Harvey, William Petty, Walter Charleton and John Evelyn, for whom his opinions, if a little extreme, were not as impossibly unorthodox as his clerical critics might suggest. The controversies of the 1650s thus took place between new and conflicting accounts of what a voluntarist science might be. Both accounts shared nominalist premises which overlapped in a common emphasis upon the importance of studying matter and motion, but they crucially differed over the role which such an analysis should play with regard to theology.

What followed in the 1660s has often been portrayed as a long-running battle in which the solidly Latitudinarian Royal Society repeatedly came to blows

92 Correspondence of Thomas Hobbes, i. 271–2.
93 Ibid. 383–4. For further discussion of this point see Jacob, Henry Stubbe, 21–2.
94 S. Shapin, 'Robert Boyle and mathematics: reality, representation and experimental practice', Science in Context i (1988), 23–58, and A social history of truth: civility and science in seventeenth-century England, Chicago 1994, 310–54.
95 Pope, Seth, lord bishop of Salisbury, 117.

with the increasingly disreputable Hobbes. It should be pointed out, however, that although Wilkins and his allies did come to dominate the ruling body of the Society, their view of natural philosophy was not accepted without question as a statement of the Society's aims and purposes. Indeed, the deliberately vague constitution of the Society's 'Baconianism' was designed to cover over the diversity of views with an empiricism to which all could subscribe. It was evident nevertheless, from the number of Hobbes's friends and sympathisers from the 1650s who had joined the Fellowship, that the Society was far from being united and characterised by an anti-Hobbesian stance. Even at the beginning of the 1660s, Hobbes was a figure with a double-edged reputation; the personification of a new and insidious brand of Epicurean atheism (as his clerical critics had suggested), but at the same time a 'grand old man' (Hobbes was seventy-two in 1660) of English natural philosophy, enjoying the patronage of the king.[96]

It was all the more ironic that Hobbes was not a Fellow given his recorded enthusiasm for such a lay-academy, free from the corrupting influence of Scholastic clerics, 'wherein lay-men should have the reading of physics, mathematics, moral philosophy and politics, as the clergy now have the sole teaching of divinity'.[97] Such enthusiasm lends credence to the suggestion that Hobbes might have been involved in passing on blue-prints for such a society, based on the constitution of the Montmor group in Paris sent to him by Sorbière.[98] If Hobbes was not a Fellow, it probably was, as Hobbes protested, through the fault of his clerical adversaries. The clergymen may have found themselves deprived of their university posts, and under suspicion for their complicity with the Interregnum regime, but they were in a position to dominate a Society from which they could exclude Hobbes.

The partisan undercurrents to the Society's activities sometimes reflected Hobbesian sympathies. The author of the remarkably Hobbesian and Epicurean *Ballad of Gresham Colledge* [sic] argued in verse five that

> Oxford and Cambridge are our laughter
> Their Learning is but Pedantry
> These Collegiates doe assure us
> Aristotle's an Asse to Epicurus

In verse six, the writer appears to describe a Hobbesian system of natural philosophy:

> By demonstrative Philosophy
> They playnly prove all things are bodyes

---

96 Tuck, *Philosophy and government*, 336.
97 Hobbes, *EW* vii. 345.
98 Malcolm, 'Hobbes and the Royal Society', 56–9.

And those that talke of Qualitie
They count them all to be meer Noddyes[99]

The existence and persistence of such views adds weight to Aubrey's comment that many in the Society 'had the like' for Hobbes, and that the major obstacle to his membership was the opposition of a small group, whom Hobbes variously identified as 'Schoolmen', 'Divines', and 'new algebraists', by which he meant Ward, Wilkins, Wallis and their particular colleagues.[100]

If Hobbes saw the Society as something of a battleground in this respect, he was not alone in doing so. The same picture emerges clearly from Sorbière's account of the Royal Society, in which he described the opposition between Cartesian mathematicians and Gassendist *literati*. It is perhaps significant that Sprat's indignant assertion of the Society's independence was weighted against Hobbes and in favour of Wallis. Sprat was a protégé of Wilkins, and, as such, was hardly likely to present the Society any other way. It is also worth noting that the attempt to strip Sorbière of his Fellowship, for his comments in the *Voyage*, came to nothing.[101]

The Latitude-men may have taken over the Society, but it is clear that Hobbes remained attached to it, and to the possibility of winning converts from its ranks. He frequently submitted mathematical papers for the Society's scrutiny and he was reputed to have fallen out with Stubbe over the latter's attacks on the Society in the later 1660s.[102] He even tried to influence the shape of Robert Boyle's experimental protocols. The occasion was the publication of Boyle's first experimental findings in the *New experiments physico-mechanical, touching the spring of the air* (1660). The work laid out the foundations of Boyle's empirical theory, with its methodological emphasis upon the simple production of what Boyle called 'matters of fact'. By producing simple facts rather than generating speculative hypotheses about causal mechanisms, Boyle satisfied the rigours of his nominalism, and simultaneously evaded the problematic theoretical conflicts which had clouded discussion of natural philosophy during the 1650s.[103]

Hobbes responded to Boyle's work in his *Dialogus physicus* of 1661. His mood was conciliatory although tinged with the magisterial arrogance which did so much to blacken his reputation. The work displayed a qualified respect for Boyle, and also for the Society itself. According to Hobbes, the Society abounded with 'the most excellent ingenious men', but all they, and in particular Boyle, lacked to complete their science was a proper consideration of

---

99 D. Stimson, 'The ballad of Gresham Colledge [sic]', *Isis* xviii (1932), 103–17.
100 John Aubrey, *Brief lives*, ed. A. Clark, Oxford 1898, i. 371; T. Hobbes, *Behemoth*, ed. F. Tönnies, London 1889, 96–7.
101 Sprat, *Observations*, 241, and *History of the Royal Society*, p. v.
102 Birch, *History*, i. 42; Aubrey, *Lives*, i. 371.
103 Boyle, *Works*, i. 303.

causes.[104] This was, of course, the kind of science which Hobbes had developed himself.

Predictably, the first response to the *Dialogus* came from John Wallis, in the *Hobbius heauton-timorumenos* (1662). He protested that Hobbes's objections to Boyle were prompted by Boyle's association with Wallis and Ward. Wallis mixed derision at Hobbes's advancing years (Hobbes was seventy-four) with a repetition of his attacks from the previous decade, stressing that Hobbes was not only unoriginal, but also out of date.[105] By contrast, Boyle's own response, the *Examen of Mr T. Hobbes*, also published in 1662, deliberately avoided the kind of hysterically abusive style associated with Hobbes's clerical critics. Boyle sought instead to compose a sober response to Hobbes's objections to his air-pump experiments, for fear that Hobbes's 'fame and confident way of writing might prejudice experimental philosophy in the minds of those who are yet strangers to it'.[106] Boyle significantly conceded that Hobbes's hypotheses might be true in parts, but at the same time argued that it was impossible to suggest with as much confidence as Hobbes did, that the local motion of particles within a plenum was the only way to explain his experimental results. Other hypotheses, he argued, could be deployed to the same effect. Boyle refused to be drawn into the dispute over causes, and preferred instead to restrict his activities to simple experiment. [107]

Robert Boyle's personal exclusion of a Hobbesian natural philosophy should not, as he himself was to observe in the *Examen*, be taken as representative of the Society's stance upon such matters. It was clear that within the loosely empirical framework, other natural philosophers were willing to talk about causal mechanisms, and this meant that there remained scope for discussion of a Hobbesian science. William Neile, who like the young Isaac Newton, found much to recommend the natural philosophy of the *De corpore*, used Hobbes's philosophy to demand a causal interpretation of Wren's natural laws of motion.[108]

In many ways, Hobbes's ideas were simply too useful to discard lightly. His work upon optical theory and refraction was particularly influential amongst Royal Society members. Robert Hooke, in considering the role of local motion in governing the behaviour of light in refraction, solicited materials from Hobbes.[109] Perhaps the most interesting example of this partial com-

104 Hobbes, *EW* iv. 236.
105 John Wallis, *Hobbius heauton-timorumenos*, London 1662, 7–8.
106 Boyle, *Works*, i. 118.
107 Ibid.
108 For Newton's early interests in Hobbes see Isaac Newton, *Certain philosophical questions: Newton's Trinity notebook*, ed. J. E. McGuire and M. Tamny, Cambridge 1983, 219–21, 451.
109 For Hooke's work see Birch, *History*, iii. 194; for Hobbes's response see *Correspondence of Thomas Hobbes*, ii. 751–2. Hooke's attitude was not always quite so charitable towards Hobbes, and this enquiry may have had something to do with the ongoing rivalry between Hooke and Wallis. For Hooke's personal encounters with the aged Hobbes see R. Gunther, *Early science in Oxford*, Oxford 1923–45, vi. 139.

patibility, even with Hobbes's enemies, was Isaac Barrow's *Lectiones opticae*, which received its *imprimatur* in March 1668. In the course of the book Barrow proposed a description of refraction which proceeded entirely from a mechanical theory of local motion. What he failed to mention was that the theory, complete with its accompanying diagrams (although reversed and slightly altered) were directly copied from Hobbes's *Tractatus opticus*.[110]

The theology of the *De legibus naturae*

In the light of Barrow's plagiarism and the persistence of 'Hobbesian' science within the Royal Society, it becomes clear why Cumberland should have chosen to use Hobbes's own philosophy to clear the common ground of suspicion of atheism. The *De legibus* constituted the most ambitious attempt to provide a coherent view of the relationship between natural philosophy and ethics. Hobbes was ironically the only writer to have done this in a systematic fashion. Cumberland's work would set out an alternative account based upon the English Cartesianism developed by Ward and Wallis.

Cumberland's task was to show that the study of matter and motion could be applied to the discovery of the moral obligation that Hobbes had denied. This was necessary because Hobbes's materialism, and his geometrical foundation, were too useful to be jettisoned entirely, but too dangerous in the form which Hobbes had made notorious. To release natural philosophy from the suspicion of atheism, it was necessary to show that use of Hobbesian physics did not automatically imply a Hobbesian ethic.

To do this the theological obstacles which had led Hobbes to his controversial conclusions had to be overcome. Cumberland needed to show that individuals could come to an understanding of God's will. He had agreed with Hobbes, however, that natural reason could not provide automatic access to knowledge about the divine will. The essential question was whether a rational analysis of nature could improve upon this situation, and reveal anything about God's willing natural moral obligation. For Hobbes, this idea was an absurdity. The principles of natural science, he had written, were 'so far from teaching us any thing of God's nature, as they cannot teach us our own Nature, nor of the smallest Creature living'.[111] Hobbes could acknowledge that God was an omnipotent first cause, but the suggestion that human reason could provide any information about God's reasons or purposes was, in his terms, impossible. God's justice was not evident from the nature of the world. As he meditated upon his favourite Book of Job, Job's afflictions were merely the product of God's power, and were certainly not any kind of natural justice for his sins. In his response to Thomas White, he made it clear that there was no reason why God's omnipotence should be constrained by

110 F. Brandt, *Thomas Hobbes's mechanical conception of nature*, Copenhagen 1927, 211–16.
111 Hobbes, *Leviathan*, 252.

anthropomorphic assumptions of reason, virtue and justice: 'And as regards justice, if it be examined either according to the laws of nature, or against the premises contained in the Holy Scripture, God has an obligation to his creatures no more than the potter to his clay.'[112] It was for these reasons that Hobbes's laws of nature could only ever be theorems invented by man and binding only upon the conscience. They could only bear obligatory external force when a competent law-giver was capable of enforcing them. This for Hobbes could only be the civil authority.

Cumberland and his colleagues shared Hobbes's veneration for God's *potentia absoluta*, and also God's freedom of will in establishing the universe. This meant that Cumberland, Tillotson, Stillingfleet and Wilkins were reluctant to make the intellectual leap by which God could be judged according to human standards of reason. This led to some tension in their attempts to reconcile their theology with their Scholastic rationality. Cumberland felt that he must 'beg the readers pardon for sometimes ascribing reason to God, and ranking him amongst rational beings'. He went on to explain that 'these expressions are not properly and in the same sense said of God, in which we use them when we speak of man'.[113] Cumberland refused to rest his argument upon descriptions of God's attributes as human perfections, primarily because Hobbes rejected such arguments.

Cumberland's solution to the problem was to suggest that there was one characteristic of God's will which could be allowed, that of non-contradiction. Although God was ultimately free to do anything, God could not do something that would be internally inconsistent. This, argued Cumberland, is 'the only method, by which anything can be proved impossible to God; for he can do anything, which does not imply a contradiction'.[114] Cumberland's argument allows God's creative act of will in causing the universe to function as a kind restriction upon his freedom of will. That statement acts as a guarantee that God's will can be related to regularities in nature. If God is the first cause, as Hobbes agrees, Cumberland argued that clearly and scientifically observed regularities in nature do indicate God's will. This is because 'neither the wisdom, nor the will of God can be thought capable of appointing a contrary law whilst the nature of things remains such as it now is'.[115] God's will in creating the world as he had implied that God was the source of the regularities found within it. Because God could not contradict himself, those regularities must be expressions of his will. This was important for Cumberland, because if he could show that there were clear moral relationships discoverable in the natural world, then these, too, could be attributed to the will of God.

---

112 Idem, *White's De mundo examined*, 461; *Leviathan*, 469.
113 Cumberland, *DLN*, introduction, sect. 10.
114 Ibid. 1.23.
115 Ibid.

This was a proposition that it was difficult for nominalists of any persuasion to accept without question. The suggestion that God could be bound by the mathematical regularities of nature reeked of anthropomorphism. Henry Stubbe, whose flirtation with Hobbes has been alluded to, had complained in 1670 that 'it seems additional to God's freedom to say that he is restricted thus . . . if God Almighty be regulated by the rule of Geometry, and Mechanical Motion in the management of the world, and that the fabrick of these things is necessarily established upon these hypotheses, I cannot in any way comprehend how God can do miracles'.[116] Robert Boyle, too, was equally sceptical about the divines' attempts to circumscribe God's powers through an analysis of nature: 'it is not without indignation', he wrote, 'that I see many men, and some of them divines too, who, little considering what God is, and what they themselves are, presume to talk of him and his attributes as freely, and as unpremeditatedly, as if they were talking of a geometrical figure, or a mechanical engine'.[117]

For figures like Boyle and Stubbe, the restriction of God's power to the laws of nature was a dangerous assumption. Cumberland, too, was aware that such an argument carried with it an implication that God was bound by the laws of created nature. As a thorough-going voluntarist, however, Cumberland sought to deny that this was the case. 'No-one in his senses', he argued, 'can imagine that the first cause is bounded by any laws.'[118] Cumberland argued that if laws were rules of action issuing from the will of a superior with rewards and punishments annexed, then it was absurd to say that God was bound by laws. God could have no superior to whom he could be obliged. If this was the case, however, there was still the problem of explaining how the regularities in nature were related to God's will.

Cumberland's answer to this was virtually identical to that given by Nathaniel Culverwell in the *Discourse*. God wills the regularities in the nature of things, and binds himself to the continued observance of them. Cumberland argued that this was not a law in a strict voluntarist sense, but instead an analogous 'law of the divine actions'. Because God cannot contradict himself, God's willing a certain dictate binds him to its observation. Thus the dictates of the divine understanding 'pass into laws, binding him by the immutability of his own perfections, as we use to say that the oath of God is ratified when he swears by himself or by his own life, that is, by his immutable perfections, which will endure forever'.[119]

This was the same quasi-voluntarist 'middle way' discussed extensively in Suarez's *De legibus*, the principal influence behind Culverwell's *Discourse*. Suarez had argued that natural law was a law that God had imposed upon himself, in order that he should perform his works in accordance with it, 'For

---

[116] Stubbe, *Plus ultra reduced to a non-plus*, 170–2.
[117] Boyle, *Works*, iv. 339.
[118] Cumberland, *DLN* 7.6.
[119] Ibid.

God', wrote Suarez, 'although he might have made and ruled the world in any one of various ways, has determined to constitute and govern it according to a certain definite law.'[120]

We can see a similar adaptation of this idea in the work of Samuel Parker, who endorsed exactly the same argument in his *Extent of the divine dominion* of 1666:

> And, therefore, though the Rights of God's Power be not streightened by any External obligation (because that is tied on by a superior Authority, and so cannot agree to him whose Prerogative is Supream) yet they are bounded by an Internal Principle, for God's goodnesse may be properly said to tye and restrain him not to do anything repugnant to itself.[121]

Parker went on to argue that this was not a limitation upon God's power, 'but is rather a Circumscription set and chose by himself, which he cannot Transgresse because he will not'.[122] As in so much else, Parker's formulation is almost identical to Cumberland's own in stressing the role of God's self-obligation in maintaining moral and physical relationships in the natural world.

This theological position formed the essential background for Cumberland's belief that God had willed natural laws which governed moral as well as physical behaviour. Natural law, once detected from a scientific examination of the nature of things, could constitute the basis of moral obligation. If man reasoned correctly from nature that the common good was more important than the good of the individual, then it was highly probable that this relationship was also God's will. Proof that this was the case, for Cumberland, came when this same natural investigation revealed that God, 'in his ordinary government of the World, has so ordered or adjusted the Powers of all things, that such [virtuous] actions should be rewarded, and the contrary punished'.[123]

Cumberland's use of this quasi-voluntarist argument provided a distinctive solution to the problems raised by Hobbes's ethical theory. It reopened the possibility of using nature to identify moral obligation without slipping into an unguarded assumption that nature alone was the source of moral authority. Cumberland's position could not provide the absolute certainty required by Hobbes – man was still a fallible creature whose rational powers were often frustrated by the evidence of the senses. But what it did offer was a much improved probability of identifying that moral laws did operate. Cumberland deployed probability theory in chapter 3 of the *De legibus* to show that even though one could never be entirely certain that one had identified the will of God, there was enough evidence to make the divine obligation to natural law

---

120 Suarez, *De legibus* 2.2.4.
121 Parker, *Divine dominion*, 150–1.
122 Ibid.
123 Cumberland, *DLN* 5.19.

a highly probable hypothesis. Statistically, it was better to live in a benevolent manner, and to assume that others would do the same, than it was to live according to Hobbes's theory, and guarantee an anti-social result. In this way, Cumberland's use of this idea of moral certainty allowed him to escape from the Hobbesian implications of nominalism, while avoiding a deist interpretation of God. Critics would later argue whether Cumberland's attribution of natural rewards and punishments to God's ordinary government of the world was a legitimate voluntarist move, but the theory of the De legibus nevertheless allowed the reconciliation of Protestant theology with a Scholastic and scientific understanding of nature.

6

De Legibus Naturae *II*

The debate over the Royal Society and the nature of science provides the essential context for Cumberland's use of natural philosophy in the *De legibus naturae*. At a time when science, and in particular the science of the Royal Society, was coming under scrutiny for its apparently atheist implications, Latitudinarian writers needed to demonstrate that natural philosophy did not automatically lead to the ethics and politics of the *Leviathan*. Cumberland's contribution was to give natural philosophy an essential role in the discovery of moral obligation. In doing this he sought to cleanse mechanical science of the taint of Hobbism, and to expose Hobbes as a poor scientist.

This process of recovering science for religion and ethics against Hobbes would go a long way towards defining the basis of Latitudinarian natural theology, a set of beliefs which would dominate the Anglican doctrine throughout the eighteenth century. The early confrontation with Hobbes contributed a great deal to the peculiarly institutionalised and clerical nature of what some have called the 'English Enlightenment'. Cumberland's *De legibus naturae*, for all its modern obscurity, was one of the founding, and possibly most enduring texts of Anglican rationalism. For this reason above all, Cumberland's treatment of science deserves to be rescued from oblivion.

One of Cumberland's fundamental tenets was that the study of men and morality could not be divorced from the study of matter and motion. The laws of nature that operated in the physical world had implications for the moral and divinely ordained laws that governed the behaviour of men. From the beginning of the *De legibus naturae*, Cumberland was keen to emphasise that the natural world could act as a guide for moral and metaphysical propositions. This was, of course, a Latitudinarian commonplace. Ward's *Essay* had stressed the text of Romans i.20 that 'the invisible things of him from the creation of the world are clearly seen, being understood by the things that are made'. Cumberland echoed Ward's sentiment but argued in addition that the recent advances in natural philosophy marked a new age of discovery:

> We congratulate indeed the happy genius of this learned age, that the intellectual part of the world has been much illustrated by that great accession of light, which former proofs of the being of God, and immortality of the soul have received from the daily increasing knowledge of the inferior parts of nature.[1]

---

[1] Cumberland, *DLN* 1.3

Moral philosophy in particular could be entirely resolved in this fashion. 'It is sufficient for us', he wrote, 'to have admonished the reader, that the whole of moral philosophy, and of the laws of nature, is ultimately resolved into natural observations known by the experience of all men, or into conclusions of true natural philosophy.' The application of natural philosophy to morality was not necessarily new. Cicero outlined the same kind of relationship in his account of Stoic ethics in the *De finibus*, so often a major source for Cumberland's work. In book III of that work, Marcus Cato, Cicero's Stoic interlocutor, argues that anyone who wishes to live in accordance with their nature 'must base his principles upon the system and government of the entire world'. Nor again can anyone judge firmly of things good and evil, save 'by a knowledge of the whole plan of nature . . . no-one without natural philosophy can discern the value of the ancient maxims and the precepts of the wise men'.[2]

Cato's insight represented the ideal relationship between science and morality, but in seventeenth-century England that relationship was under threat. The materialism of the new science appeared to work against conventional ethics. Richard Baxter, who had decried this trend in the 1667 *Reasons of the Christian religion*, complained that 'I never yet saw a scheme or method of physics or theology which gave any satisfaction to my reason.' Simply accepting the split between theology and science could not, he argued, be a satisfactory answer. A unified science was needed. Anticipating Cumberland's own work, he maintained that

> as physics are presupposed in ethics and . . . morality is but the ordering of the rational nature and its actions, so that part of physics and metaphysics which governed the Nature of Man and of God . . . is more nearly pertinent to a method of theology, and should have a larger place in it than is commonly thought and given to it.[3]

This was the kind of reconciliation which Cumberland sought to bring about in the *De legibus*. Using Cicero's model in the *De finibus* as a Stoic template, Cumberland attempted to show that modern natural philosophy should be used to discuss natural law and moral obligation.

The Stoic case for the relationship between physical and moral relationships rested upon an understanding of the universe as an integrated, organic system. This concept is central to understanding Cumberland's adaptation of Stoic ideas in the *De legibus*. For Cumberland, as for the Stoics, each part of the creation, whether spiritual, moral or material, occupied a place in an inter-related system obeying the same fundamental laws of nature.[4] This assumption allowed Cumberland to apply the methods and experimental

---

2 Cicero, *De finibus* III.xxii.73
3 Baxter, *Reliquiae*, iii. 69–70.
4 For possible Stoic sources see Marcus Aurelius, *Meditations*, trans M. Staniforth, London 1964, II.3; IV.40; VI.38.

findings of all manner of scientific enquiry to ethics, in the belief that they could illuminate fundamental laws governing the whole system. He would find moral lessons in biology, anatomy, mechanics and geometry through the use of analogical and metaphorical reasoning.

While Cumberland's systematic understanding of nature owed much to ancient writers, his analysis was given a fashionably modern appearance by his use of mathematics. Mathematical order, for Cumberland, was the common currency of all natural phenomena. Cumberland's usage of this idea betrays the clear and considerable influence of Descartes's *mathesis universalis*. Cumberland explicitly refers to the Cartesian idea of a universal science in the first chapter of the *De legibus*, where he shows that apparently abstract mathematical reasoning can be used in the demonstration of any kind of theorem.[5] This is the source of the geometrical framework that underlies Cumberland's attempt to rationalise the moral behaviour of man. If the moral and the physical worlds were based upon analogously ordered systems, a demonstrable notion of morality was possible. Demonstrating morality, of course, had been the objective of Hobbes's ethical project, an objective that Cumberland intended to appropriate with his own *scientia moralis*.

Moral science

Cumberland argued that there could be a geometrically axiomatic, and thus demonstrably certain, core to moral theory. This was a break with conventional Aristotelian ethics, in that Aristotle had argued that ethics, like politics, was an empirical subject that was based upon probability and not certainty.[6] Hobbes was the first writer to challenge this position with his alternative *scientia* of definitions. The possibility of an axiomatic morality was one that tantalised many moral philosophers after Hobbes. Samuel Pufendorf had already taken Hobbes's insight that a rigorous approach to the definition of moral terms could provide demonstrable certainty in ethics. Moral ideas, inasmuch as they existed as abstract concepts, could be known with the definitive certainty of mathematical propositions. If ethics consisted of the relationships between moral ideas or axioms, then it was theoretically possible to have a science of ethics. Pufendorf applied this Hobbesian logic in his *Elementorum jurisprudentiae universalis* of 1660, where he argued that 'Morality is capable of Demonstration, as well as Mathematicks: since the real Essence of Things Moral Words stand for, may be perfectly known; and so the Congruity and Incongruity of things themselves, be certainly discovered, in which consists perfect knowledge.'[7]

In England, Benjamin Whichcote had argued that in morality 'we can be

---

5 Cumberland, *DLN* 1.9.
6 Aristotle, *The ethics of Aristotle*, trans. J. A. K. Thompson, London 1953, I.iii.
7 Pufendorf, *Elementorum* 1.3; 11.16.

sure as in mathematics'. Henry More, in the *Divine dialogues* of 1668, expressed the same faith in the axiomatic nature of morality when he suggested that 'the chief Parts of *Morality* are no less demonstrable than *Mathematics*; nor is the subtility greater in Moral Theorems than in Mathematicall'. John Locke, whose early drafts of the *Essay concerning human understanding* (c. 1671) may have been composed to combat the same Hobbesian problems confronted by Cumberland, echoed Pufendorf when he argued that

> the idea of ourselves, as understanding, rational creatures . . . would, I suppose, if duly considered and pursued, afford such foundations of our duty and rules of action as might place morality among the sciences capable of demonstration: wherein I doubt not but from self-evident propositions by necessary consequences as incontestable as those in mathematics, the measures of right and wrong might be made out.[8]

Cumberland's own version of this moral *scientia* proceeded from his understanding that there were essentially two kinds of knowledge: firstly, knowledge deriving from the senses, and secondly, knowledge produced by the mind reflecting upon its own activity in intellection. This reflexive knowledge was capable of producing true statements because the object of the understanding was necessarily perfectly understood.[9]

The probable source for Cumberland here may have been Henry More, who used the same argument in the establishment of what he called 'noetic' moral axioms in his *Enchiridion ethicum* of 1668.[10] More argued that the mind could draw reflexive and undeniable conclusions, such as that the whole was greater than the part, and that good should be chosen and evil avoided. These could be listed and combined to construct more complex moral theorems. More's list would be influential; it was reproduced in John Wilkins's *Principles and duties of natural religion* (1675), and also in James Tyrrell's adapted translation of Cumberland's own work in 1692.[11] Cumberland appears to have endorsed More's conception of axiomatic knowledge while remaining sceptical about his claim that such knowledge was necessarily innate.

The most distinctive feature of Cumberland's moral science was his characteristic, possibly unique, use of *benevolentia*. Cumberland understood *benevolentia* in its literal sense of willing good. As such, *benevolentia* is the 'intrinsic cause of present, and the efficient cause of future happiness'.[12] This idea, for Cumberland, was one which proceeded from the mind's reflection

---

[8] Whichcote, *Aphorisms*, no. 298, p. 36; More, *Divine dialogues*, 6; Locke, *Essay concerning human understanding* 4.3.18.
[9] Aristotle, *Ethics* I. iii.
[10] More, *Enchiridion ethicum*, 17–24.
[11] Wilkins, *Principles and duties*, 12–21; J. Tyrrell, *A brief disquisition of the law of nature according to the principles and method laid down in the Reverend Dr Cumberland's Latin treatise on that subject*, London 1692, 88–9.
[12] Cumberland, *DLN* 1.4.

upon its own activities. The operation of *benevolentia* could thus be understood definitively. *Benevolentia* would be a clearly defined term in Cumberland's mathematical ethics. It could be understood as an ethical cause, and thus the basis for a causal science. *Benevolentia* necessarily produces good actions in the same way as a point produces a line, and therefore any analysis of ethical actions needed to take benevolence as its subject.[13] Cumberland is careful to distinguish the term from its ambiguous popular meaning, and from the even more anomalous association with the idea of passion-dominated 'love'. In avoiding the latter association, Cumberland was keen to avoid any implication that his notion of *benevolentia* was characterised by irrational instinct.[14]

His reason for doing this may have been a reaction to Platonist excesses. Henry More had appealed to intellectual love as the motivating force of his boniform faculty, and it is possible to suggest that Cumberland's concern to purge his terms of passionate 'enthusiastic' excess was partially a response to More's less restrained rhetoric. Cumberland's rationalising project sought to reform ambiguous moral language through logical and coherent redefinition.

The result of this redefinition is that *benevolentia*, or the will to good, became the basic 'mathematical' function of Cumberland's ethics. The greatest good that individuals can pursue is, as Cumberland seeks to demonstrate in chapter 3, the greatest good of all rational agents. Combining benevolence and the greatest end allows Cumberland to formulate the *a priori* moral theorem that, based upon his definitions, 'the greatest benevolence of every rational agent towards all, forms the happiest state of every, and of all the benevolent . . . and is necessarily requisite to the happiest state which they can attain, and therefore the common good is the supreme law'.[15]

Cumberland's reasoning is tautological, and deliberately so. Cumberland regards highly abstract reasoning as a process that frees moral discussion from contingencies, and which allows a theoretical and demonstrably certain connection of terms. Hypothetical propositions can then be applied to practical ethical questions. To illuminate his process here, Cumberland draws a comparison with the relationship between theoretical and applied mathematics:

> General mathematical theorems, necessary to the construction of problems, are freed from the uncertainty of such guesses as are made concerning future contingencies, by not affirming that such constructions shall be, only demonstrating their properties and effects, if ever such constructions are produced. I have thought fit to proceed in the same method, and to deliver some evident principles, concerning the natural effects, the parts and various respects of universal love, without assuming that there is such love. However, because

---

[13] Ibid. 1.8.
[14] Ibid.
[15] Ibid. 1.3.

such benevolence is possible, many consequences may thence be drawn which may direct us to the practice of morality.[16]

Cumberland stressed that theoretical activity did not rule out practical application. Although theoretical mathematicians did not make any reference to the practical application of the principles which they lay down, this did not mean that their work had no practical application. Just as the postulates of geometricians were applied in the construction of geometrical and physical problems, so the principles of moral behaviour related to the direction of the practice of morality.[17]

This argument constituted Cumberland's case for the speculative 'geometrical' part of his science of morality. Cumberland's willingness to assert a connection between theoretical and practical sciences was also bolstered by examples drawn from Royal Society research, which had proved that theoretical research could have practical consequences. Cumberland drew upon the account of Wren's geometrically designed lens-grinding machine in the *Philosophical Transactions* when he argued that 'men are excited to the making of parabolic specula, or hyperbolic telescopes, for the sake of effects which mathematicians have demonstrated will thence follow'.[18]

The role of empiricism

Cumberland's *scientia moralis* was, as he admitted, a theoretical product of reflexive reasoning. But the products of reasoning alone, as he had agreed with Hobbes and Selden, could not constitute the basis of moral obligation. They were, like Hobbes's laws of nature, merely theorems. What he needed to prove was that the moral theorems which he had produced in this way were in fact necessary and obligatory expressions of the will of God.

This was where the 'nature of things' would play a vital part in Cumberland's theory. Cumberland agreed with Hobbes that reason could not be understood as an infallible faculty, but reason could nevertheless still be understood as a faculty 'not false in the act of judging'.[19] Cumberland argued that Hobbes's analysis had started from the correct premises, but had reasoned to the wrong conclusions when Hobbes had argued that in the natural state 'no man can know right reason from false, but by comparing it with his own'. In making this move Hobbes had argued that each man's reason was necessarily subjective, removing a common standard of judgement. What the Scholastic philosophers had called 'right reason' was nothing other than an individual reasoning on a particular matter. Cumberland denied that this was

---

[16] Ibid. 1.8; see also 1.15.
[17] Ibid. 1.9.
[18] Cumberland's source for Wren's engine is the *Philosophical Transactions* xlviii (1669), 961.
[19] Cumberland, *DLN* 2.5; cf. Hobbes, *De cive*, 52.

the case. Although reason could not provide an infallible guide by itself, it still operated upon, and judged its conclusions according to, sensory information derived from the natural world. The 'nature of things' was invariable and objective. Reason, although unable to derive conclusions by itself, could draw correct and objectively true conclusions upon the evidence provided by nature. In reply to Hobbes, Cumberland argued that the 'nature of things' constituted a common standard by which individuals could try their reason. The truth of a theoretical proposition did not rely upon a subjective judgement but rather proceeded from the objective relationship of things in the external world. 'It is most certain', argued Cumberland, 'that the truth or rectitude of propositions concerning things and actions . . . consist in their conformity with the things themselves, concerning which they are formed.'[20] If two individuals reason correctly from nature, then their conclusions must necessarily be the same. Right reason for one person is therefore the same as for everyone else. Hobbes's blunder, according to Cumberland, was to ignore the fact 'that there was the same standard to all, by which the reason of everyone is to be tried, whether it be right or no; namely, the nature of things'.[21]

By laying his stress upon the 'nature of things' Cumberland was reopening the possibility that nature could offer a route back to the right reason of the Scholastic philosophers. If nature was the expression of God's will, then objective rational conclusions drawn from natural relationships must be congruent with God's intentions. Hobbes and other voluntarists like Charleton had been sceptical about such a simple equation. They had agreed that God was the first cause, and that providence operated in a determinative manner. Whether man's natural reason was adequate to the task of revealing God's will in this way was a very different matter. Cumberland's response was his use of empirical natural philosophy. Careful, routinised observation of natural phenomena, of the kind associated with the new natural philosophy, would be used to overcome Hobbes's Carneadean scepticism. Cumberland combined the rhetoric of Cartesian clear and distinct ideas with the protocols of experimental knowledge when he wrote that

> In order to preserve our reason right, we ought not only to avoid false deduction, but especially the rash admission of any thing as self-evident, without proof. And we ought to take care, in the first place, that our simple ideas be both clear, from strong and frequent impressions of the same thing known in various circumstances; and distinct, by a separate observation of the parts singly.[22]

The concept of clear and distinct ideas had been used by Latitudinarian writers before. Stillingfleet, in his *Origines sacrae*, used them to convey a sense that disciplined perception could give a true picture of the 'nature of

[20] Cumberland, *DLN* 2.5.
[21] Ibid. 2.6.
[22] Ibid. 2.9.

things'.[23] Cumberland developed this argument when he suggested that natural philosophy could provide a more detailed and compelling view of all kinds of natural relationships.

Cumberland argued that a scientific empirical investigation could reveal the natural connections in the universal system with a higher degree of certainty than simple observation. If clear and distinct ideas from the nature of things could support the theoretical propositions of Cumberland's *scientia moralis*, then there were probable grounds for suggesting that those propositions did in fact represent the will of God. Empirical natural philosophy thus became a new and essential tool for revealing natural moral relationships. He concluded that: 'a philosophical contemplation of nature does very much assist the minds of men, in forming a more distinct notion of that general law'. It could do this because natural philosophy could 'very distinctly explain what things, or powers and motions of things are to others either good or evil, and how necessarily and unchangeably this is brought about'.

This position also meant that natural philosophy could become an essential tool in identifying objective good and evil:

> For seeing it is the only scope of this science to discover the causes of generation, duration and corruption . . . and seeing as it is certain that the causes generating and preserving man, for example, by the efficacy of which he continues for some time and flourishes in faculties, as well of body as mind, enlarged and determined to their proper function, are called good to him, but that the causes of grief and trouble are naturally evil.[24]

Science could therefore identify natural good and evil, but the ethical implications of natural philosophy could go further than a purely material analysis. Although the voluntary character of moral acts was not easily analysed in terms of matter and motion, moral actions did have physical consequences. This feature enabled them to be considered by methods properly pertaining to natural philosophy:

> although the voluntary actions of men, whose effects are external, do not take their rise in the same manner with motions merely natural from the impulse of other bodies, but are determined by our reason and free-will, nevertheless, since they are true motions produced by and received their measure and proportion from the powers of our body, which are of the same nature as the powers of other natural bodies, they must, after they exist, by a like necessity, and in the same manner as other natural motions, produce their effects according to the laws of motion.[25]

---

[23] Stillingfleet, *Origines sacrae: or a rational account of the grounds of Christian faith*, London 1662, 396–7.
[24] Cumberland, *DLN* 1.16.
[25] Ibid. 1.17.

The fact that even free moral acts have a physical dimension allowed Cumberland to blur the distinction between physical and moral acts. By arguing this point, Cumberland suggested the possibility that morality could be securely grounded, and analysed objectively, as a product of nature. Hobbes's 'scientific' account of nature had suggested that there was no necessary moral order to the world, and that moral obligation was created artificially by men. In response, Cumberland deployed his science to demonstrate that morality was inherent in nature, and obligatory moral laws were accessible to those who would take the care to look for them properly.

Moral physics: the defence of mechanism

Hobbes's uncompromising materialism was clearly linked to his ethical theory, as the objections of Baxter and More had shown. Hobbes's deterministic view of the universe as a material, necessitarian mechanism appeared to banish ideas of free will and moral responsibility. Although Hobbes's argument against free will was one endorsed by some Protestant theologians, the connection of it with mechanistic determinism worried Latitudinarians. One of Cumberland's main tasks in the *De legibus naturae* was to prove that mechanical principles, or the science of matter in motion, could support forms of morality that were not Hobbesian. Joseph Glanvill had set about the same task in his *Philosophia pia*, published in 1671, commenting that 'the modern atheists are pretenders to Mechanick principles, and their pretensions cannot be shamed, or defeated by any so well, as by those who thoroughly understand them'.[26]

Cumberland's strategy in using physics against Hobbes was not to argue against Hobbes's science *per se*. The analysis of the effects of local motion had played a large part in Cartesian science, and Hobbes's own theories in the *De corpore*, as the previous chapter has shown, were taken by many scientists to be a valid means of accounting for physical phenomena. This was the part of the Hobbesian heritage which needed to be either appropriated or neutralised. In order to recast the moral implications of Hobbesian science, Cumberland developed his own model of the relationship between physics and ethics, and used this to undermine the relationship between Hobbes's science and his ethics.

To focus upon the link between Hobbes's science and ethics might seem a little unfair, since Hobbes did not explicitly relate his physical to his ethical theories in a literal fashion. Hobbes did believe that people, like particles, were predetermined to act in certain ways, even if they were under the impression that they exercised free will. Ethics could be demonstrably certain if it was based upon self-preservation, just as physics could have a demonstra-

---

[26] Glanvill, *Philosophia pia*, 23.

bly certain core by being based upon the study of matter in motion, and that alone. But Hobbes did not labour this connection and rarely drew direct inferences from physics to ethics. Cumberland's reaction stemmed more from the popular equation between science and Hobbism which had developed in the twenty years after the publication of the *Leviathan*, and which was threatening the science of the Royal Society in the later 1660s.

Cumberland's response was to refute Hobbes by taking his idea of mechanism, but to apply conclusions from the study of physical bodies directly to ethics. In this way, Cumberland sought to show that Hobbes's own conclusions did not flow from his physics, and that the two were separable. The examples that Cumberland deployed were simple and straightforward, and in many cases they used a scientific explanation to reinforce common-sense conclusions. This was typical of Cumberland's 'strategy', which was designed to use a scientific appraisal of 'the nature of things' as a means of providing authority for conventional moral statements.

In one example he argues that 'it is not unusual in other causes whose force is only mechanical to observe an evident effect, producing an advantage or disadvantage to many'. This phenomenon could be seen, he explains, in the means by which the rays of the sun (a single cause) provide nourishment to 'innumerable vegetables over the whole earth, and necessary heat to the blood of all animals'. Cumberland argues that common sense observation can be reinforced by a 'more accurate inquiry into nature', which does, 'upon several occasions, demonstrate that every motion of every corporeal particle does very widely extend its force, and consequently, in some measure, however, little, necessarily concur with many other causes, to produce many effects'.[27]

Having made this point, Cumberland then deploys one of Hobbes's own observations upon mechanical motion from the *De corpore*. He draws attention to the penultimate paragraph of Hobbes's Latin work.[28] Cumberland says that here Hobbes 'expressly asserts that there can be no motion in a medium admitting of no vacuity, unless the next part of the medium give way, and so on infinitely, so that particular motions of every particular body contribute somewhat to every effect'.[29] Plenism was an essential feature of Hobbes's mechanistic science. Hobbes famously denied that there could be a vacuum in a material universe. This meant that local motion was the only conceivable cause of physical phenomena in a plenum, motion being preserved through the circulatory movement of matter throughout the whole system.

Cumberland takes the physical theory from the *De corpore*, but then uses it to demolish Hobbes's ethical theory. Hobbes is clearly not aware, says Cumberland, that his physical theory will have the implication that 'any human

[27] Cumberland, *DLN* 1.19.
[28] Thomas Hobbes, *Opera philosophica*, ed. W. Molesworth, London 1839–45, i. 430–1.
[29] Cumberland, *DLN* 1.20.

action, by its own nature, will contribute something to this effect, viz. the preservation and perfection of many who do not desire it'. One action for an individual might constitute a natural good to many. Cumberland has in mind social externalities produced by individual actions. The notion that such a natural good might be considered an objective phenomenon subverts Hobbes's idea that the notion of 'good' can only mean the good of a particular individual, defined in terms of self-preservation. If Hobbes had been aware of the implications of his own physical theory, 'he would not so crudely assert that good respects only him who desires it, and hence infer that the nature of good and evil is variable, at the pleasure of a single person in the state of nature'.[30]

Hobbes's ethical discussion is thus not properly related to the mechanical premises which he and Cumberland share. This is one example of Cumberland binding physics and ethics much more tightly than Hobbes himself had done, and Cumberland goes on to use this closer relationship to form both his positive theory and his attack upon Hobbes. In this way, Cumberland sought to prove that true natural philosophy based upon mechanistic principles could be used to defend conventional moral positions.

The key to much of Cumberland's positive theory is his emphasis upon the physical powers and limits which govern moral actions. These physical limits and powers are governed by the laws of nature, and in turn they govern the parameters of moral action. One example of this proposition is Cumberland's stress upon the finite quality of matter in general. It is a natural precept, he announces grandly, that

> the same bodies cannot at the same time be in more than one place; that the same bodies cannot at the same time be moved towards several places . . . so as to be subservient to the opposite wills of several men; but that they are so limited, that they can be determined by the will of one only, unless several conspire to one and the same effects or use.[31]

This 'natural precept' argues Cumberland, is of the highest ethical importance. It is the foundation for the Stoic distinction between those actions 'in our power' and those that are not. Cumberland was particularly influenced by Stoic thought, and this was one of several examples where he attempted to marry the new science and his Roman Stoic ethics. Stoicism provided a theory in which materialism and empiricism were associated with a strongly providential theology.

In this instance, Cumberland's inspiration was not Cicero, but Epictetus' first *Discourse*, which stressed that man had not been created with the essential liberty of the gods, but rather as a corporeal being with physical powers and limitations. Happiness on this account arose from a knowledge and

---

30 Ibid; the reference is to Hobbes's *De homine* XI.iv.
31 Cumberland, *DLN* 1.21.

acceptance of things within our power, and an acknowledgement of those things that were controlled by God through nature.[32] 'This distinction', commented Cumberland,

> constantly attended to, is of great use in forming our manners and regulating our affections, for hence we are taught not to seek any other happiness to alleviate our labours than that which arises from prudential management of our faculties, and from those aids, which we know the providence of God in the administration of the universe, will afford us.[33]

Cumberland uses Epictetus' distinction to define physical parameters to human actions in an ethically relevant way. Among the useful conclusions he draws is the fact that because the powers of individuals are limited, then they will necessarily require the assistance of others to achieve happiness. The physical circumstances of human existence require moral responses. Moving from construction to criticism, he also uses the same argument to attack Hobbes's rights theory.

Hobbes had argued, and Cumberland quoted him doing so, that it was possible to have a right to all things.[34] A right, in Hobbes's theory, was derived from the subjective assessment of what conduced to self-preservation. Because an individual in the state of nature was necessarily the only judge of what was necessary for his or her own preservation, then it was possible for that individual to have a potential right to anything.

For Cumberland, this notional subjective right was unacceptable. He argued that it was physically impossible for one person to own, or more importantly to use, all things. This physical limitation therefore produced a limitation of right to legitimate use. Cumberland's conclusion was that his natural principle required an objective division of property according to man's capacity to use physical objects productively. This provided the basis for Cumberland's theory of property, which suggested, again against Hobbes, that because the use of things is physically limited, then there are objective natural limitations upon property rights even in the state of nature.[35]

Cumberland's use of natural philosophy in these instances may seem like a long-winded way to go about analysing something which even Cumberland could concede was fairly obvious. However, to dismiss the scientific allusion on this basis is to miss the point that Cumberland was trying to address. In finding a role for science in supporting a naturalistic Stoic account of ethics, Cumberland was both grounding natural philosophy in ancient ethical practice and at the same time using it to offer a response to Hobbes's ethical scepticism.

Cumberland's use of mechanism also went beyond scientific justifications

---

[32] Epictetus, *Moral discourses*, trans. E. Carter, London 1910, 3–5.
[33] Cumberland, *DLN* 1.21.
[34] Ibid. 1.22; cf. Hobbes, *Leviathan*, 91.
[35] Cumberland, *DLN* 1.28, 7.

of commonplaces. One of the more complex uses of the analogy, and one of the recurrent themes throughout the *De legibus*, is his ethical use of the characteristics of physical systems. The properties of mechanical systems were a source of constant fascination to Cumberland, whether it was through modelling the solar system in his orrery, or considering the internal constructions of biological organisms. In the *De legibus* he argued that the behaviour of motion in physical systems could have moral implications.

His initial premise is to posit a closed system in which all acts (productive of physical motion) have inter-relating physical causes and consequences.[36] Cumberland draws two ethical conclusions from this. Firstly he argues that all motions which preserve the life, health and strength of an individual are necessarily complicated with, and to a certain extent dependent upon, the motions of other parts of the corporeal system. The moral lesson is that the good of an individual is necessarily bound up with the motion in the whole system. Again, patterning his argument upon Hobbesian local motion, Cumberland argues that no moral or physical action can take place in a vacuum. Cumberland's second and related observation is that any motion is 'propagated far and wide, and does not perish, but concurs with other motions to perpetuate the succession of things to preserve the whole'. Cumberland's physical theory is taken directly from Descartes's conservation theory, which argued that the amount of motion within the corporeal system was a constant. Any single action therefore generated motion which was sustained throughout the system of bodies. Cumberland's point is that individual acts must have implications for the whole system; in other words, the moral actions of individuals necessarily affect the common good.

Cumberland's purpose is to dissolve the distinction between the interest of the individual and the common good. Just as a particle is a determined and determining part of the motion of the whole system, so individuals cannot act without reference to the good of the whole community because those actions are necessarily inter-related through one collective order:

> In both these complicated motions, namely, that by which almost all things concur in some measure to the preservation of any particular body for some time, and that by which any particular body concurs with others to the preservation of the whole system, a certain order is preserved by which some motions are determined by others in a continual series, and all are governed by the continued circular motion of the whole system.[37]

This order is natural law. Cumberland acknowledges that this might seem a touch speculative, but he argues that its value lies in conceptualising the proper foundation of moral reasoning. By such demonstrable statements, it can be acknowledged that universal causes do operate in the world, that individual actions may cause multiple effects, and that such actions are inter-

---

36 Ibid. 2.13.
37 Ibid.

related. Recognising the moral implications of natural systems thus allows an individual to identify the necessity of moral obligation more clearly. 'If we embrace this opinion', argued Cumberland, 'from a thorough examination of the nature of things, it will doubtless oblige us to pay obedience to all the laws of nature and to take diligent care, that the same be paid by others.' This was, he argued, 'the utmost we can do, to make ourselves as well as others happy; nor can Reason propose to any one a greater end'.[38]

Cumberland had made a case for deriving morality from mechanism, but it was still a controversial strategy to adopt. Using Hobbes's own premises implied acceptance of his materialism and his determinism, both unacceptable features of a Hobbesian science. Cumberland attempted to defuse this by anticipating the objection that men are not, in fact, like matter at all. Cumberland acknowledges that there are obvious differences between the system of rational agents and other mechanical systems. In physical systems, motion occurs through the contiguity between bodies, and particles do not contain free will. Men, by contrast, act often at considerable distances, and 'make much use of their reason and liberty'.[39]

The argument that men were not like other physical bodies was a powerful objection to Cumberland's notion of moral physics, but he makes two points in response. His first is to defend his idea of the physical quality of moral acts. Men cannot be characterised as determined agents in their intellectual decisions, but the outcome of their free deliberation is still a corporeal act, and is therefore subject to the mechanistic laws of motion. Cumberland's second point is that the physical effect of moral action does still preserve a level of contiguity between human actors, which can still be regarded as interacting in the same manner as within a physical system. Physical juxtaposition is replaced by other, and in some cases, intellectual, media. Men live in societies where they meet frequently and act through words, written and spoken, communicating both good and harm to other men at great distances. Cumberland argues that if one takes his concept of 'system' to incorporate intellectual as well as physical contact, this does in fact preserve the analogy between physical and moral systems. As a consequence,

> the whole race of mankind ought to be considered as one system of bodies, so that nothing of any moment can be done by any man, relating to the life, fortune or posterity of any one which may not in some way affect those things which are alike dear to others, as the motion of every body, in the system of the world, communicates its motion to many others, especially neighbouring ones.[40]

Intellectual contact thus stands in for its physical counterpart. Man's natural sensibility to the least signals 'whether natural or arbitrary' ensures that

---

38 Ibid.
39 Ibid. 2.14.
40 Ibid.

individuals do respond to and influence each other. They also retain memory of deeds done and are excited to retaliate. They are also provident and plan ahead to avoid future evils and secure probable future advantages. These distinctively human characteristics in fact make men unusually sensitive 'particles', reacting to the actions of others in the same moral and intellectual system. Naturally, says Cumberland, this sensitivity differs from man to man 'according to their different degrees of sagacity in apprehending causes or hindrances to the common good', but this does not make the difference any less natural, he argues, than the differential communication of motion between subtle and gross matter in a fluid plenum.[41]

Cumberland's theory relied upon Hobbesian and Cartesian assumptions about the nature of local motion for its ethical insights. It was perhaps a measure of progress in the physical sciences that, as he was writing the *De legibus*, the experiments of Wren and Huygens were finding evidence of entropic tendencies in ballistic impacts. Motion, far from being conserved, was being dissipated, a fact which reduced the impact of Cumberland's moral theory. The attachment of Cumberland's insights to Cartesian natural philosophy was one of the reasons why his scientific interest for contemporaries soon waned, as new, more exciting, and theologically respectable accounts made their appearance.[42] Nevertheless, Cumberland's fascination for moral mechanism and the notion of a systematic morality modelled upon it would form an important template for Latitudinarian clergymen such as Samuel Clarke and Richard Bentley. In this respect Cumberland's peculiarly physicalist moral theory would survive the specific controversy over the role of mechanism in the 1660s.

Moral biology

Alongside his use of geometry and mechanical physics, Cumberland drew extensively from the life sciences in the *De legibus naturae*. This was common for anti-Hobbesian/Epicurean writers of the period. Stillingfleet's *Origines sacrae* (1662), John Wilkins's *Of the principles and duties of natural religion* (1674) and John Ray's classic *Wisdom of God manifested in the works of creation* (1690, but composed in the 1660s), all deployed scientific information to prove against Hobbes and Epicurus that the world had been designed by God, and was not, as Epicurus was supposed to have argued, the chance result of a casual concourse of atoms. Like Cumberland, these writers all deployed the classical design arguments against Epicureanism drawn from Cicero's *De natura deorum*, Pliny's *Natural history*, and book II of Galen's *Usefulness of the*

---

41 Ibid.
42 For Royal Society discussion of the consequences of Wren's work see Birch, *History*, ii. 381; *Correspondence of Henry Oldenburg*, v. 571–2; W. L. Scott, *The conflict between atomism and conservation theory 1644–1860*, New York 1970, 6–13.

parts of the body.[43] Cumberland used all of these sources, but he did more than regurgitate classical examples. He actively deployed and interpreted recent biological science in accordance with his theory about the analogical con-nection between nature and morality. This usage not only reflects Cumber-land's own enthusiasms and medical training, but again focuses upon the kind of observations which Hobbes himself had used in support of his ethics.

Hobbes had represented the dark side of mechanism, and this repute extended to his varied use of psychology, anatomy and biology. Hobbes had called the science of man's body 'the most profitable part of natural science' and some of his analysis of the emotions and the passions rested upon physio-logical observations about the vital motion of the blood and spirits.[44] The result had been that Hobbes's view of human nature, upon which his contro-versial ethical positions rested, appeared to have a 'scientific' basis.[45]

Cumberland deployed the same methods that he had used to defend mechanism. Hobbes's use of physiology and biology had been sketchily related to his political and ethical observations. Cumberland attempted to bind science and ethics much more closely by extracting moral lessons from biological observations. These could then be used to refute Hobbes's ethics apparently upon Hobbes's own terms.

The first major example of this occurs in chapter 2 of the *De legibus*, where Cumberland investigates the extent to which the study of animals sheds light upon the concept of mutual need.[46] Cumberland argues that the study of living organisms proves that their physical limitations require them to co-operate. Each living organism has only small powers and lives for a short time. As a result, any animal's capacity for action is finite, and in order to achieve the maximum happiness of which the organism is capable, in many cases it can be proved that animals require assistance and co-operation of others of the species.

By the same token, the physical limitations of organisms mean that the essential requirements of self-preservation alone are necessarily quite low. Cumberland introduces this observation to combat Hobbes's thesis that self-preservation is the sole motivation for man. If Cumberland could prove, physiologically, that self-preservation, although a primary stimulus, was easily satisfied, then he could attack Hobbes's dependence upon it as the sole basis of rights.

Cumberland discusses the point with reference to the circulation of the blood. This was particularly appropriate terrain over which to engage

---

[43] For the ethical use of biology and the argument from design see N. C. Gillespie, 'Natural history, natural theology and social order: John Ray and the Newtonian ideology', *Journal of the History of Biology* xx (1987), 1–50; I. Rivers, 'Galen's muscles: Wilkins, Hume and the educational use of the argument from design', *Historical Journal* xxxvi (1993), 577–97.

[44] Hobbes, *EW* i. p. viii; *Leviathan*, 13–14.

[45] See particularly the first chapter of *De homine*: *Opera philosophica*, ii. 1–6.

[46] Cumberland, *DLN* 2.17–18.

Hobbes, because both Hobbes and Cumberland shared admiration for Harvey's work. Hobbes deployed analysis of the 'vital motion' of the blood and spirits in order to lend physiological authority to his work.[47] Cumberland argued that the extent of the blood supply, bounded by tissue, effectively

> sets limits to those necessities, which urge it to self-preservation. All the necessities of the body are enclosed within the circumference of the circle described by the blood of the animal: those few things which are sufficient to fan and repair this vital fluid are sufficient to the preservation of life, health and natural strength.[48]

Although self-preservation is essential, its requirements are easily satisfied. The anti-Hobbesian point is that there is a natural limit to what individuals and animals will regard as necessary for their self-preservation. Cumberland argues that those things necessary to maintain the blood-producing vessels are so small 'that I believe it evident, that no animal, even of the brute-kind, ever fell into Hobbes's error, so as to think all things necessary to its own preservation'. Cumberland reinforces his point about natural and physical limits upon subjective right; even if an animal should form a mistaken assessment of its physical needs, the limitations of its physiology mean that there is only so much that can be consumed. Nature thus provides natural limits 'whence naturally arises some kind of division of things amongst several animals, in which is laid the foundation of concord and mutual benevolence, which we are enquiring after'.[49]

Property here becomes a characteristic of all animals, based upon legitimate use rights. If there are natural limits to consumption, it therefore follows that once the limited requirements of self-preservation are satisfied, then there is no reason to oppose the self-preservation of others. In Hobbes, subjective assessment of right had resulted in a state of war. For Cumberland, given the natural limits to subjective right, a state of war could not be considered normative because there would be no reason to attack one's neighbour if one were sated. The state of nature was thus a state of peace. If Hobbes had argued that subjective assessment governed moral action, Cumberland argued that subjective assessment would always be qualified by natural law.

Much of the *De legibus* is devoted to refuting Hobbes's idea that the state of nature is a state of war, and Cumberland uses his biological observations to reinforce this critique. Cumberland's argument rests on the assumption that hostility between animals of the same species is unnatural. Homogeneity of features generates a species loyalty and mutual affection based upon recognition of similarity and interdependence. Behaviour to the contrary is simply

---

47 Hobbes, *EW* i. 406–7. Hobbes is said to have attended dissections with Harvey, who left Hobbes £10 in his will to 'buy something to keep in remembrance of me': G. Keynes, *The life of William Harvey*, Oxford 1978, 388, 462.
48 Cumberland, *DLN* 2.17.
49 Ibid.

unnatural, and the Hobbesian state of war should be seen as an aberration 'as all who look upon it as a distemper and praeternatural disposition of a dog, who through rage or madness, is unusually excited to bite every other dog he sees'. Actions which are contrary to the natural desire to associate peaceably should therefore be viewed as 'a certain distemper of the blood and brain, and somewhat akin to the rage of a mad dog'.[50]

Excessive attachment to certain passions should also be seen the same way, according to Cumberland, in attack upon Hobbes's preoccupation with fear. Hobbes's exclusive concentration upon fear alone is unnatural and militates against self-preservation. In animals, writes Cumberland, excessive fear 'like other distempers . . . prejudices their health, by reducing them to sadness, solitariness and unseasonable watchings, with other symptoms of a predominant melancholy, which hastens untimely death'. Antisocial behaviour and excessive fear, far from being the natural and essential forces that Hobbes suggests, are rather the product of a disturbed imagination.[51]

Observation of the social good, by contrast, is beneficial. To show this, Cumberland returns to discussion of the circulation of the blood. 'Natural philosophers', he wrote, 'know very well that the motion of the blood and heart, which is necessary to life, is befriended by love, desire, hope and joy, especially when conversant about a great good.' The physiological effects of considering greater goods involve the arteries being 'filled with better and more flowing juices, brisker spirits are produced and consequently all the animal functions are performed with greater ease'.[52] The greater the good, according to Cumberland, the greater the effect. Contemplating moral good is literally good for the health! Cumberland argues that this is an effect which is obvious to animals and men, even if they do not necessarily understand the science involved.

With negative passions, however, such as envy, hatred, fear and grief, Cumberland argues that the physiological effects are detrimental. The motion of the blood is retarded and the heart is clogged, 'whence the countenance of man becomes pale, and numberless mischiefs in the whole animal economy, but especially in the function of the brains and nerves follow; such are the distempers usually ascribed to the spleen and melancholy'.[53] Unnatural passions thus cause blockage in the vital motion, and Cumberland cites an example from Harvey's De generatione (1651), where the physiologist, while conducting the autopsy of a 'high-spirited man' allegedly suffering from a pent-up desire for revenge, 'found the aorta so distended, and stuffed with blood, that the size of the heart and cavities were as great as those of an ox'.[54]

---

[50] Ibid. 2.18.
[51] Ibid.
[52] Ibid. 2.19.
[53] Ibid.
[54] Ibid.

Cumberland uses this discussion to suggest that the design of the human body requires control of the passions, and also contemplation of moral goods. The rewards of right thinking, and the natural penalties attached to excessive fear, hatred or grief make it evident that 'the very nature of an animal, and of the passions, admonishes men that it will be of advantage to them, to be of a benevolent disposition towards others'. Again, Cumberland has derived natural limits to Hobbesian passions; the physiological make-up of animals requires that they do in fact observe restraint. Not to do so effectively endangers their well-being.

Cumberland also uses discussion of biology to reinforce his stress upon the interdependence of the individual and the collectivity. His thesis here is that the same causes which promote individual preservation also necessarily contribute to the continuation of the species. Here Cumberland again draws upon Harvey's *De generatione animalium* for his example. Harvey's work had been published in the 1650s, but the theme that Cumberland was addressing, that of generation, had been discussed by the Royal Society in November 1668.[55] Harvey had observed that the same processes which formed the nutritive organs in the egg (stomach, heart etc.) also simultaneously formed the reproductive organs. Nourishment not only went into sustaining the organism, but was also used for stocking its reproductive capacity, a capacity which was not directly linked to the self-preservation of the organism.[56] Cumberland views this as a classic example of nominally selfish action (obtaining nutrition) being necessarily structured for the wider good through biological necessity. He brings out the political relevance of the example by arguing that the same biological structure which preserves the individual is simultaneously designed also to serve the common good through that individual's reproductive capacity:

> The whole circulation of the blood, and every thing instrumental thereto, as the muscular force of the heart, and the individual contrivance of the valves in the veins, is at the same time subservient to the private nourishment of the individual, and to the public good by propagating the species, whilst it sends off the material of the seed to the spermatic vessels.[57]

As with his discussion of mechanism, Cumberland is alive to the objection that such observations do not actually tell us much about voluntary moral actions. While animals might automatically and necessarily behave in ways which benefit the common good, can Cumberland seriously apply this reasoning to moral laws when benevolence appears to be the accidental side-effect of a more essential selfishness? Cumberland addresses this objection, which he sees as coming from those, like Hobbes, who wish to evade the

---

[55] Birch, *History*, ii. 323.
[56] William Harvey, *De generatione animalium*, London 1651, exert. 69, 305–14.
[57] Cumberland, *DLN* 2.20.

evidence of natural inclinations, whether voluntary or not.[58] His answer is interesting because it goes some way towards explaining the tension that seems to exist in his account between apparently self-interested behaviour and the genuine benevolence which was the didactic message of the book.

His first point is that his main priority is to identify obligatory laws of nature rather than the possibly erroneous perceptions that animals might have of their own ends. His second point is that the formulation of the objection may be incorrect, in that it was entirely possible that animals might simultaneously will their own good and that of others at the same time. Hobbes was wrong, argued Cumberland, to argue that the good of the individual and the good of all necessarily require different forms of actions. Hobbes was therefore wrong, or at least only giving a partial account of moral motivation, when he argued that self-preservation was the only possible source of moral obligation. For Hobbes to say that animals perform apparently benevolent actions merely because they seek advantage to themselves merely illustrates his failure to acknowledge that actions which can benefit the individual can also benefit others.[59]

Cumberland's use of biology thus undermined Hobbes's emphasis upon self-preservation. Hobbes had, according to Cumberland, proposed 'this little end as the rule of all human action', but the evidence of nature had indicated a far more complex reality, in which the behaviour of all animals was more likely to be aimed at mutual assistance than its opposite.[60] It was not that Hobbes had been wrong; individuals, as Cumberland noted on many occasions are motivated by self-interest, but whereas Hobbes had used self-preservation as the *reductio* for a demonstrative science of morality, Cumberland was urging acknowledgement of the natural boundaries of all forms of action. Hobbes had sought philosophical closure by abstracting human behaviour from nature; Cumberland, by contrast, in the attempt to re-establish the divine origin of moral obligation, sought to place human behaviour in its natural context. Ironically, although Hobbes was often accused of reducing humanity to the status of ravening animals, Cumberland came closer to upholding the continuities between human and animal behaviour.

This contrast can be seen in a long passage where Cumberland systematically confronts Hobbes's controversial comments upon social animals. The natural community of social animals such as ants and bees was standard evidence for natural sociability in Aristotelian political theory. For Hobbes to uphold his thesis about man's natural antisocial tendencies, he had to develop the argument that man was not the same as other animals. This is what he did in chapter 5 of the *De cive*.[61] Cumberland, by contrast, wished to re-establish this kind of natural connection. Man was precisely the same as

---

[58] Ibid.
[59] Ibid.
[60] Ibid. 2.20.
[61] Hobbes, *De cive*, 87.

other animals in respect of their sociability. For this reason he attempted to counter each of Hobbes's claims for the essential differences between men and animals.[62]

Hobbes's first objection to considering man as a social animal was that, unlike other creatures, 'men are continually in competition for honour and dignity'. The consequence of this is that 'amongst men there ariseth on that ground Envy and Hatred, and finally Warre'. Cumberland's response focuses upon Hobbes's understanding of honour and dignity. True honour and dignity, he argues, are properly won by serving the common good. To value honour and dignity by themselves in such a destructive fashion is an unnatural aberration. Again Cumberland argues that Hobbes has mistaken dysfunctional behaviour for natural tendencies. Also he argues that Hobbes is internally inconsistent in discussing competition for social honours in a presocial context. In the state of nature, only true honour and dignity would command respect.

Hobbes's second objection is that 'amongst these creatures [meaning ants and bees], the Common Good differeth not from the Private, and being by nature enclined to their private, they procure thereby the common benefit. But man, whose joy consisteth in comparing himselfe with other men, can relish nothing but what is eminent.' The first part of what Hobbes says is, of course, precisely what Cumberland wanted to argue about men. Cumberland uses Hobbes's assertion that there is in fact a common good as evidence that Hobbes was being disingenuous.[63] Hobbes could acknowledge the existence of a common good but he refuses to recognise its influence upon individuals. As a result he fails to provide a genuine and necessary insight into the 'nature of things'. Hobbes may have asserted that man relishes his own eminence, but this, suggests Cumberland, is less an empirically demonstrable fact of human nature than Hobbes's analysis of his own defective personality.[64]

Hobbes's third objection is to point to the irrationality of animals. They cannot, as a result of their lack of reason, see any fault in the administration of their public business. Men, by contrast, are always ready to think themselves able to govern better than the rest. Cumberland regards this treatment of man's fractious character as unconvincing. Men may complain, but more often faults of public administration are borne for the public good. Can it be the case, he appeals, that reason made the condition of man worse than brutes?

Hobbes's answer to this question would probably have been yes. His next objection focuses upon the destructive consequences of some of man's 'higher' abilities, which do indeed compromise the chances of a peaceful social existence. Hobbes draws the reader's attention to man's peculiar use

---

62 Cumberland, *DLN* 2.22.
63 An example of Hobbes's use of the common good can be found in the *De homine* XI. iv, translated in *Man and citizen*, ed. B. Gert, Indianapolis 1991, 47.
64 Cumberland, *DLN* 2.22.

and abuse of language. Bees, although they can be considered to have some voice, 'yet want the art of words by which some men represent to others, that which is good, in the likeness of evill, and evill, in the likeness of that which is good; and augment, or diminish the apparent Greatenesse of Good and Evill; discontenting men and troubling their peace at their pleasure'.[65] This problem of *paradiastole* was central to Hobbes's analysis of the instability of moral language.[66] The labels of good and evil, promiscuously used, lead to rhetorical confusion, and this rhetorical confusion lay at the heart of moral and political dysfunction. Hobbes's philosophical project was built around the suggestion that with clear definitions and clearly demonstrated propositions, the problem of rhetorical instability, and its political consequences, could be avoided.

Cumberland's objection to this signals some of the fundamental differences between *De legibus* and the *Leviathan*. His position was very close to that of Wilkins and Tillotson in the *Essay towards a real character*, a work that Cumberland referred to in his *Jewish measures and weights* of 1686.[67] Hobbes's position presupposed language to be an arbitrary system of signs whose meaning was conventional. Cumberland agreed that language itself was an arbitrary imposition, but with the crucial difference that the relationships established by those signs reflected real and objective relationships in the nature of things. As a result, although meaning could be confused, the fact that language was based upon cognisable relationships evident from nature meant that in most cases individuals would be unlikely to be taken in by 'the empty sound of words'. Because objective natural relationships are the foundation of language, argued Cumberland, language therefore had greater capacity to establish peace rather than to destroy it, by facilitating meaningful communication. The contrast between Cumberland and Hobbes could not be clearer, in that where Hobbes claims that man's peculiar features serve to distance him from 'nature', Cumberland argues that, if anything, the ability to use language and reason binds mankind more closely to the observation of natural law.

This contrast is pursued in Hobbes's last objection to the equation between humanity and social animals. Here Hobbes argues that the agreement of such animals is 'natural'. The agreement of men, however, is by rational agreement or covenant only, 'and therefore it is no wonder if there be somewhat else required (beside covenant) to make their Agreement constant and lasting, which is a Common Power, to keep them in awe, and to direct their actions to the common benefit'. Cumberland rejects this distinction between the natural agreement of animals and the artificial agreement of men. For Hobbes to suppose that the use of reason is artificial is to ignore

---

65 This is Cumberland's translation of the passage of *De cive*; cf. Hobbes, *De cive*, 88.
66 Q. R. D. Skinner, 'Thomas Hobbes: rhetoric and the construction of morality', *Proceedings of the British Academy* lxxvi (1990), 1–61.
67 Cumberland, *Jewish measures and weights*, 56.

the fact that it is, as Hobbes himself has conceded, a natural faculty.[68] Cumberland argues that what Hobbes considers to be artificial proceeds from nature in the same way that mathematics is a rational skill that is learned naturally. Again, the problem goes back to Hobbes's analysis of language. Cumberland agrees that words are indeed arbitrary signs, but because reason and speech identify real relationships, the agreement of men through speech is thus as natural as that of animals.[69]

Cumberland's engagement with Hobbes over social animals serves to clarify the essential differences as well as the similarities between their positions. Hobbes's *scientia moralis* rested its demonstrable quality upon the possibility of abstracting human characteristics from nature. Cumberland's agenda was to locate man within the physical realities of a law-bound universe. Although this meant accepting some of what Hobbes had said, particularly about self-preservation and the role of local motion, Cumberland's characteristic emphasis upon the 'nature of things' served to provide a corrective to Hobbes's emphasis upon rights alone, by revealing the physical boundaries or natural laws which governed the exercise of rights. By showing that Hobbes's ethics rested only upon introspective and invalid assumptions about human nature, rather than a detailed application of his science to his ethics, Cumberland also sought to discredit Hobbes as a natural philosopher. Cumberland's message was that biology and ethics, if joined more closely together, could form a harmonious and profitable relationship.

The moral anatomy of man

Cumberland had argued that the structure and behaviour of animals did offer moral lessons applicable to mankind. His responses to Hobbes's writing on social animals revealed that he saw animals and humans as operating upon the same natural moral principles. Cumberland was not, however, about to abandon the idea that mankind was just another species of animal. Indeed, as Cumberland would repeatedly argue throughout the *De legibus*, human characteristics made man even more sensitive to the laws of nature than any other animal. Man was far more likely to behave in a moral manner than Hobbes's inadequate analysis would suggest.

Cumberland's sources in this discussion reflect his medical interests, going back to his experiences in the 1650s. But the material is not merely illustrative; it proposes a physiological basis for human moral capacities. One implication of this, already hinted at by Cumberland, is that immorality is a form of dysfunction or illness. This type of argument was uncommon, but it did have an interesting precedent. Cumberland appears to have adapted the ethical use of anatomical material directly from Samuel Parker's discussion in

---

68 Hobbes, *De cive*, 41, 52.
69 Cumberland, *DLN* 2.22.

the *Free and impartial censure* of 1666. One sinister implication of such work could be read through the anti-toleration literature of the later 1660s. Both Simon Patrick and Samuel Parker spoke of religious dissent as a form of physical disorder. Cumberland's analysis of moral anatomy could have political as well as moral dimensions.

Cumberland begins by sketching out those features which distinguish man from other animals. Although they share a similar organic framework to other creatures men have a greater quantity of brain mass and blood volume. Citing Bartholin's *History of anatomy*, Cumberland notes that the ratio of brain to body mass in man is eight times that of an ox, an observation borne out by his own dissections of sheep and hogs, which reveal a similar ratio.[70] The influence of the brain on the government of the actions, he reasons, is thus much greater in men than in beasts. Cumberland draws the ethical conclusion that if the brain is the seat of perception, this will also mean that man's observation of sensible objects is not only going to be more accurate, but thereby better able to consider what things in our power 'can bring of Good and Evil to men singly or jointly consider'd'.[71] He also makes the observation that, as Thomas Willis had suggested in his *Anatome cerebri* (1664), the nervous system originates in the brain. Cumberland concludes that 'both the greater quantity and force of the brain, which are visible in man, are naturally of use to him, to direct the various actions or motions depending with more circumspect deliberation, counsel and care, which are the peculiar offices of the brain'.[72] The size and scope of the organ also indicates its use for higher purposes than self-preservation alone. Cumberland comments that 'certainly, a more simple apparatus of organs, such as is found in trees, is sufficient for the preservation of one individual'. Given that even fish and birds, whose brains are as small as their eyes, have enough understanding to live peaceably, 'how much less can it be wanting in men in general . . . who have the largest organs for acquiring knowledge'. Cumberland confirms his observation with evidence from Willis, who records that during the dissection of 'one who was a fool from his birth' there was 'nothing amiss in the Brain, but that it was extremely small'. Cumberland also uses Willis's observation that a monkey's brain is the same size as that of a dog or a fox, but because it had a greater ratio of brain-matter to body-weight with a developed nervous system, this explained why 'this animal makes nearer approaches than the rest, to the understanding of man'.[73]

Another distinctively human feature is the unusual 'quantity, purity and vigour' of the blood and spirits 'which may justly be reckoned among the helps of the fancy and memory, and consequently of prudence itself'. Study of

---

[70] Ibid. 2.23; Thomas Bartholin, *History of anatomy*, London 1668, 133–4.

[71] Ibid.

[72] Ibid; Thomas Willis, *Cerebri anatome, cui accessit nervorum descripto et usus*, London 1664.

[73] Cumberland, *DLN* 2.23; Willis, *Cerebri anatome*, 184–91.

the blood had been a major concern of Royal Society natural philosophers in the later 1660s. Cumberland reflected this interest in his deployment of recent research both directly as example, and indirectly as a metaphor for the body politic and the intellectual system. As with the brain, Cumberland notes that 'the quantity of blood varies, for several reasons, in all animals and consequently in man'.[74] Cumberland cites estimates for human blood volume from Walter Charleton, Richard Lower and Francis Glisson to the effect that it constitutes between one-eleventh and one-twelfth of human body weight. Cumberland compares this to his own observations upon animal dissections where 'in a sheep, calf and hog, I have often found, that the blood in proportion to their bloodless body, as one to twenty, or at most, to eighteen'. The amount of blood in the human body is thus proportionately double that of other animals, and more than this when compared to smaller animals such as fish and birds. Cumberland also notes that anatomists have agreed that man's blood is warmer, something which Cumberland accounts for by the 'plenty and briskness' of the spirits.

The moral import of this information is derived from the relationship between the blood and the nervous system. Cumberland, possibly following Descartes's *Traité de l'homme* (1664) asserts that the spiritous part of the blood constitutes the basis of the nervous system.[75] His conclusion is that the greater proportion, and heat of the blood in the human body therefore implies a greater quantity of spirits than are to be found in any other animal. The consequence of this is that man has a more sensitive and complex network of nerves. Cumberland refers to Francis Glisson's treatise *De rachitide* (1650) in support of his claim, noting Glisson's observation that in children with rickets, where other body parts have wasted away, the head would grow larger 'and at the same time the understanding is enlarged in proportion to the brain, by means of the affluence of a greater quantity of blood'.[76]

Even man's upright posture gives distinct physiological aids to moral government, and Cumberland presses his knowledge of statics into service, 'the influence of which principles, though they may seem impertinent, and foreign to our present purpose, appears to me to be extended through the material world; and consequently to have no inconsiderable effect upon human bodies'.[77] Cumberland's argument here betrays his enthusiasm for extrapolating from his universal principles. He argues that the blood consists of different elements, some thicker and heavier than others. Motion imparted to the mixture has a differential effect on the blood's constituent parts. This, combined with the brisker motion of the spiritous parts of the blood in the arteries will mean that 'the blood is somewhat brisker, which rises in the narrow ascending trunk, than that which passes into the wider descending trunk

---

74 Cumberland, *DLN* 2.23.
75 Ibid.; cf. Descartes, *Philosophical writings*, i. 100.
76 Cumberland, *DLN* 2.23; cf. Francis Glisson, *De rachitide*, London 1650, 15–16.
77 Cumberland, *DLN* 2.24.

through which the greater and heavier blood is forced with greater ease'. This, combined with the perpendicular situation of the ascending arteries ensures the swift circulation of spiritous blood to the head, thus enabling it to operate more acutely than animals who do not have an upright posture.[78] Cumberland's use of such esoteric evidence is designed to reinforce the suggestion that mankind is designed for more extensive and complicated purposes than Hobbes's limited psychology will allow.

One of the most interesting examples of Cumberland's ethical use of physiological material occurs when he examines those properties of the human body 'which seem more nearly to respect the government and determination of the affections to preserve, rather the good, than hurt of others'.[79] Cumberland's discussion examines anatomical evidence that men are by nature equipped to govern the passions. Establishing the medical basis for the proper relationship between reason and the passions was a major issue for Anglican writers. Not only had Hobbes's cognitive model laid emphasis upon the passions as principal stimulus to action, but emotional and passionate excess was part of the sickness that Parker had diagnosed in dissenters. Demonstration of the rational control of the passions was thus an essential part of the Latitudinarian rhetoric of godly sobriety, with political as well as moral implications.

Cumberland's stated reason for introducing the topic is that the regulation of the strongest passions is usually the object of laws. All those things which either excite or allay the passions therefore have a considerable role to play in discussion of the laws of nature. He refers the reader to a plate in Thomas Willis's *Cerebri anatome*, where Willis refers to the way in which the network of nerves spreads over the region of the heart, with its associated arteries and veins carrying the blood supply to the head.[80] The key passage for Cumberland is the one in which Willis draws out his conclusion:

> the intercostal nerve, by these branches, supplies the place of an extraordinary courier, communicating to and fro, the mutual sensations of the heart and brain. By means of this communication, the conceptions of the brain affect the heart, and move the vessels thereof with the diaphragm, whence the motion of the blood, and the respiration, receive various alterations, and the state of the spirits, which are thence formed, is somewhat changed.[81]

The flow and the quality of the blood can thus be controlled by the brain acting through the nervous system. Cumberland argues that this reveals the moral capacity of man to moderate and control his own passions: 'It is sufficient to have shown', he writes, 'that man is naturally furnished with these instruments . . . for the government of his affections . . . since these things are

---

[78] Ibid.
[79] Ibid. 2.26.
[80] Ibid: the reference is to plate nine in ch. xxvi, reproduced in Maxwell's translation.
[81] Cumberland, *DLN* 2.26.

peculiar to man, it cannot but suggest to his mind that it is its province diligently to attend the Helm committed to its care, and to steer skillfully.' Cumberland may have taken this example directly from Samuel Parker. In the *Free and impartial censure*, Parker uses the same passage from Willis to argue that the nervous system enables the mind to control the body.[82] The nerves allow the soul to 'be able to restrain and check the Impetuosity of the Blood's Motion, and consequently curb the eager and unruly passions'. Cumberland and Parker both argue that passionate excess can be controlled through physiological links between body and mind. For Cumberland this is evidence that the passions were not determinative, as Hobbes had appeared to suggest, but rather that they should be controlled according to the dictates of the law of nature: 'How much it conduces to our present argument', wrote Cumberland, 'that, from the very structure of our body, we are continually admonished of the necessity of governing our affections with a strict hand.'[83] All of the virtues, he claims, and the whole observance of the law of nature are ultimately related to the government of the passions. The use of reason to curb passionate excess forms the foundation for morality, sociability and the settling of property.

Cumberland's moral physiology thus demonstrated that the internal structure of man provided particular advantages in the exercise of morality. This was enough to cast doubt upon the suggestion that Hobbes had offered compelling evidence for his analysis of human nature. As Cumberland triumphantly remarks, 'Hobbes has nowhere offered anything in this manner natural or essential to the mind or body of man, which can suggest to anyone a necessary argument.'[84] The problem here was not that Hobbes had used science, but rather that he had not been scientific enough in his observations. Hobbes's abstraction of human nature relied upon dubious analysis of his own problematic personality and generalisations based upon atypical behaviour. Cumberland complained that 'the manners, which a few sometimes rashly fall into, from which the conduct of most others, and often of themselves too, differs, are not to be imputed by the nature of man, nor of the universe'.[85] Aberrant anti-social behaviour is a contingent circumstance resulting not from man's essential nature, but the 'rash determination' of his free will. Hobbes's bad science had led to a mistaken ethical theory; Cumberland's true science, on the other hand, offered new and better ways of understanding ethics and obligation.

---

82 Parker, *Censure*, 66. See also his *Tentamina physico-theologica de Deo*, Oxford 1665, 79–98, 100–8, 116–20, 138–9. Robert Sharrock also uses Willis in *De finibus virtutis Christianae*, Oxford 1673, 114–15.
83 Cumberland, *DLN* 2.27.
84 Ibid. 2.31.
85 Ibid.

Analogy and metaphor

The nature of Cumberland's project meant that even where there were no direct lessons to be drawn from natural philosophy, science could be used analogically to illustrate the application of the laws of nature throughout the universal system. This usage was part of a well-established tradition in early-modern natural philosophy. Robert Boyle argued that 'by example, analogy . . . we are, as it were, led by the hand to the discovery of divers useful notions. . . . And, indeed, the world is a great book, not so much of nature, as of the God of nature which we should find crowded with instructive lessons, if we but had the skill, and would take the pains . . . to pick them out.'[86] Boyle may have been sceptical about the skills that individuals could possess in this art, but for English Cartesians, the use of analogical reasoning fitted well with a systematic understanding of nature. One example of this at a practical scientific level was Henry Power's *Analogia physico-chymica* (1666) which compared physical and chemical processes side by side.

For Cumberland, the physical operations of nature could be used analogically to illustrate the broad application of similar laws throughout the physical and intellectual system. Again, Cumberland's emphasis was upon identifying the common laws of nature governing all created things, locating man and rational morality in a law-bound universe. Cumberland's most elaborate use of analogy occurs in chapter 5 of the *De legibus*, where he lays out his theory of obligation. Here, Cumberland uses the air as a metaphor for the benevolence and agreement of men. Both air and benevolence are necessary for the sustenance of life, and Cumberland lingers on the comparison because 'hence may be illustrated the mutual offices of men, which I have chiefly undertaken to explain'.[87]

Cumberland points out that the necessity of air to man is something that has been long known and which philosophers have demonstrated 'by the instructive experiments, which they have found out'. Cumberland takes this opportunity to show the ways in which the Royal Society's work has helped in this respect:

> This has been proved by means of animals endowed with blood which immediately died in the Air Pump (the Hon. Robert Boyle's most ingenious contrivance) upon the air being exhausted. Dogs dissected by the learned Mr Hook, testify the same; who, after the Asperia Asteria was cut below the epiglottis, and the ribs, diaphragm and pericardium were cut away, lived above an hour, by the help of fresh air blown into the lungs by the help of a pair of bellows.[88]

---

[86] Boyle, *Works*, ii. 149,155.
[87] Cumberland, *DLN* 5.34.
[88] Ibid.

The air pump experiments were recounted in Boyle's *New experiments physico-mechanical* (1660), and the experiments with birds were carried out by Hooke in 1659.[89] The gruesome experiment with the dog (which Evelyn found 'of more cruelty than pleased me') was performed in October 1667.[90] Cumberland concludes that 'it is therefore certain . . . that the air is one of the necessary causes of life, and that which is healthful is everywhere sought, although its essential properties, and the manner of its acting upon us, be not yet fully discovered'. Cumberland then argues that agreement to men is as air is to life. Cumberland makes the simile that individuals should always endeavour to obtain agreement 'though we no more understand the inward constitution of men, than of the air'. This transforms into an argument for unilateral moral action. If seeking agreement is as natural as respiration, then agreement should be sought in every circumstance for fear of the consequences of not seeking it, just as it is necessary to breathe even in a situation where the consequences are uncertain:

> nor can we foresee all that, whether good or harm, which may arise from [others'] society, as in like manner we are ignorant what draught of air is perfectly healthful and which will bring with it a contagious distemper; yet we know that certain death is the consequence of respiration stopped, but that continuance thereof, for the most part, is a vast advantage to life.[91]

Just as the human body does not impede the natural tendency to breathe, so reason should unilaterally promote the social virtues. Respiration also provides Cumberland with an analogy for moral reciprocity:

> The air, which we have drawn into our lungs, we immediately breathe back again; or, if a small portion thereof be retained for some little time, for the refreshing of our blood and vital spirits, it is afterwards, along with the blood itself and vital spirits, as it were, with interest, restored by insensible perspiration to the common mass of the air; this reciprocal natural motion, which is intermixt with somewhat voluntary, thus resembles gratitude, and points out its necessity for the good of the whole.[92]

Respiration thus 'shadows out some slight touches of humanity' and 'yet this shadow exactly represents the particular part of living virtue, and this mutual connexion, with their real motions, or effects'. Cumberland's fascination with reciprocal motion recurs throughout the *De legibus naturae*. In some cases it was combined with a circulatory metaphor, in which natural systems were compared with the circular transmission of benevolence. The circulation of the blood, carrying nutrition to every part of the corporeal system, is

89 R. G. Frank, *Harvey and the Oxford physiologists*, Berkeley 1980, 200–1.
90 John Evelyn, *Diary*, ed. E. S. de Beer, Oxford 1955, iii. 497–8; *Philosophical Transactions* ii (1667), 539–40.
91 Cumberland, *DLN* 5.34.
92 Ibid.

compared with the circulation of good offices in society. Most commonly, the circulatory metaphor is used in the context of mechanics. In chapter 2, Cumberland argued that in all things, 'a certain order is preserved, by which some motions are determined by others in a continual series, and all are governed by the continued circular motion of the whole system'.[93] In chapter 9, Cumberland wrote that: 'The material system is indeed preserv'd by a motion communicated to all its parts; but it is necessary that such a motion should return unto itself and, by that means, be perpetuated.' Cumberland perceives the same structure to moral acts: 'In like manner, in the moral system, a universal benevolence, once begun, is daily renewed by the reciprocal force of gratitude, and by its aid, or even by a prospect or hope thereof gain new strength, and an eternal youth.'[94] The operation of gratitude acts to preserve benevolence in the moral system, just as collision produces reaction in a mechanical system.

This last example highlights Cumberland's objectives in incorporating natural philosophy into his ethical system. Motion and circulation had been central concepts in Hobbes's account of a nominalist science, but Cumberland had appropriated that territory, and even Hobbes's own scientific writings, for his own ethical ends.[95] This appropriation was Cumberland's essential purpose in using as much science as he did. Natural philosophy in general, and experimental philosophy in particular, could provide clear and distinct evidence both of the physical limits to moral action and the physical potential for moral behaviour. The first Cumberland used to discredit Hobbes's theory of subjective right. The second formed the basis for Cumberland's constructive theory. Both demonstrated in a novel fashion that the laws of nature were obligatory and inescapable. In the course of his critique Cumberland had identified Hobbes's theory as unjustly abstracting mankind from the rest of nature. Nature was ruled by the same pattern of God-given laws, and man was essentially part of nature and subject to the same legislation. Indeed, if man had any distinct advantage over the rest of creation, it lay in a greater sensitivity to God's government, a sensitivity accompanied by the gift of free will. Hobbes's error stemmed from his wilful disregard for the evidence of nature, a fault not of too much science, but paradoxically, of too little.

It is perhaps a measure of Cumberland's success, and that of others who wrote in this genre, such as Ward, Wallis, Wilkins and Stillingfleet, that Hobbes was so thoroughly discredited as a natural philosopher by the close of the seventeenth century. This was not because his science was necessarily wrong or inadequate, but rather because his account of a nominalist science, with its ethically reductive implications, was so unacceptable. Hobbes had to be detached from the useful aspects of his natural philosophy for that kind of materialist science to be used at all. Ironically, it was the work of writers like

---

[93] Ibid. 2.13; cf. H. Burton, *A second volume of discourses*, London 1685, 516.
[94] Cumberland, *DLN* 9.4.
[95] For Hobbes's use of circular local motion see *EW* vii. 7–10, 95.

Cumberland in defending mechanism against its critics, that ensured that the lessons of the *De corpore*, and Hobbes's optics, could be absorbed and transformed within Newton's science and the Latitudinarian cosmology that accompanied it. As with his politics, Hobbes was too near the bone to be ignored, but too dangerous to be openly endorsed. His reputation as a natural philosopher had to be destroyed in order for the idea of mechanistic natural philosophy to survive and develop. It is still underestimated today.

Cumberland's own usage of natural philosophy quickly dated. Even while he wrote, Cartesian conservation theory was coming under attack, and this undermined the force of Cumberland's plenistic systems of bodies, rational agents and benevolence. What in 1672 would have seemed exotic, novel and strikingly original deployments of very recent research soon paled in the wake of Newton's *Principia*. The apologetic work for the Royal Society in the 1660s nevertheless left its mark. In forcing an early confrontation with Hobbes, Descartes and Gassendi, the works from this period constructed the shape of the Anglican accommodation with natural philosophy. Confronting Hobbes required an alternative conception of the relationship between science and religion. The anti-religious tendencies of natural philosophy were neutralised in the works of writers like Cumberland. The elevation of the Latitude-men, and Cumberland himself, to the episcopal bench in the last decade of the century ensured that this view became institutionalised, a feature which must go some way towards accounting for the peculiarly institutionalised and clerical nature of the English Enlightenment.

Frontispiece to Jean Barbeyrac's French translation of the *De legibus*, the *Traité philosophique des loix naturelles* (1744).

The illustration perceptively represents Cumberland's project. The original captions reads: 'La LOI NATURELLE, embrasse L'EQUITÉ; LA SCIENCE la decouvre, & la VERITÉ l'eclaire, pendant que le GENIE de CUMBERLAND terrasse L'ERREUR, & le GENIE de HOBBES'.

7

De Legibus Naturae
and the Natural Law Tradition

Cumberland's work had been conceived to exonerate the apparently Hobbesian ideas of his colleagues in both science and politics. It demonstrated that it was possible to make the voluntarist critique of natural law without abandoning the idea of natural sociability. In addition Cumberland had retained the positive fruits of Hobbes's theories. The emphasis upon self-preservation and the *Leviathan*'s solution to the problems of political and religious conflict, could be sustained without resorting to a warlike state of nature, or the argument that all obligation was sourced in the state. In short, Cumberland had proved that one did not have to endorse Hobbes in order to use the natural law language to which he had contributed.

This argument became important for other writers accused of maintaining Hobbesian positions. The defensive use of Cumberland's work was his most significant legacy. The *De legibus* could be used to inoculate natural law theory against the charge of Hobbism. In providing this service, Cumberland's theory allowed the continued development and acceptance of post-Hobbesian natural law theory. The most interesting examples of this process can be seen at work in the natural law theories of John Locke and Samuel Pufendorf. Both of these writers would be scrutinised for their apparent Hobbism. In both cases, Cumberland's solution to the problem of Hobbism would be deployed to meet the objections. In this way both Locke and Pufendorf would demonstrate the continuing importance of Cumberland's theory of obligation.

Samuel Pufendorf

Pufendorf was an exact contemporary of Cumberland. He also shared Cumberland's interest in developing a Cartesian *scientia moralis*, an approach which gave rise to his *Elementorum jurisprudentiae universalis* (1660). Pufendorf's thesis proposed that morality could be established upon a geometrical framework of principles, axioms and observations. Its spare, mathematical style owed much to his Cartesian mentor at Jena, Erhard Weigel, but Pufendorf's geometrical ethics drew on other sources as well. He remarked in the preface that 'No small debt likewise do we owe to Thomas Hobbes, whose basic conception in his book De Cive, although it savours somewhat of the profane, is nevertheless for the most part extremely acute and sound.'[1] This equivocal reaction could be considered a fair summary of much of the reaction, both in England and on the continent, to Hobbes's first major attempt at a demonstrative ethics. It is important to note, however, that Pufendorf's Hobbesian borrowings were selective and critical, even at this stage.

The most obvious similarity between the *De cive* and the *Elementorum* was Pufendorf's use of self-preservation. But although this was a distinctive element of Hobbes's natural law theory, it was also the common property and commonplace of all those theorists who, after Grotius, had returned to Ciceronian natural law. However, Pufendorf's theory seemed to take on a more Hobbesian dimension when it came to the discussion of natural sociability. Pufendorf was dissatisfied with Grotius' vague ascription to man of a natural tendency to a social existence. He sought to anatomise sociability much more rigorously in terms of self-interest alone. Pufendorf argued that good extended to others was no different from self-love in nature. In addition he suggested that sociability resulted in physical needs as well as natural propensity: 'Such is the state of need, of human life, that were not a number to unite upon a mutual task, life could only be preserved with the utmost difficulty.'[2] Apparently following Hobbes, Pufendorf argued that it was not unreasonable to suggest that man should be made fit for society not by nature but by discipline. The dramatic tension between natural and artificial sociability seems to owe something to Hobbes, but Pufendorf ameliorates this by suggesting that nature and artifice can work together. The coincidence between self-interest and sociability can be a design of nature: 'nature has not bidden us to cultivate societies with the purpose of neglecting the care of ourselves; since, forsooth, societies bring about in the very highest degree the conditions that, through the mutual sharing of aid and of blessing with a number, we can more conveniently look out for our own blessing'.[3]

Pufendorf's concentration upon a narrowly selfish and utilitarian analysis and simultaneous emphasis on the primary importance of the social good, resembles the contrasting approaches in chapters 1 and 2 of the *De legibus*. Rather than misguided allegiance to Hobbesian theory, both represent attempts to understand the process by which the individual comes to identify their own good with that of the social unit. Both demonstrated a willingness to consider a range of motives for a sociable existence. Pufendorf might have considered self-interest first, but this did not mean that he ruled out the possibility of mutual benevolence, which as Cumberland would later argue, was also compatible with self-preservation.[4]

His mixed assessment of human motivation meant that Pufendorf un-

---

[1] Pufendorf, *Elementorum*, ii, p. xxx.
[2] Ibid. 2.3.2; cf. Cumberland, *DLN* 1.11 later cited in the second edition of *De jure naturae* 2.3.14.
[3] Pufendorf, *Elementorum* 2.3.4; 2.3.5.
[4] Ibid.

equivocally refused to see the state of nature as a state of war. He argued that 'this status would be utterly repugnant to the conservation and security of men, and would bring with it infinite troubles and miseries'. As a result of this, 'the inconveniences . . . directly resulting from such a state ought not to be substituted as the foundations of the law of nature; but rather this, namely, that God has directly determined man to cultivate a social life'.[5] For Pufendorf, natural sociability was a basic natural moral obligation. Pufendorf was always critical of Hobbes's position, in which sociability arises artificially as a way of escaping a hostile state of war. In Pufendorf's account, the natural law of *socialitas* was God-given and obligatory, even in the state of nature.

Pufendorf's *De jure naturae et gentium* was published in the same year as the *De legibus*, and developed the natural law position of the *Elementorum*. The natural law theory worked out in book II was remarkably similar to Cumberland's treatise. It discussed the contents of the law of nature and the source of its obligatory force, divorced from the complications of theology and civil law. Pufendorf developed the theme of *indigentia* or need as an incentive to sociability, emphasising the convergence of positive and negative motives to common association. 'It is quite clear', he wrote, 'that man is an animal extremely desirous of his own preservation, in himself exposed to want, unable to exist without the help of his fellow creatures.' At the same time, he noted, man is 'fitted in a remarkable way to contribute to the common good, and yet at all times malicious, petulent, and easily irritated, as well as quick and powerful to do injury'. The pessimistic aspects of Pufendorf's analysis recall Hobbes's negative assessment of human nature, but Pufendorf turns the stress upon need into a motive for sociability:

> For such an animal to live and enjoy the good things that in this world would attend his condition, it is necessary that he be sociable, that is, willing to join with others like him, and conduct themselves towards him in such a way that, far from having any cause to do him harm, they may feel that there is reason to preserve and increase his good fortune.[6]

As a result of this prudential sociability, the law of nature thus dictated that 'every man so far as in him lies, should cultivate and preserve towards others a sociable attitude which is peaceful and agreeable at all times to the nature and end of the human race'. Pufendorf's account of sociability had absorbed some of the potential for evil that Hobbes identified in his work, but it also mixed this with a recognition that there could be a social group and that self-interest and sociability were not mutually exclusive. Pufendorf's theory thus lay midway between the rigid self-interest of Hobbes's theory and the antithetical universal benevolence of Cumberland.

Unfortunately for Pufendorf, it was this ambiguous position which left the

---

5   Ibid. 2.3.6.
6   Samuel Pufendorf, *De jure naturae et gentium*, ed. and trans. C. H. Oldfather and W. A. Oldfather, ii, Oxford 1934 (hereinafter cited as *DJN*), 2.3.15.

theory open to the charge that the law of nature could be reduced to the utilitarian assessments made by self-interested individuals. Without a convincing account of natural obligation, Pufendorf's laws of nature were in danger of being dissolved into Hobbesian 'theorems'. As Palladini has pointed out, the 'as far as in him lies' condition recalls Hobbes's qualification that laws of nature could be disregarded where there was a threat to the life of the individual.[7] Pufendorf had made it clear that he accepted the voluntarist critique of right reason. To count as laws, natural precepts required the binding obligation of a superior.[8]

Like Cumberland, Pufendorf appealed to an essentially free God, who had bound himself to natural laws, in order to make his natural law binding.[9] Pufendorf argued from this that if man were genuinely sociable then this was also the will of God:

> He so formed the nature of the world and man that the latter cannot exist without leading a social life, and for this reason gave him a mind capable of grasping the ideas that lead to this end . . . it is surely to be recognised that he also willed man to regulate his actions by that native endowment which God himself appears to given him in a special way over the beasts.[10]

Such laws were backed up by the pangs of conscience which intimated retribution for unpunished earthly transgression. Pufendorf's appeal to a 'higher principle' authorising the conclusions of reason established the binding and universal obligation to God's imposed, but rational, law.

Despite this discussion of divine obligation Pufendorf was attacked as a Hobbesian. Two of Pufendorf's colleagues at Lund, Nikolaus Beckmann, Professor of Roman Law, and Joshua Schwartz, Professor of Theology, led an assault on what they perceived to be the moral relativism of the *De jure naturae*.[11] Pufendorf was forced to defend himself, and in a series of works during the 1670s he attempted to clarify and distinguish his position from that of Hobbes. Given the congruence between their projects it is no surprise to find Pufendorf turning to Cumberland's more explicitly anti-Hobbesian work to provide support for his case. One of Pufendorf's earliest references to the *De legibus naturae* comes in his *Epistola ad scherzerum*, where he defends his usage of *socialitas* as the sole organising foundation for natural law.

---

[7] For the similarities between Hobbes and Pufendorf in this regard see F. Palladini, *Samuel Pufendorf: discepolo di Hobbes: per una reinterpretazione del giusnaturalismo moderno*, Bologna 1990, 135–9.

[8] Pufendorf, *DJN* 1.6.4.

[9] Ibid. 2.3.4–5; cf. Cumberland, *DLN* 7.6.

[10] Pufendorf, *DJN* 2.3.20.

[11] Beckmann led the assault with his *Index novitatum*, Lund 1673. Other assailants included Friedrich Gesen, a Lutheran minister from Magdeburg, Valentin Veltem, Professor of Theology at Jena, and Valentin Alberti, Professor of Theology at Leipzig. The arguments of Pufendorf's critics are discussed in F. Palladini, *Discussioni seicentesche su Samuel Pufendorf*, Bologna 1987, 99–122, and Haakonssen, *Natural law and moral philosophy*, 43–6.

Sociability is the 'chief principle in the study of natural law derived from the observation of the nature of things and the desires of men'. It is an opinion held by Plato, Aristotle and especially the Stoics, 'as it is completely opposed to the Hobbesian doctrine of self-preservation, which Cumberland joins me in attacking'.[12] More explicitly approving references came in the *Specimen controversarium* of 1677, which, together with the *Eris scandia* (written at the same time but published in 1686), aimed to defuse the accusations of Hobbism. Pufendorf's tactic was to cast himself as a Stoic alongside Cumberland, against the maverick Epicureanism of Hobbes, thus effacing the points of contact between them. After mentioning that Hobbes had probably gained inspiration for his moral science from Gassendi's natural philosophy, Pufendorf sang Cumberland's praises:

> In my opinion, however, the Englishman, Richard Cumberland has most soundly refuted his [Hobbes's] theories in his most learned and excellent book, De Legibus Naturae; and he has securely erected a counter-philosophy which agrees very closely with the views of the Stoics. I, too, had planned to do both of these things. And I must admit I was delighted to see this work published abroad in the same year (rather different in form) but nonetheless agreeing with my philosophy and demolishing very many tenets of Hobbes which I had criticised. Nor is the work of either of us the less valuable, because each has particular merits of its own in addition to those which they have in common.[13]

Pufendorf repeatedly argued that he had 'expressly refuted' Hobbes's innovations in religion, and had consistently sided with the Stoics against the Epicurean Hobbes. Again, Cumberland was wheeled on as evidence of Pufendorf's good faith: 'If anyone carefully compares with mine the work of Richard Cumberland . . . he will see practically all his criticisms of Hobbes had been made by me too, though whereas his declared purpose was to demolish Hobbes's philosophy, I counted it as merely an ancillary task to refute his errors.'[14]

Pufendorf took his admiration for Cumberland one step further in the second edition of the *De jure naturae*, published in 1684. Pufendorf included no fewer than forty references to the *De legibus naturae*, of varying length and importance. Palladini has argued that Pufendorf used these quotations from Cumberland to conceal a Hobbesian utilitarianism rendered unusable by the criticism of the *De jure*.[15] However, as the brief examination of the *Elementorum* has shown, Pufendorf had always maintained a sceptical attitude towards

---

12 Pufendorf, *Epistola ad scherzerum*, 74, quoted in Palladini, *Samuel Pufendorf*, 179–80.
13 Pufendorf, *Specimen controversarium* 1.6; translated in Kirk, *Cumberland*, 80.
14 Ibid.
15 Palladini, *Samuel Pufendorf*. Palladini's extreme interpretation appears to rest upon the misconception that Pufendorf's voluntarism and his emphasis upon self-preservation and the state of nature both mean that he was a disciple of Hobbes. In fact such elements were the common property of all writers in the natural law tradition. They had been compro-

Hobbesian theory, particularly the suggestion that the state of nature was a state of war. Pufendorf was prepared to quote Hobbes on self-preservation with approval, but he consistently objected to Hobbes's suggestion that individuals were only obliged to the law of nature through their own self-interest.[16] According to Pufendorf, rational reflection would always lead men to arrive at sociable conclusions. Hobbes might have been right to start from the premise of self-preservation, but wrong to assume that this would automatically result in a state of war. Pufendorf, like Cumberland, was attempting to develop Grotius' thesis about natural sociability, but in a way that avoided Hobbes's controversial arguments about moral obligation. In other words, Pufendorf was maintaining a Stoic thesis against those Epicurean elements which had characterised Hobbes's subversion of the language of natural law. The problem for Pufendorf, as for Hobbes's English critics, was that Hobbes mixed acceptable premises with unorthodox and subversive conclusions. Pufendorf found himself facing the same problem that writers like Parker had encountered in deploying useful Hobbesian theses. As a result it was natural that he should find Cumberland's Ciceronian opposition between Stoic and Epicurean a useful way of complementing his own position.

In addition to reinforcing Pufendorf's anti-Hobbesian stance,[17] the positive theory of the De legibus also added weight to Pufendorf's obligation theory. Like Hobbes, Pufendorf had rested his moral observations upon an examination of the nature of man alone.[18] Cumberland's thesis, with its attempt to place human nature in the context of a law-bound universe, extended the range of observations which could prove the existence of obligatory natural law from the 'nature of things'.[19] Following Cumberland, Pufendorf argued that reason tried against the nature of things could provide an objective standard for apprehending natural law: 'Now this reason in a state of nature has a common, and furthermore, an abiding and uniform standard of judgement, namely, the nature of things, which offers a free and distinct service in pointing out general rules for living, and the law of nature.'[20] Pufendorf thus added this new method of seeing obligation to enhance his original position. Empirical examination of nature refined through the use of

---

mised by Hobbes's subversion of the genre, hence Pufendorf's desire to distance himself from Hobbes.

16 Pufendorf, DJN 2.3.16

17 There are numerous examples of this, see particularly Pufendorf, DJN 2.2.8; cf. Cumberland DLN 2.29. See also Pufendorf, DJN 1.7.13; cf. Cumberland, DLN, 8.6.

18 Pufendorf, DJN 2.3.9.

19 Ibid. 1.4.8: 'Richard Cumberland shows how man has been endowed by nature with special powers to curb the passions, and how at the same time his life and strength are more seriously threatened, than are those of other animals, from violent and ill-controlled passions, and how, therefore, he is under greater necessity to restrain them.' Cf. Cumberland, DLN 2.26–7.

20 Pufendorf, DJN 2.2.9.

clear and distinct Cartesian ideas could reveal objectively true moral relationships.[21]

Pufendorf's revisions benefit most from Cumberland's theory where Pufendorf deals with formal obligation theory. The paragraph dealing with the obligation to natural law was amended to include a linkage between ideas of
natural sociability and God's causal agency in producing them through
nature (the 1684 addition is in italics):

> Since He has so formed the world and man that the latter cannot exist with-
> out leading a social life, and for this reason gave him a mind capable of grasp-
> ing the ideas that lead to this end, *and since He suggests these ideas to men's
> minds by the course of natural events as they come from Him as the first Cause, and
> represent clearly their necessary relationship and truth*, it is surely recognised that
> He also willed for man to regulate his actions by that native endowment
> which God Himself appears to have given him in a special way above the
> beasts.[22]

Pufendorf also added Cumberland's master-thesis about the possibility of
natural rewards and punishments in order to strengthen the probability that
God was indeed the author of moral obligation. Pufendorf argued that 'the
Creator has assigned to every act agreeable with His Law its regular and
natural effect, which tends to the advantage of man. These good things
Richard Cumberland calls natural rewards.' Pufendorf comments that
although God could have demanded obedience without earthly sanction, in
fact it 'pleased his goodness so to constitute the nature of the world and of
men that certain good things follow by a natural connexion the observance
of natural laws and certain evils their violation'.[23] It should be noted that
Pufendorf was not arguing that natural rewards and punishments are the
source of natural obligation. As in Cumberland's work, obligation is still formally and materially derived from God the legislator. Natural rewards and
punishments are merely coincidental indicators of the divine intention. The
existence of such rewards and punishments makes it clear that even if good
actions do not always produce rewards, they nevertheless make it a more reli-
able guide for human action than pure self-interest.[24]

The adaptation of Cumberland allowed Pufendorf to dissociate himself
from Hobbes by providing a more convincing material framework for the
obligation to *socialitas*. Cumberland helped to neutralise the critics' charges
that Pufendorf's moral obligation proceeded primarily from utility, and not
from conformity with the laws of a superior. As a result, Pufendorf could argue

---

21 Ibid. 1.3.2; cf. Cumberland, *DLN* 2.9: See also Pufendorf, *DJN* 1.3.3; cf. Cumberland,
DLN 2.10.
22 Pufendorf, *DJN* 2.3.20.
23 Ibid. 2.3.21; cf. Cumberland, *DLN* 5.25.
24 Pufendorf, *DJN* 2.3.21.

that Cumberland's law of nature, which merged the good of the individual and the community, was no different from his own:

> The law of nature as stated by Richard Cumberland . . . regarding zeal for the common welfare and the greatest possible exhibition of good will towards others does not differ from our fundamental law. For in saying that man is a social animal we do not intimate that he should hold his own advantage, distinct from that of others, as his good, but the advantage of others as well, not that anyone should seek his own advancement to the oppression or neglect of others, not that man should hope for happiness if he disregards and injures others.[25]

Pufendorf thus attempted to rescue his thesis by the introduction of Cumberland's arguments. The new emphasis upon natural sanctions and the nature of things allowed him to establish an objective reference point for his obligation theory. Self-preservation could then be stressed safely within the context of a law-bound state of nature. As a result, Pufendorf could use those aspects of Hobbesian theory that remained useful to him. He puts this quite aptly after giving an apparently Hobbesian discussion of rights. An individual may have a right to do what conduces to self-preservation, but, writes Pufendorf, 'one can by no means conclude that a man has any right to do as he pleases to any one he pleases, if one bears in mind that the man discussed by Hobbes in such a state is still subject to the rules of natural law and right reason'.[26]

The English context

The continuing controversy over Hobbes and Hobbism meant that the *De legibus naturae* would be read and used throughout the Restoration period. The original but flawed text was cited as one of the best responses to Hobbes's theory in England and on the continent, but it was through translations that Cumberland found a wider market and popular appreciation in his own country. There were two major attempts to translate and popularise the arguments of the book. It is no surprise to find that one of Cumberland's earliest interpreters was Samuel Parker, now archdeacon of Canterbury, whose *Demonstration of the divine authority of the law of nature* was published in 1681.

The many connections between Parker and the *De legibus* have already been discussed at length, and it is clear that Parker had every reason to associate himself with a thesis which strengthened the anti-Hobbesian tenor of his natural law ideas. Parker's book was designed to be a popularisation of all aspects of moral obligation theory available to Protestants, and it was produced in the vernacular because it was the 'ignorant and the unlearned who were most likely to slip into scepticism'. Hobbism had become a live issue in

---

[25] Ibid. 2.3.15.
[26] Ibid. 2.2.3.

the late 1670s and early 1680s for a number of reasons. The lapse of the licensing laws provided an opportunity to publish unauthorised copies of *Behemoth*, Hobbes's banned history of the civil wars, and even the *Leviathan* itself. Hobbes's death in 1679 prompted printed comment and a posthumous reprinting of many of his works. At a deeper level, the crisis in Church and State created a demand for Hobbes's writing. As John Marshall has shown, anti-toleration sentiments expressed by Tillotson and Stillingfleet resurrected the charges of Anglican Hobbism. The debate over exclusion, popery and arbitrary government also revived an interest in contract theory. As with the later 1660s, the recurring tensions in the polity returned the ideas of the *Leviathan* to the political stage.[27]

Parker's preface indicated that the dangers of Hobbism were at the top of his agenda. With characteristic venom, Parker berated the 'unlearned herd' of 'plebeians and mechanics' who have 'philosophized themselves into principles of Impiety, and read the Lectures of Atheism in the Street and the High-Ways'. He went on:

> And they are able to demonstrate out of the Leviathan that there is no God or Providence, but that all things come to pass by an eternal Chain of Natural Causes: That there are no principles of every-Man's self-interest, nor any self-interest but onely of this present Life: That humane Nature is a meer Machine and that all the contrivances of Men are nothing but the Mechanical Results of Matter and Motion.[28]

The rabble were clearly becoming infected with this kind of enthusiasm and Parker's self-appointed task was to intercede with plain language and common sense, 'to step in between the dead and the living, the infected and the sound, and, if possible, to give some stop to the contagion, or at least to keep the disease from descending to Posterity'.[29] Parker had lost none of the rhetorical vigour that had characterised his dispute with the nonconformists, and his revulsion was driven by the identification of the same impious disease, with Hobbism as its common ideological symptom. Parker's antidote was to demonstrate the divine source of moral obligation with every means at his disposal, from Cumberland's arguments in the *De legibus* through to the Scriptures themselves.

Parker begins by sketching out the inadequacies of natural law to date. The Civilians, Canonists and Schoolmen, he argues, have merely defined it. Even Grotius has mistaken its nature by proposing that it is 'obligatory

27 For the concerns about *Behemoth* and *Leviathan*, and the response to Hobbes's death see Mark Knights, *Politics and opinion in crisis, 1678–81*, Cambridge 1994, 208n., 254–5; Marshall, 'Ecclesiology of the Latitude-Men', 407–27.

28 Samuel Parker, *A demonstration of the divine authority of the law of nature*, London 1681, p. iii.

29 Ibid. p. v.

without the supposition of a Deity'.[30] Parker notes that Pufendorf 'has indeed of late hapned upon its right definition in general, but has neither described its particular Branches, nor demonstrated any of the grounds of its obligation'. Parker's remark about the first edition of the *De jure naturae* reflects the general dissatisfaction with Pufendorf's treatment of obligation. The solution to the deficiency, argues Pufendorf, is Cumberland's *De legibus naturae*. Cicero's *De republica* may have been lost, he comments,

> but by those fragments that are remaining of it, I am apt to think that this loss has been compensated by the learned and judicious Treatise of our Country-man Dr Cumberland upon this Argument, who has not onely hit upon the right Notion of the Law of Nature, but has, in a method heretofore proper only to Mathematicks, demonstrated its obligation.

Parker comments that the original text, with its complicated scientific allusions was hard to understand. As a result he has taken Cumberland's 'main notion alone stript of all accessional Ornaments of Learning and prosecuted the demonstration of it in my own way in a similar stile and an easie method'.[31]

Despite his claims, it should be noted that Parker does not remove all the references to natural philosophy in the *De legibus*. Parker was aiming his argument at careless use of the mechanical philosophy. He had consistently been interested in the godly use of science from his first published work in 1665 through to his *magnum opus*, the *Disputationes de deo et providentia divina* of 1678. Throughout his writings, Parker had been passionately interested in the new science, but at the same time alive to the dangers of atheistic interpretations of mechanism. The *Disputationes* attacked the limitations of Cartesianism and Epicureanism as systems with a potential for atheism. In particular Parker was concerned by the dangers of endorsing a science of matter and motion alone; he wrote of the

> folly and nonesense of meer Mechanism . . . accounting for the nature of Things onely by Matter or Motion, or any other second Causes, is so notorious that all the Philosophers in the World never were, nor ever will be able to give any the least account how so much a stone should fall to the ground without a Divine Providence.[32]

This was not an ill-informed rant but rather a popular expression of his more detailed work. Parker's concern, which dovetailed with Cumberland's project, was to emphasise the role of God in nature. Some 'mechanicks', he commented, indulge in the 'building of stately Worlds without an Artificer . . . whereas if they would take the Divine Wisedom into their Mechanicks, and make their several ways of mechanism the effects of his contrivance and

30 Ibid. p. viii.
31 Ibid. p. ix.
32 Ibid.

not the results of blind and stupid Matter, for me they might play at *mechaniz-ing* as long and as variously as they please'.[33]

Although Parker agreed with this aspect of the *De legibus naturae*, he parted company with Cumberland in his emphasis upon the sanctions of the after-life. This may have been an implicit critique of Cumberland's reluctance to discuss the after-life, a function of his desire to confront Hobbes on his *Leviathan's* own ground. Parker argued that the same providence that had created the world would ensure a future state in which the injustices of this life could be remedied. The existence of natural law necessarily presupposed future justice.[34] Parker agreed with Cumberland that natural philosophy could be used to identify God and his providential government, but ultimately the most convincing demonstration of moral obligation came from the awareness of a future state in which a provident God dispensed justice. That alone, argued Parker, 'far exceeds the evidence of all other demonstrations'.[35]

Parker's dissatisfaction with Cumberland's rigorous adherence to Hobbes's agenda led him to place his borrowings from the *De legibus* in a more conventional theological setting. Some eighty-eight pages of loosely translated and freely adapted Cumberland is qualified with a critical Ciceronian appraisal of Epicureanism and also the more unacceptably materialistic tendencies of Stoicism. Parker's text then moves on to a full-blooded defence of Scripture as a detailed revelation of the full content of natural law. His resort to Scripture was, of course, like the more traditional voluntarist explanation of moral obligation used by Jeremy Taylor, and even by Hobbes in the *De cive*. The continued need to combat and deflect charges of Hobbism meant that Cumberland's thesis remained a part of the polemical weaponry of Anglican rationalism.

Locke, Tyrrell and the *Brief disquisition*

It would be less than ten years before Cumberland's thesis made a major reappearance. The occasion was yet another resurgence of Hobbism, but this time in the pages of John Locke's *Essay concerning human understanding*. James Tyrrell, Locke's friend, wrote to him from Oxford in June 1690 describing the reaction of some 'thinkeing men' to the *Essay*: 'I found them dissatisfyed', he wrote, 'with what you have sayed concerning the Law of nature, (or reason) whereby we distinguish moral good, from evil and vertue, from vice.'[36] The critics were concerned with the way that Locke had derived moral obligation from three laws: divine law, the law of the commonwealth and thirdly the law

---

33 Ibid. pp. xvi–xvii.
34 Ibid. p. xxi.
35 Ibid. p. xxiii.
36 *Correspondence of John Locke*, ed. E. S. de Beer, Oxford 1976, iv. 101–2.

of opinion or reputation. In the first edition of the *Essay*, the divine law was described in such a way that it could easily be taken to refer to revelation alone.[37] This left a question mark hanging over the third law, that of opinion, or fashion, where Locke seemed to entertain the possibility of a purely conventional ethics remote from the natural obligation of God:

> Nor is it to be thought strange, that Men everywhere should give the name *Vertue* to those actions, which amongst them are judged praiseworthy; and call that *Vice* which they account blameable: Since otherwise they would condemn themselves, if they should think anything *Right*, to which they allowed not Commendation; anything *Wrong*, which they let pass without Blame.[38]

Locke partially escapes moral relativism by insisting that conventional understandings of virtue and vice tend to coincide with God's law because a 'correct' understanding of God's law is incidentally in the individual's interest.[39] This, however, was not enough for the Oxford critics. Tyrrell reported that Locke's laws, particularly the third law of fashion 'come very near what is so much cried out upon in Mr:Hobs; when he asserts that in a state of nature and out of a commonwealth, there is no moral good or evil: virtue, or vice but in respect to those persons, that practice it, or think it so'.[40] By appearing to leave nothing between revelation and the law of opinion, Locke seemed to be denying that morality could be discerned by the light of nature.

This drawback to Locke's moral theory had its roots in the *Essays on the law of nature*. It was clear to Locke that the Hobbesian emphasis upon self-preservation was not sufficient to generate moral obligation but his voluntarist alternative was weakly developed. The proof that a sociable law of nature was externally imposed by God the legislator came from the idea of God as the architect of man's natural impulse to society. Locke's solution was thus to argue that moral obligation stemmed from the omnipotence of God, and that His law was advertised with sufficient clearness in the constitution of human nature. Locke was reluctant to go beyond this and to provide a detailed account of exactly how such obligation could be detected. Rewards and punishments were rejected because they were not an efficient cause of obligation. Locke's stress rested uncertainly upon reason: it was the 'rational apprehension of what is right, puts us under an obligation, and conscience passes judgement on morals, and, if we are guilty, declares that we deserve punishment'.[41]

Locke never published this discussion of moral obligation, but clues to its possible development can be identified in the *Two treatises*, which clearly rest upon an anti-Hobbesian natural law foundation. Here, Locke argues that

---

[37] Locke, *Essay concerning human understanding* 2.28.8.
[38] Ibid. 2.28.10.
[39] Ibid. 2.28.11.
[40] *Correspondence of John Locke*, iv. 102.
[41] Locke, *Essays on the law of nature*, 199.

although the state of nature is a state of liberty, it is not a Hobbesian state of licence, and this is because natural law operated in the state of nature:

> The State of Nature has a Law of Nature to govern it, which obliges every one: And Reason, which is that Law, teaches all Mankind, who will but consult it, that being all equal and independent, no-one ought to harm another in his Life, Health, Liberty, or Possessions. [42]

Locke then develops what appears to be Pufendorf's definition of the law of nature, which ties together self-preservation with the greater good. Locke suggests that 'Every one, as he is bound to preserve himself, and not to quit his station; so by the like reason when his own Preservation comes not into competition, ought he, as much as he can, to preserve the rest of mankind.' But Locke's theory is not simply Pufendorfian or Grotian, because he also considers a kind of natural punishment which is attached to the law of nature. This sanction becomes crucial because it provides the origin of the right of war against anyone who breaks the law of nature. This was the basis for Locke's right of resistance.

Locke's argument is that in transgressing the law of nature, an offender puts himself outside that law. As a result, he becomes dangerous to all:

> Which being a trespass against the whole Species, and the Peace and Safety of it, provided for by the Law of Nature, every man upon this score, by the Right he hath to preserve Mankind in general, may restrain, or where it is necessary, destroy things noxious to them, and so may bring such evil on any one, who hath transgressed that Law, as may make him repent the doing of it, and thereby deter him, and by his example others, from doing the like mischief. And upon this case, and upon this ground, *every Man hath a Right to punish the Offender, and be Executioner of the Law of Nature*.[43]

This description of individuals acting as executioners of the law of nature resembles Cumberland's argument in the *De legibus naturae*. Cumberland had remarked in chapter 1 that 'if someone is so unnatural as to commit a villainy, he cannot be secure because men whose interest it is universally that a most extensive benevolence and that justice should take place are almost certain to punish'.[44] Committing acts against the natural law gives a right of punishment to other individuals whose good is materially affected. This applies even in society; Cumberland argues that the attempt of a burglar to violate property rights gives his victim a right of war.[45] Locke uses a similar examples of petty crime to make the same point in the second *Treatise*: 'Thus a Thief, whom I cannot harm but by appeal to the law, for having stolen all that I am

---

42 Idem, *Two treatises of government*, ed. P. Laslett, Cambridge 1960, II.6, pp. 288–9.
43 Ibid. II.8, pp. 290.
44 Cumberland, *DLN* 1.26.
45 Ibid. 5.3; 5.29.

worth, I may kill, when he sets on to rob me, but of my horse or coat.'[46] In both cases the impossibility of referring the case to an arbiter gives a right under natural law to punish the offender with death. There is no direct evidence that Locke borrowed what he called this 'strange' doctrine from Cumberland but the similarities are striking. Just as Cumberland had found a role for the state of war as a punishment for anti-social behaviour, so Locke had found the same idea useful as a means of legitimating resistance.

Locke's thinking was thus moving in directions which brought it into line with Cumberland's De legibus naturae. Locke made it clear, however, that the second Treatise was not designed to give a definitive account of obligation theory.[47] The question of how individuals come to recognise moral obligation was, on the other hand, one of the problems that underlay the detailed project in the Essay, which makes an interesting comparison with the De legibus.

The Essay concerning human understanding had been written in draft form as early as 1671, and had resulted from discussions between Locke and his friends.[48] Locke's preface described five or six of his friends meeting at his chamber 'and discoursing on a Subject very remote from this, found themselves quickly at a stand, by the Difficulties that rose on every side'.[49] After puzzling over the problem, Locke wrote that 'it came into my thoughts, that we took a wrong course; and that, before we set ourselves upon Enquiries of that Nature, it was necessary to examine our own Abilities, and see, what objects our Understandings were, or were not fitted to deal with'. A manuscript note in Tyrrell's copy of the Essay suggested that the topics of the discussion were 'the Principles of Morality and reveal'd Religion'.[50] It is tempting to speculate from the dating and topic that the Essay was a response to the same debate about moral obligation and Hobbism that had produced the De legibus naturae at the same time.[51] This would certainly explain why it seemed strange to Tyrrell that Locke should not have provided a detailed account of moral obligation.

Locke's reply to Tyrrell's letter from Oxford referred Tyrrell back to his argument about divine law. Locke argued that natural law was included within divine law, and this was the answer which Tyrrell gave to Locke's critics. They were not convinced. Tyrrell wrote back to Locke reporting that they had repeated the charge that Locke was only referring to revelation in his use of the divine law, and also that he only referred to rewards and punish-

---

[46] Locke, Two treatises II.19, pp. 298; cf. Cumberland, DLN 5.25.
[47] Locke, Two treatises II.12, pp. 293.
[48] Idem, Drafts for the Essay concerning human understanding, and other philosophical works, ed. P. Nidditch and G. A. J. Rogers, Oxford 1990.
[49] Idem, Essay concerning human understanding, 7.
[50] R. S. Woolhouse, Locke, Brighton 1983, 7.
[51] James Tully takes the view that the Essay concerning human understanding is Locke's response to Hobbes, which accords with this view: An approach to political philosophy: John Locke in contexts, Cambridge 1993.

ments in the after-life. Although Tyrrell meekly accepted Locke's claim that divine and natural law were the same thing, he nevertheless urged Locke to consider developing his account of natural law along the lines indicated by Cumberland and Parker:

> I conceive men for the most part lye under sufficient obligations to observe the Laws of nature from those natural rewards to Duty, and punishments for sin, which God hath by the natures of the things themselves appointed in this life; and where those fall short, that God will make it up in the life to come, as Dr:Cumberland hath very fully proved in his booke of the Laws of nature against Mr:Hobs. And Dr:Parker as to the necessity of a future state hath more fully made out in his Demonstration of the Law of nature according to Mr:Cum: Principles. and I could wish you would publish your own thoughts upon this excellent; and material subject; since I know you have made long since a Treatise or Lectures upon the Law of natur which I wish you could revise and make publick, since I know none more able, then your selfe to doe it, and which would likewise make a second part to the former worke.[52]

Tyrrell might well have seen Locke's *Essays* in notebook drafts left with him during Locke's exile in Holland between 1683 and 1689.[53] It was clear to Tyrrell that the substance of Locke's position on obligation, revised in the light of Cumberland's work on rewards and punishments, would be sufficient not only to silence Locke's Oxford critics, but also to complete the project for which the *Essay* laid the foundation.

In his next letter, at the beginning of August 1690, Locke refused to be drawn by Tyrrell's suggestion. He argued that there was no case for him to answer; the divine law included the natural law, and that was all that he would say. As far as natural rewards and punishments were concerned, Locke categorically rejected Tyrrell's argument. He was scathing about the suggestion that the sanctions of the after-life should be insufficient for moral obligation; to argue that there were sufficient punishments and rewards in this life only undermined the importance of divine judgement later. If his critics wanted a simple and natural account of moral obligation, "tis easy to see what a kinde of Morality they intend to make of it'. Locke was clearly sceptical about Cumberland's system of rewards and punishments and reluctant to be drawn into speculations about the problematic operation of natural justice. This explained why he preferred to subsume natural under a more general divine law, which incorporated all the forms of God's justice. The same doubts led Locke to reject Tyrrell's invitation to demonstrate morality:

> Another thing that stumbles you is that it is much doubted by some whether the rewards and punishments I mention can be demonstrated as established by my divine law. Will nothing then passe with you in Religion or Morality but what you can demonstrate? If you are of so nice a stomach I am afraid If I

---

52 *Correspondence of John Locke*, iv. 107–9.
53 Locke, *Essays on the law of nature*, 87–8.

should examine how much of your Religion of Morality you could demon-strate how much you would have left.[54]

Locke went on to comment that demonstration in such matters might indeed 'be carried a great deale farther than it is', but he made it clear that this was nevertheless a difficult task. There are millions of propositions in mathemat-ics, he commented, that are demonstrable in theory, but which no-one has demonstrated or perhaps will do so before the end of the world. The implica-tion seems to have been that he felt the same about morality, the subtlety of which would evade the kind of analysis Tyrrell was proposing. 'The probabil-ity of rewards and punishments in another life', he concluded, 'I should think might serve for an inforcement of the Divine law if that were the business in hand.'[55]

Locke made it clear that it was not his business in the *Essay* to demonstrate the grounds of natural obligation, and he said so in no uncertain terms. The *Essay*, he claimed, did no more nor less than it claimed; it explained how individuals came by their ideas. Locke would only entertain criticism about omission if Tyrrell could prove that Locke had been internally inconsistent.

The exchange reveals much about Locke's attitude to moral obligation. His position was that excessive interest in natural rewards and punishments was dangerous. Not only was it difficult to demonstrate, but it led one back to the danger of substituting nature for the judgement of God. Locke's nominal-ist position made him shrink back from the bolder assumptions of the *Two treatises* towards the more introspectively voluntarist solution of positing pos-sible sanctions in the after-life as a source of moral obligation. One had the freedom to behave immorally, but as Pascal's wager made clear, immoral be-haviour was not worth the risk of eternal damnation. This would suggest that Locke's desire to formulate his own demonstration of morality was frustrated by the difficulties of founding moral obligation upon the imperfectly-known will of a deity whose intentions were not easily reduced to simple formulae. Locke did not share Cumberland's Cartesian faith in the ability to decode God's will in nature mathematically, and this was a facet of his empirical nominalism which linked him to Hobbes's rejection of the same position.

Locke may not have been prepared to defend his natural law theory from accusations of Hobbism, but his earnest friend Tyrrell effectively decided to do the job for him. In March 1692 he wrote to Locke announcing that he was about to publish his own 'epitome' of Cumberland's *De legibus*. Tyrrell, who had already sent a copy to Cumberland, asked Locke to read the manuscript. His intention in doing so was to encourage Locke 'to publish somewhat more perfect: which will be a great satisfaction not only to the learned, but to your affectionate servant'.[56] Tyrrell's book was published in June 1692, with

---

[54] *Correspondence of John Locke*, iv. 110–13.
[55] Ibid.
[56] Ibid. 242–4.

Cumberland's personal endorsement, as *A brief disquisition of the law of nature according to the principles and method laid down in the Reverend Dr Cumberland's Latin treatise on that subject.* He stated that he had read the *De legibus* when it was first published and that he had taken some notes which friends, including Robert Boyle, had encouraged him to make public.[57] This would supersede Parker's version, because Parker's use of Cumberland, according to Tyrrell, had been too brief to do Cumberland justice. This was especially the case when it came to 'setting forth of those Rewards and Punishments derived (by God's appointment) from the Nature of Men, and the Frame of Things; which can only be according to that exact Method your Lordship hath here laid down'.[58] This was, of course, the section that Tyrrell thought that Locke would benefit most from adapting.

Tyrrell decided to omit the difficult science. He also placed the criticism of Hobbes in a special appendix at the back of the work, on the basis that it 'disturbed the sense' of the argument. The relocation had the effect of containing Cumberland's contact with the dangerous Hobbes.[59] As a result, Tyrrell generated a discrete anti-Hobbesian work, and saved Cumberland's thesis from dubious association with his opponent. Tyrrell also incorporated sections of Wilkins's *The principles and duties of natural religion* and the parts of More's *Enchiridion ethicum* which listed demonstrable moral axioms.

Another deliberate borrowing was from Locke's *Essay.* If Tyrrell could not get Locke to approve Cumberland's thesis publicly, he could juxtapose the *Essays* and the *De legibus* in such a way that they appeared to be compatible. Tyrrell argued that the inclusion of the excerpts from the *Essay* was justified because Locke 'proceeds upon the same Principles with your Lordship and hath divers very new and useful Notions concerning the Manner of Attaining the knowledge of all Truths, as well Natural, as Divine, and the Certainty we have of them'.[60] Some of the Lockeian insertions are predictable; Locke is cited against innate ideas and Platonist doctrines in general;[61] but others are more interesting. Tyrrell cites Locke's discussion of ideas together with Cumberland's description of the manner in which individuals move from simple to more complex conceptions in developing a notion of the common good. It was precisely these aspects of Locke's work that one would pick out as the foundation of an axiomatic moral science.[62] It is clear from the borrowings that Tyrrell saw Cumberland's work as an unpolished prototype for the kind of natural law treatise that he would like to see from Locke. Even more intriguing from this perspective were Tyrrell's unattributed borrowings from

---

[57] Tyrrell, *Brief disquisition,* sig. A3v.

[58] Ibid. sig. A5r. Tyrrell would nevertheless borrow some of Parker's work; see, for example, p. 191.

[59] Ibid. sig. B2r.

[60] Ibid. sig. B2v–3r.

[61] Ibid. 4, 195–7; cf. Locke, *Essay concerning human understanding* 1.2.12.

[62] Tyrrell, *Brief disquisition,* 214–16; cf. Locke, *Essay concerning human understanding* 2.24.

Locke. Tyrrell reproduced a passage from Locke's sixth essay, which dealt with obligation, spliced into his translation of the *De legibus*. Consciously or unconsciously, Tyrrell was determined to place Cumberland and Locke in the same theory.[63]

Tyrrell tried to get Locke to react. He sent Locke a copy of the book in August 1692, along with a letter expressing the hope that

> this treatise may give the world a better account of the Law of nature; and its obligation, then what hath bin allready performed: as also to confute with better Reasons the Epicurean Principles of Mr:Hobs: for the doeing of which, I know no man more capable than yourself if you please to undertake it.[64]

Locke made no response. There was no more mention in their correspondence of the book, or of Locke's views upon it. All Tyrrell earned for his pains was a small amendment to the second addition of the *Essay*. Locke now wrote that the divine law also included the law of nature, which could be known by the light of reason.

The Locke episode shows both the popular esteem for Cumberland's solution to the problem of obligation, and also the difficulties of its implementation. For a nominalist like Locke, Cumberland's reliance upon natural rewards and punishments was too problematic to endorse. This was in spite of the fact that such ideas, and that of *scientia moralis*, held a continual fascination for him. In this respect, as Tyrrell, Parker and Pufendorf suggested, Locke was unusual in rejecting the aspects of Cumberland which rendered natural law theory proof against implication with Hobbes. This may have been one of the reasons why Locke would never escape the accusation of Hobbism.[65]

These examples also indicate Cumberland's wider importance to the natural law genre. If Cumberland rejected the more shocking elements of Hobbes's work, he also managed thereby to preserve some of his more useful insights into the nature and role of *scientia moralis*. As the discussion of Pufendorf suggests, it was vital in this respect that the Leviathan should be tamed and not killed. Cumberland's popularity may have waned after what Richard Tuck has called the 'heroic' period of natural law theory, but it was mainly because the Hobbesian threat to natural law theory had diminished. In this changed context, it would be difficult to understand what all the fuss had been about. Cumberland would be seen as a rather strange deist, or proto-utilitarian, whose ethical and political discussion of the common good was so far ahead of its time.

---

[63] Tyrrell, *Brief disquisition*, 116; cf. Locke, *Essays on the law of nature*, 181–3.
[64] *Correspondence of John Locke*, iv. 493–6.
[65] Locke, *Two treatises*, introduction, 72.

Conclusion: Taming the Leviathan

Cumberland's *De legibus naturae* had been designed to neutralise the threat to natural law doctrine posed by Hobbes. Contemporaries like Pufendorf recognised this fact even if modern historians have been reluctant to view Cumberland this way. As this study has shown, the argument of the *De legibus naturae* only makes sense when it is considered as a reaction to Hobbes and the problem of 'Hobbism' in politics and natural philosophy. Cumberland's aim was, first and foremost, to confront the *Leviathan*. But he did so not just to kill it, but rather to tame it. In doing so he preserved and developed the insights offered by ethical naturalism, including much of what Hobbes had contributed to the sciences of politics, morality and natural philosophy.

Cumberland's engagement with Hobbes, with its parallel processes of criticism and construction, helps us to understand Cumberland's work, but also to understand the continuing relevance of Hobbes's philosophy to the political thinkers of the Restoration period. As this study has shown, criticism of Hobbes was not an idle exercise in the demolition of a discredited theory. Hobbes, and Hobbesian solutions to political and moral problems, remained at the heart of Restoration culture and debate. To criticise Hobbes was to contribute to contemporary political discussion.

This feature of Hobbes's reception was not merely a function of Hobbes's notoriety as a political theorist. It is true that Hobbes had provided the most shocking theoretical response to the political disturbances of the mid century, but he had done so within the terms of a natural law discourse which acknowledged the role of the state as a means of resolving conflict. Although most natural law writers may have rejected the state of war as the basis of sovereignty, they were only too aware of the importance of the role of the state as arbiter, most crucially when it came to the resolution of religious disputes, arguably the most important single cause of conflict in seventeenth-century Europe.

The persistence of religious conflict in Britain made it inevitable that Hobbes would be a consistent feature of the political debate after the Restoration. The dangerous combination of a broad political and narrow ecclesiastical settlement institutionalised the religious disputes of the civil wars and Interregnum. As a result England was fated to revisit the problems which had torn the country apart in the mid century.[1] At moments of tension, the polity was threatened with the kind of conflict and dissolution to which Hobbes

---

[1] For this view see J. Scott, 'England's troubles 1603–1702', in R. Malcolm Smuts (ed.), *The Stuart court and Europe*, Cambridge 1996, 24–7.

had responded so trenchantly in the 1650s. Hobbes's work kept its political relevance, particularly at times of stress, because the very issues that the *Leviathan* had addressed in the 1650s recurred throughout the Restoration.[2]

Works like Cumberland's *De legibus* had a crucial role to play in mediating this Hobbesian legacy. Like Hobbes, Cumberland and his Latitudinarian colleagues were forced to deal with a political environment in which religious division and conflict had become inescapable facts of political life. Again, like Grotius, Hobbes and Pufendorf, they were drawn to natural law theory as one possible solution to sectarian controversy. Unlike Hobbes, however, they also wished to reassert the natural basis of sociability and to defend the natural basis of the restored society. The enthusiasm of Wilkins, Tillotson, Stillingfleet and their colleagues for a comprehensive society of believers in the Church of England, was matched by their aspiration for a broadly based Royal Society. Both projects demonstrated a political commitment to a unified society based on an interpretation of the requirements of natural law. This implied placing less emphasis upon specific doctrines, and more upon the importance of natural communities and the role of the state in resolving religious controversy. Diversity could be tolerated, but within the natural community regulated by the state. Unfortunately such eirenic aspirations were complicated by the religious divisions lying at the heart of the Restoration settlement. The polarisation of politics in the later 1660s, and what has been called the first 'Restoration crisis', led to the failure of plans for a comprehensive Church and the near failure of the Royal Society. In the increasingly heated debate between the Established Church and non-conformists, the Latitudinarian faith in natural society appeared to be supplanted by a reliance upon the state as the ultimate means of resolving social conflict. Parker may have argued that state prescription in religious matters was a requirement of natural law, but this, as we have seen, did little to save his work from the accusation of Hobbism. At the same time, the problems with establishing a non-sectarian political identity for the Royal Society led to its fatal association with Hobbist doctrine.

In this situation it was vital that Latitudinarian writers should attempt to redefine their relationship with the *Leviathan*. Parker's responses to his critics, Tenison's *The creed of Mr Hobbes examined* (1670), Fowler's *The principles and practices of certain moderate divines* (1670) all attempted this kind of reorientation. This was also the purpose of Cumberland's *De legibus naturae*. Cumberland carefully attacked those aspects of Hobbes's thought which were widely associated with atheism, but he did not reject Hobbes's ideas outright. Rather, he attempted to reconcile the use of self-interest, political sovereignty and materialism with a faith in natural law and natural sociability. In 1651 Hobbes had portrayed a world in which political and religious conflict was the central feature of human relations; the state of war was the essential

[2] Particularly in the periods 1658–62, 1667–72, 1678–82.

badge of his political doctrine. Twenty years later Cumberland painted a more complex picture in which conflict and sociability coexisted. Peace and co-operation were man's natural condition, but conflict did exist as the divine punishment written into the fabric of nature. Cumberland did not reject Hobbes's observations, but rather sought to reinterpret them. Hobbes's observations about human behaviour had been partially correct even if Hobbes had drawn the wrong conclusions about what was truly 'natural'. Where Hobbes had sought to replace the vague promptings of God and nature with the more compelling authority of the state, Cumberland attempted to show that moral and political obligation, indeed the state itself, could be seen as the products of the divine will and natural law. To live in accordance with nature, according to Cumberland, was ultimately to live in accordance with the rules of the state. By making this argument, Cumberland effectively domesticated the *Leviathan*.

We have also observed the same process at work in Cumberland's treatment of natural philosophy. Cumberland sought to show that the science of local motion did not automatically imply the atheistic beliefs imputed to Hobbes. As with his politics, Cumberland sieved Hobbes's work for its errors in order that valuable insights about matter and motion should not be tainted by their association with the *Leviathan*. Just as Glanvill had sought to vindicate mechanistic philosophy in the *Philosophia pia* (1671), so Cumberland attempted to recover natural philosophy for a godly purpose. In the *De legibus naturae*, natural philosophy became a means of discovering moral and political obligation. If Hobbes had attempted to make science a means of separating the realms of faith and reason, Cumberland sought to show how even Hobbesian natural philosophy could be used to illustrate and emphasise the connection between the two. The investigation of nature revealed the divine obligation to both society and the state. In this respect, Cumberland took ideas of *scientia moralis* much further than even Hobbes had been prepared to. Cumberland's conception of nature as a mechanism filled with providential meaning offered the possibility that natural philosophy could provide an objective and scientific basis to both political and moral behaviour.

This process of filtering and reconstructing Hobbesian ideas is what gives Cumberland's work its historical significance. It also provides interesting clues as to the nature of Hobbes's philosophical legacy, so often supposed to have been barren. If the argument of this book is correct, then it may be true to say that Hobbes's true influence lies not so much in the few writers who openly endorsed his doctrines, but among his many critics whose criticism served as a means of reacting to, and taking the lessons from, his moral, political and scientific theories. Samuel Mintz observed in *The hunting of Leviathan* that Hobbes exercised a powerful influence upon the logical standards of his critics, demanding greater rigour and rationality than they might otherwise have practised.[3] In Cumberland's case this is undoubtedly true. In order to

---

[3] Mintz, *The hunting of Leviathan*, 149.

meet Hobbes upon his own ground Cumberland had to couch his argument in Hobbesian terms, and this should certainly be taken as one form of direct influence. But the effect of the confrontation was perhaps more profound than one of style and logical rigour. In confronting Hobbes, and taming the *Leviathan*, theorists like Cumberland were forced to come to terms with the philosophical legacy of the English Revolution, and to come to an early engagement with the potentially destabilising forces of ethical naturalism and scientific rationalism. Reconciling these forces to traditional ethics and the Established Church helped to contain and defuse long-term conflict between them. The unique role of Restoration writers like Cumberland, in responding to Hobbes as early and as carefully as they did, must go some considerable way towards explaining the eventual triumph of a Latitudinarian and Newtonian Whig ideology, the terms of which were often forged in combat with Hobbes. It is perhaps significant that the debate over Hobbism in the later 1660s should have produced texts as influential as the *De legibus naturae* and Locke's *Essay concerning human understanding*. With this in mind, it is perhaps no exaggeration to regard the protracted confrontation with Hobbes as an essential factor lying behind the distinctively Latitudinarian character of the English Enlightenment.

Such a role perhaps allows us to explain Cumberland's peculiar 'modernity', so often cited in connection with his thesis. It should be clear that Cumberland was far from being a 'modern' proto-utilitarian. What utilitarian elements exist in his thesis are the product of his engagement with Hobbes. Equally, Cumberland's abandonment of scriptural evidence was not a statement of secular intent, so much as a response to Hobbes's scepticism about scriptural evidence in general. Throughout his works, Cumberland wished to underpin Scripture more securely with the forces of reason, just as in the *De legibus* he wished to reconnect natural law with the will of God. Ironically the main tensions between the sacred and the secular in his theory are fuelled by his choice of Cicero as the main response to Hobbes's Epicureanism. This humanist adaptation of a classical 'script' for the debate with Hobbes is paradoxically what lends the *De legibus* its 'modern' and secular tone. In this instance, it was Cicero's synthesis of Stoic ethics rather than any novel doctrine, which heralded the forces of secular enlightenment.

It is perhaps a measure of Cumberland's success, and that of his Latitudinarian colleagues, that much of the argument of the *De legibus* had become commonplace by the middle of the eighteenth century. Cumberland is often referred to, alongside Grotius and Pufendorf, but rarely discussed in any depth. His discussion of moral obligation and his dated science increasingly diminished his appeal to an audience, for whom the threat of Hobbes was a dim and receding memory.[4] But in this respect his work had been done; some

---

4 See Kirk, *Cumberland*, 100–31.

of the most important lessons of Hobbes's political theory, and indeed of English Revolution, had been absorbed into the bloodstream of English political thought. The *Leviathan* had been tamed.[5]

---

[5] *Taming the Leviathan* is the projected title for my next book. This will examine the response to Hobbes's ideas from the 1640s through to the early eighteenth century along the lines suggested here.

Bibliography

Unpublished primary sources

Cambridge University Library
MS Add. 6
MS Add. 36
Grace Book, supplicats 1677–80

Cambridge, Magdalene College
College register

London, British Library
MS Add. 4274

London, City of Westminster Public Library
St Paul's Church, Covent Garden, marriage register

London, Lambeth Palace Library
MS 934 Gibson papers
MS 999
MS Faculty Office

Northamptonshire Records Office
Brampton Ash parish records no. 36, 44, 45

Oxford, Bodleian Library
Lincoln MS B.14.15
Rawlinson MSS A170
Selden MS supra. 109
Tanner MS cccv

Oxford, Lincoln College
Address of the bishop of Peterborough to his clergy, 1701

Printed primary sources

Anon., *The inconveniences of toleration*, London 1667
Anon., *Insolence and impudence triumphant*, London 1669
Anon., *A letter to a member of this present parliament for liberty of conscience*, London 1668
Anon., *A proposition for the safety and happiness of the king and kingdom*, London 1667

Anon., *A second discourse of the religion of England*, London 1668

Anon., *True effigies of the monster of Malmesbury: or, Thomas Hobbes in his proper colours*, London 1680

Aquinas, T., *Summa theologia*, general ed. T. Gilby, London 1964–81

Aristotle, *De anima*, trans. R. D. Hicks, Cambridge 1907

—————— *The ethics of Aristotle*, trans J. A. K. Thompson, London 1953

—————— *Nicomachean ethics*, trans. T. Irwin, Indianapolis 1985

—————— *The politics*, ed. S. Everson, Cambridge 1988

Aubrey, J., *Brief lives*, ed. A. Clark, Oxford 1898

Aurelius, M., *Meditations*, trans. M. Staniforth, London 1964

Bacon, F., *Works*, ed. J. Spedding, R. C. Ellis and D. Heath, London 1858–74

Bagshaw, E., *The great question concerning religious worship*, London 1660

Barrow, I., *The usefulnesse of mathematical learning*, trans. J. Kirkby, London 1684

—————— *Works*, ed. J. Tillotson, London 1686–7

—————— *Theological works*, ed. J. Napier, London 1858

Bartholin, T., *History of anatomy*, London 1668

Baxter, R., *The reasons of the Christian religion*, London 1667

—————— *Reliquiae Baxterianae*, London 1696

Beckmann, N., *Index novitatum*, Lund 1673

Birch, T., *The life of the Most Reverend Dr John Tillotson*, London 1753

—————— *A history of the Royal Society of London*, New York 1968

Boyle, R., *New experiments physico-mechanical touching the spring of the air*, London 1660

—————— *A defence of the doctrine concerning the spring and weight of the air*, London 1662

—————— *Some considerations concerning the usefulness of experimental philosophy*, Oxford 1663

—————— *The works of the Honourable Robert Boyle*, ed. T. Birch, London 1772

Bramhall, J., *Castigations of Mr Hobbes his last animadversions*, London 1658

—————— *The catching of the Leviathan, or the Great Whale*, London 1658

—————— *The works of John Bramhall*, Dublin 1677

Burnet, G., *History of his own time*, London 1734

Burthogge, R., *Divine goodness explicated and asserted*, London 1671

Burton, H., *Several discourses*, London 1684

—————— *A second volume of discourses*, London 1685

Bysshe, E., *Bibliotheca Bissaeana*, London 1679

Calamy, E., *Calamy revis'd: being a revision of Edmund Calamy's account of the ministers and others ejected and silenced, 1660–2*, ed. A. G. Matthews, Oxford 1934

Calendar of state papers, domestic series, of the reign of Charles II, ed. E. Green, F. H. B. Daniell and F. Bickley, London 1860–1938

Casaubon, M., *A treatise concerning enthusiasm*, London 1655

—————— *Concerning experimental natural philosophie*, London 1669

—————— *Of credulity and incredulity in things divine & spiritual*, London 1670

Charleton, W., *Deliramenta catarrhi*, London 1650

—————— *The darkness of atheism dispelled by the light of nature*, London 1654

—————— *Physiologia-Epicuro-Gassendo-Charletonia: or a fabrick of science natural, upon the hypothesis of atoms*, London 1654

—————— *The harmony of natural and positive divine laws*, London 1682

Cicero, M. T., *De finibus bonorum et malorum*, trans. H. Rackham, London 1914

——— *Tusculan disputations*, trans. J. E. King, London 1927

——— *De re publica; De legibus*, trans. C. W. Keyes, London 1928

——— *De natura deorum*, trans. H. Rackham, London 1933

——— *On duties*, ed. M. T. Griffin and E. M. Atkins, Cambridge 1991

Coke, R., *A survey of the politicks of Mr Thomas White, Mr Thomas Hobbs, and Mr Hugo Grotius*, London 1662

Correspondence of Anne, viscountess Conway, Henry More and their friends, 1642–1684, ed. M. H. Nicholson, rev. edn S. Hutton, Oxford 1992.

Correspondence of Henry Oldenburg, ed. A. Rupert Hall and M. B. Hall, Madison 1965–75

Cudworth, R., *A sermon preached . . . March 31st, 1647*, Cambridge 1647

——— *The true intellectual system of the universe*, London 1678

Culverwell, N., *An elegant and learned discourse of the light of nature*, ed. R. A. Greene and H. MacCallum, Toronto 1971

Cumberland, R., *De legibus naturae disquisitio philosophia, in qua earum forma, summa capita, ordo, promulgatio & obligatio e rerum natura investigantur: quinetiam elementa philosophiae Hobbianae cum moralis tum civilis, considerantur & refutantur*, London 1672

——— *De legibus naturae, editio secunda*, Lubeck–Frankfurt 1683

——— *An essay towards the recovery of Jewish measures and weights*, London 1686

——— *De legibus naturae, editio tertia*, Lubeck–Frankfurt 1694

——— *De legibus naturae*, Dublin 1720

——— *Sanchoniatho's Phoenician history*, London 1720

——— *Origines gentium antiquissimae*, London 1724

——— *A treatise of the laws of nature*, ed. J. Maxwell, London 1727

——— *Traité philosophique des loix naturelles*, ed. and trans. J. Barbeyrac, Amsterdam 1744

——— *A philosophical enquiry into the laws of nature*, trans. J. Towers, Dublin 1750

——— 'The motives to liberality considered', *The English preacher*, London 1774, ix

Descartes, R., *The philosophical writings of Descartes*, trans. J. Cottingham, R. Stoothoff and D. Murdoch, Cambridge 1985

Diogenes, *De clarorum philosophorum vitis*, trans. R. D. Hicks, London 1925

Eachard, J., *Mr Hobbs state of nature consider'd in a dialogue between Philautus and Timothy*, London 1672

——— *Some opinions of Mr Hobbs considered in a second dialogue between Philautus and Timothy*, London 1673

Epictetus, *Moral discourses*, trans. E. Carter, London 1910

Evelyn, J., *An essay on the first book of T. Lucretius Carus De rerum natura interpreted and made English by John Evelyn*, London 1656

——— *Diary and correspondence of John Evelyn*, ed. W. Bray, London 1908

——— *Diary*, ed. E. S. de Beer, Oxford 1955

Ferguson, R., *A sober enquiry into the nature, measure and principles of moral virtue*, London 1673

——— *The role of reason in religion*, London 1675

Fowler, E., *The principles and practices of certain moderate divines of the Church of England (greatly misunderstood) truly represented and defended*, London 1670

——— *The design of Christianity*, London 1671

Fuller, T., *History of the University of Cambridge*, London 1655

Gassendi, P., *Opera omnia*, Lyons 1658

Glanvill, J., *The vanity of dogmatizing*, London 1661

——— *Scepsis scientifica*, London 1665

——— *A blow at modern sadducism*, London 1668

——— *Plus Ultra, or the progress and advancement of knowledge since the days of Aristotle in an account of some of the most remarkable later improvements of practical useful learning*, London 1668

——— *Philosophia pia, or, a discourse of the religious temper and tendencies of the experimental philosophy which is profest by the Royal Society*, London 1671

——— *Essays on several important subjects*, London 1676

Glisson, F., *De rachitide*, London 1650

——— *De natura substantiae energetica*, London 1672

Grotius, H., *The truth of the Christian religion*, trans. S. Patrick, London 1680

——— *De jure belli ac pacis*, trans. F. Kelsey, Oxford 1925

——— *De iure praedae commentarius*, trans. G L. Williams, Oxford 1950

Hale, M., 'Reflections by the Lrd. Cheife Justice Hale on Mr Hobbes his dialogue of the lawe', in W. S. Holdsworth, *A history of English law*, Boston 1924, v. 500–13

Hall, J., *The advancement of learning*, ed. A. K. Crosten, Liverpool 1953

Harvey, W., *De generatione animalium*, London 1651

Hobbes, T., *An antidote against atheism*, London 1653

——— *Opera*, Amsterdam 1668

——— *The moral and political works of Thomas Hobbes*, London 1750

——— *Opera philosophica*, ed. W. Molesworth, London 1839–45

——— *The English works of Thomas Hobbes*, ed. W. Molesworth, London 1839–45

——— *Behemoth*, ed. F. Tönnies, London 1889

——— *Elements of law natural and politic*, ed. F. Tönnies, 2nd edn, intro. M. M. Goldsmith, London 1969

——— *Thomas White's De mundo examined*, trans. H. W. Jones, Bradford 1976

——— *De cive: the English version*, ed. H. Warrender, Oxford 1983

——— *Leviathan*, ed. R. Tuck, Cambridge 1991

——— *Man and citizen*, ed. B. Gert, Indianapolis 1991

——— *The correspondence of Thomas Hobbes*, ed. N. Malcolm, Oxford 1994

Holder, W., *Elements of speech: an essay of inquiry into the natural production of letters*, London 1669

Humfrey, J., *A case of conscience*, London 1669

Huygens, C., *Oeuvres*, La Haye 1889

Hyde, E., *A brief view and survey of the dangerous and pernicious errors to Church and State in Mr Hobbes' book entitled Leviathan*, Oxford 1676

Lactantius, *Divine institutions*, trans. M. F. McDonald, Washington, DC 1964

Lawson, G., *An examination of the political part of Mr Hobbs his Leviathan*, London 1657

Locke, J., *Essays on the law of nature*, ed. W. von Leyden, Oxford 1954

——— *Two treatises of government*, ed. P. Laslett, Cambridge 1960

——— *Two tracts on government*, ed. P. Abrams, Cambridge 1967

——— *An essay concerning human understanding*, ed. P. H. Nidditch, Oxford 1975

——— *Correspondence of John Locke*, ed. E. S. de Beer, Oxford 1976

————— *Drafts for the Essay concerning human understanding, and other philosophical works*, ed. P. Nidditch and G. A. J. Rogers, Oxford 1990

Lowde, J. A., *A discourse concerning the nature of man, both in his natural and political capacity*, London 1694

Lower, R., *Tractatus de corde*, London 1669

Lucretius, *De rerum natura*, ed. and trans. C. Bailey, Oxford 1947

Lucy, W., *Observations, censures and confutations of divers errors in the first two chapters of Mr Hobbes his Leviathan*, London 1656

Marvell, A., *The rehearsal transpros'd and the rehearsal transpros'd: the second part*, ed. D. I. B. Smith, Oxford 1971

More, H., *An antidote against atheism*, London 1653

————— *The immortality of the soul*, London 1659

————— *Collection of several philosophical writings*, London 1662

————— *Divine dialogues*, London 1668

————— *Enchiridion ethicum*, London 1668

————— *An account of virtue: or, Dr Henry More's abridgement of morals, put into English*, London 1690

Newton, I., *Certain philosophical questions: Newton's Trinity notebook*, ed. J. E. McGuire and M. Tamny, Cambridge 1983

Owen, J., *Two questions concerning the power of the supream magistrate about religion*, London 1659

————— *Truth and innocence defended*, London 1669

Parker, S., *Tentamina physico-theologica de deo*, Oxford 1665

————— *A free and impartiall censure of the Platonick philosophy*, Oxford 1666

————— *The nature and extent of the divine dominion*, Oxford 1666

————— *A discourse of ecclesiastical politie*, London 1669

————— *A defence and continuation of the ecclesiastical politie*, London 1671

————— *Disputationes de deo et providentia divina*, London 1678

————— *A demonstration of the divine authority of the law of nature*, London 1681

————— *A history of his own time*, London 1728

Patrick, S., *A friendly debate betwixt two neighbours*, London 1668

————— *A defence and continuation of the friendly debate*, London 1669

Payne, S., 'Brief account of the life . . . of the author', preface to Cumberland, *Sanchoniatho's Phoenician history*

Pepys, S., *The diary of Samuel Pepys*, ed. R. Latham and W. Matthews, London 1970–83

Pope, W., *Life of the Right Reverend Father in God, Seth, lord bishop of Salisbury*, London 1697

Power, H., *Experimental philosophy*, London 1664

Pufendorf, S., *De jure naturali*, Lund 1672

————— *Elementorum jurisprudentiae universalis*, trans. W. A. Oldfather, Oxford 1931

————— *De jure naturae et gentium*, ed. and trans. C. H. Oldfather and W. A. Oldfather, Oxford 1934

————— *On the natural state of men*, ed. and trans. M. Seidler, New York 1990

Ray, J., *Wisdom of God manifested in the works of creation*, London 1690

Rolle, S., *A sober answer to the friendly debate*, London 1669

Rosse, A., *The new planet no planet, or, the earth no wandring star, except in the wandring heads of Galileans*, London 1646

———— *Leviathan drawn out with a hook*, London 1653

Royal Society, *Philosophical Transactions of the Royal Society of London*, London 1665–1886

Sanderson, R., *De obligatione conscientiae*, trans. C. Wordsworth, Lincoln 1877

Scargill, D., *The recantation of Daniel Scargill*, Cambridge 1669

Selden, J., *De jure naturali & gentium iuxta disciplinam Ebraeorum libri septem*, London 1640

———— *Table talk*, ed. F. Pollock, London 1927

Sergeant, J., *Sure footing in Christianity, or rational discourses on the rule of faith*, London 1665

Shafte, J., *The great law of nature*, London 1673

Sharrock, R., *History of the propagation and improvement of vegetables*, Oxford 1660

———— *Ypothesis ethike: de officiis secundum naturae jus*, Oxford 1660

———— *De finibus virtutis Christianae*, Oxford 1673

Sherlock, W., *A vindication of the rights of ecclesiastical authority*, London 1685

Smith, J., *Select discourses*, ed. J. Worthington, London 1660

South, R., *Sermons preached upon several occasions*, Oxford 1823

S. P., *A brief account of the new sect of Latitude-men together with some reflections on the new philosophy*, Cambridge 1662

Sprat, T., *Observations on monsieur de Sorbière's voyage into England*, London 1665

———— *The history of the Royal Society of London for the improving of natural knowledge*, ed. J. I. Cope and H. W. Jones, St Louis 1958

Stanley, T., *The history of philosophy*, London 1655–62

Stillingfleet, E., *Irenicum: a weapon-salve for the churches wounds, or the divine right of particular forms of church government discuss'd and examin'd according to the principles of the law of nature*, London 1661

———— *Irenicum, second edition*, London 1662

———— *Origines sacrae: or a rational account of the grounds of Christian faith*, London 1662

———— *The unreasonableness of separation*, London 1681

———— *Works*, London 1709–10

Stubbe, H., *A severe equiry into the late oneirocritica*, London 1657

———— *The Savilian Professor's case stated*, London 1658

———— *The Indian nectar, or a discourse concerning chocolata*, London 1662

———— *Campanella revived: or an enquiry into the history of the Royal Society, whether the virtuosi there do not pursue the projects of Campanella for the reducing of England unto popery*, Oxford 1670

———— *A censure upon certaine passages contained in the History of the Royal Society, as being destructive to the established religion and Church of England*, Oxford 1670

———— *Plus ultra reduced to a non-plus*, London 1670

———— *A letter to Dr Henry More*, London 1671

———— *Rosemary & Bayes*, London 1672

Suarez, F., *Selections from three works*, trans. G. L. Williams, A. Brown and J. Waldron, Oxford 1944.

Taylor, J., *Ductor dubitantium*, London 1660

Tenison, T., *The creed of Mr Hobbs examined*, London 1670

Tillotson, J., *The Protestant religion vindicated*, London 1680

———— *A sermon preached at the funeral of the Reverend Benjamin Whichcot . . .*, May 24th, London 1683

————— *Sermons*, ed. R. Barker, London 1704

————— *The works of the Most Reverend Dr John Tillotson*, ed. R. Barker, London 1728

Towerson, G., *An explication of the decalogue or ten commandments*, London 1676

Traherne, T., *Centuries, poems & thanksgivings*, ed. H. M. Margoliouth, Oxford 1958

————— *Christian ethicks*, ed. C. L. Marks and G. R. Guffey, New York 1968

Tyrrell, J., *A brief disquisition of the law of nature according to the principles and method laid down in the Reverend Dr Cumberland's Latin treatise on that subject*, London 1692

Wallis, J., *Truth tried*, Cambridge 1643

————— *Arithmetica infinitorum*, London 1655

————— *De sectionibus conicis*, London 1655

————— *Elenchus geometriae Hobbianae*, London 1655

————— *Due correction for Mr Hobbes*, Oxford 1656

————— *Hobbius heauton-timorumenos*, London 1662

————— *Mechanica: sive, de motu*, London 1670

Ward, S., *A philosophicall essay towards an eviction of the being and attributes of God*, Oxford 1652

————— *Astronomiae geometricae*, Oxford 1656

————— *In Thomae Hobbii philosophiam exercitatio epistolica*, Oxford 1656

————— and J. Wilkins, *Vindiciae academiarum*, Oxford 1654

Whichcote, B., *Select notions*, London 1685

————— *Works*, Aberdeen 1751

————— *Moral and religious aphorisms*, ed. J. Jeffery, London 1753

White, T., *Sciri, sive scepti et scepticorum a iure disputationis exclusio*, London 1663

————— *An exclusion of sceptics from all title to dispute*, London 1665

Wilkins, J., *A discourse concerning a new planet*, Oxford 1640

————— *An essay towards a real character and a philosophical language*, London 1668

————— *Of the principles and duties of natural religion*, London 1675

Willis, T., *Cerebri anatome, cui accessit nervorum descripto et usus*, London 1664

Wolseley, C., *Liberty of conscience in the magistrate's interest*, London 1668

————— *The unreasonableness of atheism*, London 1669

————— *The reasonableness of Scripture-belief*, London 1672

Wood, A., *Athenae Oxoniensis*, ed. P. Bliss, Oxford 1813–20

Worthington, J., *Diary and correspondence*, ed. J. Crossley and R. C. Christie, Manchester 1847

Secondary sources

Albee, E., *A history of English utilitarianism*, London 1901

Allison, P., *The rise of moralism: the proclamation of the Gospel from Hooker to Baxter*, London 1966

Applebaum, W., 'Boyle and Hobbes: a reconsideration', *Journal of the History of Ideas* xxv (1964), 117–19

Arber, E., *The term catalogues 1668-1709*, London 1903–6

Armitage, A., 'René Descartes (1596–1650) and the early Royal Society', *Notes and Records of the Royal Society* viii (1950), 1–19

Ashcraft, R., *Revolutionary politics and Locke's Two treatises of government*, Princeton 1986

———— 'Latitudinarianism and toleration: historical myth versus political history', in Kroll and Ashcraft, *Philosophy, science and religion 1640–1700*, 151–77

Axtell, J., 'The mechanics of opposition: Restoration Cambridge v. Daniel Scargill', *Bulletin of the Institute of Historical Research* xxxviii (1965), 102–11

Bloch, O., *La philosophie de Gassendi, nominalisme, materialisme et metaphysique*, The Hague 1971

Blom, H., *Morality and causality: the rise of naturalism in Dutch seventeenth-century political thought*, Utrecht 1995

Boas, M., *Robert Boyle*, Cambridge 1958

Bowle, J., *Hobbes and his critics: a study in seventeenth-century constitutionalism*, London 1951

Brandt, F., *Thomas Hobbes's mechanical conception of nature*, Copenhagen 1927

Bredvold, L. I., 'Dryden, Hobbes and the Royal Society', *Modern Philology* xxv (1928), 417–38

Brown, H., *Scientific organisations in seventeenth-century France*, Baltimore 1934

Brundell, B., *Pierre Gassendi: from Aristotelianism to a new natural philosophy*, Dordrecht 1987

Buckle, S., *Natural law and the theory of property*, Oxford 1991

Burns, J. H. and M. Goldie (eds), *The Cambridge history of political thought 1450–1700*, Cambridge 1991

Campbell, R. and A. S. Skinner (eds), *The origin and nature of the Scottish Enlightenment*, Edinburgh 1982

Carpenter, E., *Thomas Tenison, archbishop of Canterbury: his life and times*, London 1948

Carroll, R. T., *The commonsense philosophy of religion of Bishop Edward Stillingfleet 1635–99*, The Hague 1975

Champion, J. A., *The pillars of priestcraft shaken: the Church of England and its enemies*, Cambridge 1992

Colie, R. L., *Light and Enlightenment: a study of the Cambridge Platonists and the Dutch Arminians*, Cambridge 1957

Cope, J. I., 'The Cupri-Cosmits: Glanvill on Latitudinarian anti-enthusiasm', *Huntington Library Quarterly* ii (1954), 269–86

———— *Joseph Glanvill: Anglican apologist*, St Louis 1956

Costello, J., *The scholastic curriculum in early seventeenth century Cambridge*, Cambridge, Mass. 1958

Cragg, G. R., *From Puritanism to the age of reason*, London 1950

Cranston, M. and R. S. Peters (eds), *Hobbes and Rousseau: a collection of critical essays*, New York 1972

Cromartie, A., *Sir Matthew Hale 1609–1676: law, religion and natural philosophy*, Cambridge 1995

Cunich, P., D. Hoyle, E. Duffy and R. Hyam, *A history of Magdalene College 1428–1988*, Cambridge 1994

Damrosch, L., 'Hobbes as a reformation theologian', *Journal of the History of Ideas* xl (1979), 339–52

Davis, P., 'Thomas Hobbes's translation of Homer: epic and anticlericalism in late seventeenth-century England', *Seventeenth Century* xii (1997), 231–55.

de Pauley, W., *The candle of the Lord*, New York 1937

Dewey, J., 'The motivation of Hobbes's political philosophy', in *Studies in the History of Ideas*, i, Columbia 1918

Dietz, M. G. (ed.), *Thomas Hobbes and political theory*, Berkeley 1991

Dijksterhuis, E. J., *The mechanization of the world-picture*, Oxford 1961

Dunn, J., *The political thought of John Locke: an historical account of the argument of the two treatises of government*, Cambridge 1969

Feingold, M., 'Isaac Barrow: divine, scholar and mathematician', in M. Feingold (ed.), *Before Newton*, Cambridge 1991

Forbes, D., *Hume's philosophical politics*, Cambridge 1975

———— 'Natural law and the Scottish Enlightenment', in Campbell and Skinner, *Origin and nature of the Scottish Enlightenment*, 186–204

Forsyth, M., 'The place of Richard Cumberland in the history of natural law doctrine', *Journal of the History of Philosophy* xx (1982), 23–42

Frank, R. G., *Harvey and the Oxford physiologists*, Berkeley 1980

Gabbey, A., 'Philosophia Cartesiana triumphata: Henry More 1646–71', in Lennon, *Problems of Cartesianism*, 171–250

———— 'Henry More and the limits of mechanism', in Hutton, *Henry More*, 19–36

Gascoigne, J., *Cambridge in the age of the Enlightenment*, Cambridge 1989

Gawlick, C., 'Cicero and the Enlightenment', *Studies on Voltaire in the Eighteenth Century* xxv (1963), 657–82

Gelbart, N. R., 'The intellectual development of Walter Charleton', *Ambix* ix (1971), 149–78

George, E. A., *Seventeenth-century men of latitude*, London 1908

Gillespie, N. C., 'Natural history, natural theology and social order: John Ray and the Newtonian ideology', *Journal of the History of Biology* xx (1987), 1–50

Goldie, M., 'The reception of Hobbes', in Burns and Goldie (eds), *Cambridge history of political thought*, 589–615

———— 'The theory of religious intolerance in Restoration England' in O. P. Grell, J. I. Israel and N. Tyacke (eds.), *From persecution to toleration: the Glorious Revolution and religion in England*, Oxford 1991, 331–68

Gough, J. W., 'James Tyrrell, Whig historian and friend of John Locke', *Historical Journal* xix (1973), 581–610

Goyard-Fabre, S., 'Pufendorf, adversaire de Hobbes', *Hobbes Studies* ii (1989), 65–86

Grafton, A., *Defenders of the text: the tradition of scholarship in an age of science*, Harvard 1991

Grant, H., 'Hobbes and mathematics', in Sorrell, *Cambridge companion to Hobbes*, 108–28

Greene, R. A., 'Whichcote, Wilkins, ingenuity and the reasonableness of Christianity', *Journal of the History of Ideas* xli (1981), 227–52

Gunn, J. A. W., *Politics and the public interest in the seventeenth-century*, London 1969

Gunther, R., *Early science in Oxford*, Oxford 1923–45

———— *Early science in Cambridge*, Oxford 1937

Haakonssen, K., 'Moral philosophy and natural law: from the Cambridge Platonists to the Scottish Enlightenment', *Political Studies* xl (1988), 97–110

———— *Natural law and moral philosophy: from Grotius to the Scottish Enlightenment*, Cambridge 1996

———— 'The character and obligation of natural law according to Richard Cumberland', in Stewart, *English philosophy in the age of Locke*

Hall, M. B., 'The establishment of the mechanical philosophy', *Osiris* x (1952), 412–541

———— *Promoting experimental learning: experiment and the Royal Society 1660–1723*, Cambridge 1991

Harris, T., P. Seaward, and M. Goldie (eds), *The politics of religion in Restoration England*, Cambridge 1990

Harrison, J. and P. Laslett, *The library of John Locke*, Oxford 1965

Harrisson, P., *'Religion' and religions in the English Enlightenment*, Cambridge 1990

Henry, J., 'Atomism and eschatology: Catholicism and natural philosophy in the Interregnum', *British Journal for the History of Science* li (1982), 211–40

Hervada, J., 'The old and the new in the hypothesis etiamsi daremus of Grotius', *Grotiana* iv (1983), 3–20

Hont, I., 'The language of natural sociability and commerce: Samuel Pufendorf and the theoretical foundation of the four-stages theory', in Pagden, *Languages of political theory*, 253–76

Hookyaas, R., *Religion and the rise of modern science*, Edinburgh 1972

Horwitz, M., 'The Stoic synthesis of natural law', *Journal of the History of Ideas* xxxv (1974), 3–16

Hunter, M., *Science and society in Restoration England*, Cambridge 1981

———— *Science and society: the Royal Society and its Fellows*, Chalfont 1982

———— *Establishing the new science: the experience of the early Royal Society*, Woodbridge 1989

Hutton, R., *The Restoration: a political and religious history of England and Wales 1658–1667*, Oxford 1986

Hutton, S., *Henry More (1614–1687): tercentenary studies*, Dordrecht 1990

Jacob, J. R., *Henry Stubbe, radical Protestantism and the early Enlightenment*, Cambridge 1983

Jacob, M. C., *The Newtonians and the English Revolution 1689–1720*, Ithaca 1976

Jones, H., *Pierre Gassendi 1592–1655: an intellectual biography*, Nieuwkoop 1981

Joy, L. S., *Gassendi the atomist: advocate of history in an age of science*, Cambridge 1987

———— 'Epicureanism in renaissance moral and natural philosophy', *Journal of the History of Ideas* liii (1993), 573–83

Kargon, R., 'Robert Boyle and the acceptance of Epicurean atomism in England', *Isis* xlv (1964), 184–92

———— *Atomism in England from Hariot to Newton*, Oxford 1966

Katz, D., *Philo-semitism and the readmission of the Jews to England 1603–1655*, Oxford 1982

———— *Jews in the history of England*, Oxford 1994

Keynes, G., *The life of William Harvey*, Oxford 1978

Kirk, L., 'The political thought of Richard Cumberland: sovereignty and the escape from the search for origins', *Political Studies* xxv (1977), 535–48

———— *Richard Cumberland and natural law: secularisation of thought in seventeenth-century England*, Cambridge 1987

Klaaren, E., *The religious origins of modern science: belief in creation in seventeenth-century thought*, Grand Rapids 1977

Knights, M., *Politics and opinion in crisis, 1678–81*, Cambridge 1994

Krieger, L., *The politics of discretion: Pufendorf and the acceptance of natural law*, Chicago 1969

Kroll, R. F., *The material word: literate culture in the Restoration and early eighteenth century*, Baltimore 1991

Kroll, W. and R. Ashcraft (eds), *Philosophy, science and religion 1640–1700*, Cambridge 1991

Kyle, W. M., 'British ethical theories: the intuitionist reaction against Hobbes', *The Australasian Journal of Psychology and Philosophy* v (1927), 114–24

Lacey, D. R., *Dissent and parliamentary politics*, New Brunswick, NJ 1969

Lamprecht, S. P., 'The role of Descartes in seventeenth-century England', *Studies in the History of Ideas* iii (1935)

———— 'Hobbes and Hobbism', *American Political Science Review* xxxiv (1940), 31–53

Lehmberg, S., 'The writings of the English cathedral clergy 1600–1700', *Anglican Theology Review* lxxv (1993), 63–82

Leites, E. (ed.), *Conscience and casuistry in early-modern Europe*, Cambridge 1988

Lennon, T. M. (ed), *Problems of Cartesianism*, Montreal 1982

———— *The battle of the gods and giants: the legacy of Descartes and Gassendi 1655–1715*, Princeton 1993

Linnel, C. L. S., 'Daniel Scargill, a penitent Hobbist', *Church Quarterly Review* clvi (1953), 256–65

McAdoo, H. R., *The structure of Caroline moral theology*, London 1949

———— *The spirit of Anglicanism: a survey of Anglican theological method in the seventeenth century*, London 1965

McGuire, J. E., 'Boyle's conception of nature', *Journal of the History of Ideas* xxxiii (1972), 523–42

MacIntosh, J. J., 'Robert Boyle on Epicurean atheism and atomism', in Osler, *Atoms, pneuma and tranquility*, 197–220

Malcolm, N., 'Hobbes and the Royal Society', in Rogers and Ryan, *Perspectives on Thomas Hobbes*, 43–86

Manuel, F. E., *Isaac Newton: historian*, Cambridge 1963

Marshall, J., 'The ecclesiology of the Latitude-Men', *Journal of Ecclesiastical History* xxxvi (1985), 407–27

———— *John Locke: resistance, religion and responsibility*, Cambridge 1994

Mathias, P. (ed.), *Science and society 1600–1900*, Cambridge 1972

Mayo, T. F., *Epicurus in England 1650–1725*, Dallas 1934

Millburn, J. R., 'William Stukeley and the early history of the orrery', *Annals of Science* xxxi (1974), 511–28

Mintz, S., *The hunting of Leviathan: seventeenth-century reactions to the materialism and moral philosophy of Thomas Hobbes*, Cambridge 1969

Moncosu, P. and E. Vailati, 'Torricelli's infinitely long solid and its philosophical reception in the seventeenth century', *Isis* lxxxii (1991), 50–70

Moore, J. and M. Silverthorne, 'Gerschom Carmichael and the natural jurisprudence tradition in eighteenth-century Scotland', in I. Hont and M. Ignatieff, *Wealth and virtue: the shaping of political economy in the Scottish Enlightenment*, Cambridge 1983, 73–88

Mulligan, L., 'Anglicanism, Latitudinarianism and science in seventeenth-century England', *Annals of Science* iii (1973), 213–19

——— 'Civil war politics, religion and the Royal Society', *Past and Present* lix (1973), 92–116

——— 'Robert Boyle, right reason and the meaning of metaphor', *Journal of the History of Ideas* lv (1994), 235–58

Mullinger, J. B., *The University of Cambridge from the election to the chancellorship in 1626 to the decline of the Platonist movement*, Cambridge 1911

Nicolson, M., 'Christ's College and the Latitude Men', *Modern Philology* xxvii (1929–30), 35–53

——— 'The early stages of Cartesianism in England', *Studies in Philology* xxvi (1929), 356–74

Niebyl, P. H., 'Science and metaphor in the medicine of Restoration England', *Bulletin of the History of Medicine* xlvii (1973), 356–74

Nuttall, G. F. and O. Chadwick (eds), *From uniformity to unity*, London 1962

Oakley, F., *Omnipotence, covenant and order: an excursion into the history of ideas from Abelard to Leibniz*, Ithaca 1984

——— and E. W. Urdang, 'Locke, natural law and God', *Natural Law Forum* xi (1966), 92–109

Osler, M. J., 'Descartes and Walter Charleton on nature and God', *Journal of the History of Ideas* xl (1979), 445–56

——— 'Baptising Epicurean atomism: Pierre Gassendi on the immortality of the soul', in M. J. Osler and P. L. Farber, *Religion, science and world-view: essays in honour of R. S. Westfall*, Cambridge 1985, 163–84

——— 'Fortune, fate and divination: Gassendi's voluntarist theology and the baptism of Epicureanism', in Osler, *Atoms, pneuma and tranquillity*, 155–74

——— *The divine will and the mechanical philosophy: Gassendi and Descartes on contingency and necessity in the created world*, Cambridge 1994

——— (ed.) *Atoms, pneuma and tranquillity*, Cambridge 1991

Pagden, A., *The languages of political theory in early-modern Europe*, Cambridge 1987

Palladini, F., *Discussioni seicentesche su Samuel Pufendorf*, Bologna 1987

——— *Samuel Pufendorf: discepolo di Hobbes: per una reinterpretazione del giusnaturalismo moderno*, Bologna 1990

Parkin, J., 'Hobbism in the later 1660s: Daniel Scargill and Samuel Parker', *Historical Journal* xl (1999), 85–108

Parkinson, G. H. R. (ed.), *The renaissance of seventeenth-century rationalism*, London 1993

Parry, G., *The trophies of time: English antiquarians of the seventeenth century*, Oxford 1995

Patrides, C. A. (ed.), *The Cambridge Platonists*, London 1969

Phillipson, N. and Q. R. D. Skinner, *Political discourse in early-modern Britain*, Cambridge 1993

Plomer, H. R., *A dictionary of the printers and booksellers who were at work in England, Scotland and Ireland from 1668 to 1725*, Oxford 1922

Pocock, J. G. A., 'Thomas Hobbes, atheist or enthusiast?: his place in Restoration debate', *History of Political Thought* xi (1990), 737–49

Popkin, R. H., 'The philosophy of Bishop Stillingfleet', *Journal of the History of Philosophy* ix (1971), 303–20

——— *The history of scepticism from Erasmus to Spinoza*, Berkeley 1979

Probst, S., 'Infinity and creation: the origin of the controversy between Thomas Hobbes and the Savilian Professors Seth Ward and John Wallis', *British Journal for the History of Science* xxvi (1993), 271–9

Purver, M., *The Royal Society: concept and creation*, London 1967

Rattansi, P., 'The social interpretation of science', in Mathias, *Science and society*, 28–32

Reedy, G., *Robert South 1634–1716: an introduction to his life and sermons*, Cambridge 1992

Rivers, I., *Reason, grace and sentiment: a study of the language of religion and grace in England*, Cambridge 1991

———— 'Galen's muscles: Wilkins, Hume and the educational use of the argument from design', *Historical Journal* xxxvi (1993), 577–97

Robertson, G. C., *Thomas Hobbes*, London 1886

Rogers, G. A. J., 'Hobbes's hidden influence', in Rogers and Ryan, *Perspectives on Thomas Hobbes*, 189–206

———— and A. Ryan (eds), *Perspectives on Thomas Hobbes*, Oxford 1988

Sacksteder, W., 'Hobbes: the art of the geometricians', *Journal of the History of Philosophy* xviii (1980), 131–46

Sarasohn, L., 'Motion and morality: Pierre Gassendi, Thomas Hobbes and the mechanical world-view', *Journal of the History of Ideas* xlvi (1985), 363–80

———— *Gassendi's ethics: freedom in a mechanistic universe*, Ithaca 1996

Saveson, J. E., 'Descarte's influence on John Smith, Cambridge Platonist', *Journal of the History of Ideas* xx (1959), 255–63

Schaffer, S., 'Wallifaction: Thomas Hobbes on school-divinity and experimental pneumatics', *Studies in the History and Philosophy of Science* xix (1988), 275–98

———— and S. Shapin, *Leviathan and the air-pump: Hobbes, Boyle and the experimental life*, Princeton 1985

Schneider, H., *Justitia universalis: Quellenstudien zur Geschichte des 'Christlichen Naturrechts' bei Gottfried Wilhelm Leibniz*, Frankfurt 1967

Schneiders, W., *Naturrecht und Liebesethik: zur Geschichte der praktischen Philosophie im Hinblick auf Christian Thomasius*, Hildesheim 1971

Schochet, G., *Patriarchalism in political thought: the authoritarian family and political speculation and attitudes, especially in seventeenth-century Britain*, Oxford 1975

———— 'Between Lambeth and Leviathan: Samuel Parker on the Church of England and political order', in Phillipson and Skinner, *Political discourse in early-modern Britain*, 189–208

Scott, J., 'The law of war: Grotius, Sydney, Locke and the political theory of rebellion', *Political Studies* xiii (1992), 565–85

———— 'England's troubles 1603–1702', in R. Malcolm Smuts (ed.), *The Stuart court and Europe*, Cambridge 1996, 24–7

Scott, J. F., *The mathematical works of John Wallis*, London 1938

Scott, W. L., *The conflict between atomism and conservation theory 1644–1860*, New York 1970

Seliger, M., 'Locke's natural law and the foundations of politics', *Journal of the History of Ideas* xxiv (1963), 337–54

Shapin, S., 'Robert Boyle and mathematics: reality, representation and experimental practice', *Science in Context* i (1988), 23–58

———— *A social history of truth: civility and science in seventeenth-century England*, Chicago 1994

Shapiro, B. J., *John Wilkins, 1614–1672: an intellectual biography*, Princeton 1969
———— *Probability and certainty in seventeenth-century England*, Princeton 1983
Sharp, F. C., 'The ethical system of Richard Cumberland and its place in the history of British ethics', *Mind* xxi (1912), 371–98
Sharp, L., 'Walter Charleton's early life 1620–59, and his relation to natural philosophy in mid seventeenth-century England', *Annals of Science* xxx (1973), 311–40
Sidgwick, H., *Outlines of the history of ethics for English readers*, London 1886
Simon, I., *Three Restoration divines: Barrow, South, Tillotson*, Paris 1967
Simon, W. G., 'Comprehension in the age of Charles II', *Church History* xxxi (1962), 440–8
Skinner, Q. R. D., 'Thomas Hobbes and his disciples in France and England', *Comparative Studies in Society and History* viii (1965–6), 153–67
———— 'Thomas Hobbes and the nature of the early Royal Society', *Historical Journal* xii (1969), 217–39
———— 'The context of Hobbes's theory of political obligation', in Cranston and Peters, *Hobbes and Rousseau*, 109–42
———— 'Thomas Hobbes: rhetoric and the construction of morality', *Proceedings of the British Academy* lxxvi (1990), 1–61
———— *Reason and rhetoric in the philosophy of Hobbes*, Cambridge 1996
Sommerville, J. P., 'John Selden, the law of nature, and the origin of government', *Historical Journal* xxvii (1984), 437–47
———— *Thomas Hobbes: political ideas in historical context*, London 1992
Sorrell, T., *Hobbes*, London 1986
———— 'Seventeenth century materialism: Gassendi and Hobbes', in Parkinson, *The renaissance of seventeenth-century rationalism*, 235–72
———— (ed.), *The Cambridge companion to Hobbes*, Cambridge 1996
Southgate, B. C., 'Cauterising the tumour of Pyrrhonism: Blackloism vs skepticism', *Journal of the History of Ideas* liii (1992), 631–45
Spaulding, F., *Richard Cumberland, als Begruender der Englischen Ethik*, Leipzig 1894
Spellman, W. M., *The Latitudinarians and the Church of England 1660–1700*, Athens, Georgia 1993
Spiller, M. R. G., *Concerning natural experimental philosophie: Meric Casaubon and the Royal Society*, The Hague 1980
Spragens, T., *The politics of motion: the world of Thomas Hobbes*, Lexington 1973
Springborg, P., 'Hobbes's biblical beasts: Leviathan and Behemoth', *Political Theory* xxiii (1995), 353–75
Spurr, J., 'Latitudinarianism and the Restoration Church', *Historical Journal* xxxi (1988), 61–82
———— 'Rational religion in Restoration England', *Journal of the History of Ideas* xlix (1988), 1–23
———— 'The Church of England, comprehension and the Toleration Act of 1689', *English Historical Review* civ (1989), 927–47
———— ' "Virtue, religion and government": the Anglican uses of providence', in *The politics of religion in Restoration England*, ed. T. Harris, P. Seaward and M. Goldie, Cambridge 1990, 29–48
———— *The Restoration Church of England 1660–1689*, New Haven 1991

Steneck, N. H., 'The "Ballad of Robert Crosse and Joseph Glanvill", and the background to *Plus ultra*', *British Journal for the History of Science* xlvi (1981), 59–74

Stewart, L., *The rise of public science: rhetoric, technology and natural philosophy in Newtonian Britain, 1660–1750*, Cambridge 1992

Stewart, M. A., 'Critical notice of "Questions concerning the laws of nature" ', *Locke Newsletter* xxiii (1992), 145–66

—— (ed.), *English philosophy in the age of Locke*, Oxford forthcoming

Stimson, D., 'The ballad of Gresham Colledge [sic]', *Isis* xviii (1932), 103–17

Stradenbauer, C. A., 'Platonism, theosophy and immaterialism: recent views of the Cambridge Platonists', *Journal of the History of Ideas* xxxv (1974), 157–69

Syfret, R. H., 'Some early critics of the Royal Society', *Notes and Records of the Royal Society* viii (1950), 20–64

Sykes, N., *From Sheldon to Secker: aspects of English church history 1660–1768*, Cambridge 1959

Thomas, A., 'Comprehension and toleration', in Nuttall and Chadwick, *From uniformity to unity*, 191–253

Thorpe, C. D., *The aesthetic theory of Thomas Hobbes*, Michigan 1940

Tierney, B., *The idea of natural rights*, Atlanta 1997

Toon, P., *God's statesman: the life and work of John Owen*, Exeter 1971

Tuck, R., *Natural rights theories: their origin and development*, Cambridge 1979

—— 'Grotius, Carneades and Hobbes', *Grotiana* iv (1983), 43–62

—— 'The "modern" theory of natural law', in Pagden, *Languages of political theory in early-modern Europe*, 99–122

—— *Hobbes*, Oxford 1989

—— *Philosophy and government*, Cambridge 1993

Tulloch, J., *Rational theology and Christian philosophy in England in the seventeenth century*, London 1872

Tully, J., *A discourse on property: John Locke and his adversaries*, Cambridge 1980

—— 'Governing conduct', in Leites, *Conscience and casuistry in early-modern Europe*, 12–71

—— *An approach to political philosophy: John Locke in contexts*, Cambridge 1993

Twigg, J., *The University of Cambridge and the English Revolution 1625–88*, Woodbridge 1990

Van Leeuwen, H. G., *The problem of certainty in English thought 1630–1690*, The Hague 1963

Von Leyden, W., 'John Locke and natural law', *Philosophy* xxxi (1956), 23–35

Watkins, J. W. N., *Hobbes's system of ideas*, London 1973

Webster, C., 'Henry More and Descartes: some new sources', *British Journal for the History of Science* iv (1969), 359–77

—— *The great instauration: science, medicine and reform 1620–1660*, London 1975

Westfall, R., 'On ye atomicall philosophy: unpublished papers of Robert Boyle', *Annals of Science* xii (1956), 111

—— *Science and religion in seventeenth-century England*, New Haven 1958

Wood, A. H., *Church unity without uniformity*, London 1963

Wood, P. B., 'Methodology and apologetics: Thomas Sprat's History of the Royal Society', *British Journal for the History of Science* xliii (1980), 1–26

Woolhouse, R. S., *Locke*, Brighton 1983

Yolton, J. W., 'Locke on the law of nature', *Philosophical Review* lvii (1958), 477–98

Unpublished theses etc.

Balaguer, M., 'Law as the basis of morality in the philosophy of Hobbes, Cumberland and Locke', unpubl. PhD diss. London 1937

Carey, A., 'Richard Cumberland and the epistemology of ethics', unpubl. PhD diss. Washington State 1967

Hochstrasser, T. J., 'Natural law theory: its historiography and development in the French and German Enlightenment *c.* 1670–1780', unpubl. PhD diss. Cambridge 1990

Kirk, L., 'Richard Cumberland (1632–1718) and his political theory', unpubl. PhD diss. London 1976

Malcolm, N., 'Thomas Hobbes and voluntarist theology', unpubl. PhD diss. Cambridge 1982

Palladini, F., 'Is the *socialitas* of Pufendorf really anti-Hobbesian?', unpubl. paper written for The Workshop on Modern Natural Law, convened by I. Hont and H. E. Bodecker, Gottingen, 26–30 June 1989

Index